A Practical Reference Applying Technology
Concepts to the Practice of Law

THE DIGITAL PRACTICE OF LAW

4th. Edition

Michael R. Arkfeld

Law Partner Publishing
Phoenix * Arizona
1999

Library of Congress Catalog Card Number: 98-94865

Printed in the USA by

MORRIS PUBLISHING

3212 East Highway 30 • Kearney, NE 68847 • 1-800-650-7888

About the Author:

Michael R. Arkfeld is a practicing attorney specializing in civil tort litigation. His practice includes multimillion-dollar cases involving personal injury, medical malpractice, wrongful termination, and a host of other tort claims. He has appeared before both federal and state appellate courts and has tried over 30 cases to a jury. His duties include preparation of case management plans, investigation and deposing of expert and lay witnesses, pretrial preparation of witnesses and document organization, pretrial filing of documents, and appearances for motion hearings, pretrial conferences, trials, and appellate arguments.

Since 1985, Michael has incorporated personal computers extensively in his legal practice and lectures frequently throughout the United States on the impact of technology on the practice of law. His approach to using computers in the practice of law includes calendaring, case action plans, full text document management, imaging, document assembly, databases, spreadsheet applications, graphics, Internet applications and computer-generated simulations.

Michael is a licensed attorney in the State of Arizona, member of the American Bar Association and a member of the Litigation and Law Practice Management Sections. Michael has been the assistant editor of the Litigation Applications Newsletter and a Board Member for TechShows 1996, 1997 and 1998. He was appointed Chair of the Technology Committee for the Judicial Division for 1997-98 to plan technology programs for the Judicial Division.

In 1995 he was appointed chairman of the Task Force on Integrating Technology into the Justice System for the Arizona State Bar. This task force facilitates the integration of technology in the justice system in the State of Arizona. Committee members include representatives from the courts, legislative, executive, state bar and law schools. He is a monthly columnist for the Arizona Attorney magazine and a contributing writer to the American Bar Association Journal and a variety of other legal publications.

Copyright:

Warranties:

Cover Design and Quantity Book Discounts:

Cover design by Scott Neeley.

Quantity book discounts are available from the publisher. Special quantity discounts are available for education, business, sales or for use in legal training programs. Contact Law Partner Publishing, 2615 South Sierra Vista Circle, Tempe, Arizona 85282, or contact the author at Michael@Arkfeld.com.

Table of Contents

1 — The Necessity for Automating the Practice of Law

2 — Hardware and Software

_3_   *Networking and Group Computing*

4 — *The Internet and Telecommunications*

Management and Personnel Technology Considerations

6 Computer Concepts and Applications

7 — *Managing Litigation Information Using Technology*

_8_ _Using Multimedia in Legal Proceedings_

Acknowledgements

A special acknowledgement to my family and supporters for their assistance as I continue my journey down the road of applying technology to the practice of law and the justice system. To Louraine, Luke, Dawn, Adam, William, Colby and Courtney for your patience and understanding. A special acknowledgement to my brother Dan and his son Cory who have recently passed away. Their free spirits and love of life will not be forgotten. To my brothers and sisters Bill, Phil, Anne and Rosemary who taught me the meaning of perseverance and determination. Finally, to all those people who have patiently listened and provided valuable insight, information and criticism as I struggle to apply technology to the practice of law and the justice system.

Preface

My experiences as a trial attorney, law office manager, and computer enthusiast convinced me of the necessity and importance of using computers in the practice of law. The demands of our profession require easy access and control of case information. Computers can meet these demands by providing immediate control over the documents, facts, and law of a case. In effect, computers can literally give you the winning edge in today's legal arena. Automation is definitely the key to staying competitive into the 21st century.

Today's case management and litigation process is more complex than ever. In a routine case, it is not uncommon to have many docketing dates, multiple depositions, sets of interrogatories, requests for production of records, and several pretrial motions before ever selecting a jury. By using PIM's, document assembly, CD-ROM technology, full text search and retrieval, databases, imaging, outlining, graphics, and animation, you can maintain control of your case. From the moment you get the case to the last appeal, every fact and every exhibit can be at your command, instantly, easily, and consistently.

The desktop and the laptop computers have literally revolutionized the practice of law, as we know it today. Besides acting as a communication device, the computer's capacities to store, assemble, retrieve, and manipulate information and images provides a decided edge for the attorneys who use it in their cases. It greatly decreases the amount of time spent organizing your case and instead allows attorneys to focus on the presentation of their cases. Computer concepts need to be understood by all practitioners in order to integrate these powerful concepts into your firm's practice. Without them, you will always be at a decided disadvantage to your adversaries who are now automating their practice.

The " lawyering processes" are not part of the software packages you purchase. Software is merely a tool that you use to organize and control your case. Whether it is outlining, word-processing, databases, full text or imaging software, they are tools to organize and have instant access to all the facts and documents in your case. To integrate your lawyering processes with computer software will, without question, save time and enhance your field of expertise. Your time will be spent on analyzing your case instead of shuffling paper or trying to locate the information. The payoff is well worth your investment of time.

The technology revolution in the last 10 years is not slowing down. It is accelerating at a faster pace with the introduction of Windows 98, CD-ROM, and Internet applications. It is an exciting and fascinating time, but it is important that you begin the journey now, toward what will truly be "paperless" litigation and "virtual" law firms.

I welcome any comments, criticisms, or suggestions regarding this book. Please forward all comments to Michael@Arkfeld.com.

Introduction & Book Layout

Introduction

This book is based on years of my practicing law with a computer at my side. The focus has always been and will continue to be to use computers and software as a tool to replicate the lawyering method of storing, accessing, and retrieving critical information in the practice of law. My focus is upon the work, not upon the software and hardware.

This book is not designed to provide everything you want to know about computers and software. Volumes of materials are prepared monthly providing the latest and greatest. This book is designed to give you the information on the basics of computer technology and how to apply computer concepts to the legal processes which will take you on the way to the virtual law practice of today and tomorrow. This book is designed to permit first time or advanced users to use lawyering processes with software applications without the necessity of "reinventing the wheel". Each chapter is illustrated with screens and points on how to use computers to their best advantage in the practice of law.

The book takes a comprehensive approach to using technology in the law office. Many of the articles written over the last few years have focused upon certain computer software and sometimes their functionality to the practice of law. The goal of this book is to approach the technology implementation from a "total" approach. All aspects of a case - case management, billing, interrogatories, documents, transcripts, graphics, Internet applications, in-court presentation and so on are discussed in this book to provide an understanding of how the pieces fit together. This total approach is intended to place you in the center of your case with instant computer access to the law and facts for your analysis.

Book Layout

This book has been organized into eight chapters to guide you through the process of automating your practice.

Chapter 1 entitled **The Necessity for Automating the Practice of Law** presents persuasive reasons for the automation of your practice. It is intended to challenge you to begin the visualization of how law will be practiced and to start the strategic planning for this revolution. The focus will be on the reasons for automating your practice , visualizing and implementing the "virtual law office".

Chapter 2 is entitled **Hardware and Software** and provides basic information as to the hardware and software needed to automate your practice. From how much RAM you need for your computer to factors when considering a software upgrade this chapter explains the hardware and software concepts and practical considerations.

Chapter 3 entitled **Networking and Group Computing** explores the role of computer networking and Intranets in your practice as well as a discussion of the emergence of workgroup computing as we transition into the digital age.

Chapter 4 entitled **The Internet and Telecommunications** explores the exciting world of the Internet and the role of telecommunications in the practice of law. It explains the different digital information channels and the many modules of the most powerful communication device of all times – The Internet. Among the many topics it provides pointers on accessing the Internet, selecting an Internet service provider (ISP), building your web site and a list of Internet sites to assist you in your practice.

Chapter 5 entitled **Management and Personnel Technology Considerations** focuses on engineering and re-engineering technology from a human resource perspective. Issues such as management support for technology integration, training approaches and competency testing for law firm personnel are discussed.

Chapter 6 entitled **Computer Concepts and Legal Applications** will discuss computer concepts and their application to the legal profession. It is necessary to understand basic computer concepts in order to integrate them into your practice. Document assembly, databases, full text systems and multimedia are a few of the concepts discussed.

Chapter 7 entitled **Using Information Technology (IT) in Your Cases** will focus on the office and litigation process on how to integrate IT into your cases. This chapter focuses on the practical steps and considerations of managing the legal and factual details of your case from the perspective of the litigation process.

Chapter 8 entitled **Using Multimedia in Legal Proceedings** will discuss using computers and technology in legal proceedings to assist you in persuading the trier of fact of your position. It discusses the practical considerations of presenting your case in a digital format and the courtroom issues that may affect your presentation. Techniques and tips on how to present your case and whether real-time reporting should be used are a few of the technology issues discussed.

The **Glossary explains** explain key computer definitions.

Chapter 1

The Necessity for Automating the Practice of Law

Just as the Industrial Revolution dramatically expanded the strength of man's muscles and the reach of his hand, so the smart-machine revolution will magnify the power of his brain. But unlike the Industrial Revolution, which depended on finite resources such as iron and oil, the new information age will be fired by a seemingly limitless resource - inexhaustible supply of knowledge itself.

- author unknown

Is Your Legal Future Secure?

The technology revolution has forever changed society and the practice of law. When I graduated from law school in 1975 an office, law books, legal pads, typewriters, and pens were the primary tools of an attorney. The preparation of pleadings took many hours in the library and the services of a typist to produce a professional product. Now, over 20 years later the primary tools for a lawyer are a computer, CD-ROM drive, modem, printer and an Internet connection. The preparation of a pleading takes half the time then it took 20 years ago, based on legal research more accurate then 20 years ago, in a "virtual" office located  wherever you are physically located. The digital revolution has substantially altered and will continue to alter the way law is practiced.

The cornerstone of this transition is the change from a paper and analog based society to a digital society. Analog devices such as video and audio recording devices record real events in real-time using film or audiotape. *Digital* is the recording of information in a binary manner as 1's and 0's for use by a computer. Once in a digital format all forms of information - data, sound, graphics, text, video - can be stored, accessed, retrieved, manipulated, organized and sent over the Internet using computers anytime and anywhere.

There are many differences between digital and analog information. Digital media is non-linear. It enables the user to instantly jump to any part of a digital book, video or sound. Traditionally one reads a book sequentially or had to view a VCR tape from beginning to end or fast-forward it. Digital information enables one to be interactive with the information - picking and choosing depending upon one's response to the feedback from the information. It allows you to interact with the media to move to different areas of the information depending upon the user's needs such as hypertext links on WWW pages.

The world is moving from the age of paper and machines to the age of digital information. This move will impose technology changes upon the legal profession and radically alter the time, place and manner of how we practice law. Competition in this new digital age will intensify and the law practice will lose its physical boundaries and will result in a global law practice. Lawyers are already starting the transition and will increase the automation of their practices. The dramatic increase in the number of lawyers and non-lawyers practicing law and technology efficiencies will put pressure on changing from the billable hour to a value based billing system. Marketing to clients will involve digital connections through the Internet and direct connections. Intranets and extranets will become commonplace.

We will increasingly be defined by our ability to communicate and access digital information. Case strategies and status, billing and communications will be done increasing by e-mail, extranets and other digitized communication methods. The ethical implications will be numerous as we struggle to understand the impact of this digitized changing world. Depending on the practitioner's skills a lawyer's quality of life can dramatically increase with these new efficiencies. We are living in an exciting transitional period and if we take the proper steps now to visualize and implement the digital practice of law our legal future will be secure.

The Necessity for Automating

The traditional method of practicing law has many limitations that impact the quality and quantity of services to your clients. For example, searching through law books can take hours where the same search through the Internet or on a CD-ROM can take seconds. Using document assembly software one can assemble a complex or routine legal document quickly and accurately as compared to retyping a document or using cut and paste to modify it for a different client.

The digitization of legal information has changed the competitive nature of the legal profession and has had a corresponding impact upon the economics of the practice of law. To properly service the needs of our clients and to stay competitive we need to fully automate our practice. There are several significant factors that necessitate the automation of the practice of law.

Competitive Technology Changes

The threshold issue that confronts firms and lawyers today is to what extent should they automate their practice. Most practitioners today were taught in law school and by their mentors to use books, paper, typewriters and pens to practice law. The billable hour was and is generally the measure of payment for the law firm. We were taught in law school that the practice is a "profession" and ignored business efficiency techniques. However, just over 10 years ago a technology revolution began that imposed and will continue to impose significant competitive, economic and social changes upon the practice of law.

To understand the vast technological changes that have occurred we need to examine where we have been as a profession. What "tools" did we use in the past and how has the use of those tools changed?

When Abraham Lincoln practiced law he studied from law books, drafted his own pleadings with a quill pen and charged his clients on a "value based" system. In 1985, over 120 years later, we still studied from law books, prepared our pleadings with a pen and typewriter instead of a quill pen but now billed by the "hour". The technological advances were not significant and generally did not give an edge to a practitioner. The use of brute force by using a lot of staff was a formidable factor to an opponent as large firms were commonplace. Typewriters were plentiful and used for only one purpose.

Most practitioners were billing by the hour, except personal injury attorneys and some others.

In 1985 the personal computer with its ability to process information at phenomenal rates moved into the mainstream. In 1995 the Internet burst into the forefront with phenomenal communication potential. Now, information could be stored, instantly retrieved, reused, and organized at the whim and control of the user. What used to take a lot of personnel to accomplish could be done with fewer people and more computer power. The last 10 years has forced the legal profession and the whole society to rethink how to use the new tools to store, locate and use legal information, now in a digitized format.

Famous Last Words

I think there is a world market for maybe five computers. – Thomas Watson, chairman of IBM, 1943.

I have traveled the length and breadth of this country and walked with the best people, and I can assure you that data processing is a fad that won't last out the year. – The editor in charge of business books for Prentice Hall, 1957.

But what . . . is it good for? – Engineer at the Advanced Computing Systems Division of IBM, 1968, commenting on the microchip.

There is no reason anyone would want a computer in their home. – Ken Olson, president, chairman and founder of Digital Equipment Corp., 1977.

640K ought to be enough for anybody. – Bill Gates, 1981.

Timeline - The History and Role of Technology

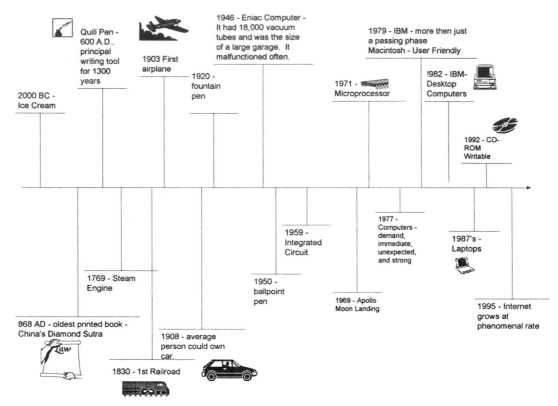

Technology has become a great equalizer. With technology sole practitioners or small firms can compete against large firms. The reason for this is that computers are relatively inexpensive and are able to organize, store, access and retrieve a voluminous amount of information without the need for manual support. No longer is the number of personnel working on a case a significant advantage, instead the strategic use of technology can provide a definite competitive edge.

What is in store for the practice of law by the year 2001? The year 2001 will bring global competition and increased communication. We can be assured that we will be globally connected and sharing information on a worldwide basis for very little cost. We are constantly reading and hearing about the super information highway - the Internet. To properly understand the evolution of the Internet system is to compare it to the railroads and highways in America. As these infrastructures were being built in America the lifeblood of towns were determined as to where the track was being laid or the highway built. These tracks and roads were the connecting commerce links. It was a common occurrence for towns to die out if they were not included on the railroad companies' or governing body's transportation plan. With the Internet there will be no physical track. Instead anyone from anywhere who has a connection to the Internet will be part of this revolutionary infrastructure.

The "law firm" as we know it today will not exist in the year 2001 if it fails to "connect" onto the information superhighway. The capability to link directly with your clients will create immediate connection with your client's problems. The capability to locate information throughout the world in seconds will impact the advice you provide to your clients. The capability to "conference" with your clients, fellow employees and other practitioners anytime and anyplace using video and conferencing software will change where and how one practices law. Can we accurately predict with 100% accuracy what the year 2001 will look like? No. But we can make calculated reasonable judgments based on the technology available today, with an understanding of the legal workflow and the needs of our clients.

The focus of this entire book is to lay the foundation and describe legal technology applications that will enable one to stay competitive in the new digital age. Below are some examples of computer applications that significantly change how law is practiced:

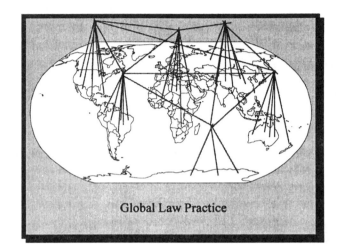

Global Law Practice

- A deposition can be searched and information retrieved in seconds using full text software;
- Trial graphics can be created and modified easily using graphics software;
- Past pleadings and workproduct can be easily accessed electronically to prevent the reinvention of the wheel;
- Case management systems can provide docketing reminders, pleading dates, witness contact list, calendars, etc.;
- Group computing platforms such as an Intranet, Lotus Notes, etc. can provide remote group assistance on cases;
- Video testimony of witnesses can be viewed on line anywhere in the world within seconds after a witness testifies in a deposition or at trial;
- Spreadsheets can automatically calculate settlement and damage proposals;
- Legal issues can be electronically linked to the factual information to prove your cases;
- Witness trial books can be created quickly linking vital documents and other data to a specific witness;
- Using document assembly techniques one can generate routine legal documents in a matter of seconds;
- One study revealed that a manual search of 10,000 documents took 67 paralegal hours and yielded 15 relevant documents seeking information about a witness. A computer search took seconds and yielded 20 relevant documents;
- The digital image of your case documents can be retrieved in seconds;
- Up to 15,000 documents images can be stored on a CD-ROM and accessed through a portable computer;
- Legal research can be completed over the Internet or on a CD-ROM anytime and anywhere in seconds;

> "If a man write a better book, preach a better sermon or make a better mousetrap than his neighbor, though he build his house in the woods, the world will make a beaten path to his door." - Ralph Waldo Emerson

- A day of trial per week can be saved by using "paperless" trial techniques;
- Unlimited access to caselaw anytime, anywhere on CD-ROM is available and for one low fixed cost;
- Invaluable research on individuals, partnerships or companies can be completed over the WWW;
- E-mail and attached text, audio or video files can be sent to clients or anyone anytime, from anywhere, to anywhere for pennies; and
- Information from millions of computers can be instantly accessed on the Internet.

These are but a few examples of how technology is changing the competitive nature of the practice of law.

Changing Law Practice Economics

The process of lawyering is providing the best representation at a fair fee. Over the last 1400 hundred years the manual tools we have used in our law practice have changed very little until the last 10 years. In that short period of time technology has changed the rules of practicing law. The last 10 years has forced the legal profession and our whole society to rethink the way we store, locate and use information, now in a digitized format. Computers and technology can free us from the drudgery of physically handling and organizing documents and physically searching for cases through law books. Time is saved. This forces us to reexamine the economics of the practice of law.

The Death of the Billable Hour?

Abraham Lincoln said that our time and advice are our stock in trade. These two elements - time and advice - form the foundation of the practice of law. We advise our clients on how to conduct their personal and business affairs. This advice must be based upon the best and latest reflections of the state of the law as applied to our client's circumstances. Time is our commodity. Generally we provide our time for money, usually by the hour.

However, there has been an obvious clash between implementing technology in the law firm, which produce results in less time than those reached manually. Most of this clash surrounds the controversy in "billing by the hour." Clients complain that there is a lack of predictability of what the total cost will be when hourly billing is used, the lack of any risk sharing between lawyer and client when hours spent is the sole criteria in setting fees and a lack of incentive for efficiently handling a case.

The billable hour encourages a firm to hire a lot of staff and for the staff to work a lot of hours. If one can show that a computer can do in seconds what an associate attorney can do in 10 hours at $150 per hour what course will the firm follow? This is especially true when "time-saving" hardware and software costs $50,000 to install.

Corporate counsel is carefully the billable hour issue. In the January, 1993, issue of Corporate Legal Times, it was observed that while "The rest of corporate America is downsizing . . . in-house law departments are expanding . . . The driving forces behind in-house expansion . . . are the desire to control legal costs and a perceived need for preventive legal counseling." Over 51% of corporate counsel said they use "fixed fees" as an effective manner of controlling outside counsel costs.

> Price of services is a major consideration by corporate counsel in selecting outside counsel. In a technology roundtable discussion I attended in 1991 a vice-president of a major insurance company asked an attorney from one of their outside counsel law firms whether they would consider a flat fee for a breach of agency lawsuit instead of an hourly billing rate. The vice-president said that it costs his company, on the average, $58,000 in legal fees for each similar case. He asked the attorney, "If I give you $45,000 for each case with no questions of how the money is spent, would you accept it? If it cost you $25,000 because of the application of computers, CD-ROM, imaging, etc., to handle the case, then we both win-win. If it cost you $50,000, then not only is part of the risk shared, but the value of services using traditional methods of "lawyering" may not reflect your implementation of the advancements of technology." There was no response to the question.

> The Wall Street Journal of January 13, 1992 reported that a major national law firm had been making agreements with their clients to handle their cases for fixed fees . . . "Law firms have traditionally billed on an hourly basis but the system has come under increasing attack by clients." Business Week, on August 17, 1992, suggested that "law firms that don't adapt to a clockless era may find their time has passed."

Law firms are going to have to deal with the issue of how clients' value the legal services provided by the firm. Clients are increasingly looking at the perception of value of the services provided rather than the number of hours invested in providing the service. As Richard C. Reed, an expert in value based billing, stated:

> **In a price-sensitive economy, lawyers compete not only on the basis of price, but also on the basis of quality of product. Indeed, price or quality of product, or both, serves to differentiate one lawyer or law firm from another.**

It is not uncommon for corporate clients to suggest and even mandate that mediation, arbitration, and "private" courts be used to resolve a dispute. They are pushing hard to obtain the highest value for their litigation dollar. Some corporate clients are beginning to pay a flat fee for a portion of services requested and a "contingency fee" depending on the outcome of the litigation.

The ABA and in-house counsel passed standards for a task based billing system known as the Uniform Task Based Management System-Litigation. This uniform task based billing system sets fees based upon the task performed as opposed to the billable hour. These type of standards underlines the importance of knowing your costs no matter which type of billing system is used. Under these standards the technologically sophisticated will benefit. The standards are available from the ABA by calling the Member Services Department at 312-988-5522.

The 1997 ABA Small Firm Survey found that 88% of the attorneys offered hourly rates, 64% offered fixed fee, 55.8 % itemized billing, 48.6% flat fee, 33.5% negotiated fees, and 24.5% blended hourly rates.

One solution to the billable hour dilemma is to use value based or fixed fee billing. Fees under this system should measure the value of services as perceived by the clients. For practical approaches to this problem I would recommend two books by Richard C. Reed - WIN-WIN BILLING STRATEGIES and BEYOND THE BILLABLE HOUR. Both books are available through the American Bar Association. (www.abanet.org/abapubs/lawoffice.html).

Without a doubt we are transitioning through difficult times in trying to implement law firm technology in a sometimes resistant environment while at the same time maintaining the financial health of our organization. This transition requires a new way of thinking as we strive to provide advice to our clients while fairly measuring our time and the technology infrastructure cost.

Price, Billing and Profitability

Price is of utmost importance to your clients. The price to our clients is reflected in the amount of time that we spend on their case. Technology will enable us to spend less time on a case and thus lower billable hours to our client. It is not uncommon for the cost of legal services to be carefully reviewed by our clients. Corporate law departments will continue to scrutinize the services, fees, and use of technology by outside law firms to ensure lower costs.

Shortsighted attorneys may argue that lawyers should spend more time doing things manually because there will be more billable time. The nature of such a system discourages incentive for efficiency and early resolution of your client's case if billable hours are the sole measure of the value of your services. In the long run the legal work product should be judged by its value to the client. The rewards for a firm in lowered billing by using technology are obtaining more business from a client.

Law firms are going to have to deal with the issue of how clients' value the legal services provided by the firm. Clients are increasingly looking at the value of the services provided rather than the number of hours invested in providing the service.

In the National Law Journal of April 4, 1994, the lead story was about one of the top trial attorneys in the country "Fred H. Bartlett Jr. - ex-Army Ranger, titan-trial lawyer - is a man with a mission. At 61, he and two dozen colleagues who launched a new firm last year want to do away with hourly billing and, as a result, are inciting revolution in the legal profession." Managing partner Sidney Herman says they do not want to make money on the hourly billing method of doing business. Instead they will earn their profits by" capitalizing on computer technology and partner experience will help make the firm profitable. Mr. Bartlett says "The law business ought to be the best way in the world to make a living . . . instead it is the most inefficient industry in the world." The hourly billing arrangement is an incentive not to be efficient. Besides the cutting edge approach to alternative billing arrangements the firm has invested heavily into computer technology. "At a cost of about $60,000 per lawyer, it has the latest computer hardware, software, and office equipment. Each attorney can network with colleagues and clients, process documents, retrieve internal precedents and search depositions or databases with a high-powered portable laptop computer from any location." Mr. Bartlett used to think that trial lawyers who used the technology were "sissies". Now both he and the managing partners are both staunch supporters of the computer productivity which both admit has improved their work product.

Analysis - Billable Hour Without Technology vs. Value Based Billing with Technology

Below is an analysis of investing technology dollars into your law firm operation. The numbers are fictional but are made to emphasize the point about the billable hour vs. value based billing after technology is acquired. It also shows the effect if you invest in technology to make you more efficient but continue to bill by the hour.

	BILLABLE HOUR No Technology		BILLABLE HOUR Technology Acquired		VALUE BASED FEE STRUCTURE Technology Acquired	
Technology Investment	$0	$0	$300	$300	$300	$300
# of Cases/Tasks	20	30	40	60	40	60
Hours per Case/Task	2	2	1	1	1	1
TOTAL HOURS/WK.	**40**	**60**	**40**	**60**	**40**	**60**
Billable hour	$100	$100	$100	$100	N/A	N/A
Value Based Billing per case/ task	N/A	N/A	N/A	N/A	$150	$150
Client Fees (Per case or task)	$200	$200	$100	$100	$150/case	$150
Number of cases/ tasks	20	30	40	60	40	60
NET REVENUE/WK.	**$4000**	**$6000**	**$3,700**	**$5,700**	**$5,700**	**$8,700**

Billable Hour - No Technology Acquired - Under this scenario a lawyer chooses not to automate and continues to charge by the hour. If a lawyer works **40 hours** or **60 hours** per week then his gross revenue would be **$4000** or **$6000** per week based upon an hourly rate of $100 per hour. It is assumed that he would complete work on **20 or 30 cases or tasks** at an average time of **2 hours per case or task.**

Billable Hour - Technology Acquired - Under this scenario the lawyer makes a technology investment of an average of $300 per week. If a lawyer works **40 hours** per week then his gross revenue would be **$4000** per week based upon an hourly rate of $100 per hour minus $300 for the technology investment. His net revenue would be $3,700 for the week. It is assumed that he would complete work on **40 cases** or tasks at an average time of **1 hour per case or task.** The lawyer would be more efficient but his net income per week would decrease by $300 since he has invested in technology but continues to bill by the hour.

Value Based Fee Structure - Technology Acquired - Under this scenario if a lawyer works **40 hours per week** and invests $300 per week into technology, his gross revenue would be **$6,000** per week based upon a value based rate of $150 per case. It is assumed that he would complete work on **40 cases** at an average time of **1 hour per case. His weekly net income would be $5,700 per week or a $1,700 increase over the billable hour where no technology is acquired and he would only work a forty-hour week.**

Under the 60-hour scenario, after a lawyer's technology investment of $300 per week, his gross revenue would be **$9,000** per week based upon a value based rate of $150 per case. It is assumed that he would complete work on **60 cases** at an average time of **1 hour per case. His weekly net income would be $8,700 per week as compared to $6000 per week if no technology was acquired and the billable hour rate was used.**

Government and Plaintiff Lawyers. If you are a plaintiff's attorney working on a contingent fee basis or a salaried government employee then your entire office should be automated. Why? Because efficiency will reward your efforts as long as the employer does not measure productivity by the number of hours worked. If you can now handle 40 cases in a normal 40-hour workweek, then you should be able to handle more cases in the same workweek if technology has made you more productive.

> In today's world, customers of all types of businesses and clients of all types of professionals are demanding ever better service. Some say responsiveness standards are set by expectations at fast food restaurants and with fax machines. Today, many clients now expect quicker access to and results from their lawyers. Cellular telephones, once a luxury, are now often a necessity. . . If law firms successfully implement technology [Videoconferencing, remote access, fax/modems, etc.], then they can accommodate client demands for quick turnaround and instant communication. . *Reality Today, A Prototype of the Law Firm of the Future,* Nicholas Wallwork, Muchmore and Wallwork, P.C. (www.mmww.com)

Quality of Legal Services

Law firms manufacture intellectual work. Its product is constantly reviewed for its quality and price. If you compete, not only on price but also on quality, and if technology will deliver a better quality product for your client, shouldn't it be used? Ronald S. Beard, managing partner in the law firm of Gibson, Dunn, & Crutcher, Los Angeles, discussing Total Quality Management tools in his firm, said:

> The primary ones [TQM] are in the quality relations' areas: reducing our costs and improving our technological capabilities including access to research and access to prior work product. By the end of 1992 we should have our local area networks completely in place, linking all 18 offices and probably some clients as well. A young associate sitting at his or her desk will be able to access all of our research by pushing a button. I remember how it was when you had to look around. A constant waste of time. Now, it's just a matter of seconds. Now the product is immediately available to all members of the firm. This immediate access to past work product will provide a better present work product.

Some of the important quality concerns of clients are:

1. Turnaround time;
2. Respect for budget concerns;
3. Promptly returning phone calls or e-mail inquiries; and

4. Thoughtful problem solving.

All of these concerns can be addressed by using automation. Legal research can be turned around faster using automated legal research, prior work product can be easily located, legal materials can be easily transmitted, and so on. However there definitely is a downside to not using technology. Some ramifications to consider:

- **Losing Clients** - You can realistically expect to lose clients if you fail to incorporate computerized technology into your law firm. Recently, one law firm was "informally" visited by one of their corporate clients. Later it was learned that they were being evaluated on their technological sophistication and had "flunked" the evaluation. The recommendation was to stop using the firm for their legal services.

- **Losing Opportunities for New Business** - Clients are requesting proposals from firms on how they would handle specific litigation. Those proposals outline, not only the lawyer's expertise, but also the "cost" of handling the litigation. The client who expects you to use this technology or risk losing their business knows about automation – full text retrieval, imaging, etc.

- **Tainted Reputation** - Your firm's reputation can be seriously damaged if it becomes known that you are unable, because of "old methods," to quickly respond to changing litigation.

- **Space Cost** - Your firm must consider the square foot charge for storing documents and other legal research. If these same documents can imaged and stored on a CD-ROM disk, the savings become immense.

- **Case Management Fees, Computer Use Fees, and Personnel Costs** - A per page cost for coding, computer use fees, and set fees for particular personnel can be presented to the client for approval

> ### Clients Force Tech on Firms.
> **Corporate counsel tell lawyers to use e-mail, Intranets, etc., to cut firm fees.**
>
> Two years ago, Mr. Morgan [O. Forrest Morgan, Associate General Counsel at Pittsburgh Westinghouse Electric Corp.] called a meeting of the company's top 25 outside counsel. " I wanted to establish basic things – like electronic mail connections so they could send us documents via e-mail . . . The reaction was not enthusiastic . . .Together with many corporate counsel throughout the country, he began using technology as a cattle prod to reduce outside counsel's fees . . . Technology facilitates alternative fee arrangements he says, from task based billing to flat fee arrangements. . . ."The bottom line is, technology brings down legal fees . . .", - National Law Journal, April 14, 1997

> In a radical move DuPont Chemical decided to reengineer its relationship with its outside counsel by using technology to save money. They severed ties with more than 300 of its outside counsel and established a WAN of 50 primary firms. The WAN will tie over 60 offices together and provide a common library of research, trial documents, strategy notes among other materials. The primary firms' incentive will be that they will obtain a larger amount of DuPont's work for a lower billable hour cost. DuPont has made it clear that they not only expect the firm's to begin investing and learning about the use of technology but also welcome new technology changes. The primary firms coming on board range from 13 person firms to firms with hundreds of lawyers. As Daniel B. Mahoney, DuPont's in-house lawyer who led the reengineering task said, " This is an earthquake just starting to happen." Reengineer Your Lawyers, Forbes Magazine ASAP

Dramatic Increase in the Number of Lawyers

Since 1776 the number of lawyers has increased to almost a million practitioners and firm sizes have increased dramatically. The increase in lawyers since 1970 has been unprecedented. Law schools are graduating more than 35,000 attorneys who are very comfortable using technology.

This is occurring in the midst of a technology revolution that is changing the way we practice law. This increase in lawyers, digital technology changes and the downward pressure on the billable hour and firm size will significantly

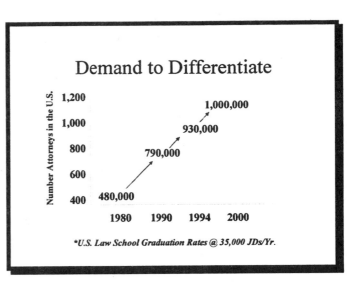

> "The present technology has vast implications for young lawyers and for legal education. I personally believe we have 60% too many lawyers today when you consider what can be done with technology. This means that there will be survival of the fittest. The few survivors will be those who can do things that others cannot. The survivors will have the field to themselves." - Fred Bartlitt, Jr.

impact the practice of law over the next 10 years.

Over the past 200 years we have changed from a profession of few lawyers, small firms, few pleadings and a value based billing system to many lawyers, large firms, voluminous pleadings and the billable hour. Most seers are predicting the digital information and communication changes will reduce the firm size, there will be a resurgence of value based billing and digital data will replace paper.

Year	# of Lawyers in America	Firm Sizes	Fees	Pleadings	Litigation Materials	Caselaw & Statutes
1776	Unknown	Small	Value Based	Quill Pen & Paper	Manual Index & Paper	Books
1865	Unknown	Small	Value Based	Quill Pen & Paper	Manual Index & Paper	Books
1915	120,000	Small	Value Based	Fountain Pen & Paper	Manual Index & Paper	Books
1950	160,000	Small	Value Based	Typewriter & Paper	Manual Index & Paper	Books
1960	209,000	Increased	Billable Hour	Typewriter & Paper	Manual Index & Paper	Books
1985	620,000	Increased	Billable Hour & Value Billing	Typewriters, Computers & Paper	Electronic Index & Paper	Books & Electronic Research
1995	800,000	Reduced	Billable Hour & Value Billing	Computers	Electronic Index &	Electronic

				Paper	Images (paperless)	Research
2000	1,100,000	Reduced	Value Billing Billable Hour?	Computers & Paper?	Electronic Index & Images (paperless)	Electronic Research

Client Marketing and Retention

Since the 1977 United States Supreme Court decision of Bates v. State Bar of Arizona, 97 S. Ct. 2691 (1977), lawyer advertising has been permitted. TV commercials, yellow page ads, seminars, and law firm newsletters attest to the fact that the legal profession has taken the message seriously. Marketing has become a major focus of law practice. Firms compete and seek to differentiate their services from those provided by competitors. Remember differentiation is primarily based on quality of product and cost.

Clients, private citizens, private corporations and governmental organizations, are sophisticated purchasers of legal services. They look carefully at how services are performed by outside counsel. They want to know which lawyers will be employed, what expertise is available, how effectively you employ modern technology, and whether you are conscious of the cost of production of services. From a marketing perspective, how would technology applications assist in marketing the services your firm offers and in retaining clients?

> ### Your Clients Have PC's in Their Business & Personal Lives
>
> - PCs purchased for the home will comprise nearly half of the entire U.S. market by 1998
> - 28.5 Million PC's will be shipped in 1998.
>
> | | 1993 | 1994 | 1995 | 1996 | 1997 | 1998 |
> |---|---|---|---|---|---|---|
> | **Professional** | 9.4 | 10.3 | 11.4 | 12.5 | 13.5 | 14.6 |
> | **Home** | 5.3 | 6.9 | 8.2 | 9.8 | 11.8 | 13.9 |
>
> Source: Dataquest (July 1994: millions)

- Will promotion of the uses of technology in the firm attract new clients and differentiate your firm from other firms?
- Will a direct on-line computer connection with my business clients enhance the services your firm provides them?
- Will electronic imaging, which provides ready access to my client's business documents, benefit the advice that one gives them?
- Will ASCII copies of business documents from my client, for example accident investigation reports from my client's insurance carrier, reduce litigation costs and provide a closer tie-in between my firm and my client?
- Will an electronic trial notebook, linking testimony, documents, and exhibits, provide the necessary information for my client to consider the practical resolution to his case?
- Will real-time transcription of testimony over the Internet during the deposition of an expert witness ensure that his opinions and the basis of his opinions are disclosed and examined to maintain the competitive edge for serious settlement negotiations?
- Will a marketing database assist in tracking the firm's marketing efforts? Periodic reports can be generated quickly to determine the success of your marketing plans. Client referral sources - who and how are clients referred to your firm. What bankers, insurance agents, etc. refer your clients and how are they acknowledged?
- Will a database marketing program ensure that an individual attorney follow his/her proposed marketing plan? This type of system permits you to track when the firm is retained by a particular client and which attorney was involved in the marketing of the firm; and
- Will an Internet World Wide Web site provide marketing and access to the firm's expertise for potential clients?

These are a few examples of how technology can win over clients as well as retaining them.

Survey of Automation Changes in Small and Large Firms

ABA 1998 *Small* Law Firm Technology Survey

The survey confirms that 82% of sole practitioners use computers and approximately the same percentage of lawyers in small firms (2-20) have computers on their desk and are now focusing on implementing computer software applications. More then 90% use WINDOWS and 11% use DOS as an operating system. Lawyers are increasingly purchasing computers with enhanced hardware capability with over 70% using Pentium based systems.

Though WordPerfect is still the leader with 59% of the market share Microsoft Word has made strides capturing 38% of the respondents (Some law firms use both packages). At least 73% of firms have one lawyer with full Internet access 36% of the without full access plan to gain full access in 1998. 86% of attorneys use the Internet for legal research, 52% communicate with colleagues and 53% communicate with their clients. Netscape is the primary browser for the Internet.

79% of firms use CD-ROMs for legal and factual research. There are over 1,100 CD-ROM law-related titles available.

Software used in firms:	1998 (%)	Software used in firms:	1998 (%)
Word Processing	91.8	Contact management/client list	25.4
Accounting	65.8	Desktop Publishing	23.9
Legal Research	62.5	Case management	23.1
WWW browser	59.6	Citation checking	18.8
Time & Billing	56.4	Generic document assembly	18.1
Forms	52.4	Conflict of Interest checking	17.3
External e-mail	51.7	Internal e-mail	15.8
Online services	51.4	Document management	14.6
Spreadsheet	47.9	Presentation graphics	10
Docket control	45.0	Litigation support	8.1
Personal Dairy/Calendar	41.8	Imaging	7.9
Database	36.6	Website development	6.7
Tax Preparation	26.4	Groupware	3.2
OCR	25.5		

ABA 1998 *Large* Law Firm Technology Survey

The survey confirms that 98% of all or most lawyers have computers on their desk and are now focusing on implementing computer software applications. More them 91% of the firms use WINDOWS and 7% use DOS as their operating system. Lawyers are increasingly purchasing computers with enhanced hardware capability with over 90% using Pentium or higher based systems.

WordPerfect is still the leader with 60% of the market share and Microsoft Word has 40% of the respondents (Many firms use both packages).

87.4 of the lawyers have full Internet access. 42% of the firms have T-1 access. 95% of attorneys use the Internet for legal research, 84% communicate with colleagues and 94% communicate with their clients. 52% use Internet Explorer and 48% use Netscape Navigator. 98% use CD-ROMs for legal and factual research.

Software used in firms:	1998 (%)	Software used in firms:	1998 (%)
Word Processing	100	Fax	73.2
Accounting	98.7	Desktop Publishing	72
Time & Billing	97.5	Tax research	70.7
External e-mail	96.8	Forms	65
Spreadsheet	96.8	Tax Preparation	64.3
Online service	95.5	Imaging	63.7
Database	94.9	Groupware	63.1
Internal e-mail	94.3	Integrated desktop Suite	61.1
WWW browser	94.3	Marketing database	59.2
Legal Research	91.7	Project management	56.1
Document management	91.1	Website development	53.5
Remote Access	91.1	Case Management	45.9
OCR	89.8	Brief bank / Workproduct	43.9
Presentation graphics	89.8	Generic Document Assembly	43.9
Litigation Support	87.9	Substantive practice area document	33.8
Personal Dairy/Calendar	87.3	assembly	
Docket/Calendar	85.4	Real-time document sharing	30.6
Conflict of Interest	84.1	Voice Recognition	27.4
Citation checking	83.4	Integrated law firm/practice management	22.3
Contact management/client list	73.9		

To purchase a complete copy of these excellent surveys contact the ABA Legal Technology Resource Center 312-988-5465 or visit their site at www.abanet.org.

Technology Ethical Considerations

As technology changes and impacts the practice of law, how does it affect the scope of liability for our actions? At what point does technological advancement cease to be merely our preference, but instead mandated by our ethical obligations as lawyers? Do we have an obligation to incorporate automated legal and non-legal research, document assembly, full text search systems, and the latest document imaging? If technology is available at a low cost to search a deposition in seconds for key testimony is it unethical to charge your client for the hours it takes you to do it manually? These are becoming difficult questions as we transition into the technology age. The recurring question is have our actions been reasonable in light of the changing technology environment?

Once we begin using technology then whole new sets of ethical issues arise such as whether the use of e-mail without any safeguards is ethical.

Failure to Use Technology in your Practice

Failure to use a computer for certain tasks of

For an excellent up-to-date ethics discussion site see www.legalethics.com. Noted legal ethics expert Peter Krakaur discusses the many issues of technology and legal ethics.

"By using computers to make the system more accessible, lawyers can "increase public satisfaction with the system and with all those - including lawyers - who work in it." . . . "Another area in which computers can be helpful is in making all of us not only more efficient lawyers, but more competent lawyers, " says O'Connor, "one of the saddest things about a judge's job is seeing possibly meritorious cases lost because of lawyer error . . .Naturally, no computer can make a competent lawyer out of an incompetent one. But technology can help keep otherwise good lawyers from making mistakes." What really is important is that "the organized Bar . . . aggressively seek out newer and better ways of doing things. " Justice Sandra Day O'Connor, Dec 1993 Arizona Attorney.

legal and nonlegal research may be an act of professional negligence. The question is whether the failure to use computers is reasonable under the circumstances? O'Connell, "Legal Malpractice: Does the Lawyer Have a Duty to Use Computerized Research?," 35 Federation of Insurance Counsel Quarterly 77 (1984). In California an attorney lost a malpractice suit because of failure to conduct thorough research and properly represent his client in a divorce proceeding, Smith v Lewis, 13 Cal.3d 349, 530 P.2d 589 (1975), overruled on other grounds, 126 Cal.Rptr. 633, 641 (1976). Also see Pritchard, Attorneys in the Electronic Age: Is There a Duty to Make the Transition?, 62 FLA. B.J., 17 (March 1988); Davis v. Damrell, 119 Cal.App.3d 883, 174 Cal.Rptr. 257 (1981) found that where an attorney had engaged " in a through, contemporaneous research effort" including a computerized online search the bad advice was not malpractice. Also see, The T.J. Hooper, 60 F.2d 737(2nd Cir.1932); Helling v. Carey, 83 Wash.2d 514, 519 P.2d 981 (1974); and Warrick v. Giram, 290 NW 2d 166 (Minn. 1980).

The Seventh Circuit in a recent "duty to browse" decision seems to impose a duty on litigants to 'browse" the Internet for certain financial information. Whirlpool Financial Corporation v. GN Holdings, Inc., 67 F3rd 605, 610 (7th Cir. 1995.) The court stated:

> "Moreover, once the significant discrepancies between the projections and actual results placed Whirlpool on notice regarding the possibility of fraud, the information Whirlpool says it needed to "uncover" the alleged fraud was in the public domain. In today's society, with the advent of the "information superhighway," federal and state legislation and regulations, as well as information regarding industry trends, are easily accessed. A reasonable investor is presumed to have information available in the public domain, and therefore Whirlpool is imputed with constructive knowledge of this information. See Eckstein v. Balcor Film Investors, 58 F.3d 1162, 1169 (7th Cir.1995)."

Ethical Issues Involved in Using Technology

Once we begin automating in our law offices what are our ethical obligations? New ethical issues requiring new standards of care arc constantly arising as a result of the technology changeover. Losing client data or allowing client confidences to be accessible by unauthorized individuals are a few of the ethical issues that must be addressed. Always check the latest ethics opinions. Many office computer disasters and possible ethical violations can be avoided if certain precautions are taken. The following is a short list of the increased scrutiny the legal profession will be expected to address as the technology revolution continues.

Office systems:

- Prevent unauthorized users from using your desktop;
- Ensure passwords are locked up and unusual;
- Back up your system and have a disaster recovery plan;
- Diligently use anti-virus software, even on manufacturer's disks;
- Have two or more people familiar with your computer system, preferably one being an outside consultant;
- Select an outside consultant who maintains confidences;
- Surge protectors and temporary power suppliers should be installed and checked on a routine basis;
- Decide who gets access to information and provide consequences for unauthorized access or attempt to access;
- Preclude access to key areas of the computer operating system;
- Immediately determine the risks of disgruntled employees and act accordingly;
- Use anti-virus on e-mail that has an attachment;

- Do not keep passwords out in the open;
- Learn how the paralegal and secretary use their computers and where certain case computer files are located; and
- Keep kids and others away from your computer at home or at work.

Work product

- Use the spell checker and grammar corrector before submitting documents, however grammar checkers and spell checkers are not proofreaders;
- Proofread documents that are produced from document assembly systems;
- Determine if you have a year 2000 crisis– law firms may have problems with their own computers – visit the www.year2000.com Internet site;
- Understand the changing jurisdictional issues as a result of the Internet;
- Request electronic data from the opposing party during discovery;
- Use a computer for legal and factual research;
- In word processors there is a feature called UNDO that enables a user to undo the last command. For example if you send an electronic note as part of draft contract to your client and your client read and then deleted the note it can still be retrieved. The other party would just have to UNDO the last command and they could see the note to your client in the electronic contract. Some word processors allow you to UNDO up to 300 of your last changes. Be sure and remove the UNDO feature from the document before it is sent on to the opposing party; and
- Do not send old diskettes to opposing counsel, files can be easily undeleted.

Internet and e-mail usage:

- Maintain an e-mail policy with employees. Tell them e-mail is subject to review and disclosure pursuant to court order, public record law or office policy;
- Advise clients on use of e-mail and the need for encryption;
- Can a hacker get into my system? Even if you are not on the Internet, can he call up our office's computer and see sensitive information? What security measures have I put in place?
- Stop unauthorized use of your name to any e-mail;
- Ensure e-mail confidentiality – use encryption. However, hackers generally will hack into the server where the e-mail resides, not intercept it on the Internet.
- Is your advertising and solicitation on the WWW in conformance with ethical standards?
- What are the implications of providing legal advice over the Internet?

Phones

- Conversations on cellular phones can be intercepted; Cellular phones pose significant risks as to the confidentiality of attorney client communications.

Non-Lawyers and Machines Practicing Law

There is continued growth of nonlawyers and machines practicing law throughout the United States. Whether they be "document preparers", real estate agents, personal injury advisors, accountants or others there has been significant inroads into the practice of law by those that do not understand the legal issues such as attorney/client privilege, the impact of a pension on a dissolution proceeding or key contractual clauses that should be inserted in a buy/sell agreement. Yet, they advertise and many people feel they perform a valuable service. Why is that? Wouldn't a person be more inclined to trust the judgment of a legal professional as opposed to a "document preparer"? The fact of the matter is that in a recent ABA Gallop Poll the reason people go to paralegals are:

- 97% - lower fees;
- 43% - convenience;
- 41% - responsiveness;
- 35% - dislike attorneys; and
- 14% - quality of service.

Attorneys are losing business to paralegals, nonlawyers and computers. Forty seven percent (47%) of attorneys say they have lost between 10% to 49% of business to nonlawyers. However, the "bright spot" is that the legal needs of most families still go unmet. In fact *"about half of all low- and moderate- income families in America have a legal need . . . but never turn to the justice system . . . " A Shunned Justice System, ABA Journal, April 1994*

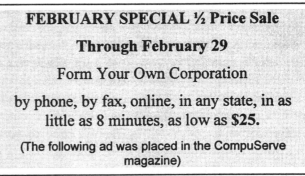

FEBRUARY SPECIAL ½ Price Sale

Through February 29

Form Your Own Corporation

by phone, by fax, online, in any state, in as little as 8 minutes, as low as $25.

(The following ad was placed in the CompuServe magazine)

This article reported "that 47 percent of low-income households and 52% of moderate-income households had at least one new or ongoing legal problem in 1992." where a lawyer was not consulted. One article strongly proposed using more paralegals stating that " recent estimates indicate that about three-quarters of the legal needs of low-income Americans remain unmet, as do almost two-thirds of such needs among middle-income households." *Meet Needs with Nonlawyers*, American Bar Journal, January, 1996.

Non-lawyers are increasing their role in providing legal services. For example, nonlawyer document preparers in Arizona charge $99.00 plus additional fees to complete the paperwork for a dissolution proceeding. The ABA has acknowledged the growing role of nonlawyers in providing legal services in the United States. Regulating Nonlawyers, ABA Magazine, October 1995, James Podgers. The report sets out a process for the states to follow in assessing what continuing role nonlawyers might play in the legal system and how to regulate their role.

With the approval and control of the Arizona Supreme Court computer kiosks have been installed that provide instructions to litigants, produce legal documents for court cases and increase access to the courts. These kiosks were installed to meet the needs of low-income citizens as attorneys generally agree that this "low end" business is not desirable. These kiosks known as QuickCourt is an interactive, multimedia computer system that uses text, graphics and an on-screen narrator. The forms and instructions available for a fee include domestic relations, landlord tenant, probate and small claims. Fees range from $6.00 to $30.00.

Quicken Business Law Partner – Use more than 60 legally binding documents, letters and worksheets to protect the future of your growing business – they're easy to use and they're as handy as your PC. ... Designed by a team of expert attorneys . . . . . Valid in all 50 states and the District of Columbia. $29.95

Integration into the Courts and Law Schools

Applications of Technology in the Courts - The courts are integrating computer technology in the resolution of cases from the day they are filed until the case has its last appeal. Many of the same information technology skills that you develop in the preparation of your cases can be applied in electronic filing or presentations in the courtroom. Many courtrooms across the country are computer-integrated with terminals on the desks of court personnel and the litigating parties. If a courtroom is not computer-integrated, the

portability and cost of making them computer ready for any trial has been substantially reduced. Testimony is being instantly translated real-time for use by the judge and the parties. The first truly "paperless trial" was held in Cincinnati, Ohio in the Federal District Court of the late Judge Carl Rubin. All of the documentary evidence in this securities case was to the jury and parties by courtroom.

electronically imaged and shown video monitors set up in the

Many courts have on- such as ACES (Federal Appellate CITE. These are electronic

> The National Center for State Courts in Williamsburg, Virginia is an active clearinghouse in coordinating and disseminating information on actual applications and successes in applying technology in the courts. www.ncsc.dni.us/.

line database systems Court Electronic Services) or bulletin boards or Internet

systems where attorneys can access published slip opinions, view oral argument calendars, court rules, notices, and press releases. PACER (Public Access to Court Electronic Records) allows attorneys to retrieve computerized docket information in federal district courts for a fee.

Courts across the country are rapidly adopting technological advances in computer applications to effectively and efficiently administer cases. As the courts continue to automate it is important that practitioners automate to provide open and continuous access to the courts.

Application of Technology in the Law Schools - Law schools are starting to take a leadership role in the integration and teaching of digital technology to new law students. There are two technology programs that should not go unnoticed. At the University of Arizona Law School Professor Winton Woods is spearheading a the "Courtroom of the Future" and "Law Office of the Future" projects which provides students and practitioners a technology equipped courtroom and office to learn presentation and digital office skills. (www.law.arizona.edu/courtroom.html).. At the William & Mary College of Law the school has developed one of the most advanced technology courtrooms of the future and includes services such as providing students videoconferencing access time to interview with potential out-of-state employers. (www.courtroom21.net/index.html)

> West Group is sponsoring the "virtual law school" group computing where professors and students can continue classroom discussions with on-line discussion forums

The Virtual Law Office

> Every few hundred years, throughout Western history, a sharp transformation has occurred. In a matter of decades, society altogether rearranges itself. Its worldview, its basic values, its social and political structures, its arts and institutions. Fifty years later, a New World exists. Our age is in such a period of transition.
> - *Peter Drucker, Harvard Business Review*

The word "virtual" means being "in effect but not actually". For example, when you research law using either CD-ROM or on-line services from your desk you have made a "virtual" appearance in the law library. In effect you have reviewed the "actual" books using electronic media. This virtual library revolution has been so fast and total that we hardly realize it. Faxing a document to opposing counsel - he or she has made a virtual appearance to the opposing counsel's office. Video settlement conferencing with

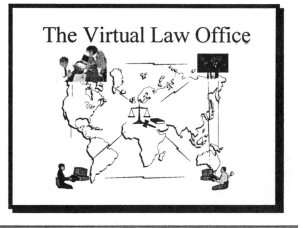

The Virtual Law Office

cameras - the two lawyers have met virtually and discussed settlement of case.

Fundamentally the essence of the law firm is changing. The virtual law office will have no permanent physical location but will exist electronically wherever the legal professional is located. An attorney's "tools of the trade" such as law books, case documents, case histories and so forth can reside on his computer or he can be networked by modem to his law office, his client, or the court. The law firm will be become an information center for the practitioner as he works on a case or teams up with others to work on a case. For example, the virtual law library is reality today.

In order to implement the virtual law practice it is imperative that you visualize what the "office " will be. Sit back and daydream what impact certain technologies and implementation of those technologies will have upon your firm. For example video conferencing which is the viewing of persons or places using video cameras at both ends of a telephone line will be reality in the near future. Most telephone companies are installing special ISDN and DSL lines for customers to view high quality video anytime.

So what impact will this have upon the legal industry as "video conferencing" is implemented? If I can view clearly a witness's nonverbal expressions in a deposition using video conferencing is it necessary for me to be in person? What impact will conferencing have upon the need to appear "in person" for court hearings? Will there be "virtual trials"? The virtual law practice will in essence be what it is today without the actual paper and other any physical limitations -

The law firm of Muchmore and Wallwork (www.mmww.com) located in Phoenix, Arizona may be the virtual prototype law firm of the future. Specializing in civil litigation this eight-person firm places a strong emphasis on the use of technology with its employees and cases. The eight person lawyer staff has one lawyer devoted exclusively to being a locator of legal and factual information using the Internet and on-line services to gather information either for there clients or about the opposing parties. One staff person is the MIS director and focuses exclusively on the network and other technology in the office. It is generally unheard of for an office this size to devote one person exclusively to the location, retrieval and organization of information and another person devoted exclusively to the hardware and software integration. The firm uses Windows NT, Windows 95 and the Professional Office Suite. Microsoft PowerPoint on the lawyers' laptops is used for client and in-court presentations. One lawyer employee working out of her home is connected to the office using ISDN Proshare videoconferencing. Cases are imaged and connection to the Internet is through a direct fiberoptics connection.

As early as 1994 one real estate firm in California set up a computer for homeowners associations, which enabled lawyers, accountants, appraisers and others to communicate by e-mail. Also, they post legislative materials on-line that affect associations, summaries of cases that affect them and have a file of commonly asked questions from associations that are posted free. Eventually, the firm will be charging for online advice. *Opening the Computer Door*, ABA Journal, August 1994.

There are three principal means of acquiring knowledge available to us: observation of nature, reflection, and experimentation. Observation collects facts; reflection combines them; experimentation verifies the result of that combination. Our observation of nature must be diligent, our reflection profound, and our experiments exact. We rarely see these three means combined; and for this reason, creative geniuses are not common. - *Denis Diderot*

A New Breed of Lawyer – The Information Expert. Many law firms do not understand the fundamental change in the way information is obtained and used. Kathy Shimpock is the lawyer in charge of information at our firm. She holds not only a law degree, but master's degree in both business administration and law librarianship. In addition to these academic qualifications, Kathy is an experienced researcher and skilled computer user. She literally wrote the books not only on Arizona legal research, but on online business and legal research as well. (Her latest book is *Business Research Handbook: Methods and Sources for Lawyers and Business Professionals,* Aspen Law & Business, 1-800-638-8437). . . Most firms do not have anyone with Kathy's skills because most firms have not recognized just how dramatic the change has been in how information is obtained. *Reality Today, A Prototype of the Law Firm of the Future,* Nicholas Wallwork, Muchmore and Wallwork, P.C. (www.mmww.com).

including your office.

Once you understand technology and its benefits, you can predict its effect upon the legal profession. From this prediction you then can plan for your "virtual law office" of the future and what strategic decisions your firm will need to make to stay competitive. As you proceed through this book it is important for you to "visualize" how the different computer concepts and technology will be strategically implemented in your office.

The visualization should encompass at a minimum the following legal or office functions upon the impact of planning of your virtual law office:

> Justice Sandra Day O'Connor sees technology as a valuable tool for improving not only the quality and efficiency of legal services delivered but also the quality of life of those in the legal profession. Acknowledging that great strides have been made in the delivery of legal services through technology she suggests that we seize the opportunity to improve services even further through the use of legal materials to be in a digital format such as images or full text, videoconferencing and other specialized computer applications. As she so eloquently states, " Technology is never panacea. It won't make our laws more just, or make lawyers more ethical or more collegial. But it is a valuable tool: a tool for making ourselves more efficient and more competent; a tool for making the legal system more accessible; a tool for making the legal profession easier on the legal professional." The Role of Technology in the Legal Profession, Law Practice Management Magazine, March, 1994, Justice Sandra Day O'Connor

- Virtual secretary's desk - will I need a secretary or will that person become my "electronic case manager"?
- Will your firm's office space decrease as virtual home and branch offices become more common? Is it necessary to have associates when specialized legal memorandum can be contracted for over the Internet with hundreds of lawyers.
- Will the traditional few partners and many associates give way to the many partners and few associates change since our fees will be based on value and not hours?
- Virtual filing of court documents - documents in the future will be filed electronically with the court.
- Virtual information – information is voluminous on the Internet and will be your gateway to newsletters, newspapers, magazines and all other information.
- Information experts – every firm will contract or will have in-house information experts to locate information over the Internet.
- Virtual depositions - Depositions will no longer be handled by traveling to the remote locations. With fiber optics, ISDN lines and video cameras, audio, and graphics depositions will be handled virtually.

> Technology moves work to where and when I want to do it, in a way that I want it done. – Fred Bartlitt, Jr.

- Virtual communications with clients - networked connections with your client will enable the transmission of information, documents, photographs, and voice at any time.
- Paperless offices - The paper will be stored digitally and there will not be any requirement for large bookshelves and storage area for your office or case documents.
- Information, documents, etc. can be transmitted anywhere in the world immediately
- Virtual courtroom - If a trial is held will it be videoconference? If held with parties, what electronic form should my evidence be to persuade the trier of fact?

- Virtual Library - The location of factual and legal data will reside throughout the world and will be available on-line.
- Parties can be anywhere -clients, lawyers, judges, witnesses, etc. can be physically located anywhere and still meaningfully participate in legal

proceedings or meetings.

We are beginning to see the "lessening of the requirement of physical co-location". Since the work of a legal professional can be done anytime and anywhere then is it necessary that person be physically present in a law office to complete the work? The earthquake in Los Angeles forced some law firms to set up satellite offices away from the downtown because their staff was unable to drive to their law offices. Computers to their main office connected these satellite offices. These proved to be very productive and are still in use even after the traffic problems were resolved because of the significant savings in not having to commute in traffic at least 2 hours a day. The physical location of attorney will be largely irrelevant in the future.

There are personnel and logistic problems that need to be addressed under the "virtual law office ". The loyalty and trust to a firm is partially generated by daily person to person interactions and meetings. Would clients appreciate that the new law firms will not occupy a significant amount of space in commercial buildings? Law firms of the future are being designed to facilitate conferencing with clients, the court, witnesses, or others but not to house a large number of attorneys and associates in professional offices. What about the need " to press the flesh" of clients and others? There will also be a need to realize that to maintain your quality of life that at times you need to turn off the pagers, faxes and computers and commit to your family and community.

Conclusion

Digital technology will transform the practice of law and allow us to "practice" law. Digital technology will free us from the drudgery of locating and organizing paper and the large cost and the ineffective time consuming search for cases will end. It will enable a practitioner to settle from a position of strength. It will give you control of the facts and law of your case and the time to analyze those facts to assess the strengths and weaknesses of your case. The capital investment in computers is cheap compared to investment into additional employees. The cost of accessing the law has dropped sharply. The time to search for legal precedent and statutes is minutes instead of hours or days. Corporate attorneys are demanding better services for less cost. Discounted legal services are being demanded based on volume, value-based billing, task-based billing and blended billing. There are tremendous opportunities for growth and for reduction. Some predict that 200 out of the largest 500 large firms as we know of them today will no longer be in existence or substantially changed by the year 2001.

Technology for the year 2001 has already been invented. The chips for the computers and their capacity have been already been designed for the next decade. Technology will change but the computerized lawyering process of handling of information will remain the same. The concepts of full text, databases, images, hypertext linking will remain static. The tools will get to be more sophisticated but the objectives will be the same – to provide quality service for your clients. The application of the technology process is not easy and does not result from chance - it must be learned, practiced and upgraded. Think in terms of information technology tools and the people that can actuate those tools for your cases. Think in terms of your clients' needs and how application of technology can meet those needs.

However, the computer is only a tool. It does not have a brain and think like a lawyer. It can free you from the paper shuffle. It can assist you in digging out facts quickly and efficiently. It cannot prepare a clear opening statement. It cannot judge the demeanor of a witness, when to make objections, how to sell your case to a jury, or the most effective way to present your evidence. It will never take the place of the lead attorney. The computer is only a tool and will not replace you as an attorney. However, it can assist you in each phase of the trial, and it can free you to use your considerable skills as a trained trial attorney, thereby making this impossible job of ours a lot easier. Even though computers will not replace lawyers, an attorney who uses a computer may replace one who doesn't.

But how can I as a busy practitioner implement digital technology solutions in my practice? The focus for the remainder of this book will demonstrate how implementation of existing computer based solutions, with an ever-watchful eye toward the future, can assist you as a practitioner in representing your clients.

Chapter 2

Hardware and Software

Man is still the most extraordinary computer of all.

- John F. Kennedy (1917–1963),
U.S. Democratic politician, president.
Speech, 21 May 1963.

Introduction – Why Understand the Basics?

Computers are found in all areas of the justice system, from the lawyer's office to the Supreme Court of the United States. Though they are in widespread use most legal professionals are unaware of how they work and how they can be used in the practice of law. Just as it is necessary to understand some of the basic features of an automobile it is necessary to learn the basic features of computers and software. This section will provide insights into the basic infrastructure of hardware and software.

Without a doubt computer technology has and will continue to revolutionize the way law firms, companies and individuals communicate and conduct business. In the practice of law we will continually have to address basic hardware and software questions. Hardware questions such as what type of processor to buy, how much memory should be installed and whether a CD-ROM drive should be installed will have to be answered. Software questions will include what operating system to purchase, case management, database or full text software should one use. The questions will impact the efficiency of your firm and the allocation of resources for technology. Also, it is important in understanding these issues in order to intelligently converse with the court, opposing counsel and vendors and even your kids about technology issues. They also are automating and to communicate one must understand the basic computer hardware and software concepts. It is not expected that one will become a computer technologist but understanding computers will become a necessary adjunct to every legal professional's practice.

What is a computer and how does it work?

A computer is an electronic machine that enables one to input, manipulate, store and output information. One can use it to create documents, multimedia presentations, calculate numerical formulas, organize large amounts of data and provide entertainment.

The main piece of a PC is the system unit. Inside are dozens of hardware parts. These include the microprocessor (CPU) which acts as the brains of the computer, memory chips which store data as it's being processed, hard drives and more. Hardware peripherals reside outside the system unit and include printers, scanners, keyboards, etc. Expansion cards fit within the main system and are installed to operate different hardware parts such as a modem or CD-ROM.

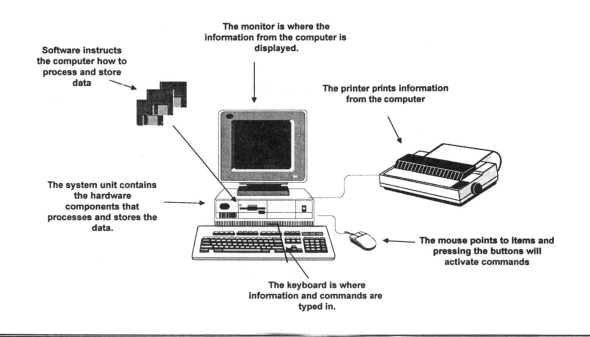

Software instructs the computer how to process and store data

The monitor is where the information from the computer is displayed.

The printer prints information from the computer

The system unit contains the hardware components that processes and stores the data.

The mouse points to items and pressing the buttons will activate commands

The keyboard is where information and commands are typed in.

Data is entered through a keyboard or other input device and stored in RAM (Random Access Memory). The Central Processing Unit (CPU) moves the stored data from RAM and processes it and places the results back in RAM. Output from the processing is sent to a monitor or printer where it can be viewed.

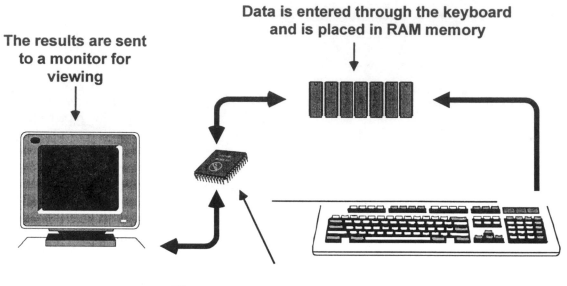

Data is entered through the keyboard and is placed in RAM memory

The results are sent to a monitor for viewing

The processor processes the data stored in the RAM memory

Hardware - Revolutionary Changes

Hardware is the physical equipment that comprises a computer system. The monitor, keyboard, printer and so forth are the hardware of a computer. The hardware works with computer software to perform tasks on the computer. The software is the program that tells the computer what to do with the hardware and how to process data.

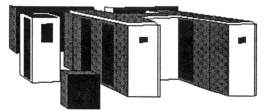

One of the first computers was the ENIAC that stood for Electronic Numerical Integrator, Analyzer and Computer. This computer was two stories high, weighed 30 tons and covered 15,000 feet. The leading manufacturer of computer mainframes was IBM who ruled the marketplace until the 1960's. In the sixties the minicomputer appeared which was smaller, easier to program and challenged the dominance of the mainframe computer. Minicomputers were affordable to more businesses since they did not require air-conditioned housing and were easier to program. The dominant minicomputer manufacturer was Digital Equipment Company (DEC) which became the second largest manufacturer in the world.

During the seventies the microprocessor was furthered developed which has forever changed the computing industry.

> Computers in the future may weigh no more than 1.5 tons. – Popular Mechanics – 1949.

The IBM PC was developed in 1981 based upon a microprocessor chip that was first introduced in 1974. One of the first processors, the Intel 8088, became the seed from which the computer PC market has mushroomed. The first systems had an 8088 processor with two floppy drives and 64 kilobytes of RAM. To complement the chip IBM went to a small company called Microsoft for development of the operating system. The rest is history with over 100,000,000 microcomputers being sold since 1981.

The microcomputer connotes a computer designed for use by one person. The terms microcomputer, PC and personal computer are interchangeable. The words *IBM compatibles* and *clones* are personal computers made by a non-IBM manufacturer.

Purchasing a computer

Before considering the purchase of computer hardware and software one needs to focus upon the particular needs of your law practice. Where do you do work - at the office, at home or on the road? Is it necessary to connect to your office from your home or while you are working on the road? Do you sit in front of the computer all day preparing documents or reviewing images of litigation documents? Do you need remote access to your office's computers? Do you need to access deposition information while on the road or in depositions? Do you visit your clients or do they come to your office? Do you need a

> **Network Computers**
> An alternative to purchasing a desktop computer is to buy a network computer. A network computer, depending on its configuration, relies upon a central server for its application programs and files. It is a throwback to the mainframe computers and the "dumb" terminals attached to them. These stripped down computers cost less.

desktop, a portable or both? Do you need the latest and greatest equipment or can you wait until the prices come down since you usually have to pay a premium for the latest processor, etc. Though waiting may save you money will you have enough computing power for your needs? Finally, do you have the necessary amount of money to purchase what you want?

There are many factors to consider when deciding upon what computer hardware to buy. Computer catalogs and magazines such as *Computer Shopper* and *PC Magazine* list weekly or monthly the changing prices and features offered to the consumer. The following are some of the key features that one must consider when purchasing computer hardware.

PC Architecture & Performance

Processor Speed. Microprocessors act as the computer's brains and carry out the software commands, perform calculations and communicate with the different hardware components needed to operate the computer. The processor speed is the speed of the microprocessor chip in your computer. This plays a significant role in the performance of your computer. Intel produced one of the earliest microprocessors in 1971 called the 4004 chip. The 8086 chip produced in 1978 had 29,000 transistors and a 16-bit data bus. The Pentium chip has over 3,000,000 transistors and a 64-bit data bus. The generation of  processors has evolved from the early 4004 processors to the 8088, 8086, 286, 386, 486, and Pentium™ I and II processors. When a processor such as the Pentium II is first introduced it sells at a premium. If you wait a few months it usually drops in price.

Year	1971	1974	1978	1982	1985	1989	1993	1995
Chip	4004	8080	8086	80286	386DX	486	Pentium	Pentium Pro
*Transistors	2300	6000	29,000	134,000	275,000	1.2 million	3.1 million	5.5. million

*The number of transistors enables new chips to do more work.
- Source, Byte, December, 1996.

Bit Operating System. The architecture and performance of a personal computer is partially dependent on whether the system is a 16 or 32-bit operating system. When we discuss bit operating systems we are referring to the width of the data path. A byte, which is the same as a character, is 8 bits wide. Therefore in a 16 bit system data is transferred two characters at a time since two bytes equals 16 bits. In a 32-bit operating system 4 characters are transferred at a time. Whether your computer is a 16 or 32-bit system is one indication of the performance value of your computer. The underlying architecture should be designed to support the new 32-bit operating system. Windows 95/98 is a 32-bit operating system. Plans are already designed to increase computers to 64 bit and then 128 bit systems.

Memory - RAM is the acronym for Random Access Memory. This is where the data is stored during the actual operation of the computer. A Windows program because of its graphical user interface requires a lot of RAM to store program data. The amount of RAM is an important indicator for the performance of the computer. Since RAM costs only about $3.00 per megabyte it is suggested that a minimum of 16 megabytes of RAM be installed to run Windows based programs. Many programs run faster with 64-120 megabytes of memory such as video and voice recognition.

Cache - is a memory chip that is in-between the CPU (Central Processing Unit) and the RAM. Its function is to speed the processing of the data. It is generally low cost and at least 256 Kilobytes are recommended. It will store previous data screens to allow quicker retrieval speeds.

Hertz and Megahertz - Hertz is a measurement of frequency that is defined as one cycle per second. A megahertz is 1,000,000 cycles per second. Microprocessors run at speeds that are measured in MHz or millions of cycles per second. The higher the MHz the faster the computer runs

Bus Speed. The bus is the communication hub for the computer. Connected to it are the memory, CPU and input/output devices. The bits are routed through the bus so the speed of the bus is important to how fast the computer will run. If you have a slow bus then the speed of the processor may not make a difference.

MMX Technology. Intel's MMX processor (www.intel.com) improves multimedia playback capability 20% to 80% depending on the software and the application. It improves streaming video over the web.

Design. All computers are not designed equally. The design of the computer in terms of the RAM, bus type and processor speeds are important in the overall performance of the computer. Benchmark tests for various manufacturers systems are routinely placed in major computer publications like PC Magazine™, Computer Shopper™ and PC Week™.

Input Devices

The following are different devices to input data into your computer.

Keyboards is the primary device used to input data into a computer. The pressing of a key on a keyboard produces an electrical signal to the processor which converts the signal into digital data such as the letter A or number 4. There are many different configurations of keyboards with many different layouts. Keyboards can have trackballs, touchpads or even scanners built in.

Mouse is a device used to point to and select items on a screen. Similar in appearance to a real mouse with a tail, as it is moved the cursor on the screen moves. It is used primarily on Graphical User Interfaces (GUI) interfaces and generally has two buttons that are pressed to activate commands. It rolls on a rubber ball that translates the movement into input signals that the computer reads. A pointing device or mouse type device is a must with Windows-based applications.

Trackball is a close relative of the mouse and has the ball mounted in a permanent position on top. It is an upside down mouse. When you move the ball the cursor on your computer will move. It also has buttons to press to activate commands on the computer screen. They are generally used in small areas where space to move a mouse is unavailable such as on a laptop. They may be valuable in a courtroom or other setting where space is unavailable.

Touchpad is another relative of the mouse and is a small smooth surface where a finger can be placed and moved to control the cursor on a computer screen. Tapping the touchpad once or twice will act as a "button" to activate computer commands.

Joystick is also an input device used to control on-screen object movement. They are generally used for game software to control a plane in flight simulation, spaceships or characters in adventure games. Buttons on the sides allow the user to activate computer commands.

Scanners are used to scan a piece of paper or graphic into digital data that a computer can read. Once in the computer one can view the "electronic picture or graphic" and edit the image. These electronic images can be stored or printed. The two most popular scanners are flatbed and hand-held scanners. Also, with a scanner you can scan paper and use Optical Character Recognition (OCR) software to convert the words on paper to ASCII readable text. Then this ASCII text from briefs or interrogatories can be imported into your word processing for changes. A high quality scanner can be purchased for $150 - $350. Options to consider are multiple paper feeder trays, DPI (dots per inch) rate - the higher the dpi the sharper the imaged document, color scanning capability, image formats supported by the scanning software, whether OCR and image editing software is included, and scalability to larger systems. Some scanners are built directly into the keyboard such as Visioneer's PaperPort™ (www.visioneer.com) and Pagis Pro™ (www.xerox.com).

A hand held scanner can be used for smaller jobs or to convert text from books. WordWand ™ (www.wordwand.com) is like a highlighter hooked up to your PC. Whatever you "highlight" on a printed page drops into your computer as if you just typed it. The text can be edited and spell checked just like a word processing file.

Voice Recognition gives you the ability to insert text or data directly into your computer application or control the Windows command interface *using a microphone*. As the user says a word or number the computer interprets the word or number and compares it to a dictionary of tens of thousands of words and inserts it instantly into your word processing program or other application. The same process translates speech into computer commands.

The new continuous speech recognition programs - speak to your computer without pausing between words - permits you to talk naturally at speeds of 120 words per minute or greater which is generally considered conversational speed or normal speaking. The actual output of words per minute will decrease as time is needed to format text, correct errors and add new words. Additional accuracy will increase as phrase, concept and context recognition become more sophisticated.

The basic cost for voice recognition software is approximately $200. Costs increase as additional features are incorporated into the software and additional specialized vocabularies are purchased. To learn more about voice recognition software check out the following WWW sites: DigitalDictate™ – www.digitaldictate.com; IBM VoiceType™ - www.software.ibm.com/workgroup/voicetype; Dragon NaturallySpeaking™ - www.dragonsystems.com; and Typhoon™ Software - www.typhoon.com.

Pay attention to the hardware requirements since voice recognition performs best with the fastest microprocessor available on the market. At a minimum you need a processor equivalent to Intel Pentium™ 150MHz with MMX or faster. You will need Windows 95/98 or Windows NT 5.0 and 32 MB of RAM for Windows 95/98 and 48 MB RAM for Windows NT 5.0. You need at least 125-MB available hard disk space, a headset microphone, Creative Labs SoundBlaster™ 16 or 100% compatible sound card and a CD-ROM drive. SoundBlaster™ (www.creativelabs.com).

Graphics tablet is a special input device that has a soft tablet and a pen or stylus to draw on it. When a stylus is pressed on the tablet the tablet converts the exact image drawn onto the computer screen where it can be edited. They are generally used with graphics programs. They can be used to draw on documents and other exhibits for courtroom presentations.

Pen Computing is using a pen or pointing device to write or perform other functions on a computer screen. This developing technology enables a person to use a pen, similar to a pen and yellow pad, and write on a computer screen that is usually horizontal. The writing will be converted into ASCII text. They are generally used today to fill in forms by checking boxes since the accuracy of converting actual handwriting is still low.

Digital Camcorders and Cameras are recent new input devices that enable one to take photos or digital video and then easily download or transfer them directly into a computer from the camera.

Digital camcorders can act as a camcorder or as a still camera. The camcorder can record full motion video in MPEG-1 video format with sound along with JPEG photographs. You can take up to 5,400 still shots on one tape. Check out JVC Digital CyberCam™ – www.jvc.com and www.hitachi.com.

With digital cameras there is no more waiting for film development or photo scanning. Still digital camera buying considerations include resolution quality, color, memory, number of pictures, LCD display availability, flash, focus free and zoom, self-timer and whether software is bundled with the camera. Check out sites at Kodak™ (www.kodak.com); Epson™ – (www.epson.com); Ricoh™ – (www.ricohcpg.com); Casio™ – (www.casio-usa.com) and Hewlett Packard Photosmart PC™ home photography system (www.hp.com) that includes a digital camera, scanner and color printer.

To capture still pictures from a VCR, TV, etc consider the Snappy™ product. Just plug the Snappy™ hardware module into your PC or laptop parallel port. Then connect any camcorder, VCR or TV with the included cable. Watch your PC screen and when you see a picture you want, click SNAP. The Snappy™ product can be seen at www.play.com.

Output Devices

After the data has been entered into a computer the two primary ways of outputting the information is through the use of a monitor or printer.

Monitors display the text, graphics and video from your computer programs. Commands and data can be seen on the monitor as the user enters commands through various input devices. They not only look like a television set but have the capability of receiving television channels with new video adapter cards. Monitors come in various sizes, resolution and color. Black and white monitors are primarily on laptops because they are less expensive. The resolution of a monitor is important since it displays the sharpness of the displayed text or images. The number of dots or pixels that are on a screen measures resolution. The greater the number of dots the sharper the displayed information. VGA monitors normally display images at 640 X 480 dpi (dots per inch) with 256 colors. Enhanced VGA can display images at 800 X 600 dpi. Super VGA displays images at 1,024 X 768 dpi. Screensavers protect monitors from "burn-in" which leaves an after image on computers. Non-interlaced monitors are preferred over interlaced monitors since they display the entire image each time. A monitor should have a dot pitch of .28 or lower.

The monitor size is important. We will be spending more time in front of a computer monitor as the practice of law becomes more automated and the Internet connections increase. A 17" color monitor is generally ideal when performing basic computing functions. At a minimum a 15" flat screen is preferable. Flat screens cost more than conventional curved screens but are less susceptible to glare and distorted images. The 17" monitor is large so see what it looks like on your desk before purchasing. If you are involved with high-end graphics work then a larger monitor may be necessary. If you have gone or are going "paperless" then a 21" black and white or color monitor is suggested to view the paper images on the screen.

Portrait™ Display Labs manufacturers a model Pivot™ 1700 that allows for landscape or portrait views that is great for document viewing. You can view a full page in a brief or memo without scrolling. It pivots from a horizontal to a vertical position. Check it out at www.portrait.com.

The merging of computer monitors and television monitors will accelerate over the next several years to enable users to use the television or monitor for either computer applications or to watch a television broadcast.

The LCD technology available on laptops is transitioning for use on desktop systems. The screens are only 2 inches thick and newer models provide crisp clear images. It saves the intrusive look of a regular monitor. However, the costs can range from $3,000 to $10,000. Check out the sites at NEC™ (www.nec.com), SigmaData's™ (www.sigmadata.com) and Fujitsu's™ (www.fujitsu.com) for more information.

Printers allow the user to see a printout of ones work. There is a wide assortment of printers available for all price ranges and in all sizes. From the immensely useful travel size printers to the large 40 page plus per minute office printer the selection and prices change on a monthly basis. Before purchasing it is wise to check the latest computer magazines for comparisons and recommendations on printers. Printers print text and graphics using a variety of methods such as impact, laser, inkjet or bubble-jet. Laser printers use lasers to draw characters and graphics on a dry ink drum that turns and transfers ink to paper. Inkjet and bubble-jet use liquid ink to spray ink onto a paper to form characters and graphics. Impact printers prints characters and graphics by impacting a spoke such as the letter against an inked ribbon onto a piece of paper. Some considerations:

- Don't forget to get a multi-bin paper feeder for your printer to handle both regular size paper, legal size paper and envelopes;
- Color printers are the rage as their price decreases and as more lawyers understand their value in including graphics into their briefs, motions and trial exhibits;
- Consider purchasing a duplex printer that is a printer that prints on both sides 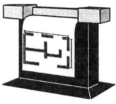 of a piece of paper;
- Don't forget to factor in the cost of additional RAM needed to handle your PC or network needs;
- Do you need collating capability?
- Print out photographic samples as well as presentation and text samples on the printers you are considering;
- Speed is important for network printers and standalone printers. Speeds range from 2 pages a minute up to 90 plus pages per minute;
- The higher the resolution of the printer the better quality the text or graphic will be. Normal resolution is 300 dpi. Enhanced resolution is 600 dpi with some printers able to print at 2500 dpi and up.

Audio Speakers can be attached to computers and digitized audio sound can be played from a computer through the speakers. This is useful for videotaped depositions, wiretaps and other data that has been digitized. One other significant application is to utilize the capability of the computer to convert text to sound to listen to your documents. The computer can convert the text of a document like a motion to dismiss into audio. As more information on the Internet is presented in a multimedia format, speakers and other multimedia equipment is a must.

Other Hardware Considerations

Integration. Many separate hardware components are being integrated into one piece of equipment. For example, reputable manufacturers are integrating the capabilities of scanners, printers, faxes, copiers and telephones into one piece of equipment. This saves space and money. Some examples:

- ZyXEL™ Elite 28641 is an ISDN modem, interactive voice mail, voice data encryption, and standalone fax storage unit. (www.zyxel.com)
- Toshiba Infinia™ is a TV, radio and computer. (www.toshiba.com)
- Toshiba has built a LCD projector and visualizer that is contained in one unit. (www.toshiba.com)
- Mita has available a machine, that copies, laser prints, digitally scans color or black or white documents and faxing capability. (www.mita.com)
- Gateway produces the Gateway 2000™ destination system that is a combination PC presentation TV and monitor. It is a Pentium™ based multimedia computer featuring a 30-inch TV. It is compatible with a VCR and accepts video feeds from cable and TV antennas. (www.gateway.com).

Plug and Play. The plug and play standard in Windows 95/98™ lets you add hardware peripherals to your computer without worrying about jumpers, dipswitches, or any other hardware adjustments. The software will search for any new hardware components on startup and then configure the appropriate drivers to play the device. Plug and play configures your PC for you.

Service and Reliability. In my opinion, this is one of my main priorities in purchasing software or hardware. Over the years, I have had to rely upon many service departments to support both hardware and software products. Some software vendors require that you call long distance, and then put you on hold for 20 - 40 minutes, even though you may have a major problem while preparing for trial. On the other hand, I was to present at a major seminar and could not locate the key to switch my computer screen to a LCD projector and the manufacturer's technical service representative was available at 7:00 P.M. to solve my problem in minutes. Before purchasing a piece of equipment call the service department or technical support for the manufacturer several times to determine their responsiveness.

Upgrading and Obsolescence. The greatest promise of computers is the speed at which they are improving. The processor speed is doubling every 18 months but without an increase in cost. Other hardware components such as storage drive space are increasing in capacity by 20 to 30 percent every year. The price/performance in hardware will continue to cause software developers to bring new applications that will take advantage of this new power. This in turn results in many new and improved software applications that can only run on the new machines. This causes the computers and software to become obsolete within 18 to 24 months. This also results in the need for more training. Older technology may be cheaper to purchase but may end up costing you more because of its limited life span. Repairing older machines and software becomes difficult if the manufacturer does not support earlier models and versions. Newer versions of software may not support earlier version formats. It is suggested that organizations replace ¼ of the computers each year with the older models being given to staff with less demanding needs than the power users.

Modems

This is a must buy. To get onto the information highway you need a computer, modem, and communication software. Communications through the Internet for on-line legal or factual research or to access your computer system at the office are available if your computer has an internal or external modem. Files can be sent or received through telephone contact with your computer. It's perfect for sending briefs, motions, or any legal material you are working on to the office or to co-counsel.

Modem - stands for "**mo**dulator-**dem**odulator". Essentially a modem changes information from a computer into electrical signals that can be transmitted over analog telephone lines. When a modem receives the information it changes the information back into digital information the computer understands. Modem is the device that converts between analog and digital signals. Modems are used to enable computers to communicate with each other across telephone lines. If both modems can transmit data to each other simultaneously, the modems are operating in full duplex mode; if only one modem can transmit at a time, the modems are operating in half duplex mode.

If you have decided to purchase or upgrade your modem review popular computer magazines to determine the best value for your money. The modem should be Hayes compatible. This ensures that a standard set of commands called Hayes AT commands will work with other software. Purchase the fastest modem transmission rate available. Modems can now transit at 56,000 BPS (U S Robotics – www.3com.com) with the X2 technology. At a minimum purchase a 33,600 BPS (bits per second) modem with fax and sound capability.

Modems differ depending upon your connection. Connections can be through telephone lines including POTS (plain old telephone system), ISDN lines, DSL lines and cable lines among others. A different modem may be needed for each different type of connection. For example, ISDN modems are available for around $200 but may not work with a regular phone line.

Modem and communications software is needed to connect your

computer to the office computer and the information highway. Generally the modem or computer hardware that you buy will come with basic communications software. Windows 95/98™ comes with the Terminal communications software. There are a number of communications software packages on the market with a variety of features. *See Chapter 4, The Internet and Telecommunications, Communication and Remote Access Software.*

Wireless modem. Using the same technology for a cellular phone call you can connect onto the Internet or access your office's computer using a wireless modem. A cellular modem card can be inserted into the PC Card or PCMCIA slot of your laptop computer. A connecting cable plugs into your cellular phone and you can dial into a remote location such as your office's computer, Internet and so forth. With Windows 95/98 built-in fax capability you could fax back or receive documents from your office. The performance is generally slower using cellular as opposed to a regular telephone line,

Trend: Modems are now available which enable two parties to connect their computers and also talk with each other *using only one telephone line.* Prior to this time if you wanted to connect your computer real-time to your co-counsel's computer then you needed a telephone line to talk with him and another line to transmit information. Now modems are available to transmit data and your voice simultaneously on one telephone line. Modems are an important link in your communication center. Features to consider are what communication software comes with it, voice mail features, voice communication, fax capability, voice transmission, capability to send and receive files, share computer applications and on-line service software. The transmission rates for modems over telephone lines have increased from 33,600 bits per second to 56,000 bits per second and will continue to increase.

Data Storage Devices

Data storage devices store data from operating and application programs onto a fixed media. Storage devices range from the basic 5 ¼" floppy disk holding 360 kilobytes of data to hard drives that hold upwards of 2.5 gigabytes of data. The type of media used to store your data will depend upon your needs and cost considerations. All storage devices measure their capacity in how many bytes it will store.

Bytes. A byte is the basic unit of storage measurement. A byte is a group of 8 bits. A bit is a basic unit of information in a computer. A byte is formed by combining eight bits together to store the equivalent of one character or single digit number. For example, the letter A (a single byte) is made up of 8 bits represented as 01000001. To represent a number greater than 9 two bytes are needed. The sequence of 8 bits to make up a particular byte is determined by an internal table called ASCII – American Standard Code for Information Interchange. The eight bits are represented within a computer by the changing voltage of an electrical current passing through a particular circuit.

The size of data storage devices, capacity of a disk or the amount of computer memory can all be measured in bits and bytes.

Storage Unit	Number of Bytes (roughly)	Full Text Pages (double spaced)
One Byte	One	-
Kilobyte	1000	½
Megabyte	1,000,000	500
Gigabyte	1,000,000,000	500,000

Floppy Disks. A floppy, also called a disk or diskette, is a removable storage device used to store computer files. Floppy disks come in two sizes, 5 ¼" and 3 ½". The larger floppy holds between 360 kilobytes to 1.2 megabytes depending on the density of

the disk. The smaller floppy, 3 ½" disk, holds between 720 kilobytes up to 1.44 megabytes depending on the disk density. Before writing on a floppy disk it must be formatted. After formatting they are inserted into floppy drives to transfer data and are generally used to transport data between two computers.

The standard file compression utility for floppies is the popular *PKZip™ (DOS) and WinZip for Windows™*. (www.winzip.com). Depending on the type of data on your files can be compressed to 1/5 of their normal size.

Hard Drives are devices used to write and read information that is stored on metal platters. They are usually inside the computer system unit. Hard drives storage capacity ranges from 20 megabytes to 2.5 gigabytes and beyond. It must be formatted before using. Buy more than you can afford. A hard drive for a desktop should be a minimum of 1.5 gigabytes. Windows-based programs can easily use up to 10 megabytes of storage for a single program. 2.4 gigabytes of hard drive space generally costs around $200 and the price will continue to drop as the size of the drive increases. Hard drives are becoming smaller, faster and less expensive. Removable hard drives are becoming increasingly popular to secure and protect confidential data and to provide easy sharing of expensive laptops.

If your hard drive is running slow consider running two utilities, scandisk.exe and defrag.exe, that are available in DOS and Windows 95/98™. Backup your data and run the scandisk.exe program first. Also, part of Windows 95/98™ and Microsoft Plus™ is DoubleSpace™ that compresses and doubles the size of your hard drive. Performance is a bit slower but the added storage may be worth it.

Zip Drives can be internal or external and are similar in operation and appearance to a floppy drive and disk. The main features are that they hold 100 Megabytes of storage on each cartridge and cost about $130 for the drive and $20 for additional removable cartridges. They are as fast as hard drives and hold as much data as 70 floppies. Check out zip drives at Iomega™ (www.iomega.com).

Jaz Drives can be external or internal and feature removable 1-Gigabyte cartridges for around $400. Additional 1 Gigabyte cartridges can be purchased for around $100. (www.iomega.com). A competing brand is EZflyer Disk™ by SyQuest™ that features 230-megabyte 3.5-inch cartridge. (www.syquest.com). Also available is Syjet's™ 1.5-gigabyte storage cartridge. It can hold 80 minutes of broadcast quality video. (www.syquest.com)

CD-ROM. A CD-ROM (Compact Disk-Read Only Memory) is an injection-molded aluminized disc, which stores digital data in high-density microscopic pits. It is the same size as and uses the same technology as musical CD disks. Once written to, the contents cannot be deleted or changed by the user. Multi-session CD-ROM allows for additional data to be added after the initial CD is "burned" with data. Many people are familiar with the compact disc as an audio device for playing music, but it can hold a staggering amount of text, graphics, images, animation, video, and sound data.

The 4.72-inch compact disk stores approximately 650 megabytes (650 million characters) on a single side, compared to only 1.2 megabytes on a 3.5-inch floppy disk and 500 megabytes on a typical hard disk. The truly breathtaking fact is that the capacity of a compact disk is approximately 250,000 to 300,000 pages of full text or 15,000 document page images (assuming 50,000 kilobytes per image).

The CD-ROM disk fits into a CD-ROM reader or drive that can be internal or attached to your computer. It can only read data off of the disk. It cannot write to or alter the data on a disk, unless the reader is also a CD-ROM (CD-R) writer. The CD-ROM is essentially another storage device, similar to your

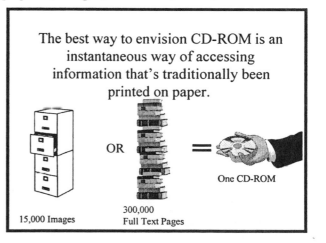

The best way to envision CD-ROM is an instantaneous way of accessing information that's traditionally been printed on paper.

15,000 Images   OR   300,000 Full Text Pages   =   One CD-ROM hard drive or floppy.

CD-ROM writers are available that allow one to produce your own CD-ROM's. Pinnacle Micro™ (www.pinnaclemicro.com) and Kodak™ (www.kodak.com) have introduced CD-ROM authoring hardware and software for under $600. Separate disks to write on costs approximately $1. Now vast amounts of data, text, or images can be transferred to these disks *by anyone* with a CD-ROM authoring system. For example, legal-related service bureaus are now routinely providing CD-ROM disks containing document images at a low price for law firms.

CD-ROM Legal Applications for the legal profession include:

- *Imaging* - With the use of imaging one can place up 15,000 document pages on one CD-ROM disk. Then you can immediately view documents in your case without the need for PAPER and its inherent limitations. These digital documents can be used for witness preparation, depositions, trial, and so on.
- *Legal Research* - The major legal publishers have moved quickly to transfer their materials - case law, statutes, regulations, treatises, practice forms, and so on - onto CD-ROM.
- *Video* – DVD (see explanation below) CD-ROM's hold at least 75 minutes of video on a CD-ROM The value of CD-ROM video is the immediate accessibility of locating a certain segment of a deposition for direct or impeachment purposes in trial or to prepare a settlement video.

Purchasing a CD-ROM Drive/Reader. As the use of compact disk technology has expanded, the price of compact disk drives (readers) has been drastically reduced. Many brands of compact disk drives can be installed in an IBM-compatible PC at prices starting around $70. CD-ROM multimedia packages marketed by Creative Labs include the CD-ROM drive, sound cards, speakers, and a number of CD-ROM disks containing an encyclopedia and books for around $250. Internal 4-disk changers are available for around $300. Check out the sites at Pioneer (www.pioneerusa.com), Plextor (www.plextor.com), and Toshiba (www.toshiba.com).

There are a number of questions that must be asked when buying a CD-ROM drive:

- *How fast is it?* The speed of a CD-ROM drive is measured by its access time and transfer rate. A fast access time is important for text-based database search and retrieval applications. Access times range from 100 ms to 1,000 milliseconds. The average is 150 ms. A transfer rate of 150 kilobytes per second is required for multimedia applications using video and animation.
- *Speed of the CD-ROM.* CD-ROM speed has increased up to 30X and beyond. The speed of the CD-ROM determines whether the data transfer is seamless. For example, full motion movies can be viewed without any distortion in the pictures with the new speeds and transfer rates.
- *Is it a Multi-Session Reader?* Once a CD-ROM is "burned" with the document images or other material that you want, any of the widely available CD-ROM readers will read this CD-ROM. However, if you decide to add additional material to this same CD-ROM and reuse it, then a multi-session CD-ROM reader is recommended. Also, ask whether the drive reads multi-session Kodak Photo CD's?
- *Do I Need a Buffer?* To display graphics, video, and animation in a smooth manner you need a consistent transfer rate of 150 kilobytes per second. Most new CD-ROM's transfer data at 1000+ KB/sec. To maintain this rate, a drive should have a buffer rate of 32 kilobyte to 64 kilobyte. For text search and retrieval a buffer is not needed.
- *Does it use a SCSI (Small Computer System Interface) or Proprietary Interface?* Most new drives use SCSI controller cards. Avoid non-standard proprietary interfaces. They limit you to the manufacturer's technology and prices, and are generally slower than SCSI.
- *Is it an Internal or External Drive?* Internal drives fit into a 5 ¼ drive bay. If it is an external drive does it attach through a SCSI port, parallel port or through a PCMCIA slot? Which do you prefer and which one does your computer or laptop computer accept?
- *Is Driver Software Included?* The drive should include drivers from the manufacturer to recognize the controller. You'll need Microsoft's CD-ROM extension drivers.
- *Can it Play Audio?* Most CD-ROM drives can play musical audio disks. Audio software and headphones should be included. Will your sound card be compatible with the CD-ROM drive?

- *Warranty and Support.* Does the manufacturer offer toll free support? Do you pay the shipping charges if it needs to be repaired or do they offer onsite support?
- *Four disk changer.* Should you purchase a four-disk changer? They are available for approximately $280.00

DVD. The Digital Versatile Disk (DVD) is replacing the traditional CD-ROM, and maybe the VCR. The DVD is the next-generation optical disk standard that has already been introduced. It has a storage capacity of 2.5 GB and above. It will store at least 90 minutes of video. The storage can potentially be increased to 18 GB since the new standard allows for double sided and double layered storage. It is designed to be backward compatible, which will enable current CD-ROM's to be played. However, it may be years before real-time video can be recorded on a DVD which will lengthen the demise of the VCR. The initial price will be $500 and will be used primarily for movies. For the legal field it will primarily be used to access image databases, video depositions, etc, and any other legal application that requires a large amount of storage.

Magnetic Tape drives are portable, generally used as backup devices and cost under $300. The tape can hold approximately 100 megabytes of data up to 2 gigabytes and higher.

Magnetic-optical drives, like CD-ROMs, use lasers to read data but also have the feature of writing data on the disk. They are fast, portable and are generally not expensive. There are two main types of magnetic-optical drives, WORM which stands for Write Once Read Many and WMRM which stands for Write Many Read Many. WORM drives can hold up to 2.6 gigabytes of data or more and are generally used to keep an unalterable audit trail. They only can be written on once but can be read many times. WMRM drives can be written to many times and read many times. These portable reusable drives make them an ideal backup storage media.

Bernoulli Drives have similar capacities as hard drives and are primarily used as backup devices. This unusual storage device operates on the principle of air flowing under flexible material as it spins. The drive can be removed just like a floppy.

Backup Storage Devices. Hard drives eventually fail so critical files should be backed up so that one can later restore the files. Backing up a hard disk requires copying files to a floppy disk or other storage device like a magnetic tape. Floppies, hard drives, CD-ROM writers, magnetic tape, and other writable optical disks are often used as backup devices for servers and PC's. Backups are usually done on a timed rotation if the storage device is reusable. *See Chapter 3, Disaster Recovery for more information on backup systems.*

Standardization

With the rapid changes in technology it is important to standardize on specific hardware and software. It is difficult to support and train on different hardware platforms and different software packages that perform the same function. Standard should be defined for hardware and software. It is difficult to support a DOS, Windows 3.1™ and a Windows 95/98™ environment over the same network. E-mail, word processing and graphics programs present the same difficulties.

To begin the standardization processes take an inventory of the hardware and software present in the firm. Determine the most common standards in your firm for the different hardware and software. After deciding on what will be the standard in the firm upgrade the hardware and software technology and get rid of the nonstandard items. In this way you will have established specifications for all future purchases. Standardization will maximize your investment into technology by reducing training costs, support time and sharing of knowledge of the common technology.

Portable Computers and the Mobile Attorney

Traditional desktop computing systems are being replaced with powerful multifunctional portable computers. Portable computers are computers that can be easily carried from place to place. Portables offer all of the advantages of desktop systems but add portability.

Portable computers have fueled the capability of practicing law anytime and from anywhere. You can access your work product from the office, draft documents, check your calendar, manage your schedule and due dates, make presentations, communicate with clients and staff from home, at court or anywhere. You can take it to court, depositions or to real estate closings. You can make presentations to clients by accessing the firm's web pages. Many portable computers have a CD-ROM built-in for easy access to CD-ROM caselaw or statutes. All of your application software – word processing, spreadsheets, full text programs and so on – can all be loaded on a portable computer. Whether it is Timeslips, WordPerfect, Lexis or Internet Explorer all of your application programs can be used.

Purchasing a Portable Computer – Features.

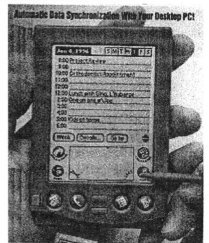

Compare, compare, and compare. Before buying a laptop, view, use and compare the various portables at tradeshows, computer stores and so on. Read the latest comparisons of the portables in computer magazines. There are many choices available from many manufacturers. Their utility depends upon a number of factors including budget, uses, lugability, and service.

For the practitioner the choice of a laptop depends upon the ones needs. Analyze your work needs and then buy accordingly. One of the threshold issues is the tradeoff between the weight and cost of a laptop and the peripherals that you need. For example:

- if you only intend to use a laptop for word processing then the weight, size and cost of a laptop is easy to determine;
- if you need to research the law on a CD-ROM or playback video depositions on your laptop them it is necessary to get a CD-ROM (internal or external) with the laptop. Also, since video requires significant computing power and at least 64 megabytes of RAM a Pentium II processor or higher will be required. This will add to the weight and cost of a laptop;
- If you need the laptop for display purposes for mediations or arbitration hearings. Then it is important to get one of the largest and brightest laptop screens to demonstrate to a mediator your client's position graphically, etc.;
- If you will be exchanging data using floppies then a floppy drive is essential;
- If you will be traveling a lot what weight is comfortable? Remember the weight adds up with peripherals, computer case, floppies, CD-ROM drive, etc.

Type - Portable computers include laptops, notebooks, palmtops and personal digital assistant computers (PDAs). Timex has even introduced a watch that immediately wirelessly downloads your schedule, telephone numbers, and court dates

One of hottest new portable computers is the PalmPilot™. Whatever's important to you -- appointments, contacts, e-mail, expense tracking -- the pocket-size It lets you enter, access, and update the information you need, whenever you need it. It synchronizes data with your PC, supports e-mail, supports applications and links to popular PIMs from thousands of developers , Size: 4.7" x 3.2" x 0.7", Weight: 6.0 oz (with batteries installed), and Windows® 3.1x, 95, NT 4.0 and Macintosh®* compatible.

from your computer into the watch for around $100. Portables range in size, price and features. Laptops and notebooks generally weigh 5-10 lbs. and are small enough to fit into a briefcase. Subnotebooks are similar to notebooks and weigh an average of 3-4 lbs. A palmtop computer is about the size of your palm and weighs about a pound. A palmtop may have some applications such as spreadsheets built in but generally are used to organize addresses and appointments. Palmtops can be linked to your desktop or portable to upload or download data.

Prices - The prices have dropped to around $1,500 for a basic color laptop. Adding on accessories such as an internal CD-ROM drive will increase the price.

Where to Buy - Portables and desktops can be purchased at local retail outlets that carry the major brands as well as many large well established mail-order vendors. Portables cost approximately 1 ½ to 2 ½ as much as a desktop with the same specifications. The *Computer Shopper™* magazine and other computer magazines that are found at most newsstands provide advertisements for large mail order computer companies. Some sites to visit include Toshiba at www.toshiba.com, Insight Computer at www.insight.com, and Gateway at www.gateway.com.

Warranties – Get a 30 day money-back guarantee. Determine the extent and terms of the long-term warranty and whether one has to send the computer into the manufacturer or whether it will be fixed at your location. Also, call the manufacturer's help line before purchasing the computer to see if you can get through to a person. Are maintenance contracts available and for what period of time and at what cost? Check out carefully the stability and reputation of the vendor.

Screens - Laptop computer screens are getting brighter, larger and increasing in resolution. Active matrix screens are preferable but sometimes it is difficult to tell the difference between active and the passive matrix screen. The trend is toward brighter, larger monitors with resolutions of 800 x 600 DPI and 1024 x 768 DPI. Since one will be staring at the screen for many hours compare the screen quality of many laptops. Also, a regular monitor can generally be easily attached to a laptop computer.

Battery Life – is most important to those who must use a computer and are not near an AC outlet. If you are on a plane or in a courtroom the length of time that the battery will last will be important. Consider purchasing extra batteries and a charger if you need the extra battery computing time. Most batteries last 3-6 hours.

Weight – Many machines are now available in the portable line from 1 lb. palmtops, 3-pound subnotebooks to 10-pound multimedia portables. The average weight has dropped to 5.0 lbs.

Memory – At least 16 megabytes of memory should be purchased to run Windows 95/98™ programs. 64-128 megabytes is ideal, and is required to view video, to use voice recognition, and other programs. One can never have to much memory.

Hard Drive – At least 1.2 gigabyte of storage should be purchased since Windows applications take a significant amount of storage.

Built in Speaker and Sound Card – Does it have a compatible SoundBlaster™ card built in along with built-in speakers or do you need to purchase these separately?

Built in AC Adapter. Does it have a built-in AC adapter or does it have an external power unit.

Disk Drives – Does it have built in or an interchangeable CD-ROM drive, 3 ½" or 5 ¼ " drives?

Portable Printers - portable printers are small and weigh very little. They may weigh as little as 1.5 lbs. and print only 2 pages per minute. Some products to consider include the Citizen™ printer (www.citizen-america.com) and the Canon Bubblejet™ (www.canon.com).

Keyboards – are smaller on a laptop and decrease in size for palmtops, etc. Before purchasing a laptop use the keyboard to see if the location and touch of the keys are acceptable to you. Remember also that you can also easily attach a regular size keyboard to a laptop computer.

Modem & Communication Software – a modem for a portable is a must buy. Normally they are PC cards and come with remote communication software that allows an attorney to access all of his office resources from anywhere. See *Chapter 4, The Internet and Telecommunication, Communication and Remote Access*

Software.

Pointing Devices – Portable computer use different pointing devices to substitute for a mouse. These include pointing devices located in the middle of the keyboard, touchpads and trackballs mounted in different locations. Some are difficult to use, so try them out before purchasing a computer. You also can attach a regular mouse to the laptop.

PC Cards (PCMCIA) - PC cards, formerly called PCMCIA (Personal Computer Memory Card International Association) cards, can be inserted into special slots on laptops. These slots, available on a number of the portables, permit plug and play for a number of products. Modems, network adapters, hard disks, sound cards, SCSI, cellular phone connector and flash memory are a few of the products that can be activated by plugging in a device the size of a credit card to your laptop. These provide the capability of adding new functions and features as your budget permits and your use of legal applications grows. It is suggested to buy a computer with two PC Cards slots. The cards are available in a Type I, II, and III format. All PC Cards are not created equal nor are compatible with all computers. Check for compatibility before purchasing. They generally run from $100 to several hundred dollars depending upon the type of card.

Docking System - A docking system consists of a desktop station where one can insert a portable computer. Once inserted the system acts a desktop computer. It provides a quick connection without having to connect cables or other devices to a network, printer, etc. The docking station is generally connected to a regular size keyboard, monitor, speakers and any other desktop peripherals such as a CD-ROM. Also, since the body of the laptop becomes your desktop it saves you time in transferring files between your laptop and desktop and having the appropriate software programs available. These stations should be seriously considered if you are a telecommuting legal practitioner. It provides ease of use along with the important desktop features such as a large keyboard and monitor. The cost is approximately $500 per station in addition to the cost of the laptop.

Synchronization and Replication - One of the problems with carrying notebook computers is that when you get back to the office your files on the laptop need to uploaded to the network or your desktop computer to update the old files. This involves copying the files onto a floppy or connecting a cable between the two computers and transferring them to your office system. This is time consuming and not always accurate. There are a number of solutions to this problem. One option is that you could use a docking station. The notebook is the primary computer that you use and when you get back to the office it "docks" into a docking station and becomes your desktop computer with a large monitor, full size keyboard, and other attachments. A second option is to connect the desktop with your laptop computer by a cable and synchronize your files. The old files on your desktop can be updated with the new files that you worked on while you were away from the office. Synchronization software such as LAPLINK™ or My Briefcase™ that is part of Windows 95/98™ enables one to keep your files updated when switching between two computers. Another common solution is to purchase Zip drives and attach them to your computers and transfer files between your computers with these 100 megabyte floppies. **Tip:** Instead of using a cable to connect your computers consider using an infrared or radio waves device to transmit the files. You never have to physically connect to the network because all of the communication between the computers is done by radio waves.

Budget for a Portable Computer and Software. Below is an example of a portable computer setup for a legal professional:

Item	*Cost*
Portable Computer	$1500

        Pentium™ II processor
        CD-ROM
        Memory: 32 Megabyte of Ram
        Harddrive: 1.2 gigabyte +
        Display- VGA, SVGA, screen size
                and maximum resolution.

Warranty

Fax/Modem/ Voice mail/Network card	$300
Portable Printer	$350
Scanner	$350
Windows 95/98™ (bundled?)	0$
Microsoft Office Pro™ –word processing, graphics, database, spreadsheets	$495
Omnipro™ Upgrade – OCR software	$79
LOIS™ – CD-ROM – statutes and caselaw	$600
HotDocs™ – document assembly software	$49
TOTAL:	**$3723**

Conclusion

Where is personal computer hardware technology headed? The power of the microprocessor is doubling every 18 months. Technology for the year 2000 has already been invented. The chips for the computers and their capacity have been already been designed for the next decade. The processor speed is important for playing full motion video on your computer and to assist voice recognition software reach its full potential. The integration of the TV, radio, phone and computer will provide a central mobile location for all of our communication needs. The key trends are faster, smaller, cheaper and integration.

The Toshiba Infinia™ lets you go from TV, to radio, to speakerphone simply by touching a button

Software - Present & Emerging Trends

Software controls and runs the hardware of your computer system. It is important too keep in mind two different software types - operating system software and applications software.

Operating System Software

Operating system software controls the overall operation of the computer. It interprets commands from the user and tells the computer what to do. The operating program directs and coordinates the commands between your computer and other hardware components such as printers, video, soundboards and so on. It also coordinates the flow of commands between application programs and the computer. The operating system loads up application programs into system memory and coordinates their execution with the rest of your system resources. It also receives and interprets the commands from your keyboard to execute programs. The first operating software was DOS that stands for Disk Operating System. Windows 3.1™ and 3.11 are *not* operating software, but instead are a graphical interface between the operating software DOS and other application software. However, Windows 95/98™ combined the DOS operating system and the Windows graphical interface into an operating system labeled Windows 95/98™. Other operating systems include OS/2™, CP/M™, PC-DOS™ and Novell DOS™. The Macintosh™ operating system is System 8.x.

The user interface depends on the operating system. The DOS operating system uses a command line system for example *C:\ DISK COPY A: B:* that means to copy the files from Drive A to Drive B. Windows 95/98™ uses a Graphical User Interface (GUI).

Graphical User Interface (GUI) refers to a computing environment that enables one to execute commands or interact with a program using graphical symbols on the screen. It is a method of depicting information on-screen. The user performs tasks by manipulating ICONS. ICONS are little pictures that represent program files and commands. It hides the details of operating and application software. For example to save a file a click on the "save" icon will instruct the computer to perform several tasks to save a file. A team of researchers at Xerox's Palo Alto Research Center created the first graphical user interface. The computing and legal industry relies upon the GUI Windows interface as the platform of choice.

Both the Windows™ and Macintosh™ programs rely heavily upon the use of icons to run their system. The problem with icons is that sometimes it is difficult to determine which icon should be used for a specific task. Also, some nearly identical icons perform different tasks. For example some programs use the magnifying glass to represent an enlargement function in the software. Others use a similar magnifying glass to represent a search or find command. The solution to this problem will be a combination of icons and words and a uniform protocol for the different programs. In some programs such as Microsoft Word™ when the pointer is placed over an icon a written word description pops up to assist the user.

Multitasking is the process of running several programs on the computer at the same time. It also refers to allowing the computer to process multiple instructions from several programs at the same time. Software operating programs such as Windows 95/98™, NT™, and OS/2™ allow for multitasking.

Files are where computer operating and application software instructions and data are contained. For example when a user creates a memo and saves it he is saving it to a file. There are different types of files. Files with an ending of .EXE or .COM normally run a program. Data files are generally files that the user creates and must have a unique name within that directory or subdirectory. Files are located in directories that are like electronic filing cabinets. For example under the directory My Documents and the subdirectory Access Databases is another subdirectory labeled "legal" which has Access database files.

When a file is deleted from a disk it is not actually erased, instead the "address" of the file is simply deleted. The file data is still there but the "address" is open for new data. Norton Utilities (www.norton.com) and Windows 95/98 software both have the capability to "undelete" files. The safest way to ensure files are erased is to reformat the disk. To ensure 100% deletion the hard drive or floppy should be destroyed.

Desktop Interface - The standard desktop interface for most users is Windows 95/98™ screen or Windows 3.X™. This is the area where one launches different programs.

As the computing world begins the shift from personal productivity to a group computing the interface will change. The Internet and Intranets are fueling this group computing change. As a result the browsers, primarily Netscape and Internet Explorer, will become the de facto desktop interface for users.

Windows 95™ is an operating system and not merely an operating environment. It is a 32-bit system providing increased computing speed since data is traveling down a 32-bit path as opposed to a 16-bit path as in Windows 3.1™. 486 and Pentium™ machines are built for this 32-bit operating system. It is a true multitasking environment. The new Plug and Play technology in Windows 95™ keeps track of interrupts and DMA assignments and automatically installs most hardware without difficulty. Compared to Windows 3.x™ Windows 95™ is much more stable and robust.

In Windows 95™ the program manager is no longer seen when you start up the computer. It has been replaced with a *Start* button and a taskbar. Pressing *Start* displays cascading menus that take the place of program groups. Minimizing an application puts a button on the taskbar that when clicked restores the application. The file manager has been replaced with the Explorer™. The right mouse button adds important and easy to use features while in the Explorer™. You can create folders and folders within folders.

Consistency has been the goal of Windows 95™. Everything looks alike with similar command buttons for easier training of new users. Running DOS applications under Windows 95™ is stable and in many cases Windows 3.x™ and DOS applications run faster. It is a significantly more stable-operating environment resulting in fewer crashes and reboots.

The preferred computing platform is at least a Pentium™ processor and 16 megabytes of RAM. Networking options are more complete and the terminology simplified. As before a Windows based system provides many other benefits:

- Common GUI interface provides same basic menuing structure that lessons the training curve;
- User Interface is much more intuitive resulting in less training and files can now be saved with long filenames;
- Communication software links are built in such as sending and receiving faxes, dial up remote access, direct cable connections and greater Internet connectivity;
- Data can be transferred easily using cut, copy and paste features,
- Object Linking and Embedding (OLE) and Dynamic Data Exchange (DDE) enables the transfer or linking of data from application to another application; and
- Suites of application programs work easily together.

Windows 98™ does not represent a dramatic leap forward from Windows 95™. However, if you are running Windows 3.1™ then an upgrade to Windows 98™ is a logical and worthwhile step assuming you have the hardware computing power. It is suggested that you use a PC with at least a Pentium 90, 16 MB of RAM and a 1-GB or larger hard disk. This was true for Windows 95™ as well, but the improvements in Windows 98™ require higher performance.

Specifically, Windows 98™ is Windows 95™ with Internet Explorer 4.0™ integrated into the program with a number of bug fixes, new device drivers, and additional user interface improvements. Windows 98™ adds support for multiple monitors, color management, Intel's MMX, DirectX 5.0 and WebTV. It also adds support for the Universal Serial Bus (USB) found in Pentium II machines. Windows 98™ uses a USB to offer plug-and-play support for scanners, joysticks and video cameras supporting that standard.

There are also a number of aesthetic touches that have been added to Windows 98™, including gradient shading of the top bar of each window, subtler color hues in general, and a built-in Explorer interface for accessing information on both local and distributed disks. Windows 98™ comes with many more device drivers than does Windows 95™. Windows 98™ is also much less likely to crash. It is easier to use, robust and has many new features geared toward maximizing multimedia and video performance. Windows 98™ is an important operating system upgrade if video, multimedia and other high end uses are needed.

Windows NT Workstation™ - Windows NT Workstation™ is another desktop operating system from Microsoft that closely resembles Windows 95/98™. NT is a 32 bit stable operating system. NT Workstation™ is not to be confused with Windows NT™ server that is a network operating system. The NT Workstation™ has the Windows 95/98™ interface, and has built in access to the Internet and Intranet. Like Windows 95/98™ it is widely supported, features multitasking, information can easily be copied from one program to another, and it supports complex messaging and groupware applications. Windows 95/98™ and NT™ are both more stable than Windows 3.X™. NT™ can run on a variety of different processors including Intel 486 and Pentium™, RISC and MIPS. Security and performance on Windows NT™ has been increased. Some considerations for choosing Windows 95/98™ or a Windows NT Workstation™ as your operating system include:

- Will your existing programs and hardware run on either platform?
- Are there available drivers for hardware and software running on Windows NT™?
- Will your existing network operating system work on it?
- Will it cost more to install on each system then Windows 95/98™?

- Do you have the needed hardware to run NT™?
- Do you have the resident expertise to manage NT™ installations?

Application Software Programs

Application software programs have specific uses such as writing, dealing with numbers, organizing large amounts of data, etc. Application software includes word processors, spreadsheets, database managers, graphics, money managers and games. They are generally created using programming language such as BASIC, C++, Delphi and more.

The most common application software:

- *Word processing* programs that are designed to allow the user to create letters, briefs, memos and other written documents. Microsoft Word™ and WordPerfect™ are word processing application programs.
- *Spreadsheet* programs that are used to manipulate numbers, perform calculations, handle mathematical formulas and organize data. Quattro Pro™, Lotus 123™ and Microsoft Excel™ are spreadsheet programs.
- *Database* programs are used to organize large quantities of data. They are generally used to compile document indexes, exhibit tracking, case management and more. Database programs include Microsoft Access™, Paradox, and Filemaker Pro™.
- *Graphic* programs are used for drawing and designing on the computer. Exhibits, charts, graphs, bulleted items and more can be created using graphics programs. Microsoft PowerPoint™, Corel Draw™, Paintbrush™ and Visio™ are some graphic programs.
- *Game* programs are designed for fun. They include action/adventure, flight simulation, golf and others. Quest™, Golf™, Where in the U.S. is Carmen SanDiego™ are a few game programs.

Other Application Software Considerations. The primary application software packages - spreadsheets, databases, word processing and graphics programs - are not legal industry specific. Instead they are developed for the mass business and consumer market. Focusing on the mass-market sales these general application packages generate revenues for further sophisticated development of software which is provided for at substantially lower prices then if the software was developed only for the legal industry. However, this does require someone to do some amount of customization to this general software to utilize its features in the practice of law. This has been made easier by the inclusion in some application software programs of software wizards, coaches, or other experts to walk you through setting up databases or word processing legal pleadings.

General application software can contain many computer applications in one product. It is difficult to categorize a specific software product as a word processor, a database or a spreadsheet product because some products have multiple capabilities. For example a word processor generally has a built in outliner which can be used to "outline" your case. However it may not have certain features as "standalone" outlining programs that have the ability to launch into a different program from the outliner to access other case information. Some spreadsheet programs have charting and graphic publishing capabilities. Another product such as Summation Blaze™ has an integrated outliner, full text, database and imaging features. The point is that it is important to determine the extent of different software features a product has and the integration of the product not only within itself but its integration features with other popular software.

Many "all in one" programs do not have the full features that are found in standalone versions of word processing, spreadsheets and so on. However, standalone packages when integrated - such as Microsoft Office™ - are amazingly powerful and can share data effortlessly. As you evaluate software see actual demonstrations of how software integrates with other software to ensure that the software applications "talk" to each other and share information easily.

One of the emerging trends in the software industry is for programmers to obtain a license to use a general application software "engine" such as a database (Microsoft Access™) and design a customized interface for use in the legal industry. This approach is rapidly taking the place of the development of an original database program because a programmer can use as much of the underlying "engine" as he desires and ensure that his customized program is built upon an industry standard that can be used in networks and enterprise computing. As the developmental dollars continue to be invested in these "engines" the customizable interfaces will keep pace with the best of the general application software benefiting the consumer and developer. However, a word of caution, recently the legal industry has seen a number of "comprehensive" litigation support products come to market built on a standard engine such as Microsoft Access. The legal developers of these products try to duplicate their particular method of practicing law onto a computer and then attempt to impose this method upon the buyer of the software. Unfortunately, if one disagrees with their particular lawyering method one cannot customize the software.

It may be more advantageous for a firm to invest in a moderate amount of "programming" to customize the standard software application. For example, a law firm can customize a powerful database to create a sophisticated document assembly system with Microsoft Word or it can create litigation support databases with Microsoft Access™ to control the information in their case. Many of these software packages permit runtime versions to be created and distributed free to co-counsel or other attorneys. Runtime versions do not require investment in the underlying application software.

Integrated Software Suites. Another important trend is the "integration" of various software applications such as word processing, databases, spreadsheets, and graphics and other programs so that the data entered into one of the programs is easily shared by the other programs. This obviously saves significant time that translates into lower costs. This is accomplished using Dynamic Data Exchange commonly referred to as DDE or Object Linking and Embedding referred to as OLE. For example, once information is entered into a database program then the information should never be reentered for use in other computer applications. The data in the databases should be easily accessed and shared by a word processing document, a spreadsheet or for charting purposes. Also, training on integrated software has been shorter because of the similarity in the command structure in the software programs.

To check out software integrated suites see Microsoft Office 98 Professional™ (www.microsoft.com); Corel Office Professional 8.0™ (WordPerfect) (www.corel.com); and Lotus SmartSuite '97™ (www.lotus.com).

These suites offer many advantages over standalone packages:
- shared utilities such as dictionaries;
- data sharing through OLE and DDE;
- similar command structures such as menus, icons, keystrokes and toolbars;
- access to other applications while working in one application;
- purchasing a suite is cheaper than purchasing separate components;
- shorter learning curve because similar packages;
- software support from one company; and
- Installation is easier and integrated.

One of the keys to this integration is the OLE control in Windows programs. OLE enables another program's data, image, chart, or other information to be stored as an "object" in the primary program. The object can execute code or cause another program to execute code. Objects that represent images, graphics, videos, etc. can be stored in the database and when activated, by clicking on the mouse, can launch other applications that store the OBJECT as a computer file. This solves the problem of having to switch from program to program and transfer your present computer files and data to new software. Instead one can embed these files in different software and activate the other software when needed to change or update the information. For example, a docketing and address program should link with your word processor and court rules program. This will enable one to easily import names to the word processor for a pleading, etc. and also determine what amount of time one has to file the pleading using the court rules.

The goal is that all the case and litigation functions of an enterprise should be integrated into a seamless web. The case functions of time, billing, docketing, document abstracts, and so on should all be available in a seamless web. For example when a case is opened the name and address should only be entered once. Whether the name is used for billing, motions, interrogatories, or a witness list it should never be reentered. The factual information should be available to all the other software applications and law firm functions.

Legal Specific Software. There are many software packages that have been developed exclusively for the legal market. For example full text search and retrieval programs such as Summation™ are used to control the data in deposition. Docketing programs such as Amicus Attorney™ provide control over pleading dates and have many other features. Legal specific software is generally priced higher but has been designed and programmed for the needs of the legal market. These "niche' products can be very robust and provide valuable functionality or can be a bad investment of your money. Since it is easy to license a major engine such as Microsoft Access™ and modify the user screens we have recently seen a number of "new" products. Buyers beware!

Software Purchase Guidelines

Focus on the work, not the software. As you review software to use in your practice, choose software that will enable you to continue to practice law as you wish, but digitally. As a tool, software should be user friendly in the sense that the basic work techniques that one uses to practice law and prepare cases is merely duplicated on a computer. Also, the software interface is a personal choice and the ease of use of the interface is very important. Unfortunately, most software is not designed for the individual preferences of lawyers and the unique characteristics of the documents and materials we deal with as lawyers. Software technicians do not understand the "lawyering process". For example, Microsoft Access™ is a database that can be customized to handle abstracts of document records. That's fine, but what do I do about depositions and the documents attached to them as exhibits? Do I summarize the entire deposition and enter the testimony in the database along with the documentary information? Or do I import the deposition into Microsoft Word™ and search for key terms of a witness's testimony? Then I will have two programs and need two different reports to analyze my case. How do I remember that I am using one, two or more programs on a particular case?

Until recently software has always been developed as standalone applications. Word processing programs did not share data with spreadsheet programs and vice versa. This obviously created additional work for the user since his real life needs required the use of both programs. The software companies are now moving away from a technology centered and more on a human centered approach. A human centered approach focuses on the needs of the user in his everyday work environment.

The lawyer is generally not interested in a particular feature of the software but instead how is it applied to the practice of law to give him a competitive edge in representing his clients. If you want to be able to cut portions of a deposition and transfer the testimony to a digest file along with the automatic transfer of the witness name, volume number and accurate page and line number then ensure the software can do this. Many full text programs cannot. The vendors are generally interested in demonstrating features and not legal functions to the attorney because they have many diverse markets to focus on or just do not understand your needs.

The implementation of technology requires selection of specific software of which there are many choices. The evaluation and analysis of software is a continuing, difficult and time-consuming process. Advertisements and salesman assertions may not live up to their claims which can cause untold anguish as one attempts to implement technology in the firm.

Suggested steps for purchasing software:
- Determine the specific legal function you wish to automate;
- Find out what software and features are available;
- Determine what the staff wants and what features are important to them;
- Have a small representative group be available for testing the software;
- Request a demo or evaluation copy of the software;
- Test drive full versions of 2 or 3 different products;
- Determine the cost to purchase, install, implement, train, upgrade and support;
- Check references;

- Select the software;
- Manage the transition; and
- Install, implement and train.

Some key considerations in selecting software are the following:

- What is the background and commitment of the technology company?
- Which firm employees will be required to use the software?
- Is the new software worth the changeover and retraining of the staff?
- Is the software scaleable? Can you add on new users? Is it networkable?
- Is the software data format proprietary? If so, why and can it be converted easily to other data formats to use in other programs?
- Can the program be integrated with other existing programs? Can the data be shared with other programs easily?
- Is it truly user friendly and easy to use? Do you personally like the interface?
- Is their security for only specific users to see data?
- Do I know others that have used the software and are they satisfied?
- Is the documentation clear and understandable?
- Is their quality on-line tutorials or other training materials?
- What do the other staff members think about the software usability and features?
- Is it easy to setup, learn and does it use standard Windows commands? What is the estimated learning curve?
- What are the support policies and how easy is it to get assistance?
- Is the software warranted to do what the vendor claims, if not what are your remedies?
- Can I get a full-featured demo of the software to use on a standalone machine for a period of time?
- What is the per user cost on a standalone and a network version?
- How does the software fit into the long-term strategy of the firm?
- Will free upgrades be covered for 3, 6, 9 months or longer?
- Will they provide quality references?
- Does it support multiple platforms such as DOS, Windows 95/98™ and Macintosh™?
- Will it handle the size of your case?
- Finally, use your good judgment as with any business decision.

Software License. When you obtain a copy of a computer program it is often referred to as a "purchase". However, it is not a purchase but acquiring a license to use the software. The software maker retains all rights to the source code and the original technology. The terms of the license disclose whether one can transfer the license or software to another person. Some permit transfer, others do not. The term of the license is usually perpetual. The license to use the source code of the program is usually never granted.

Steps to acquiring Hardware and Software from an Integrated Systems Vendor.

1. *Issue a Request for proposal (RFP).* This essentially invites bids from vendors tailored to your specifications. It should include requests for pricing, financing, warranties and ownership rights.
2. *Specifications and Implementation.* The contract should include detailed system specifications. Legal counsel should review it. The implementation section should include timelines, personnel assigned to project and the scope of their authority.
3. *Status reports and meetings.* Weekly meetings should be held with all key personnel to ensure that the timelines are being followed. Meetings should continue until it is installed, tested and operating in a live environment.

4. *Staffing.* Ensure that the key implementation personnel for the vendor stay during the entire installation period.
5. *Install by module or the entire system.* Will it be easier to make a complete changeover or should the software and hardware be installed in module?
6. *Test, test and retest.* Ensure that a viable test with an appropriate number of records is conducted. The vendor's representative should be present during the test. Before final acceptance ensure it is operating as nearly as possible under projected conditions. If you will have 300,000 database records with images make sure that a test is done using that many records and images before final acceptance.
7. *Warranties.* Insert a well-defined warranty clause into the contract. What is the length of the warranty? Is it parts only or parts and labor?
8. *Remedies for Breach.* The remedies for a breach of contract must be practical. Time requirements for correction of the problem should be included.
9. *Limitation of liability.* Generally limits a vendor's responsibility to the price of the software or hardware.
10. *Ownership of the system.* Ownership rights of the system should be clearly spelled out. This is especially true regarding creation of web sites since there is oftentimes-original graphics included in the project.
11. *3rd Party Rights Infringement.* The contract should address the issue of a possible 3rd party asserting rights to any part of the project such as software or graphics.
12. *Confidentiality.* Include a confidentiality clause to ensure the vendor does not disclose trade secrets or business practices of your firm.
13. *Price and Payment.* There are several options but generally payments are tied to completion of certain parts of the project. The final payment should be after the system is tested and accepted.
14. *Post installation Support.* Set out in detail how system failure will be handled during the warranty period. What is the acceptable response and downtime? What happens if the first level of technical support cannot solve the problem?
15. *Maintenance Contract.* Negotiate the maintenance contract while you are negotiating the purchase, installation, etc. while your negotiating leverage is the strongest. Some of the issues to consider are commencement date, options to extend, price increases, support details – response time, days of the week, problem resolution, on-site support and maintenance for prior hardware and software components.

Upgrading Software

The changes in new versions or entirely new software packages are a fact of life in this computer era. Both hardware and software are constantly being upgraded or changed as we process our work and group interactions using computers. But when is the best time to make software change or upgrade? Does the cost justify the new features and capabilities of the upgrade? These are difficult questions but ones that cannot be ignored if one hopes to continue to compete in this global legal environment.

The decision to upgrade depends upon the costs and benefits to your practice. The costs include:

- *Software.* Are the new features worth the cost of upgrading? What is the per copy charge and the actual installation charge? How much time is needed to configure the software on a firmwide and individual user basis? Will upgrades released within a certain period of time be covered with this purchase? Will old documents or other files need to be converted to use in the new system? Will the old report formats need to be redone? Can one import the old data into the new software change or upgrade? If I switch from WordPerfect™ to Microsoft Word™ will my macros have to be redone? If I don't upgrade will the old software still be supported and will there be continued training and support from third parties?
- *Hardware.* Will the new software require the hardware to be upgraded? Is the processor speed, storage or RAM sufficient for the new software? Will modems have to be purchased? Will the new software actually run faster in a Windows environment? Will larger monitors be needed to use the new "paperless" imaging software? Will other software one is considering purchasing benefit from this upgraded hardware?

- *Training.* Will this be a major change like from DOS to a Windows environment or an upgrade on a word processing package? Will the new software cause a reprocessing of the workflow? How much time will it take for the staff to learn and use the features of the software? Do we need a 24-hour help desk? Do we need individual training or will group training be sufficient? Will an integrated suite lower the training costs?
- *Time to Learn.* The time spent learning the new software will take away from billable hours and other revenue producing functions. How much time will it cost the firm?

The benefits to the firm include both objective and subjective results:

- *Clients Needs and Productivity.* Will the new software, for example case management, allow for the caseload per lawyer to increase with continued service levels? Can we reduce the lawyer per secretary ratio if everyone in the firm commits to the new software? Will the professional staff use the new software? Does it provide them value? Will this meet the client demand for lower cost services?
- *Competition.* Do other firms already provide this service to their clients? Will we stay competitive or will we gain a competitive edge by investing in this software upgrade?
- *Lower Administration Costs.* Will the new software provide lower costs by increasing the internal efficiency of the firm. Does the increased efficiency and the other factors justify the cost?
- *Marketing.* How will our clients view this? Will they understand the changes and the benefit to them? Will the decision not to upgrade negatively impact our position with our clients and in the legal community?
- *Personnel retention.* Will purchasing the technologies persuade some members of the firm to stay?

Technology - hardware and software - is an investment. Treat it as such. The evaluation and purchase of software and hardware is like purchasing furniture for your office. Your intent is to acquire the best for a fair price that will last you for a given "investment" period. However, keep an eye on the present trends and "breakthroughs" to enable you to understand the changes for when you make your next technology investment. The costs of upgrading must be measured against the benefits to your firm. Not all upgrades are necessary for your firm to operate efficiently or competitively. Use your judgment and choose wisely.

Conclusion

The software products need to reflect the way lawyers think not the way a vendor wants them to think. Software should be easily customizable to enable a lawyer to use the software in the manner in which he or she thinks. Any new product or service in the future - and this applies to software for the legal profession - should be able to be used anytime, anywhere and be customizable.

The software industry is maturing which generally results in software being more robust and reliable. Companies that have a proven track record want to maintain their buyer's loyalty and generally have reliable products. Support is getting better and upgrades are being provided on a regular basis. Though this does not lend itself to innovative products the larger companies are purchasing the smaller companies with innovative ideas. Also, we will continue to see alliances, partnerships and other relationship deals to ensure strong products for customers. As always be aware of small software companies without a proven track record.

Chapter 3

Networking and Group Computing

Networking

Introduction

Networking is commonly referred to as connecting computers together by cables or wire to share information and hardware resources. These resources include data sharing, printers, large storage disk drives, modems, CD-ROMs, communication equipment and so on. Being connected on a network is like being connected to the hard drive of many other computers. One can access files on other computers as if they were on ones own computer.

There are two types of networks – LAN and WAN. A LAN (local area network) is several computers connected together in the same general vicinity such as an office building. Computers connected together within a city, state or worldwide, but not in the same general vicinity, are referred to as a WAN (Wide Area Network). Computers on a WAN can be connected by modems and telephone lines or by satellite. A computer connected to a computer network is called a node.

A WAN can easily connect the computers of a law firm and its branches located in different parts of the city, state or world.

A LAN has a file server that acts as the central computer for the system, network-operating software and application programs such as word processing, e-mail and calendars. The network operating system runs on top of the individual PC's operating system such as Windows 95/98™. The network operating system manages files transfers, control of peripherals and other network tasks. A LAN generally has a network administrator who handles the network and ensures that things are run properly. A PC is connected to the network with a network interface card that fits into a computer's expansion slot.

Network Applications for the Practice of Law

The value of networking lies in the capability of sharing up-to-date information and software and hardware resources with the community of other users on the system.

The primary programs used in the legal field on a network are word processing, time & billing, calendar/docket/address book, E-mail, document management, conflict management, litigation support, and peripheral sharing such as printers, CD-ROM, PC fax systems, modems and any other hardware.

Word Processing. The most used network program in the law profession is word processing. The preparation and sharing of work product information such as pleadings between law firm members is critical to its operation. Special attention should be given to form letters and other standard pleadings that can be rapidly assembled using document assembly on a network.

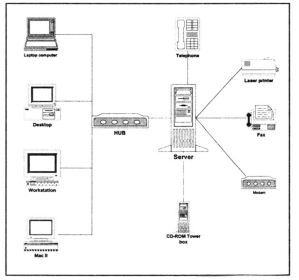

Time & Billing. The billable hour is still the primary measure of an attorney's time and the use of network time and billing programs makes it easy track and bill the time. Programs such as Timeslips™ and others keep time when working on a specific case and log the time into your client's account to be billed at a specified rate. It enables invoices to be sent and consolidates the billable efforts of staff, paralegals, associates and so on, into a central billing area.

Calendar/Docket/Address Book. A legal practitioner's practice centers on client matters that oftentimes require complex calendaring and docketing timeframes. In a litigation matter rules of procedure may dictate a host of discovery and motion deadlines that are mandated by the courts. These deadlines should be captured and shared by all members of the firm in a common and personal calendaring or docketing program. Shared calendaring is a must for the members of a firm. All firm members must use it for it to be effective. The firm's resources then are allocated depending on the scheduled events.

E-mail. Electronic messaging is the capability to send data (a message) to another user. It has become a mission critical application in the practice of law. The receiver of the message does not have to be located at his or her computer to receive the message but can retrieve it later from any location. Electronic messaging is one of the first and most productive uses of a network system. One can "broadcast" a message to several or thousands of people by the press of a button. This results in significant secretarial timesaving and keeps communication flowing. Communication can be with clients, fellow lawyers, staff, court personnel, experts and witnesses. It is becoming as commonplace as the phone system.

Document Management. For decades one of the major problems with law firms has been the inability to store, locate and retrieve the past work or even present work product of a firm. Pleadings, memos, motions, briefs and so on should be readily accessible to any member of the firm anytime and anywhere. This accessibility to past work product can solve the problem of re-inventing the wheel each time one has a similar case. This will provide better and less costly services to your clients.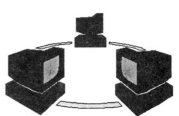

Conflict Management. With a shared network database of clients new cases can be immediately searched to ensure that there is no conflict of interest. Client names can be stored under corporate names, individuals or other identifications and can be searched in seconds for any connections.

Litigation Support. There are a number of useful network applications for litigation. Deposition of witnesses, case plans, interrogatories, image databases, graphics and other electronic trial notebooks materials can be accessible to members of your litigation team.

Peripheral Sharing. One of the main purposes of installing a network is to share hardware resources among a group of users thus lowering the overall cost of separate components. Printers, CD-ROMs, fax modems to send and receive faxes, tape backup, and modems to access the Internet can all be shared. For example, the CD-ROM caselaw and statutes for your jurisdiction can be on a network for easy access by all members of your firm.

Remote Access to the Network

Staff who are working in the courtroom, at home or anywhere can remotely access the resources on a network. They can have complete access to document management systems, litigation support databases, timekeeping entries, calendars, CD-ROM caselaw, e-mail and so on. See *also Chapter 4, The Internet and Telecommunications, Communication and Remote Access Software.*

History of Networks

Networking is not a recent phenomenon. Universities and governments have been networking for decades. What is new is that since the availability of the desktop computer in the early 1980's the value of networking is available to everyone. The history of computers and networks has evolved from huge mainframe computers that were not networked to small laptops that can be networked and connected to any other computer in the world. With the emergence of the PC networks have become commonplace.

The invasion of the PC's surprised data processing departments who lost control of the computing power in companies. Now users could take data from the mainframes or minicomputers and manipulate the data in productive ways on their own computers. Almost overnight data processing departments lost their presence and power in companies.

Data processing departments are referred to as MIS (Management Information Services), IT (Information Technology) or some name with the word INFORMATION in it. New names are starting to appear with the word KNOWLEDGE included in the title such as Chief Knowledge Officer.

The first networking systems were called "sneaker net". It implied that to share files one had to physically put on sneakers and carry a file on a floppy to a different computer if you wanted to share a document or other computer file materials. One of the first hardware sharing devices was the "data switch" which allowed several computers to share a single printer.

The first networked applications were client based. This meant that the application program such as Microsoft Access™ generally resided on the client or user PC. When the user activated the application then the server would transfer the sometimes-complete data file to the user computer for the user to work with the data. This resulted in slow searches and the network system would slow down when used by many users.

To solve this problem applications have been developed - called client/server applications - where the server does all the computing and the results are sent back to the user. This is similar to the original mainframe-computing environment. This has been met with acceptance because performance is better and more cost effective since the server can be the expensive computer and not each individual computer. Your data is better protected since only the results of your search are sent to your computer and not the whole computer file. Although it has become feasible to provide virtually every office worker with a PC, it is more cost-effective for PC users to share files and common peripherals such as printers, facsimile boards, modems, and scanners. The downside of client/server systems is the maintenance cost due to the complexity of client/server systems and the expense of the server.

The argument for the changeover from the mainframe to PC was the concept of *distributive computing*. This fancy term means that individual PC's could run programs and not have to share the programs or processing power of the mainframe. Thus the argument goes that it gives individual computing power to the individual PC user.

This distributive computing argument was successful and we have seen a huge implementation of networking systems in companies across the country. One PC server may have 5, 10, 100, or higher number of other computers connected to it. With this distributed computing came the problems of software upgrades, maintenance, systems operators, network administrators and a huge support cast for this new "productivity" tool. Also, each computing group has special needs which are often met by using off the shelf software and "end user" programming to control the information they need.

The local area network (LAN) was created in response to the need for a standardized system of linking computers together in a company. Installing cables that connect each computer to the network is still the most common linking method, but other means are being explored, such as the use of infrared radiation, radio frequency waves, and, as the conducting medium, a building's electrical wiring system.

The evolution of networking has evolved into two primary types of distributive computing, client/server and peer-to-peer networking.

Client/Server Networking

Client/server is a type of computing that intelligently divides tasks between client and servers. The client (usually the less powerful machine) requests information from the servers. The server (usually the more powerful machine) accepts the client's request, performs computations and satisfies clients' requests and sends a response. The client is sometimes referred to as the front-end component and the server is referred to as the back-end component.

Client/servers networks use a dedicated computer called a *server* to handle file and print services for *client* users. A client/server network may have several *server* computers to handle the *server* needs for the *client* group, which are all interconnected. Workstation computers connected to the *server* network are called *clients.* Client computers are at the worker's desk. They can use the server's printers or even save files to the *server* storage areas. As the network system grows separate servers for print, fax and mail can be connected. Servers called redundant file servers can be connected to your primary server that backup your data instantly and if your primary server crashes the user will not even know it.

Servers are generally high-powered machines since they are required to handle the computing needs of many client workstations. Servers can be devoted to specific network operating functions such as a mail server, print server, file server and so on. Also, since they need to handle the computing requests from several computers at once they must run an advanced operating system. Clients can also be powerful machines but can consist of a variety of low and high-powered machines connected to the same network.

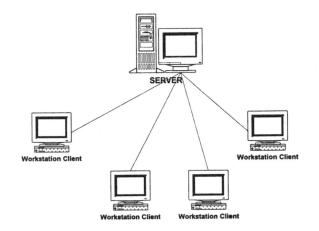

Network operating systems manage various network functions such as file storage, application software and printer use. Network operating software includes:

- Novell NetWare™
- IBM OS/2 Warp Server™
- Windows NT Server™
- Banyan Vines(Unix)™
- TCP/ISP and IPX/SPX

Specific software applications developed for this type of networking are referred to as client/server applications. Client Operating Service (COS) is the software that resides on a computer and handles the interface between the hardware and the applicable software. The most popular COS is Windows 95/98™.

Peer-to-Peer Networking

The requirements for an additional computer, network cards, etc. for a client/server networking system led to the development of peer-to-peer networking. The primary idea behind a peer-to-peer network is that each computer can be both a client and a server. Therefore, each computer can share its resources with other computers and can share resources from other computers. So if one computer has a laser printer attached a peer can request access rights to the laser printer and print a document on that printer. Similarly, if another computer has the office workproduct on it then one can as a "client" access the peer "server" to locate specific motions.

The cost of peer-to-peer is less then a client server system since you do not need a high powered standalone server computer, but one can still share data such as rolodex, accounting information and use e-mail services. However other applications such as a shared calendar and backing up the system is much more difficult if not impossible to accomplish using peer-to-peer systems.

Connections can be made through your serial port for a peer-to-peer system with Windows 95/98™ software eliminating the need for network cards. They have an advantage of flexibility and are simpler to set up. The limitations of peer-to-peer is that they are slower, one lacks the control or management over the other user's computer, and security and access are lessened. If the clients subject one peer computer to a lot of use then a significant decrease in performance can occur. Client servers are generally in a more secure environment, are not turned off, and are faster.

Peer-to-peer networks have their advocates who argue that when computing groups are small, performance is not critical, cost is important and when technical skills are generally not available then peer to peer may be the answer. Artisoft, developer of LANtastic for Windows™ or DOS, has grown to a substantial business with networks of up to 100 users using peer-to-peer networking. (www.artisoft.com). Realizing the potential of the market Novell introduced its peer-to-peer network called NetWare Lite™ (www.novell.com) and Microsoft's peer-to-peer system is Windows for Workgroups™, Windows 95/98™ and NT™ (www.microsoft.com).

As client server technology becomes simpler and peer to peer features are built into client server technology then the distinction between the two will continue to blur.

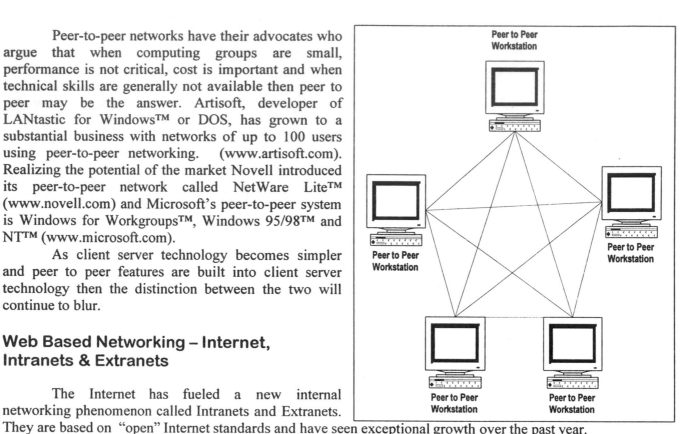

Web Based Networking – Internet, Intranets & Extranets

The Internet has fueled a new internal networking phenomenon called Intranets and Extranets. They are based on "open" Internet standards and have seen exceptional growth over the past year.

Intranets are your own personal Internet within your organization. An Intranet can be walled off and not be part of the Internet for total security from users of the Internet. It generally is located on your networked computer system within your organization. Extranets are a private "Internet" for two or more clients, firms or organizations. The same reasons that the Internet had phenomenal growth are the same reasons why Intranets and Extranets are the most talked about new infrastructures for an organization.

Technically speaking an Intranet or Extranet is an internal network that operates on "open standards". The "open standards" consist of the key standard TCP/IP (the network protocol), HTML (WWW programming language), POP3 and SMTP (Email standards), HTTP (web server language), and FTP (file transfer protocol) among others. Open standards generally result in lower cost since there are no propriety extensions to these generally simple and straightforward standards. Since they are open, low cost and not tied to proprietary vendors monopolies are not created.

The interface tool - web browser - can be used on a variety of hardware platforms – 386, 486, Pentiums™, Windows 3.1™, Windows 95/98™, Macintosh™, Unix or NT™. The browser focuses on content and not a specific software package. Intranet and Extranet costs are low compared to cost of purchasing proprietary document distribution software or other group computing software. Web sites can be configured to the group's needs – whether department wide policy matters or specific cases. They can be built and implemented quickly on a single machine, a LAN (Local Area Network) or on a WAN (Wide Area Network) which makes them easily scalable for growth of your legal organization. It can co-exist alongside other networked protocols and applications. Each person or department can update, control and publish information for his or her own area of responsibility. HTML documents can hyperlink to other documents within your organization or to outside Internet sites. It is a stable, secure environment.

The web-based interface is being used in all industries as business try to lower their total cost of ownership for computers and software. Indeed, businesses rely more and more on Intranets and Extranets to get the job done. Two of three Internet decision-makers surveyed by InformationWeek feel comfortable placing key applications on an intranet. Half say they're hooking host database and financial systems to their internal Internets. (InformationWeek, November 17, 1997).

The simplistic browser interface is one of the main attractions of an Intranet. Besides being universal, it is easy to learn to use. The primary use of the Internet or Intranets has been for publication of information such as firm policies, briefs and other work product, etc. However, applications are rapidly being developed to manage law firm and case information using Intranets. New applications such as calendars, document databases with attached images, discussion groups, full text searching of depositions or other case full text information, client information and conflict checking among others are already in use.

Web Server (Thin/Thick Client). Many application software vendors are now offering a Windows based and a Web based interface for their clients. They are generally referred to as a thick client (Windows based) and a thin client (web based). The Windows based client is referred to as thick because network and application software must be on the client computer for the system to work. It requires more disk space, administration, and computer files. The (thick) client must be loaded with network and application software to interact with a network application such as a database like Microsoft Access.

The thin client or web based client is a web browser. It can be used on a variety of hardware platforms – 386, 486, Pentiums, Windows 3,1, Windows 95/98, Macintosh, Unix or NT. The browser focuses on content and not a specific software package. Web based systems costs are low compared to cost of purchasing proprietary document distribution software or other group computing software. Applications are already developed to manage law firm and case information using the Internet, Extranet or Intranets. Applications such as calendars, document databases with attached images, discussion groups, full text searching of depositions or other case full text information, client information and conflict checking among others are already in use. Imagine the possibilities! Using a word processor, spreadsheet and database you can publish and then using an Internet browser you can have access to:

- your firm's policy and procedure manual;
- office and case memos;
- client databases;
- pleadings;
- depositions;
- calendars;
- office and case discussions;
- past work product;
- frequently asked questions and answers;
- conflict checking;
- contacts;
- commendations;

- firm list of Internet links;
- Announcements;
- training materials;
- clients – new and old;
- judges backgrounds;
- briefbanks;
- new case opinions;
- forms database;
- outlines of key work product;
- bulletins;
- specific practice area pages; and
- any other material important to your firm.

Once you have an Intranet than an Extranet is a step away. Yes, an Extranet – which is the capability to provide access to selected information to external clients. For example, a client may dial in and have access to case plans, workproduct and time and billing data on their cases. It will provide the platform for collaboration among clients and co-counsel on a case. If security is in place one can be anywhere in the world and participate in case management decisions using an Extranet.

> Extranets have proved to be extremely useful in litigation. The tobacco litigation has spawned collaborative litigation environment. The legal team is using internet protocols (Web Browsers, HTML, etc.) to access and process all transcripts, documents produced, work product, calendar, and court docket, with an integrated database, full text and document image and messaging system. Other collaborative tools are used by the lawyers for messaging, linking threaded discussions to documents, and for enhanced subjective coding by attorneys and legal staff. Hypertext (HTML) combined with databases & full text retrieval enhances the access to and viewing of all case information. To access The Tobacco Litigation Extranet Demo and for further information on Litigation Extranets contact Legal Computer Solutions, Inc. at (617) 227-4469 or their web site (www.lcsweb.com).

For example at Sun Microsystems's legal department they use an Intranet and Extranet to share contract forms, policies, status reports on cases, etc. The main interface is a web browser and can be used to access information sources such as video or databases. It provides timely access to the latest form contracts, etc., and is available 24 hours a day.

The major software companies have awakened and reacted quickly to the immense growth of the Internet and the coming explosive growth of Intranets and Extranets. They have provided simple easy to use features for converting word processing documents, spreadsheets, slideshow presentations and databases into HTML files. The HTML files can be moved to your Intranet web site with a few keystrokes and your information is readily available to all users using the standard Internet browser.

Intranet and Extranet search engines. An Intranet search engine is able to search for the information located on your private Intranet network. They are needed to locate valuable information published on your Intranet site. A quality search engine must be able to search and read data from internal and external Intranets, legacy databases, word-processing files or on any file where data is stored. Once read it must index it and then with a user-friendly interface retrieve the requested data with accuracy. These search engines are not all created equal. Depending on your specific needs such as speed, index capability, file size, amount of data and other factors specific search engines are available. Some Intranet search engines to consider:

- Verity Knowledge Base Networks™ – www.verity.com
- RetrievalWare™ – www.excalib.com
- Lycos™ – www.lycos.com
- Opentext™– www.opentext.com
- Infoseek™ – www.infoseek.com
- Alta Vista™ – www.dec.com
- ISYS™ – www.isysdev.com

Driven by open standards, low cost, hardware independent, quick to set up and low administration costs we will see this rapidly growing group computing mechanism grow in popularity.

Network Components

There are three primary components to understanding networks:

1. Physical Connections
2. Network Operating System
3. Application Component

1. Physical Connections

The physical components are the network topology and network connecting devices, which includes network interface cards (NIC), cabling, connections, and all other hardware to connect the computers.

Topologies. The different methods of connecting computers into a network are called topologies. Each topology has certain advantages and disadvantages that must be considered as one networks an office. These topologies are changing and new hybrid topologies such as Star-Bus network combining the best of both topologies are being developed.

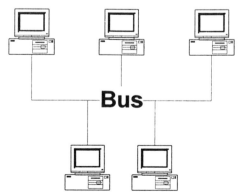

The bus topology computers are connected together to a central cable called a bus. The bus topology is one of the most common and doesn't require as much cable as other systems and thus less expensive. As new computers are added they are connected to the main backbone or bus. The system continues to work even if one of the clients cables fails. However, the whole network stops if the main cable or bus is severed or disconnected. The system may slow down as more data is transferred along this one main connection.

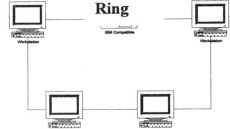

The ring topography connects each PC to two other PC's in a ring formation. Each PC is set up to pass data from one machine to the next in this relay type of system. Each computer has an in and out port. If one PC fails the entire system fails. This system uses less cable than the others and thus is less costly. Most integrators use hybrid ring systems.

In a star network all the computers are connected through a central hub to the server. The advantage to this system is that if one cable or computer is disconnected the entire network continues to function. This configuration is considered one of the most reliable, however it uses a lot of cable and thus is more expensive. If the central hub fails the system will not function.

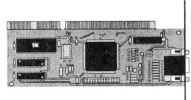

Remember that new configurations are being developed and that many networks use a combination or hybrid of the above networks to maximize performance and reliability.

Network Connecting Devices. There are a number of network physical components used to network computers. They are network interface cards, cabling, routers, bridges and hubs.

Network Interface Cards (NIC). Network interface cards are the link between your computer and the cabling to connect your computers to the other computers on the network. There are well over 50 network cards available. When choosing a new card chose the fastest technology and one that is compatible with Windows 95/98. Ethernet is a system of protocols for a computer that allows workstations to connect through NICs to other workstations. *Ethernet systems* are popular because they are relatively inexpensive. The data transmission rate is at 10 MBPS or higher and uses the bus or star topology. *Token-Ring* developed by IBM is more expensive then Ethernet but transmits data at 16 MBPS or higher.

FDDI stands for Fiber Distributed Data Interchange and requires fiber optics cabling to work. Data transmission on FDDI is 100 MBPS and faster.

ATM stands for Asynchronous Transfer Mode and can transfer data from 25 MBPS up to 155 MBPS. It is predicted that the future speeds will be 2G. It appears to be the emerging standard but still faces inoperability between vendors and backward compatibility issues.

Cabling (wire and wireless). To connect the nodes or workstations of your computer network you need cabling. Cabling here is referring to both actual physical cabling and the "wireless" variety. In either situation "cabling" is needed to connect the computers. Wire still provides the best security and integrity in data transmission at the present time.

The two primary types of wire cabling is coaxial and twisted pair. *Coaxial* cabling is generally less expensive, uses fewer other connector devices and provides good shielding from outside interference. It is more difficult to work with and to install in the walls. *Twisted pair* cabling has several pairs of wires that are braided within a plastic cover.

Direct cable networking is supported by Windows 95/98™ and enables two computers to network using either the serial or parallel ports. The parallel ports permit faster transmission but are limited to 50 feet, whereas the serial port cable can extend up to a thousand feet.

Fiber Optic network cable uses light instead of electrical impulses to carry the network signal. Fiber optic is a thin glass filament that connects to optical connectors for each of the computers. Fiber optic's signal strength enables a signal to be run a long distance without a weakening of the signal. Because of its signal strength, data speeds can increase from 10 MBPS (10,000,000 bits per second) to over 1G (1,000,000,000 bits per second) which will be sufficient for future network data needs. Fiber optic connectors and cabling are expensive but may be the choice if electrical interference is present or distance between computers is significant.

Light wave connections use either infrared light beams or lasers to communicate between two computers. Light waves cannot penetrate walls or ceilings, are subject to interference and network speeds can be quite slow.

Radio waves connections use radio signals to transmit data. They can penetrate walls and ceilings and can transmit from several hundred feet to several miles. Radio-wave connections are typically used when the need to connect mobile laptops in a business is required - such as recording the inventory in nearby warehouses with laptop computers. Radio wave networking can be used to connect buildings and mobile units within a several mile radius. Radio wave connections are subject to interference of other nearby radio transmissions.

Gateways are computers that convert one protocol to another protocol. They can convert data from TCP/IP to another protocol or e-mail from one protocol to another.

Hubs, Routers and Bridges are hardware components that connect network segments together to send and receive data between different LANs and WANS. A hub is a connecting device to connect workstations and servers to form a network. They can be used for client/server or peer-to-peer systems. To connect networks together one would use a router or bridge  to exchange data information. Routers are generally used to connect and send information from a LAN to the WAN. Bridges are hardware devices that break a large LAN into smaller ones for better management. To connect WANS together connectors called DSU/CSU's are connected to data transmission lines such as ISDN, etc.

2. Network Operating System

In order to communicate on a network, computers must use the appropriate operating protocol selected for the network. This protocol enables the computer to exchange information and ensure correct data transmission. The network operating system (NOS) is the controlling software that enables a server to accommodate multiple clients and provide the communication network between them. The most common network protocols and the products supporting the protocol are:

- TCP/IP - *Unix, Windows NT™ server, Internet products* (TCP/IP is the protocol being used on the Internet and for in*tra*nets)
- IPX/SPX - *Novell NetWare™, Windows NT Server™*
- NetBIOS - *OS/2 WARP Server™, Windows NT Server™*

3. Application Component

The value of networking lies in the capability of sharing up-to-date information, software and hardware resources with other users on the system.

The primary programs used in the legal field on a network are word processing, time & billing, calendar/docket/address book, E-mail, document management, conflict management, litigation support, and peripheral sharing such as printers, CD-ROM, PC fax systems, modems and any other hardware. See the prior part on *Network Applications for the Practice of Law* for a detailed discussion of these applications.

Network Cost

The approximate cost of a **client/server** network is set forth below. These are rough estimates and the cost will change depending upon your individual requirements such as number of workstations on the system, peripherals attached, software requirements, and remote communication needs among others.

- File Server $2,500 +
- Data Backup System $300 - $600
- Uninterruptible Power
  Supply (UPS) $300 - $1500
- Hub $300+

- Per individual PC
  - Network Interface Card $50 - $150
  - Network Software $50 - $150
  - Cabling $100
  - Install System $50 - $100
- Network Hub $125 - $1000

The approximate cost of a **peer-to-peer** network is set forth below. These are rough estimates and the cost will change depending upon your individual requirements such as number of workstations on the system, peripherals attached, software requirements, and remote communication needs among others.

The cost of a peer-to-peer system **per** PC is:

- Network Interface Card $50 - $150
- Network Software $50 - $150
- Cabling $100
- Install System $50 - $100
- Network Hub $125 - $1000

Network Internet Resource Sites.

LAN Time Magazine (www.lantimes.com); LAN Magazine (www.lanmag.com); Network Computer Magazine (www.techweb.cmp.com/nwc); Novell (www.novell.com); Microsoft (www.microsoft.com/ntworkstation/); Artisoft (www.artisoft.com); IBM (www.ibm.com); Intel (www.intel.com); and Compaq (www.compaq.com).

Disaster Recovery

Disaster recovery is a term given to the process of recovery and/or protecting your hardware, software and data from being damaged or destroyed. With the significant investment in technology and the critical role it plays in your firm's daily operations it is essential that it be given top priority.

- *Tape or optical backup.* It is essential that you back up your data. One of the most common and inexpensive backup devices is the digital audiotape (DAT). Tape drives have sufficient capacity for the new high capacity drives and are the most cost effective. However, the cost of writable optical drives is low and provides for a more secure media to store your data than a tape backup

    Whatever backup or disaster recovery system one purchases test it on the computer or network system that is being backed up to ensure it works. Practice on a standalone machine without valuable information on it. Delete a file and then actually try to restore the lost file.

Develop a regular backup schedule and have one set of weekly backup tapes or disks offsite in case of fire, theft, etc. Understand how to use the system yourself.

- *Data equipment racks* – are used to keep your servers and other equipment off the floor and securely anchored in a central location. If you live in earthquake country this additional bracing is needed.

- *File Servers with fault tolerant drives.* Fault tolerant drives are drives that mirror or contain the same data on a separate drive. In the case of failure of a drive then the other drive will take over and business can proceed as usual. In some cases more than one drive will be mirrored so more than one backup drive is available. However, if the power supply goes down or the motherboard or memory chips fail your system can still crash.

- *Surge Protectors.* A surge protector prevents a high voltage spike from seriously damaging your computer hardware. They run around $40 for a quality protector to protect computer hardware generally worth thousands of dollars. Ensure that they have electrical certifications and a warranty that provides for product damage replacement if the protector does not work. However, you may want to consider buying a combination surge protector and Uninterruptible Power Supply (UPS). The UPS battery powered UPS unit will provide approximately 10 minutes of time or more to save your data and properly shut down your system. They cost around $150 to $450. Check out the American Power Conversion site at www.apcc.com.

- *Uninterruptible Power Supply (UPS).* An UPS has an internal battery that will activate when it senses a loss of power to your system. Generally it will stay on for a specified number of minutes and advanced systems will alert the users that the system will be shutting down in a specified number of minutes. Users can then save their data and power off. Consider UPS devices on key workstations such as the MIS director's and others to allow them to continue or complete their work. Also, some UPS devices can be stacked to allow for the system to continue to operate for hours in case of a power shortage or stoppage.

- *Dial in access protection.* If you are away from the office then dial in access may be critical for you. Ensure that UPS and surge protectors protect the dial in access components of your network.

- *Maintenance and support contracts.* Have maintenance contracts in place to replace the critical components of your system in case of a disaster. In the contract set out the response time (usually 4 hours) tolerated to repair your problems. Include penalties for non-performance. Consider contracting with a company to set up an off site LAN to handle critical projects if the system cannot be fixed immediately.

- *"Smart" disaster recovery software.* Software is available to monitor the components of your system and warn you of impending failures. You can then take affirmative action before disaster strikes.

- *Off site server or Intranet server.* If you have an off site server then remote employees can have access to instructions or other material if the main system is out of order. Also, you may want to set up an off site LAN to handle mission critical tasks while the system is being fixed.

Security

Security of computer data is becoming one of the most widely discussed topics in the information age. It is wonderful that the information age has brought the capability of storing, sending and retrieving data anytime and anywhere in the world. However, the dark underside to computing technology is ensuring that your data in networks, desktops and laptops are secured from theft, tampering or outright destruction.

At the outset it must be understood that nothing is one hundred percent secure, you can only minimize your exposure. So the goal is to minimize your exposure to the risk of security breaches. Also, determine the value of the information that you are seeking to protect. If you control cash or marketable securities then security is of paramount importance. However, if you are protecting word processing documents that have been backed up then what price do you pay for security? If client confidences are in case management files then security becomes more important. However, deciding upon reasonable physical security measures such as double bolted doors, alarms or 24-hour security guards to guard your paper files, one must also decide when reasonable efforts have been made to secure your computer data system.

Virus is a program designed to duplicate itself and spread from system to system. Some are harmless, but most are designed to be destructive destroying data or entire hard drives. It is very important to invest in anti-virus programs since a virus can destroy and cause havoc if they invade your computer system. One new virus is created each day and there are over 8000 signature viruses. Remember to scan floppies even if you have been assured that they are virus free since they may have been scanned on old virus software.

Anti-virus programs can locate and destroy virus programs. Always run a virus program to check floppy disks before transferring files into your computer. Some anti-virus programs to consider are Symantec's Norton Anti-Virus™ (www.norton.com) and McAfee's VirusScan™ (www.nai.com). Norton Anti-Virus™ will also check for viruses on files one downloads from the Internet and provide the latest virus signatures for download on the Internet. See also PC-cillin II™ (www.touchstonesoftware.com)

Theft, computer viruses or hard drive failure can cause security breaches of data. A security plan including policy and procedures should be implemented. This will also assist you in avoiding arbitrary claims if you need to take action against an employee for a security breach. Such a plan should be integrated with your overall telecommunications and information system plans. Involve your staff in your security efforts.

Security Checklist:

- Encrypt laptop files or have a password to get in;
- Tell staff you will try to break into passwords;
- Passwords, keys and other security devices should be secured;
- Send staff to security courses;
- Educate staff on insecurity of e-mail;
- Plan on how to handle terminated employees. Terminate their passwords and access codes immediately;
- Ask your staff about how to set security policy since they know the weak areas;
- Training your staff on security issues is a must, security will only be as good as the people who implement it;
- Install firewalls on your servers;
- Check who is logging in and out of your network;
- Use 8 character or longer passwords that are not found in dictionaries;
- Frequently change passwords (at least once a month);
- Encrypt your files;
- Scan your data and incoming electronic information using virus software;
- Backup your system on a regular basis;
- Run virus protection software on floppies, servers and desktops and update your system as new viruses are discovered. The number one way hard drives are infected is viruses on floppies;
- Be aware of rogue Java applets – They can search your computer and upload information back to their site, delete files, crash your browser;
- Write protect your program disks. To write protect have the little switch on the back of a floppy in an open position;
- Control dial in access by using passwords, callback and/or electronic ID cards;
- Lock off certain directories from users;
- Install all vendor security features and upgrades promptly;
- Configure system options known to be accessible to security problems;
- Ensure that outside vendors do not breach your security;
- Have all staff read, sign and practice computer security policies; and
- Check users access rights on a regular basis to determine the need for staff to access certain areas on the network.

Without a doubt we are accelerating toward an interconnected world using the Internet, Intranets, Extranets and LAN's. As we transition into this interconnectivity we must always be security vigilant.

For a further discussion on security on the web see *Chapter 4, The Internet and Telecommunications, Security on the Web.*

Conclusion

During the proliferation of computers in the 80's it became apparent that the "sneaker" method (putting on your sneakers and hand carrying floppies with files to another computer) of sharing files and moving expensive printers from location to location was wasted time. Networking evolved into allowing information to be accessed and exchanged by anyone inside or outside the office without exchanging floppy disks. The value to networking is sharing information or hardware resources that enable you to be productive in your work. The capability to share data, printers, fax modems, CD-ROM towers and other hardware resources is cost effective. Working together using different application programs is more difficult to quantify in terms of cost savings but it can have a significant impact upon the sharing of work information and productivity.

In the law firm, e-mail, work product sharing and common docketing databases are a but a few of the benefits of a network. However, connectivity has increased beyond the law firm and has moved to connections with clients and others. It is not unusual to see frequent e-mail exchanges with clients and direct connections with court and other databases. It is not as important if people and businesses are physically together since they can all be connected together using networking. Networking provides the foundation to store, access and share information with co-employees, clients, courts, businesses or government agencies instantaneously.

It appears that peer-to-peer networks will continue to be a force in the network market as long as complexity and cost are factors in client/server systems. They may end up existing side by side with messaging and communication handled by peer to peer and servers handling the critical computing functioning. The distinction between the two is beginning to disappear as the features of each blend together in new products. These systems will be linked with Skytel and other messaging personal digital assistants (PDA) to enable users without their laptops or desktops to acquire information instantaneously. Wireless networks are being followed closely to determine if the cost and performance justify their installation. Network performance will transport data in the gigabyte per second range. Video conferencing will start to be used as the bandwidth for transmission of data enlarges so that full motion video is available.

Networking is the foundation for the growth of group computing. The unpredicted emergence of the Internet will form the backbone of the group computing and networking group-computing scenario. Business will become increasingly decentralized.

The Internet has now moved networking up to a new level. Besides communication within your organization the Internet, Intranet and Extranet provides the capability to network and collaborate with any person, company, court or government agency anywhere in the world.

Workgroup Computing - The Next Logical Step

Introduction

The emergence of the PC in the 1980's centered on personal productivity. It has been used mainly to automate the law firm's traditional individual work processes. Word processing, spreadsheets and graphics were a few applications that improved the quality and quantity of a legal professional's

> Knowledge in the only enduring asset in a law firm. Leveraging that knowledge by communicating, collaborating and coordinating into a computer work process is workgroup computing. Workgroup computing will enable parties to work on legal and non-legal matters from their computers anywhere and at anytime. This will be the most important computing application over the next decade. It offers the Holy Grail of Collaboration and Productivity as the reward.

work product. As these PC's became linked into networks users began to share printers and files. However, the focus was still not on the sharing and electronic collaboration of our work. This has changed with the emergence of workgroup computing software (WCS). Now the LAN, WAN, the Internet, Intranet and Extranet and workgroup computing systems provide the opportunity for attorneys and clients to electronically collaborate like they have never done before. For the first time workgroup computing allows firms to expand the capabilities of computers beyond glorified typewriters. Now law firm manual processes of sharing information, interacting with others and collaboration can be automated.

Workgroup computing is particularly useful in the legal profession. Lawyers are constantly called upon to share information, coordinate, and collaborate with many different people on many different cases. Clients, paralegals, secretaries, fellow attorneys, judges and many others need to communicate on a variety of legal and nonlegal matters. To reengineer these manual interactions and processes onto a computer system will be both cost effective and efficient.

The same time that lawyers migrate to workgroup computing platforms the legislative, executive, and judicial branches are also moving up the workgroup technology ladder. Eventually, the different components of the justice system will converge into an integrated system that will allow greater access to our justice system.

Strategic Workgroup Legal Applications

There are many strategic group-computing applications for the legal profession. In fact, all of the manual processes of practicing law are candidates for applying workgroup-computing principles. Workgroup computing essentially replicates the manual processes onto a computer platform whether they are administrative or case related. Consider the following examples:

- *Law Firm Administrative Functions.* Administrative information in a law firm is interwoven with many office and case functions and is a prime candidate for group computing. For example, client information is important for contact management, document preparation and management, timekeeping, billing, litigation databases, trial notifications, etc. A well-designed workgroup information system should share and route the same information among the different law firm functions. This can result in a substantial timesaving as the manual work process or individual computer applications are reengineered onto a workgroup-computing platform. Now information will move in a workflow on a computer instead of being handled manually.

- *Collaborating with Your Clients.* Group computing can reduce the time and provide higher quality workproduct for the client. For example, suppose a client is referred to your firm for preparation of a contract. You can immediately access the Internet for a voluminous amount of information about the business your client is involved in and the party with whom he wishes to contract. One can locate information on credit ratings, market or industry conditions and other background material. Legal forms on your network or the Internet can be used to locate clauses and whole agreements specifically addressing his needs. Using e-mail it is easy to contact many of your colleagues from across the country to solicit input on specific contract issues or to review the contract. You will be more prepared to intelligently discuss the risk and benefits of your client's contractual needs. Information can be obtained, shared and discussed wherever your client is located using e-mail or real-time virtual meeting software such as Microsoft's NetMeeting. By taking advantage of electronic workgroup resources you will service your client while tying your client and you closer together.

- *Case Management Tasks.* The all important case management tasks can be automated giving you calendar, docketing and case management control. For example, when a case is opened an electronic request can be sent to the accounting department to open an account. After conferring with the client a case plan with assigned responsibilities is electronically prepared and sent to a secretary, paralegal, an associate and anyone else associated with the case. Certain dates for completing the responsibilities can be assigned. The other workgroup members, when they access their computer, will see that they have been assigned responsibilities for a new case and their deadlines. They can electronically report on the progress or problems as they complete their duties. The communication will be constant and continuous between the members of your case team. Communication links can be set up with your client to provide status reports and obtain input on the case. Draft pleadings can be instantaneously sent to your client for review and comments. Docketing information can be obtained from the court electronically and in some courts the pleadings can be "electronically" filed.

- *Preparation of Litigation Discovery Requests.* Specific litigation tasks can be automated reducing the paper jungle and providing control of your case. For example the manual process of responding to interrogatories can be reengineered onto a computer. Once interrogatories have been received they could be OCR'ed, if received in a paper format, and processed in a workgroup computing environment. The interrogatories would first go to the lead attorney who could provide the first draft of the answers and then electronically assign certain interrogatories to certain team members. Due dates would be placed on the responses and a set could be e-mailed to the client. The team members will locate and answer the interrogatories and communicate by e-mail with the client. After receiving the second draft the lead attorney could "meet" electronically with his team members by video or document conferencing and finalize the answers. No more paper copies, postage, letters, in-baskets stuffed with paper, instead, the process would be completed electronically.

Workgroup computing systems provide a unique and exciting opportunity. All of the work we do involves the interaction and sharing of information to achieve a common purpose. If the information is always electronically available and we can work as workgroups without being physically present then the need for a "physical" place for a law firm is greatly diminished. It provides the foundation for the "virtual law office".

Defining Workgroup Computing Systems

Workgroup computing refers to any computer system that replicates the manual work process. Anytime two or more people work together sharing information on a computer system it can be defined as group computing. It is a way to electronically process human transactions. The focus is on information sharing, coordination and collaboration. When two people manually send letters or memos to each other this is a workgroup process. When two people send the same letters or memos using e-mail this is referred to as workgroup computing. Any software that supports workgroup computing can be labeled as groupware.

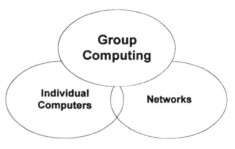

Workgroup computing is about working with other people in an electronic work environment. This collaboration can take place in offices located next to each other or in different parts of the world.

There are three different levels of group computing:
- Individual level – On this level the members individually work toward a group goal but there is no group coordination. Members use word processors, spreadsheets and databases but do not coordinate their efforts. Here, we find duplication and no sharing of work that oftentimes produces inconsistent results.
- Coordinated effort – On this level the members coordinate and actively manage the flow of work by structuring work processes. It goes beyond individual automation and provides a structured work environment. The structures are the processes that need to be completed for a legal function. It focuses on the communication in the transmitting and receiving of messages. The basic tool for information sharing is e-mail. There are no time and place barriers. It pushes information to others. Other tools that support these coordinated efforts are schedulers, project managers, shared databases and workflow automation software. This may require some development or customization of commercial software packages.
- Collaborating. Members here make concerted efforts for information sharing, discussions and obtaining other information as needed. It pulls information from many different data storage areas

for use by all the team members. It is a "virtual" workplace that allows many to many information exchanges without the constraints of time and space. Shared whiteboards, electronic brainstorming, shared editors, electronic conferencing and electronic voting are technology tools that are supportive of this group dynamic.

Groupware Computer Applications

The value of workgroup computing lies in different applications to the practice of law. Anything we do manually and with paper should be considered an opportunity to transition the manual process onto a computer. Sometimes it is easier to define and understand workgroup computing in terms of what it does and what computer software applications make up a workgroup-computing environment. The following computer

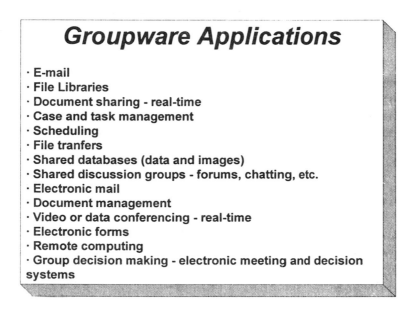

Groupware Applications

· E-mail
· File Libraries
· Document sharing - real-time
· Case and task management
· Scheduling
· File tranfers
· Shared databases (data and images)
· Shared discussion groups - forums, chatting, etc.
· Electronic mail
· Document management
· Video or data conferencing - real-time
· Electronic forms
· Remote computing
· Group decision making - electronic meeting and decision systems

applications concepts support a workgroup-computing environment.

Electronic Mail - Provides all members of a workgroup – lawyers, clients, associates, paralegals, secretaries, etc - the capability of sending electronic messages and computer files to each other or to broadcast the message to all or selected members of the workgroup. Additional features include the capability to file messages into 'file cabinets" for later retrieval, faxing the message or forwarding on the message, and replying to it. Some packages enable one to attach an audio message, graphics, video or other digitized information.

File Libraries – Computer files for pleadings, forms and any other legal material can be stored, accessed and shared by different members of the workgroup. It provides workgroup members access to past or current documents.

Document Sharing – Contracts, legal pleadings or other legal materials can be worked on at the same time or can be reviewed individually for comments from

Group Computing extends not only to members of your firms but to your clients or potential clients. The firm of Berding & Weil, an Alamo, California law firm adopted one innovative approach in January 1993. With over 800 homeowners associations as clients they developed there own group computing platform using off the shelf group computing system. All members of the association can send private e-mail messages to each other and also access numerous legal materials that affect their associations. For example, summaries of active bills affecting associations are on-line, case law abstracts regarding legal issues that affect associations and other useful information. More important the firm will phase in a fee structure to respond to member association's legal questions submitted on-line. Needless to say they were ahead of the Internet rush and realized the value of the "virtual law firm". Opening the Computer Door, ABA Journal, David Vandagriff, August, 1994.

all members of the group.

Task Management – Different case management plans and assigned tasks can be monitored to ensure timely completion of the different stages of a client's case. It provides the workgroup members the capability to see that the case or litigation plan is being timely followed by different law firm members.

Scheduling & Docketing – It is easy to schedule group meetings and ensure docketing dates are met when all the law firm members keep their schedules on a group computer-scheduling program like Microsoft Outlook or GroupWise.

File Transfer - Correspondence, pleadings and any text, graphic, sound or video files can be transferred or viewed by another person. Databases or files can be accessed for downloading by other workgroup members.

Shared Databases - If the firm has a conflict of interest database then a practitioner can immediately check to determine if there is a conflict with accepting a new client. Exhibit, depositions, witness or chronological databases can be accessed or shared by different members of the workgroup.

Image Databases - Users can share remotely or in-house case documents that have been imaged. Also, clients and co-counsel in cases can share the combined image and database analysis of the documents.

Case Management or Project Management Systems - Cases can be discussed and plans of action developed for members of the law firm. These case management systems can be on a timeline and task oriented to ensure the case is being worked on in a timely fashion.

Data and Video Conferencing - Members of the firm, opposing counsel or others can meet real-time with their computers to draft pleadings, work on settlement papers or coordinate schedules. The video component gives one the capability to assess the impact of the discussion upon the other party real-time.

Electronic Forms - law firm members or others can share uniform interrogatories, notices of depositions, and other law firm work product and materials.

Workgroup Decision Making - Electronic Meeting Software (EMS) software supports basic meeting problem solving techniques such as brainstorming, idea organization, voting, issue analyzing, policy formulation, prioritizing and stakeholder identification.

E-mail – Killer Application for the Nineties

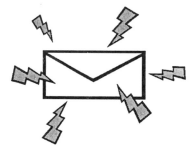

Word processing and spreadsheets were the "killer applications of the eighties".

E-mail is the "killer application of the nineties". It is one of the best-received workgroup computing applications. It is the single most compelling reason why organizations are networking internally and externally through the Internet. E-mail has become a key part of the communications networks of most modern offices. Data and messages can be transmitted from one computer to another using telephone lines, microwave links, communications satellites, or other telecommunications channels. The same message can be sent to multiple parties at different addresses simultaneously. E-mail has always been popular but now anyone can generally connect with just about anyone else. It is low cost, fast and accurate and prevents phone tag.

Benefits - An e-mail connection can support many attorney-client functions and solidify an existing relationship. With e-mail it can assist with:

- Joint document drafting;
- Legal discussion groups;
- Exchanging documents;
- Accessing billing tasks and costs;
- Avoiding telephone tag and other inefficiencies;
- Shared work product retrieval;
- Distributing information of importance to clients;
- Exchanging messages; and
- Shared case management plans and timetable.

History - Electronic mail systems have evolved over the past several years and are more sophisticated then just sending and receiving messages. The first generation supported simple interpersonal communication. Messages were usually short, did not support text enrichment and were not intended to be saved. They were intended to convey short timely information. Reports, graphics and other business information were not intended to be captured in e-mail messages.

The second generation of e-mail included the ability to attach binary or textual files. This enabled users to send along documents and other computer files containing law firm work product and other law practice materials.

The third generation of e-mail focused upon the capability of enabling the user to enhance the e-mail message itself. Now rich text format and embedded objects could be part of the message. More important was the capability of the e-mail software to store and organize e-mail materials. Now folders or other systems could be set up to save e-mail for particular projects or cases. The storage module became the law firm's storage of case and firm business. This along with the capability to broadcast e-mail to casual users increased e-mail use.

The next generation of e-mail will see a convergence of e-mail with other workgroup computing applications. E-mail will be part and parcel of workgroup computing applications such as database linking, Internet links to World Wide Web pages and a host of other integrated applications. A key feature of this 4th generation e-mail growth will be compatibility and accessibility by remote users. This will enable legal professionals to contact and interact with the firm's e-mail workgroup computing environment whether in the office or not. Microsoft Exchange™ (www.microsoft.com), Lotus™ (www.lotus.com), Netscape Communicator™ (www.netscape.com)and GroupWise™ (www.novell.com) all have developed workgroup-computing platforms primarily based on messaging between members.

Two of the "complete" messaging services are Microsoft Mail™ from Microsoft (www.microsoft.com) and cc:Mail™ from Lotus (www.lotus.com). Both the client and server software packages are included in this workgroup. These products and others provide a "gateway" to enable your LAN to receive and send mail to other messaging LANs, Internet and others through public telephone lines or other communication services. Electronic messaging features can include the capability to embed sound, graphics, video and text. Other e-mail packages include the popular Eudora™ (www.eudora.com), Netscape™ (www.netscape.com) and Internet Explorer™ (www.microsoft.com).

E-mail Connection: The simplest e-mail connection setup would be through an Internet service provider (ISP) but this poses some confidentiality problems as your mail is sitting on different computers waiting to be retrieved and then deleted. Two suggested options are to use encryption software or, though more costly, would be to set up a direct e-mail link with your client. This link would be through a dedicated telephone or leased line between the two parties. There would be no intermediate computer that your mail would reside on. A gateway computer may need to be installed if the parties are not using the same e-mail software.

E-mail Etiquette and Tips

It is important that one follows appropriate etiquette when sending e-mail. It saves time for the recipient and prevents misunderstandings or hurt feelings. Some considerations:

- Indicate the topic of your message in the subject area;
- Review before sending. Your manner of responding will create an impression on others;
- Use sarcasm and humor with care – it could be misinterpreted;
- CAUTION: An e-mail factual presentation can seem cold and even evoke anger from a recipient. Remember there is no inflection or facial read in e-mail;
- Keep the message to the point and brief. Reread it to ensure your message will not be misunderstood;
- Label messages as urgent, ASAP, etc. only when needed;
- Use a spellchecker;
- Do not put messages in all caps – it is considered shouting;
- Signature files should include name, address, phone number and e-mail address;

- Limit the recipients of e-mail to only those who need to know. Don't waste people's time;
- Use the return receipt;
- Check e-mail daily just like voice mail;
- Prevent e-mail overload by using filtering features and folders;
- Do not send e-mail when you are angry;
- Excessive use of e-mail wastes time for both the sender and receiver;
- E-mail can be altered and signatures changed – check with the alleged sender if there is any question;
- E-mails can be discovered and used in litigation. Assume everyone will be reading your e-mail. Passwords do not protect e-mails from being read. E-mail is not private;
- Assume that it will never be destroyed and that there will always be a copy on someone's server or backup system;
- Remember that an employer generally reserves the right to review and disclose all e-mails messages sent over their system. Do not use e-mail when interpersonal communication is required; and
- Backup needed e-mail messages – some programs automatically delete them after a certain number of days. Follow policies on the personal and nonbusiness use of e-mail.

Permanent E-mail Address

Have a permanent e-mail address no matter which ISP you use. There are several services that offer you a permanent e-mail address for little or no cost. Check the sites at Bigfoot Partners™ (www.bigfoot.com) and iName™ (www.iName.com). For example if your address is JohnDoe@aol.com then provide AOL your permanent e-mail address and they will forward your mail to the permanent address. So anytime, you change Internet providers your e-mail address stays the same.

Another way having a permanent e-mail address is to get a domain name. Besides identifying your address on the web a domain name can be used as your e-mail address. For example if your domain name is *crimlaw.com* then your e-mail address can be Smith@crimlaw.com. If you switch ISP's then your domain name and e-mail address will follow you to the new ISP.

Universal Inbox

According to the Gallop Organization the average person in a corporation gets 178 messages each day. A universal inbox will permit you to control these messages. The concept of a universal inbox is simply a computer capable of receiving messages from multiple sources in multiple formats. Voice mail, e-mail, faxes, and pagers all would be delivered to the same inbox. It would list all incoming messages and the user can listen to, read, delete or file the messages. (You read voice mail by playing it over your multimedia computer). It would be faster and easier to train users since only one interface is used. Your messages can be organized into folders like e-mail and text messages could be read to you like voice mail.

The universal inbox is being built upon groupware products such as GroupWise™, Lotus Notes™, etc. We will begin to see universal inboxes combining Computer Telephony Integration (CTI) with computer groupware for control of collaborative computing. See Lucent Technologies (www.lucent.com) and Octel Corporation (www.octel.com) for further product information.

Message and Database Workgroup Computing Platforms

Workgroup computing platforms have focused on a messaging or database system to store, retrieve and view information.

Messaging systems are based on e-mail platforms to communicate, collaborate and coordinate group-computing tasks. Messaging has become the genesis of groupware. It is a "push" model of communication in that information is pushed to the receiver. Due to its growing role as an information repository and platform for legal case information software companies have built messaging systems such as Microsoft Exchange based on reliability, availability, storage and, in particular, security.

Database group computing systems store information in databases. Lotus Notes is built on a database model where discrete documents are saved as database records for each occurrence as opposed to messages. However, Lotus Notes™ relies on cc: Mail™ that is one of the most robust messaging programs on the market.

The Infrastructure for Workgroup Computing

There are three major factors fueling the move to workgroup computing; one, the number of computers that have and will be purchased; two, the connectivity issue; and, three, groupware.

1. Computers. Newspapers report that 4 out of 10 households have computers now. An important fact is that approximately 15,000,000 computers will be purchased for the home in 1998.

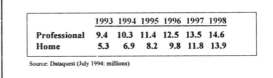

Your Clients Have PC's in Their Business & Personal Lives

- PCs purchased for the home will comprise nearly half of the entire U.S. market by 1998
- 28.5 Million PC's will be shipped in 1998.

	1993	1994	1995	1996	1997	1998
Professional	9.4	10.3	11.4	12.5	13.5	14.6
Home	5.3	6.9	8.2	9.8	11.8	13.9

Source: Dataquest (July 1994: millions)

2. Connectivity. The second major component of groupware applications is the connectivity issue to the workgroup-computing platform. How, when, where and what software can I use to connect to the workgroup computing platform? Can I use a modem with only my terminal communications program to dial into the computer? Can I use the Internet for my communication backbone? Is it accessible remotely as well as on the Local Area Network (LAN)? The goal of the connectivity issue is to be universally accessible to your users regardless of what platform they are using and what communication service.

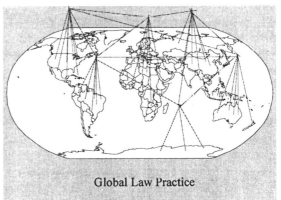

Global Law Practice

One of the keys to effective workgroup computing is ensuring interconnectivity among the various software packages. If one uses Lotus Notes as a platform the users are required to convert to a Windows based system. The hardware upgrade cost can be significant along with the $100 per copy of Notes.

Another important issue is the telecommunication charges. Using a regular telephone line to dial long distance into a computer can become expensive quickly. This is the reason why the Internet connection cannot be underestimated. Generally for $20.00 a month you can get unlimited hours per month to access the Internet. This includes any charges for sending and receiving e-mail, file transfer, participation in newsgroups and surfing the World Wide Web. If the Internet enables you to participate in your own workgroup computing environment with members of your law firm for a maximum of $20 per month then it definitely has to be seriously considered.

©1991-1998 Michael R. Arkfeld   3 - 21

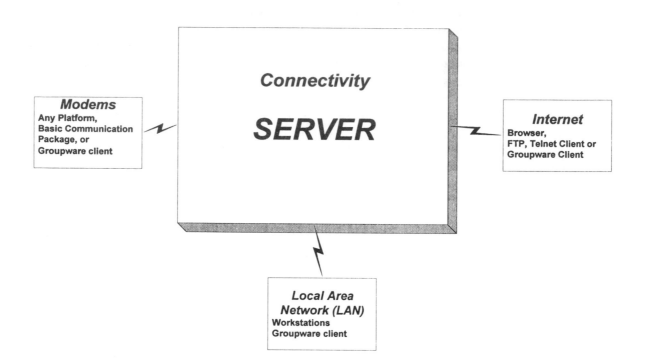

3. Groupware. The third and final piece of the group-computing infrastructure is to determine which software to use as you collaborate with your colleagues. There are two primary choices – Internet based groupware such as Netscape Communicator™ based on "open" standards and proprietary software such as Lotus Notes™ and Microsoft Exchange™. Lotus Notes™ has been available since the mid 1980's'and has developed into a robust group computing platform. However, both Netscape and Microsoft have significant group-computing features that compete effectively with Lotus Notes.

Workgroup Computing and the Internet

The Web provides a global means of publishing information that is based on a "pull" model. The Web browser specifies a specific URL and requests a copy of that HTML page which is then translated to the workstation. The WWW is developing into a true group computing system as the pull model is being complimented with a "push" model of sending information to other users. With the rapid deployment of broadcast push technology it will be just a matter of time before the Internet protocols develop into a robust group-computing platform. Some essential features needed for the Web to continue to develop into a group-computing platform are:

- *Interactivity or collaboration.* Handling a legal matter requires the interactivity between various legal and nonlegal personnel. It is not just a one–way sharing of information but requires brainstorming, idea sharing and problem solving from all members of the team.
- *Notification.* All team members must be capable of being

> Telecommuting - All of the electronic links among the people in a modern office can be extended beyond the building walls to workers at home or in satellite offices. This capability has led to a sharp increase in telecommuting. In 1991 an estimated 5.5 million U.S. workers worked at least part of the time outside the main office, a 38 percent increase over 1990. Managers and professional employees were the major participants in this trend. Early reports of increased productivity among people who no longer spent hours traveling from home to office indicated that further increases in telecommuting will occur.

reached on the system with e-mail. In addition members should be easily notified of new documents and easily retrieve the information for viewing. Document storage with an integrated messaging service provides the ability to locate key documents.

- *Triggered events.* Workgroup-computing systems built on database systems can monitor the status and initiate action based on data in a particular field. If a response to a pleading is due 10 days from a particular date then the system can be set to notify the appropriate attorney. Messaging based systems must have the same capability.
- *Customization.* How lawyers work and the different specialties require that systems be customizable. Viewing and organizing information in different ways provides the legal professional the tools to analyze and present information while conforming to his or her work processes.
- *Multiple levels of security.* To preserve client confidences different security levels should be available. Sensitive litigation data, contract negotiations among other sensitive client information have to be protected.
- *Integration with other applications and resources.* Legal professionals use a variety of desktop applications to manage and control case information. Word processing, databases, spreadsheets and other applications should be able to be seamlessly integrated into the work-group computing to allow for easy access to case information. Workgroup computing should not replace these systems but provide for tight integration. For example Lotus Notes has integrated with many popular legal applications in a complementary and not competitive mode.
- *Mobile user support.* More and more legal professionals are telecommuting and doing their work away from the office. They should be able to continue to participate in the workgroup computing process. They should be able to browse through data, compose and edit documents, and schedule legal matters.

Lotus Notes™, Microsoft Exchange™, Intranets and Extranets

Lotus Notes™ (www.lotus.com) is a client/server group computing application that allows people to share, retrieve, control and use information anywhere and anytime. Notes definitely has the market and mind share among the larger companies. However, there are some limitations to the Notes product. These include significant Notes training for the user, server resources and staff who are well trained in the complexity of administering Notes.

Lotus Notes™ can automate a variety of the law firm tasks that are presently done manually or are done on separate software applications. There is an assortment of third party products to enhance its basic foundation. Some of many different customized applications that can be found at www.lotus.com are:
- Time and Billing. REMIND™ Workgroup Time and Billing Application – allows law firms to process and distribute invoices to clients from within Lotus Notes™. It is a distributed computing program which electronically automates the collection of time entries, creation and approval of invoices, integration with industry standard accounting packages, etc.
- Document management systems. PC DOCS OPEN™ has integrated its document management databases with Notes. The recognizable Notes views are created allowing attorneys to immediately locate work product documents and other documents.
- Litigation Information Management.
  - LIT Casework's 2.0™ is a Notes litigation support module. It is built around a central caseload management application. It provides for conflict checking, case contact modules and one time data entry. It organizes pleadings, discovery, correspondence, work product and calendars. Virtual binders can be created for depositions, witness files, exhibit lists and indexes to all materials. Multiple cases can be organized, workgroup scheduling can be implemented and summary reports can be generated. Document images can be attached for easy viewing. Automatic e-mail can be generated for new items to keep team members informed.

- JFS Litigator's Notebook™. This customized interface for Lotus Notes™ allows teams of attorneys to access key case materials and memoranda on each case. It includes the capability to create binders for witnesses, issues or fact areas that can be shared with all members of the litigation team.

Intranets and Extranets (See also Chapter 3, Networking – Web Based Networking, Internet, Intranets, and Extranets.).

To the right is a screenshot from an Extranet site being used in the tobacco litigation. Extranets have proved to be extremely useful in litigation. The tobacco litigation has spawned collaborative litigation environment. The legal team is using internet protocols (Web Browsers, HTML, etc.) to access and process all transcripts, documents produced, work product, calendar, and court docket, with an integrated database, full text and document image and messaging system. Other collaborative tools are used by the lawyers for messaging, linking threaded discussions to documents, and for enhanced subjective coding by attorneys and legal staff. Hypertext (HTML) combined with

databases & full text retrieval enhances the access to and viewing of all case information. To access The Tobacco Litigation Extranet Demo and for further information on Litigation Extranets contact Legal Computer Solutions, Inc. at (617) 227-4469 or their web site (www.lcsweb.com).

Instead of building an Intranet or investing into the administration of a Notes server you may to look into a prebuilt Intranet for your firm. They come with several modules already built in such as bulletin boards, access to your e-mail, hold text based chat sessions, share documents, review individual employee benefits like vacation time, security features, personal calendars, employee directories and forums where members can post bulletin board like messages. Netopia™ (www.netopia.com)

Comparing WWW based group computing, Lotus Notes and Microsoft Exchange

Some things to consider when comparing WWW group computing software with a product like Lotus Notes™ or Microsoft Exchange™:
- *Standards on the Internet* - Technically speaking an Internet is an internal network that operates on "open standards". The "open standards" consist of the key standard TCP/IP (the network protocol), HTML (WWW programming language), POP3 and SMTP (Email standards), HTTP (web server language), and FTP (file transfer protocol) among others. Open standards generally result in lower cost since there are no propriety extensions to these generally simple and straightforward standards. Users have freedom of choice from many vendors. Since they are open, low cost and not tied to proprietary vendors monopolies are not created.

    However, for Lotus Notes™ or Microsoft Exchange™ the source code for this proprietary software is not in the public domain. One must license the software to use the API's. However, they generally are interoperable with Windows™, OS/2™, UNIX, etc.
- *The interface tool* - web browsers - can be used on a variety of hardware platforms – 386, 486, Pentiums™, Windows 3.1™, Windows 95/98™, Macintosh™, Unix or NT™. The browser focuses

on content and not a specific software package. Intranet costs are low compared to cost of purchasing proprietary document distribution software or other group computing software.

- *Security on the Internet* – still poses a problem from outside the web and within an organization. Lotus Notes™ and Exchange™ have adopted strong security measures to keep unauthorized users out.

- *Replication on the WWW* is in the development stage and focuses on updating web pages. Lotus Notes™ is noted for its unique replication features that assign each database and each document a unique ID number. These 128-byte numbers include time, location and date. If a change occurs then the two servers or computers will compare their ID lists and ask which was has changed?

- *Application Development Tools* – Other than basic programming the WWW has not totally settled on a set of robust unified programming tools. However, with Java and other languages development is rapidly occurring on the web.

    Notes™ provide a unified set of development tools used by many third party developers to create unique enterprise wide computing applications. Many have been or are being developed for the computing community.

- *Messaging Models* – Messaging is an important piece of the groupware puzzle. It is important that one can contact their co-worker and provide them access to a document or database without having to make an attachment. Instead it should point to the object stored and accessible to the user. With Notes this is a breeze since the databases and other objects are stored and easily accessible. The WWW use of hypertext pointers is catching up fast to point to other locations in an Intranet or Internet to retrieve and view the document or database.

Group-computing products: Netscape Communicator™ (www.netscape.com); Lotus Notes™ (www.lotus.com); Microsoft Exchange™ (www.microsoft.com); and Novell GroupWise™ (www. novell.com).

The groupware war is in full swing as software manufacturers strive to have you adopt their method of scheduling, etc. Remember when one had to choose between a Wang operating system and MS-DOS or between a mainframe or distributed computing? The choice of your workgroup-computing platform will also have an important impact on your organization. The scheduling, address book, threaded discussions and other workgroup functions will be enhanced if the right package is purchased.

Some issues to consider:

- Present software environment;
- Present Applications or suites. The contact manager, scheduling system and other software you are currently using will impact whether you decide to switch and to which workgroup-computing platform. If you are transitioning to a Windows environment from a DOS environment your choices are open. However, if one is using Microsoft Outlook™, Word™, and Access™ then Exchange may be the logical choice;
- Firm size;
- Software ease of use;
- Is security a significant priority?
- Is a litigation database important?
- Can I see an image of a document on-line?
- The software must allow for easy importing of address books and schedules; and
- Proprietary vs. non-proprietary solutions.

Electronic Decision Making (EDMS) Software

One of the foremost writers on the conceptual process of holding electronic meetings is Doctor Jay F. Nunamaker, Jr. from the University of Arizona Center for the Management of Information. In Dr. Nunamaker's articles on electronic meeting systems he discusses the many ramifications of holding electronic meetings.

Electronic Meeting Systems: Ten Years of Lessons Learned with Workgroup Systems, Oct. 1994. EDMS software supports basic meeting problem-solving techniques such as brainstorming, idea organization, voting, issue analyzing, policy formulation, prioritizing and stakeholder identification. The most striking features of EDMS software is that it enables all the participants to "speak" at once and share their ideas. An individual or individuals that have a preset agenda no longer control meetings. All members of the team share critical information, especially in a non-threatening manner if the participants are logged in anonymously. The actual workgroup decision making process is enhanced for the substantive strategic plan. However, a number of "people" issues have to be considered in ensuring that the team members have not only bought in on an issue basis but also on an emotional level.

EDMS software will become increasingly important over the next decade as we all become "connected" through the Internet. It has the potential of greatly increasing the effectiveness of meetings whether conducted together using EDMS software or remotely using modems, video and other virtual tools. One product to consider is GroupSystems™ (www.ventana.com).

Conclusion

The technology culture, infrastructure, telecommunications including the Internet and group software all plays a significant part in the move to the "virtual law firm." Johannes Gutenburg's construction of the printing press around 1450 started the paper and print revolution. The construction of the computer has started the digital revolution. Just as our parents transitioned into the age of the automobile with the use of the "horseless carriage," we will ease into the "virtual law office" with digital information.

The "law firm" as we know it today will not exist. It will not be necessary to be physically present with your clients if you can use low cost video conferencing to discuss their case. Legal information such as court decisions, statutes, administrative rules, security filings, deeds of trust are available digitally. Communications with other attorneys, paralegals and secretaries in your firm will be in a group computing environment such as Lotus Notes™ or Netscape's Communicator™. Pleadings will be digitally filed, court dockets digitally reviewed, oral arguments set by the parties using the World Wide Web and appeals electronically filed in the appellate court without paper. Value billing by the case and not the hour will become commonplace. Yes, it will have a dramatic effect upon the practice of law, as we know it today

Workgroup meeting and decision software systems enable a workgroup to share information, make decisions and set up a plan to accomplish objectives. In the 1980's when desktop computers started to hit the mainstream they were used primarily as personal productivity tools, hence the name PC for personal computers. Users were able to perform many tasks that were previously done on mainframe computers. Once the computers were networked then the capability to share information such as briefs, motions and interrogatories supported the workgroup law firm business. However, true workgroup meeting and decision making had not been replicated on the computer. Now, with the rapid connectivity of computers we are seeing the beginning of what will become the next generation of workgroup computing.

The traditional way companies have existed for the past hundred years will undergo a radical change as the world becomes increasingly connected through the Internet. Companies traditionally have had a central physical location where employees meet each day to work. These employees each contribute in their own way to the "product" of the company. For example, a paralegal ensures that a case is prepared for a client whether it is a business transaction or litigation matter. A file will be opened, plan of action prepared, communications with client and others will begin, and discovery pleadings will be prepared The paralegal will pass on the results of the work to an attorney who will review, modify and complete the preliminary work. STOP! Could the parties be in entirely different physical locations and complete most of this work? Could the parties use group computing and networking to serve the function of a central physical location? Yes, to a large degree. However, the parties still will need to interact with clients, each other and ensure the remote working environments are conducive to group work environments. The alternative may not be home computing but suboffices located throughout the suburbs and cities that have the latest computer technology for group computing. To stay economically competitive one must consider these alternatives and rethink the basic way the practice of law is conducted.

Chapter 4

The Internet and Telecommunications

Persons grouped around a fire or candle for warmth or light are less able to pursue independent thoughts, or even tasks, than people supplied with electric light. In the same way, the social and educational patterns latent in automation are those of self-employment and artistic autonomy.

- Marshall McLuhan

The World of Telecommunications - The Backbone of the Practice of Law

Introduction

Communication and the sharing of information tie our society together. Like the nervous system that connects the human body communications is the enduring connection for society. We organize, work and play together through communications. Exchanging our thoughts, messages and information in any form is communication.

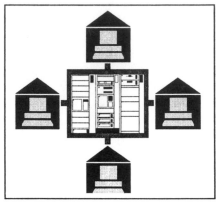

Telecommunications is the transmission of words, sounds, images, videos or data in the form of electronic or electromagnetic signals or impulses. *Tele* means distance or distant. Thus, telecommunications is the transmission of information to distant locations. The transmission of a television signal to locations throughout the United States is a powerful communication media. However, the communication impact is limited since one does not have the ability to interact or return information to the sender. It is a one way communication.

Communication has generally been separated into two types. The first type is mass communication, represented by television, radio, newspapers, magazines and any other communication where large numbers of people receive the communication. This type of communication is one way in that information is sent without having the opportunity to respond. Watching a television program does not give one the capability to directly respond and interact with the people in the program. The latest form of this type of one way communication is World Wide Web pages which disseminate huge amounts of information but provides no or limited interaction with the creator of the web site. However, this is rapidly changing.

The other type of communication is responsive communication. This is represented by the telephone, postal service, telegraph and most notable recently – digital data transmission. *This communication type represents the ability of both parties to interact in some form.* A recent innovative approach to this type of communication are Internet chat sessions or forums where participants can communicate "real-time" with other members of their group typing information using their computers. One is able to view the "conversation" of the other members on the computer screen. As the bandwidth of the connection to the Internet increases videoconferencing and other forms of two-way communication will become the norm.

In the practice of law we communicate generally in a responsive manner. From simple phone calls to mailing pleadings we communicate information in a responsive method. Traditionally these methods have included the telephone, mail, face-to-face meetings and the fax machine. This responsive method of communication requires staff support, paper, mail systems, delivery systems and a host of other support structure. Generally, these support requirements are expensive and do not contribute to the profitability of the law firm. Instead they are looked upon as overhead. What if these traditional methods of communications could be converted into a system of digital two-way communications that takes advantage of the Internet, videoconferencing and other tools? Such a system would change the economics and the practice of law.

The next few years will bring immense changes to the two-way communication structure in society. Major corporations are all positioning as the communication structure transitions from a paper into a digital communication environment. Phone companies are connecting video conferencing users across the country, television cable companies are selling phone service, video conferencing and Internet access and satellite companies are selling television and Internet access. The entire telecommunications industry is betting that consumers and businesses will pay for the capability to access and interact with large bandwidth information sources immediately from anywhere, anytime, customized for their needs, and requiring minimal equipment. Consider the following scenario:

While sitting in his home "office" in suburban Denver attorney Frank Young answers a videoconference call from his client located in San Diego, Mary Zakowski. Mary shows Frank new pictures of her children and then requests him to file an amended pleading in a pending court case in San Diego. Frank locates the original pleading and they both simultaneously make changes to the pleading. After the document is complete, Mary digitally "signs" the document on the computer screen. Frank automatically assembles the remaining part of the document including the addresses of opposing parties and then digitally signs the document. He then connects to the court and electronically "files" the amended pleading. Copies are electronically sent to opposing counsel. The court system automatically assigns a hearing date to "appear" by videoconference for oral argument on the amended pleading. Mary thanks Frank for his prompt attention to the matter and authorizes payment through her on-line credit card.

Is this science fiction? No, this is digital telecommunications and will be the backbone of the practice of law in the future. Why? Isn't time money? How much would be saved by videoconferencing with an out-of-state client? How much was saved by filing the pleadings electronically in the courthouse? How much was saved not having to provide multiple paper copies of pleadings to the court, co-counsel and others? The support staff, messenger services, postage and travel costs are all tied to many of the functions we perform as lawyers. What if those costs are eliminated? What if one could take the deposition of an out-of-state witness from one's office using videoconferencing at a reasonable price with full motion video quality? What is the value of not having to pack, go to the airport, travel, land, get a taxi or rental car, check into a hotel, go to the deposition in a strange city and return?

> *There is no pleasure to me without communication: there is not so much as a sprightly thought comes into my mind that it does not grieve me to have produced alone, and that I have no one to tell it to.*
> **Michel de Montaigne** *(1533–92), French essayist. Essays, bk. 3, ch. 9, "Of Vanity" (1588).*

Yes, the *digital information* revolution has arrived.

Benefits and Goals of Communication

There are several important strategic benefits of creating and managing an effective communication system for your firm. They are:

Connecting with Clients – The "bottom line" is your clients have to be satisfied with the service you provide them. The practice of law is a customer service business. There are many technologies to connect and stay connected with your clients as you provide them services.

Lowering costs to Clients - Clients are constantly trying to control and lower he cost of legal fees. Costs can be lowered both in the exchange of information and in substantive decision making if communications can be constant, open and ongoing.

Cost effective Access to Client, Legal and Factual Information. – The Internet provides low cost access to legal and nonlegal information. These savings can be passed on to your clients.

Global Communication of Information. – The Internet is providing a global law office with easily accessible data and people throughout the world.

Before selecting the type of telecommunications you are going to use you need to determine your communication goals with your clients and others. Consider some of the following communication goals:

- Sending and receiving e-mail;
- Joint document drafting;
- Participating in legal discussion groups;
- Exchanging documents;
- Accessing billing tasks and costs;

- Avoiding telephone tag and other inefficiencies;
- Sharing work product retrieval;
- Distributing and publishing information;
- Observing the facial expressions of a person using videoconferencing;
- Exchanging messages; and
- Sharing case management plan and timetable.

To reach your goals there are several technologies available:
- E-mail;
- Phone;
- Fax;
- Voice mail;
- Computer telephony;
- Shared computer databases and full text files;
- Document sharing software;
- Audio Internet software;
- Video conferencing;
- Workgroup computing software, and the
- Internet, Intranet and Extranet.

Selecting the appropriate technology requires consideration of a number of factors including:
- Does the product or service meet your specific goal(s)? Is it fit for its intended purpose?
- How easy will it be for the staff to use? Is it easy and fast to connect or difficult and require significant work?
- Is it a one-time cost or is there a substantial monthly charge? Can a different technology accomplish the same goal without the cost?
- Can I integrate it with other systems?
- Is the technology capable of adding new users? If not, is the company committed to further developments?
- How many parties are participating, when and what type of content will be exchanged?
- Is it stable or is it the beta or first release of the product?
- Does it allow for security from outside and inside?

Which goals you select will determine the type of communication system and technology that is best for your firm.

Digital Information Channels (Bandwidth) and Connectors

To transmit digital data from one location to another requires a *connector* to a wire or wireless *pipeline* that will carry video and other data from one location to another. In most cases this is done by wire, radio or space satellite.

The *key* to transmission of data is the pipeline width and the decoder devices or connectors on each end of the connection.

The pipeline or bandwidth of the cabling or wireless transmission (satellite) along with the connectors determines the speed that data that can be transmitted. On each end of the pipeline are connectors, such as a modem, that compress and decompress the digital data for the user. If you have unlimited pipeline width then the decoder devices to compress information are unimportant. On the other hand, if you have a finite pipeline width, then the connectors and compression and decompression techniques become important. The eventual goal is to carry four signals at once: telephone, television, radio and computer digital information.

The following are various methods of carrying digital data over different types of "pipelines" or connections. Also included is the required bandwidth to transmit different types of digital information. Other then satellite the following connectors are all cable or "hard wire" connections.

Channel Type	Bandwidth Size	Bandwidth Required for Data Type
		Text - 10 KBPS
Cellular Phones	19.2 KBPS	
POTS (Plain old telephone line)	33 KBPS, 56KBPS with 2X	
		JPEG - images full screen - 20 KBPS
ISDN(switched 56)	56 KBPS	
Wireless Cellular packet	128 KBPS	
Fractal T-1	112 KBPS +	Video MPEG-1 video quality requires a 120 to 140 KBPS datastream. VHS quality at 8 bits of color and 30 frames per second.
Twisted pair - 1 base 3	1 MBPS	Video MPEG-2 quality, quarter screen full motion requires 500 KBPS. Video MPEG-2 quality full screen & full motion requires 1 MBPS, SVHS quality.
Satellite (wireless)	1 MBPS +	
T-1	1.54 MBPS	
Cable Television	1 MBPS +	
Token ring	10 MBPS	
Switched Ethernet	10 MBPS	
Coaxial - 10 base 2	10 MBPS	
Twisted pair - 10 base T	10 MBPS	
T-3 and DS-3	45 MBPS	
Fast Ethernet	100 MBPS	
FDDI	100 MBPS	
OC-1	115 MBPS	
ATM - 155	1.26 gBPS	

* KBPS - Kilo bits per second - 10 KBPS means that data is transmitted at 10,000 bits per second
* MBPS - Million bits per second - 1 MBPS means that data is transmitted at 1, 000,000 bits per second
* GBPS - Gigabytes per second - 1 GBPS means that data is transmitted at 1,000,000,000 bits per second

Time to Download a One Megabyte File			
Type of Channel	14,400 BPS telephone	128,000 BPS ISDN	Coaxial 10,000 KBPS or 10 MBPS
Time	9.7 minutes	66 seconds	.8 seconds
Cost	$20 + per month	$45+ per month	$49+
Usage	98%	6.7 million homes by 2000	6.9 million homes by 2000

Estimates - Forrester Research, Inc.

With the recent deregulation of the communication industry we now have numerous hard wire suppliers. These include our local telephone companies, cable companies, Competitive Access Providers (CAPS), Internet Service Providers, regional bell operating companies among others.

POTS (Plain Old Telephone Lines). The most common pipeline is the regular analog copper telephone line. For a regular analog phone line the rate of transmission is approximately 1200 baud or 1,200 BPS. This is a measurement of how fast information is transferred. BPS refers to bits per second. Connectors such as modems are available to increase the transmission over a phone line at a higher rate such as 2,400; 4,800; 9,600; 14,000; 28,800; 33,600 or 56,000 bits per second. The modem encodes the data for faster transmission before sending it over the phone line and the receiver decodes it on the other end. If both parties have 28,800 modems then the faster transmission is available. However, if one party has a 14,000 modem then the other party will receive the information at that rate. Also, be aware that DSL lines discussed in the next part will transmit data at a much higher rate over POTS lines once the digital equipment is in place.

ISDN Lines. Many phone companies are digitizing existing analog telephone lines, which are then called *ISDN lines*, which creates a larger pipeline to send data. The normal phone line with a 28,000 modem can send and receive data at 28,800 bits per second. A phone line that has been digitized can send and receive information at four times that amount or 128,000 baud or 128,000 bits per second. ISDN lines can also be leased that transmit at 56,000 BPS rate.

Fractal T-1 and T-1 Lines – These lines are hardwired and offer a bandwidth ranging from 112, 000 BPS to over 1,000,000 BPS. Phone companies and others are offering T-1 connections that can transmit data at 1.54 MBPS. The competition for your connection is becoming increasingly competitive with CAPS (competitive access providers) offering full T-1 connections for as low as $800 per month.

The token ring, switched Ethernet, Coaxial – 10 base 2, Twisted pair – 10 base T and other computer networking wire connections operate generally at 10,000,000 BPS. The transmission of digital information within a LAN such as text, images and video conferencing is as important as connecting to clients across the country.

Cable TV Connection. Cable TV (CATV) companies offer Internet access to its cable customers through existing cable. They offer bandwidth at 1.5 MBAs or higher access rates which are over 30 times the current 56,000 BPS offered through regular phone lines. The increased bandwidth will enable an array of multimedia applications including full motion video, sound, graphics and so forth. The availability, pricing for the service and the cost of a required cable modem depends on what part of the country one resides. Existing systems need to be upgraded and since cables are shared by different customers the speeds will decrease as more users transmit on the same connection, like on a LAN.

Fiber Optics uses light instead of electrical impulses to carry the signal. Fiberoptics is commonly used in select parts of networking and some fiberoptics lines have been laid across our country. An optical filter is a hair-thin strand of glass. In communication it will carry four types of information at once: telephone, television, radio and computer data. Fiberoptics is one of the keys to transmitting much greater amounts of digital information over "hard wire". The increased efficiency and capacity to transmit data will enable "multimedia applications" to be sent and received. Multimedia includes text, sound, graphics, and video. Interactivity will become a product of fiber optic. Fiber optic's signal strength enables a signal to be run a long distance without a weakening of the signal. Because of its signal strength data speeds can increase from 10M (10,000,000 bits per second) to over 1G (1,000,000,000 bits per second) which will be sufficient for future network data needs.

Satellite. Satellite communications allow for the sending of television or telephone signals to small satellite dishes, as small as 12", attached to the roof of a building. Digital data can be received 40 times faster then data received over a regular telephone line or at approximately 1,000,000 BPS through $200 home satellite dishes via the Internet to recipients. However, uploading information must be through a separate connection such as a POTS line.

DSL – Digital Subscriber Lines. Plain old telephone service (POTS) may have lower bandwidth presently but the physical copper wires are adequate to deliver video if the proper digital infrastructure is built that will turn POTS lines into DSL lines. The long-term answer to video may lie with Digital Subscriber Lines (DSL). DSL is a technique for converting ordinary phone lines to run digital signals capable of Internet access at speeds ranging from 128 KBPS to 7 MBPS. DSL's can turn a pair of POTS lines into a large bandwidth digital channel when digital modems are at both ends. For example the following speeds can be achieved if the copper wires are turned into DSL lines:

NAME	Data Rate	Direction
HDSL – (high-data-rate digital subscriber line)	705 KBPS up-linked 705 KBPS down-linked	Symmetrical, bi-directional (2 phone lines needed)
SDSL – (single line digital subscriber line)	705 KBPS down-linked 128 KBPS up-linked	Asymmetrical
ADSL – (asymmetric digital subscriber line)	8 MBPS down-linked 1.54 MBPS up-linked	Asymmetrical
VDSL – (very high-data-rate digital subscriber line)	13 to 52 MBPS downlinked 1.5 to 2.3 MBPS up-linked	Asymmetrical

Wireless Solutions

One solution to the telephone and cable-wiring problem is to go wireless. Wireless transmission of data, voice and video is one of the ultimate goals of the information revolution.

Satellite - Satellite system customers are required generally to invest in the antenna, receiver, ISA interface card and software. It may be as high as $1000. Service charges may depend on usage that is measured in megabytes and not minutes. Some companies charge 80 cents per MB to download during peak hours. You also need a separate dial-up account with an Internet Service Provider since you cannot transmit data upstream to the satellite. The satellite will deliver at 400 KBPS or more and transmission upstream is 28,800 BPS or greater depending on your connection.

LMDS - Local Multipoint Distribution System. LMDS is a local service that is being built on ground based transceivers. A customer's antenna will point to a neighborhood transceiver that's mounted on a high pole or antenna. The transceiver will communicate to a central office. The downstream data delivery may be at 25 to 50 MBPS and the upstream at 5 MBPS

Cellular transmissions will continue to explode as the IRIDIUM project is set to be completed by the end of 1998. This project will provide a series of low flying satellites that will allow anyone to make a phone call from anywhere in the world. Portable data terminals will be able to hook into the system through laptop computers, personal digital assistants (PDA's) and pen computers. Two sites to visit on the wireless technology are AT&T Wireless (www.airdata.com) and Motorola Wireless Data Group (www.motorola.com) the home of the Iridium project.

Two-way Wireless Messaging Service. With a standard notebook or palmtop computer, software and a wireless PC Card modem you can send and receive e-mail or fax, receive or send a page and obtain a constant download of information. There is no logging on or connection. You simply turn on the wireless modem. Services are available through wireless messaging services and wireless carriers. Messages find you since there is no logging in. The approximate cost is $40 per month.

Communications & Remote Access Software

Communication software is needed to instruct your computer's hardware component such as a modem to interact with another computer or perform a variety of other communication tasks such as sending faxes, files, etc. over a telephone line. Windows 95/98™ provides many of the capabilities needed for on-line communication such as sending and receiving faxes, connection to remote computers and so on.

Remote access software permits a remote PC to connect to a LAN based host PC and take control of it. Key commands and mouse movements are sent from the remote PC to the host PC which are then processed as if you were physically there. In return the host computer executes the commands and sends the screen changes to your remote computer. You effectively are running the host PC computer from your remote location.

Features and Products. With communication and remote access software some of the features to consider are:

- File transfer;
- Dial up connection;
- Network shared modem connection;
- Host and terminal support;
- Chat sessions;
- Virus checking during file transfer;
- Data encryption services;
- Fax sending and receiving capability;
- Internet telephone software;
- Image manager;
- Modem support;
- Compression manager;
- OCR capability;
- Paging notification;
- Control one PC from the other;
- Voice messaging; and
- Internet faxing (saves long distance charges).

Some products to consider include: Laplink for Windows 95™, Traveling Software™ (www.trasoft.com); pcAnywhere™ (www.symantec.com); CommSuite 95™ & WinComm Pro™, Delrina™ (www.delrina.com); HyperAccess™ (www.hilgraeve.com); and WinFax Pro™ (www.symantec.com).

Computer Telephony

Computer Telephone Integration (CTI) merges the capabilities of computers and telephones, adding intelligence to the making and receiving of phone calls. This integration of computers with telephones offers the capability of controlling a variety of communication methods from one system.

CTI will allow users to extract data from the calling parties and use the data to drive and support their call processing, interactive voice response services and a host of other computer based conversation and messaging services. CTI allows transactions to be entered, edited, validated, updated, processed and tracked. Messages can be submitted, interpreted, acted upon and disseminated throughout an organization for workgroup computing and collaboration. Information can be formatted as voice, text, images, video or any other form of recordable signals.

The core CTI technologies include:
- voice recognition and voice to text processing;
- text to speech voice output;
- call processing;
- facsimile services; and
- digital signal processing.

Interactive voice response permits a telephone caller to interact with an organization's information database through the use of touch tone signals or spoken words if equipped with voice recognition to obtain or enter information. With the universal use of telephones, multilingual capability, customizable, easily modified, and speech recognition CTI will become a valuable tool for the legal profession. For example this technology can be applied to specific cases or the court can use it for system schedules for the attorneys.

Basic information of a firm such as the name, hours of operation, procedures, pager information and so forth can be easily accessible to the caller. Information can be obtained from telephony on pleadings filed, continuances, deposition schedules, payment reminders, instructions to client, case calendar and action plans, fax back for review of pleadings, posting of court rulings, ability to schedule client conferences and so forth.

The result is that voice calls will be supported with a complete set of data and information about the callers and the call process activities. The callers can access databases, create transactions and follow up on previously generated information. This will produce more efficient and effective servicing of the parties and an improvement in performance and productivity of the organization and its resources. The interacting parties will have the results of their interaction directly linked into fact and business processing systems of the organization resulting in a smoother and more automated response to the conditions and situation. This in turn should improve the business relationships between the parties and increase the potential for business. CTI will support interactive voice processing, call centers, electronic data interchange and a host of other customer/supplier interfacing. It will support dynamic response to changing conditions in the marketplace.

Application CTI toolkits include OmniVox™ (www.apexvoice.com).

Voice mail is a specialized type of E-mail system. Voice mail is a relatively simple, computer-linked technology for recording, storing, retrieving, and forwarding phone messages. It is called voice mail, or voice messaging, because the messages are spoken and left in a "voice mailbox." The telephone doubles as a computer terminal, but instead of presenting the information on a computer screen, the system reads it over the phone line, using prerecorded voice vocabulary. The systems are based on special-purpose computer chips and software that convert human speech into bits of digital code. These digitized voices are stored on magnetic disks, from which they can be instantaneously retrieved. Callers are offered a menu of choices, and the messages they select are played, left in "voice mailboxes," or they can access huge computer databases.

> **TAPI (Telephony Applications Programming Interface)**. This interface will become increasingly important as we use our computers to become the focal point of our communications. This is an API for developers that enables programs to share modems by application and share fax modems over a network. This feature in Windows 95/98™ can only be used by 32-bit Windows 95/98™ programs. If the system is set to check your E-mail while an incoming fax is arriving it will check your E-mail and then return control to the incoming fax application. With Windows 3.1 this was not available. Data modems cannot be shared over a network. All of the applications must be 32 bit TAPI supported programs for this to work.

Voice mail messages will begin appearing in the "in-box" on your computer as voice mail is integrated with computers.

Automatic Number Identification (ANI) enables the caller's phone number to be delivered to a database when the call arrives. The ANI system retrieves database records matching the caller's number. For a law firm this enables a client to be immediately routed to the appropriate associate or whoever is working on the file. The client management record can be immediately updated to reflect the call and other important client information. For the lawyer these systems can automatically track an outgoing call to client for the amount of time on the phone and subsequent invoices. Other telephone computer technology applications available include the ability to receive and send e-mail, change schedules, change meeting dates on databases by using a telephone and not a computer. The combining of the telephone and computer into a unified piece of client relation software promises strong utility and growth over the next several years.

Multifunction Telephony Boards. Multifunctional telephony devices integrate data/fax modems, fax reception and broadcasting to and from multiple users, paging services, multiple mailbox voice mail functionality, speakerphone and microphone for telephone conversations, Internet telephone capability, on-line connectivity software, and CD quality audio for around $200 to $300. These devices can provide a central management system for small or home offices. They consolidate e-mail, voice mail, and faxes making them easy to retrieve even while on the road.

Other features to consider include:
- call in voice mail retrieval;
- forward voice mail to remote locations;
- automatic paging service when messages and faxes are received;

- fax on demand services;
- password ID services for voicemail;
- caller ID;
- voice over the Internet software;
- DSVD Digital Simultaneous Voice and Data technology (modem operates at 19.2 KBPS in this mode) or Alternating Voice and Data (AVD);
- a soundchip if you don't have SoundBlaster; and
- a CD-ROM Interface connector.

Some manufacturers of CTI cards are Aztech Labs (www.aztechca.com) with model AT3300 Audio Telephony Card and 3Com's (www.3com.com) US Robotics Sportster Voice 28.8 Fax/modem PVM™.

Conclusion

Telecommunications will pay a significant role in the practice of law as we transition into the Information Age. As the bandwidth and compression and decompression techniques improve we will be able to communicate with courts, opposing counsel our clients and others over the Internet. One must keep a watchful eye on the most efficient and effective connection to the Internet in your area. Whether it be POTS, cable, satellite or other methods the increased bandwidth will save time and allow for sending and receiving of text, audio, graphics and video. It is a time that firms will have to strategically plan for the integration of these new tools and channels of communication for the law firm.

One of the noteworthy trends is the integration of computers and the telephone and increasingly television and radio. All of these electronic means of communication will enhance our ability to provide timely and quality advice to our clients.

The Internet (and Intranet and Extranet) - The Most Powerful Communication Tool of All Time.

Introduction

The Internet is the most hyped and talked about technology concept ever. It is being touted as and is the most powerful communication tool of all times. What makes this tool different and with more potential then the telephone or television? The value of the Internet is the immense capability to interactively communicate with anyone inexpensively and exchange information using text, audio, graphics or videoconferencing anytime, anywhere. Communication can be accomplished by electronic mail, sending or receiving computer files, interacting by voice, video conferencing, participating in various discussion areas and other tools. This capacity to communicate inexpensively with over 30,000,000 users on-line today and an expected 40,000,000 users on-line by the year 2000 is phenomenal. It is the most powerful communication tool of all time.

> "The Internet is a collection of information services, a communication pipeline, and file transfer protocol that spans the globe."

> Is it a fact—or have I dreamt it—that, by means of electricity, the world of matter has become a great nerve, vibrating thousands of miles in a breathless point of time? **Nathaniel Hawthorne** (1804–64), U.S. author. Clifford Pyncheon, in *The House of the Seven Gables,* ch. 17 (1851).

The Internet is an international network of computers. It links thousands of computer networks including businesses, governments, educational institutions, individual users, law firms, and clients. These links transport digital information from computer to computer until it reaches its final destination. The Internet links the continents together into a global village. There are few rules governing conduct on the Internet. There is no controlling entity or service that controls the Internet. Instead there are millions of computers that are linked together.

A law firm needs to understand the dynamics of the Internet and place it meaningfully within the context of other law firm tools and solutions. It must be able to determine if the Internet, Intranet or Extranet is the best use of its available time and resources in terms of competitiveness, productivity and strategic advantage.

Surveys

There are numerous surveys verifying the significant growth of the Internet and have a direct bearing on how legal services will be marketed and how law will be practiced in the coming years. The number and type of users and reasons they use the Internet disclose important competitive issues and marketing information for the legal industry.

- The Internet Lawyer-Microsoft Corporation survey found that 600,000 or 71% of lawyers access the Internet for e-mail, research and marketing. 72% of legal professionals use the Internet for legal research. 48% use the Net to retrieve federal court opinions, statutes, and regulations. State legal materials are accessed by 34% of those who do legal research. Other uses include finding missing people, trademark infringement issues, and medical and corporate research.

- The 1997 Survey conducted by the ABA reports that 60% of the largest law firms use the Internet for marketing. More than ½ of the firms have their own firm's web page. The Internet is used to conduct legal research (97%), to communicate with clients (91.9%) and colleagues (88%), to access court records (78%) and to participate in private discussion groups (53%).

- Survey conducted by FINF/SVP, Inc. a New York based research firm in May, 1997 found that over 20,000,000 American users regard the Internet as an "indispensable" part of their life.

- Survey conducted by Nielson in October 1995 found that 24,000,000 North American people have access to the Internet. Of that number 25% of www users had an income level of $ 80,000/year compared to 10% of the general population. 50% of web users are in a professional or management position compared with 27% of the general population. 64% have a university diploma compared to 29% of the general population.

- In a survey conducted for AT&T by Odyssey entitled *Taking Off: The State of Electronic Commerce in America* found that over 80 million Americans have access to commercial or Internet based services. Over 129 million customers have access to PC's. Key among the findings is that almost 40% of Americans say they expect to buy through Internet based services in 1997 and more than 55% expect to do so within the next 5 years.

- A BYTE magazine Survey (www.byte.com) found that the use of the Internet is prevalent among those at work and at home. 60% surveyed said they access the web from both home and work. Of that number 60% of the users use it mainly for e-mail. 40% have bought new products, 90% get new product information, 90% get general product information, 80% read on-line magazines and newspapers and 60% get general information. Intranets are used by 30% for corporate training, 40% for corporate policy distribution and 60% for information distribution.

- Another BYTE survey found that 72% of companies have web sites.

- Veronis, Suhler & Associates predict that by 1999 consumer spending will increase to 3.5 billion on the Internet

- The Internet village has seen explosive infiltration compared to all other communication devices. According to Cyberatlas it took the telephone 38 years to reach 10 million customers, fax 22 years, VCR's and cellular phones 9 years, and PC's 7 years. *The Internet only took 3 years to garner 10,000,000 users.*

Strategic Internet Legal Advantages

There are several strategic legal advantages to using the Internet in your law practice.

- *Clients and potential clients are on the Internet.* With the number and income level of the users using the Internet businesses are rushing to attract them to their products and services and communicate with them. Many of these users or businesses are clients or potential clients for your firm. Having your own web site offers a unique opportunity to reach out to clients and explain why your firm is the one to assist them. It also provides an opportunity to provide them with legal briefs, newsletters or other legal information of value such as links to government agencies of interest to your clients.

- *Other law firms and competing nonlawyers are marketing themselves on the Internet.* There are thousands of firms with web sites and more are being added daily. Nonlawyers are also finding their way onto the WWW to offer legal services. The competition for clients can sometimes be quite intense as law firms market their services. An effective way to market your firm 24 hours a day to anyone located anywhere is to have a web site. Establishing an Internet presence enables people to get information about your law firm and the services you offer.

- *Conversation among lawyers and clients creating and cementing relationships is already taking place on the web.* The ubiquitous low cost availability of e-mail has provided unparalleled access to your clients. E-mail provides the ability to send messages, documents, exhibits or spreadsheets to clients anytime and anyplace. It cements and fortifies existing attorney/client relationships especially as both parties assist each other in adapting to the new technologies. Besides e-mail many lawyers are networking by hosting or participating in discussions by using listservs and newsgroups with potential clients on the Internet. Intranets and Extranets are allowing lawyers and clients to share information and collaborate on their cases.

- *Unparalleled and cost effective access to legal and factual information.* Legal, business and financial information on the Web has been a driving force for attorneys to use the WWW. The United States Code, Code of Federal regulations (CFR), Supreme Court cases, law review articles, state statutes, caselaw and other legal information are on the WWW and more is being added daily. The Wall Street Journal, Dun & Bradstreet, stock market companies, and news services are all on the Web providing business information and services. Some states now provide UCC filing information, incorporations and doing business certificates, and court docketing information though the Internet. You also can locate expert witnesses, fact witnesses, latest standards for handling propane or how to reconstruct an accident, The Web contains a phenomenal amount of information for your litigation needs.

- *Cost effective global communication of data that includes text, voice, graphics and video.* For the first time in history we have the capability to send and receive text, voice, graphics and video to anyone located anywhere in the world at anytime. With thousands of computers linked together and passing the information from one computer to the next it provides a seamless communication link with everyone in the world for a low cost. For the price of a low-end computer, a modem and a fee of approximately $20 a month one can communicate with clients, potential clients and others. Whether that person is in Australia, Europe or North America the communication will generally be delivered in seconds or minutes.

Practical Examples of Web Usage

- *Finding People.* If you are looking for a witness, friend or whoever, there are a number of directories that allow you to search all of the phone books of the United States.

- *Finding businesses, products and services.* Yellow page electronic directories allow you to search by the type of company, area code, or zip code to help specify the location. You can find hard-to-find special item gifts or just about any book in the country by going to sites such as www.amazon.com.

□ *Research.* Lawyers and businesses are getting volumes of information off the net for which they were previously charged. Demographic unemployment statistics, genetic research and a phenomenal amount of other information are available free.

□ *Education.* The latest encyclopedias are on line. We are starting to see sophisticated long distance learning by live broadcasts over the Internet over a regular phone line. Teachers, students and parents all stay in touch using the Internet.

□ *Travel.* Cities, town, counties, states and nations are putting up a host of tourist and event information. You can find weather, maps, transportation schedules and museum hours on-line. You can purchase airline tickets at discounted rates.

□ *Marketing and Sales.* It is estimated that there will be over 3.5 billion dollars in sales by this year on the web. People are selling software, books, music disks and a host of other products over the Net. Electronic commerce will continue to grow in importance.

□ *Medicine.* Patients, doctors and others are sharing healing experiences, keeping up with the latest medical treatments and give one another support over the web. Some doctors even communicate with their patients over the web.

□ *Investing.* People are buying stocks and other securities over the web. It has revolutionized the traditional brokerage houses since one can buy and sell shares for as low as $10 a transaction.

□ *Organizing events.* Seminar, conference and trade show leaders are organizing their events over the web. They disseminate information, register and recruit speakers and perform other tasks over the web.

Connecting to the Internet

There are four basic steps to connecting to the Internet:

1. Obtain a computer capable of running Windows based programs;
2. Install a modem;
3. Obtain Internet software; and
4. Locate and sign up with an Internet Access Provider (ISP).

1. Computer. A Pentium, 486 computer or even a 386 computer running Windows based programs can easily access the web and operate at a fast speed.

2. Modem. A modem needs to be installed to convert the computer's digital signals into analog signals that can be transmitted across telephone lines. A modem costs approximately $100. Choose one that transmits at a speed of 33,600 BPS or higher. A fast modem will decrease the time to upload or download information off the Internet. For example a 1-megabyte file will take 22 minutes to download using a 9600 BPS modem, 14 minutes using a 14,400 BPS modem and 8 minutes using a 28,800 BPS modem. Recently, new 2X modems delivering information at 56,000 BPS have become available.

You will transmit and receive at the same speed modem as your ISP. If you have a 56,000 modem then your ISP must also have a 56,000 connection. Otherwise you will transmit at the modem rate that your ISP has.

A modem must be matched with your particular Internet connection service. A modem for a telephone line is not compatible with the modem used to connect to the Internet through your cable company.

3. Internet Software. Software is needed to access the various communication sources, transfer files, send e-mail and a host of other Internet services. For the WWW one needs a browser such as Netscape or Internet Explorer to surf the web or send or receive e-mail. Generally this software is provided by your ISP. Using different software to access the different Internet components is ending as major software developers are integrating the different Internet software functions into one package. Both Netscape Communicator™ and Microsoft Explorer™ are integrating new features into their "browsers" that will provide you one integrated software package for most of your Internet needs.

4. Find an Internet Service Provider (ISP). To connect to the Internet you have to go through an Internet Service provider (ISP). An ISP can be a private company such as American Online, a cable company such as Cox Communications or your local telephone company such as US West. Using a modem you connect to the ISP's host computer that is directly connected to the Internet. Most ISP's have regular phone line access transferring data at 14, 000 BPS, 28, 000 BPS or the new 56,000 BPS. Some providers offer ISDN service (Integrated Services Digital Network) with speeds up to 128,000BPS. Cable companies offer access of 1.5 MBPS or faster. The higher the BPS the faster one can surf the net and transmit data, graphics and video. See the prior part on *Digital Information Channels (Bandwidth)* and *Connectors* and *Emerging Connection Channels.*

Types of Connections to an Internet Service Provider (ISP)

There are several types of connections available to the Internet through an ISP. See the prior part on *Digital Information Channels (Bandwidth) and Connectors and Emerging Connection Channels.*

Dial-up: PPP and SLIP or Shell accounts. For an individual or for a small number of users in your company a dial-up phone connection can be made with an Internet Service Provider (ISP) in your area. If you want to use Netscape, Eudora mail and other graphical browsers you need to get a SLIP or PPP account. SLIP stands for Serial Line Internet Protocol. PPP stands for Point-to-Point Protocol. These are the TCP/IP Internet protocol over telephone lines. SLIP is a network layered protocol and PPP is a direct link protocol. *Shell accounts* are generally text only access to the Internet. They may provide some basic menuing like "1. E-mail" but it does not provide the stimulating graphical capability for viewing the WWW. They are less expensive and are mostly used for e-mail and ftp transfer.

Dedicated Dial-Up. For users that want constant access to the Internet on a regular phone line it is suggested that a "dedicated dial-up" line from an ISP be obtained. The user would dial into the ISP and would maintain the open connection all day. The cost is approximately $150-$250 per month with an initial setup charge of approximately $500. Your connection would still be at a 14,400, 28,800 BPS or higher depending on your provider and your modem.

High Speed Dial-up. Dedicated high-speed connections can increase the data transmission rate from 56,000 BPS to 1.54 million BPS. The higher the transfer rates the higher the cost. Prices generally start at $49.95 per month for a 56 KBPS and increase depending on the transfer rate.

High Speed Dedicated Dial-Up. For a number of users a high-speed dedicated phone line with a 24-hour connection may be the answer. Again the access is through an ISP and the cost is approximately $400 - $1000 per month with a $3,200 approximate setup charge. The high setup charge requires configuration of a

> TCP/IP is the standard protocol on the Internet to transfer files. TCP/IP stands for Transmission Control Protocol/Internet Program. TCP/IP was developed by the Department of Defense and is one of several software protocols that can be used to connect computers together. It is widely used in Ethernet systems and packet radio systems.

digital line, router and CSU/DSU connection.

Type of Connection	Number of Users	Monthly Cost	Setup Cost	Providers
Dial-Up	One	$10-$25	$Free - $50	- Local ISP or National ISP - Online services such as America Online, etc.
Dedicated Dial-Up	3-10 users through a local area network	$150-$250	$500 - $1000	- Local or National ISP
High Speed Dial-Up	10+ users	$400 and up plus the cost of a digital phone line.	$3000 - $4000	- Local or National ISP

Considerations for choosing an Internet Service Provider (ISP)

There are several hundred national and local ISP's who wish to connect you to the Internet for e-mail, access to the Web and for other functions:

- *Commercial National On-line Services.* America Online and Microsoft Network are a few of the well-known national providers. These services have made the Internet connection relatively painless and easy and they have local access numbers for most areas of the country. They provide information in a more organized way but you may have problems with getting on the service because of the large number of subscribers.
- *Colleges and Universities.* Most have direct connections to the Internet; and
- *National and Local Internet Service Providers.* There are several national ISP's that have local or 800 access numbers. If you travel a lot or live in a rural area then you do not have to pay long distance charges. There are many local startup companies that have begun providing access to the Internet. Look for advertisements in local newspapers, yellow pages and other local computer publications. Be aware that the ISP industry is going through a consolidation phase as more national companies like AT&T become involved. Some ISP's will be here today and gone tomorrow.

Selection Criteria. The

> Tips for Using the Internet:
> - Working offline means that you are not connected to the Internet when you are composing or reading e-mail or replying to newsgroup mail. The software will automatically send the mail or messages the next time you go on-line. This results in less time actually online.
> - Cut out the *http://* prefix. Newer versions of Netscape and Internet Explorer both recognize http:// or ftp:// and so it does not have to be typed in. For example, simply type in the address *www.azbar.org*.
> - Try to log in during off-peak hours since there are fewer busy signals and the response time is faster. During the week this time is from *8-10 AM and 3-9 PM and on weekends from 6-10 PM.*

> For a list of ISP's see www.thelist.com and www.barkers.org/online/. Ratings of ISP's can be found at www.mindspring.com/~mcgatney/isprate.html

selection of an ISP is important since generally you will get your e-mail at this address and access other web sources such as the World Wide Web. If you do not have access to your mail or cannot be on the WWW then you lose productivity. The startup time and effort to connect to an ISP can be considerable so choose your ISP carefully. This is especially important if you get your e-mail through an ISP since a change will generally require you to notify everyone of your new e-mail address.

When choosing an ISP consider:

- *Reputation in the community.* Ask your friends about ISP's they use. Are they able to get dial up access or are their lines busy? Are they down for repairs a lot? Before signing up obtain the ISP access number you would be using and call them throughout a normal day to see if you get a busy signal. How many years have they been in business? Any problem with their billing department?

- *What kind of software do you need?* Is the ISP providing it at no cost or do you need to purchase the software? What version of the software are they providing you?

- *Support.* A major factor in your decision should be the level of support of the ISP. Call their support number continuously for a few days before signing up. Does anyone answer? Do they have 7 days 24 hours a day support?

- *Price plans.* The costs of Internet access may vary widely. The cost factors to consider include:
  - Monthly and hourly charge;
  - Number of hours of access time permitted, cost of extra hours and prime vs. nonprime time access cost;
  - Out of state connection number and any additional charges; and
  - Is the cost of E-mail or file transfer services included in the basic price?

- *Web page availability.* Can you place your own home pages on their server? If so, how many megabytes of storage do you get and what is the cost of extra space?

- *Speed of the access line.* Even if you have a 28,800 modem the ISP must be connected to you at this same speed. Does the provider offer ISDN connection? Does the provider offer the new speeds such as 56,000 BPS? Does the ISP offer leased line options? If you are connecting your office to the net you may need this.

- *E-mail addresses.* Do extra e-mail addresses for employees or family members cost extra?

- *Total bandwidth of provider – Speed of the ISP's outbound line.* The ISP must maintain sufficient outbound connection to handle all of the access calls by his customers. What size line does the ISP have? Know exactly what network connection your ISP has to the Internet! This will determine whether your ISP can handle peak load periods and potential outages. Determine if the speed is actually existing or is in the planning stage.

- *Users/ modem ratio.* How many users are there per ISP modem or line? 10 users to 1 modem is a good ratio.

- *Domain name.* If you wish to use your own domain name is it part of the subscriber package or does it cost additional?

- *E-mail forwarding.* Will they forward your e-mail if you change companies?

- *Newsgroups.* How many newsgroups are carried on the ISP's host computer? Some ISP's only carry specific newsgroups. Ask them if they will add newsgroups of those you might be interested in; and

- *Newsfeeds.* How many Newsfeeds do they carry?

Internet Basics – the components

The main functions of the Internet are the capability to send and receive e-mail, publish and interact on the WWW, send and receive files and participate in discussion groups throughout the world.

E-mail (electronic mail)

The most used and popular way to communicate through the Internet is by using e-mail. You can send a message to anyone, anywhere, anytime, almost instantaneously, if both parties have access to the Internet. You can exchange e-mail with millions of people all over the world.

E-mail is used to send messages and attached computer files to other Internet users. After the e-mail is delivered the recipient can reply to the e-mail and also attach files for its return journey. The same message can be addressed to multiple recipients for fast and time saving distribution. E-mail is the primary method for participating in discussion groups on the Internet such as listservs and newsgroups. *See also Chapter 3, E-mail – Killer Application for the Nineties.*

E-mail Addresses contain the name and location protocol where the mail will be sent. They have a user's name, the @ sign, the name of the user's domain or computer, a period and the type of organization. For example my e-mail address is

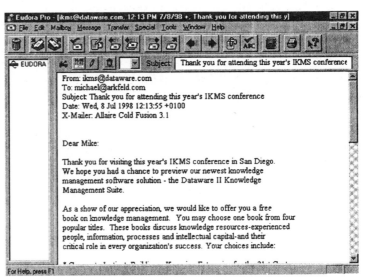

Michael@Arkfeld.com. The user's name is *Michael*, the @ sign, the user's domain or computer is *Arkfeld* and the *com* stands for commercial. Since I have my own domain name – arkfeld.com – my mail can be sent to my domain address. If I change ISP's I can keep my e-mail address the same since I can take my domain name with me to a new ISP.

When you sign up with an Internet Service Provider (ISP) they generally provide you with the last part of your e-mail address. For example if you sign up for America Online the e-mail address would be username@aol.com.

There are no two e-mail names or addresses the same. Internet addresses can come in all sizes and shapes. Some addresses are long and contain a variety of symbols such as % signs, exclamation points and so on. If unsure of the e-mail address of a person try to send e-mail and then call the person to find out if they received it or ask the person to respond if they received the e-mail.

> **Never change your e-mail address again!** Besides identifying your address on the web a domain name can be used as your e-mail address. For example if your domain name is *crimlaw.com* then your e-mail address can be Smith@crimlaw.com. If you switch ISP's then your domain name and e-mail address will follow you to the new ISP.

E-mail software lets you send computer files, generally called attachments, along with the e-mail. These attachments can be software, graphic, spreadsheet, or document files. The process of sending attachments is called MIME encoding. MIME stands for Multipurpose Internet Mail extensions.

E-mail Acronyms. The following acronyms are used frequently on the web in e-mails, listservs, etc.:
BTW – by the way
RTM – read the manual
IMHO – In my humble opinion
ROFL – Rolling on floor laughing
TIA – Thanks in Advance
YMMV – Your mileage may vary

Features and Products. Features to look for in an Internet e-mail program:
- Automatically checks for e-mail at scheduled intervals while you are performing another task on-line;
- Filtering features to prioritize your mail;
- Address book to keep e-mail addresses;
- Distribution mail lists for groups of users;

- Templates available for repetitive responses;
- Folders for organizing your e-mail; and
- Encryption features.

There are several graphical e-mail software programs available. Eudora Pro 3.0™ by Qualcomm is the web's most popular e-mail client. The lite version is free. It can be downloaded at www.qualcomm.com or www.eudora.com. Qualcomm also provides a FAQ section at www.eudora.com/techsupport/faqs.html that explains many e-mail questions. Another program, E-mail Connection, can be downloaded at www.connectsoft.com. The Netscape Communicator™ program includes an e-mail software program. (www.netscape.com) as does the Internet Explorer™ with a module called Outlook Express™ (www.microsoft.com). Free e-mail via the web is available at (mail.yahoo.com) and (www.hotmail.com).

The e-mail feature of the Internet is one of the killer applications for the nineties. Communication is considerably easier using e-mail to communicate with clients, witnesses, relatives or anyone with an Internet connection.

World Wide Web

The World Wide Web is also called the Web, WWW or W3. It is the most talked about part of the Internet and reference is often made to a person or company's "home page". It is the most exciting part of the Internet and enables individuals or companies to publish there own home page for a very low cost and interact theoretically with over 30,000,000 Internet users to access information on your web page. Web site growth has reached 1.3 million and will increase exponentially as users rush to create web sites for business, educational, government or personal reasons. Documents, images, sounds and video clips can be placed on web sites for viewing or downloading. The software used to navigate the web is known as a browser. The most popular browsers are Microsoft Internet Explorer™ and Netscape Navigator™. Most of the other parts of the Internet are text oriented but the web is graphical and sound oriented. For example, one can view Hubbell telescope images, visit a law firm in New York, download legislative bills from the Arizona State Legislature, or visit the Louve in Paris. Information on the web is in a hypertext format.

Hypertext. The idea of hypertext is simple and revolutionary. You can link information together regardless of its location and type and these links can lead to other links in an endless manner. From text to graphics to video back to text Internet pages become dynamic and interactive. Hypertext or more commonly called links opens a gateway into the world of knowledge.

Reading using hypertext becomes an interactive exciting process. The author can link information together from a variety of sources and build communication connections for the reader. As a reader you choose what details to look at and which points to follow to seek out the knowledge you desire. No longer do you need to hunt for further information on the subject by searching indexes and a table of contents. Also, no longer is the reader limited to a sequential lincar learning experience of moving from one page to the next. Instead the reader can move to the related information instantly as the reader searches for knowledge. And best of all for the reader it is merely a click on your mouse to move to the new information without having to worry about the underlying information structure.

Hypertext can be used in a variety of ways in the legal profession. One can create hypertext briefs, motions, policy manuals and any other legal document for the office, clients or for the courts. This provides a new and exciting way to read and analyze information. Information in the legal profession is particularly well suited for hypertext.

For example in several cases attorneys have filed hypertext briefs. In these briefs the links are highlighted to indicate when more information is available. A cited case is highlighted and when you click on the highlighted portion it jumps to the actual case for the reader to view. In the actual case there can be other links to audio or video of the oral argument of the case or links to other similar cases. For one of the first United states Supreme Court hypertext briefs see www.shsl.com/internet/supcourt/brief.html

Browser to Access the Web. To access the WWW one needs a Web Browser. The most popular browsers are Netscape™ (www.netscape.com) and the Internet Explorer™ (www.microsoft.com). A unique Uniform Resource Locator (URL) address identifies all web pages. On the web the URL begins with http:// which stands for Hypertext Transfer Protocol. However, newer browser versions do not require that you type in the http:// or ftp:// portion of the URL when searching for a web site. Web browsers also enable one to visit FTP sites. These sites have addresses with ftp:// beginnings.

To access WWW locations enter the URL – for example the URL for the State Bar of Arizona is www.azbar.org.

HTML Programming. Web pages are constructed using special programming language called HTML, Hypertext Markup Language. This is the language used to create hypertext pages. HTML's commands direct a web browser like Netscape how to display web pages. This language enables the user to click on a marked word or symbol and hypertext to a different page or altogether different web site. These commands pertain to graphics, text and links to other pages or web sites.

The web was initially developed as a publishing site to publish information and not as an interactive tool. However, files can be downloaded from a web site.

Developers are rapidly developing new protocols using a language called Java and ActiveX to increase the interaction on web sites. Developed by Sun Microsystems Java applications or applets provide multimedia interactivity on a web site that can include motion, sound, and other multimedia. When your browser scans a site it downloads a Java applet into your computer which runs the mini-application. For further information check out Sun Microsystems at www.sun.com or ActiveX at www.microsoft.com.

Domain Address. A domain address is an identity tag of the Internet. The address www.azbar.org is the WWW address for the State Bar of Arizona. Each domain address is unique. It can consist of 22 letters, 26 including the extension *.com*. The domain name of *legalspan.com* tells you that this is the tag of a company called *LegalSpan* with a commercial organization as depicted by the letters *com*. The last 3 letters tell you TOP LEVEL DOMAIN or hostname zone. The standard last three letters and the type of organization they represent are:

- .edu – educational institution
- .com – company or individual
- .gov - government,
- .mil - military, and
- .net – network organization
- .int – international organization
- .org - non-profit or other noncommercial organization.

If after the top-level domain name there are two letters this stands for a different country. For example *.au* stands for Australia. For the two letter country codes see net.gurus.com/countries.

The WWW is the most popular and one of the most useful of the Internet components. Accessing the WWW is easy and immensely beneficial for your practice.

Newsgroups (Usenet)

Newsgroups are discussion areas where people from all over the world meet and discuss various topics ranging from the arts to zoos. There are over 15,000 groups with each focusing on different topics. Users can view a discussion on a topic and then enter into the discussion by posting a new message or replying to an existing message.

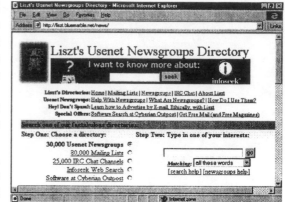

The messages are maintained on one server and are not sent to every subscriber. When the subscriber logs on one views the threaded discussions.

In order to participate in newsgroup one needs special newsgroup software. Newsgroup readers are included in the newer versions of Netscape Communicator™ and Internet Explorer. Also, your Internet provider may provide a free newsgroup reader such as Free Agent™.

There are six main categories for newsgroups that are identified by the following extensions:

- Alt – general, unmoderated topics
- Comp – computers
- Misc. – miscellaneous
- Rec. – recreation
- Sci – science
- Soc – social science

Some interesting newsgroups include:

- Misc.legal
- Misc.legal.moderated
- Misc.legal.computing
- msnews.microsoft.com
- rec.humor.funny - place for jokes and commentary
- misc.jobs.offered - job postings anywhere in the world
- rec.arts.movies.reviews - Old and new motion pictures are reviewed
- news.lists - list of most popular newsgroups

For detailed information about newsgroups visit www.liszt.com/news; net.gurus.com/usenet; Altavista (www.altavista.digital.com) search Usenet rather than the web; and www.dejanews.com.

Listserv (Mailing List)

A LISTSERV or mailing list is a discussion group similar to newsgroups where people exchange information about a variety of subjects. However, a LISTSERV uses standard Internet e-mail to exchange messages. In effect, when you subscribe to a LISTSERV you are adding your name to a mailing list. When a user sends a message it is automatically sent to everyone in the group. There are thousands of LISTSERV groups. A LISTSERV is a good way to keep current in your legal specialty area. There are LISTSERV discussion groups for real estate, probate, etc.

Subscribing. You can subscribe to a listserv via e-mail. Once you have located a LISTSERV that you wish to join you need to send an e-mail asking to subscribe. Each Listserv is different but they generally use the following subscription format.

Generally, the e-mail should be addressed to:

listserv@sitename

In the body of e-mail, not in the subject area, it should read

Subscribe listname firstname lastname

For example to subscribe to an expert witness LISTSERV send an e-mail to:

listserv@assocdir.wuacc.edu

In the body of the e-mail, not the subject area type:

Subscribe expertwitness Michael Arkfeld

To unsubscribe from the LISTSERV follow the same instructions but type in Unsubscribe in the body of the e-mail. For example send an e-mail to:

listserv@assocdir.wuacc.edu

In the body of the e-mail, not the subject area type:

Unsubscribe expertwitness Michael Arkfeld

When sending e-mail or posting a message to LISTSERV members address the e-mail to the group name: expertwitness@assocdir.wuacc.edu

Searchable directories of available listservs can be found at www.liszt.com

Internet Relay Chat (IRC)

Instead of using e-mail you have the option on the Internet to talk on-line and real-time. Online chat lets you communicate instantly with another person or persons anywhere who is logged on to the Net by typing messages back and forth to each other. So one can carry on a conversation on the net with anyone located anywhere in the world. People are talking to people all over the world about everything. They enter chat rooms to talk. AOL and CompuServe have special areas called rooms and channels where subscribers can chat with others. IRC is used with a regular Internet account.

If you are not on AOL or CompuServe specific IRC software is needed to participate in an IRC. One of the most popular shareware IRC programs is mIRC. This program can be found at shareware sites including www.tucows.com and www.mirc.co.uk. For detailed information on how to set up an IRC go to www.mirc.co.uk. Your Internet provider can give you additional information.

IRC sessions are conducted on a number of computer servers from around the country. For a list of IRC's see www.liszt.com. The three biggest ones are Undernet (www.undernet.org); iChat (www.ichat.com); and DALNet (www.dal.net).

File Transfer Protocol (FTP)

FTP or File Transfer Protocol is the Internet standard or protocol for transferring files on the Internet. An FTP enabled software program allows you to choose the computer to connect to and then lets you transfer files from the remote computer to your own. You can download programs, pictures, sounds and text to your computer such as clip art, case opinions, statutes and other information. You can download files using Internet Explorer™ or Netscape™ or by using special FTP software. Ftp software can download or UPLOAD files.

Some remote computers require a name and password to log on while others allow all users to log on using *anonymous* as the USER ID. The password is generally your e-mail address.

FTP permits either a binary or ASCII transfer. ASCII files are human readable text files. Binary files are generally software files such as ZIP or EXE file. A binary file transferred as a ASCII file will not be readable. However, an ASCII file transferred as a binary file is readable after the transfer. Binary files can contain text, bitmaps or software programs.

Both Netscape™ and Internet Explorer™ contain ftp features as part of their program. A freeware FTP program is WS_FTP available from an ISP or a number of different sites such as www.tucows.com or www.csra.net/junodj/ws_ftp.htm.

Some of the file transfer protocols you may encounter are Xmodem, Ymodem and Zmodem.

- Xmodem - Though slower than other protocols it is virtually a standard among communications programs.
- Ymodem - is the same as the Xmodem standard except for the rate of transfer that is 1,024 byte blocks as opposed to 128 byte blocks.
- Zmodem - is the fastest download protocol, reliable, host can initiate the download and multiple files can be downloaded at one time.
- Kermit - is slow and should not be used.

To use FTP you need to know the name of the computer where the file is located the directory it is in and the name of the file. A directory usually looks like this */users/lawyers*. Interesting FTP sites include:

- *ftp.ncsa.uiuc.edu* - is the National Center for Supercomputing Applications. Here is located the Mosaic browser under /Web/Mosaic/Windows.
- *ftp.cica.indiana.edu* - stands for Center for Innovative Computing. In the directory /pub/pc/win3 is located a large number of Windows programs such as utilities and templates for Word and Excel; and
- *ftp.isoc.org* is the ftp site for the Internet Society.

Other Components

The following components have been either absorbed by software integration in Netscape™ or Internet Explorer™ or the information has been transferred to WWW pages. However, the need to know these terms may arise so they are set out below.

Archie servers - Archie servers provide indexing of FTP file archives. If you have Archie client software then you can use it to search server software files and locate specific software files. Archie indexes the computer filename so if the filename is not reflective of the contents of the file it may not be able to locate the specific software you are interested in. To locate specific information contained in a file, as opposed to the filename, it is necessary to use gopher software or search the WWW.

Telnet – telnet:// - Telnet is one of the most widely used connection services on the Internet. It has been called a "dumb" or virtual type of connection. To use the Telnet feature you need to type in the name of the computer that you wish to reach and connect to it. For example if you type in *telnet://azbar.org* you will reach the computer for the State Bar of Arizona. After connecting to another computer you type in characters that are sent to the computer which processes your character request and the sends back the information in a character format or graphical format and displays it on your screen. This is most often used with resources provided by an institution such as a computerized card catalog for libraries. Telnet can save you the cost of a long distance telephone call by allowing a local computer hook up to other computers across the world. Telnet can also be used to connect to a graphical user interface Telnet location. Once at the site you will generally be given instructions on how to access the site with a password or to register as a guest or visitor.

WAIS – WAIS:// - *WAIS stands for Wide Area Information Server.* WAIS enables a user to search for indexed information in servers all over the world. This enables the searcher to locate the information in a file even if the filename is confusing or non-reflective of the subject matter. As with the gopher files the functionality of WAIS has transitioned to the WWW where many of the databases that have been indexed are now on the WWW for searching by general search engines.

Gopher – gopher:// - Gopher servers provide lists of files in many different computer locations on the Internet. If you have a gopher client (software that you run on your computer) it enables you to search many different locations for the files. Additional strong features include the ability to search descriptive comments that can be attached to filenames. Many gopher servers are also transitioning to the WWW. They have WWW menus enabling you to immediately download a file on a WWW page. It is an organized user-friendly way of accessing information. It can provide specific menu driven information such as text or sound files or other gopher menus on other networks throughout the word. All gopher menus together on the Internet are sometimes referred to as gopherspace. Your web browser can be used to access a gopher site. The initial prefix is gopher://.

Veronica is the master indexing and location service for all the gopher menus in hyperspace. Most gopher menus have a veronica search option command. Periodically gopher servers send information to Veronica regarding its menu. Veronica then indexes the information and enables the user to search its master menuing system by keywords. When you locate a specific menu then you click on the word and are taken directly to the server which contains the information. This is sort of a master hypertext link. The system is only as good as the periodic updating by the other gopher servers. An example of a Veronica site is gopher://liberty.uc.wlu.edu/11/gophers/veronica.

Netiquette & Frequently Asked Questions (FAQ's)

The Internet is not owned by anyone but is a networked group of thousands of computers so reasonable behavior or "netiquette" must be followed. Netiquette are the unwritten rules that exist to govern acceptable behavior on the Internet. Whether it is e-mail or discussion groups certain "netiquette" must be followed or the consequences can be rather severe. You may be bounced from the listserv or flamed by the other members if you violate the rules.

Listserv Netiquette rules are generally based on common sense and consideration of others. Some of the Listserv rules:

♦ Do not post a message on a listserv that is not pertaining to the subject matter of the listserv;
♦ Promotional or advertising postings are tolerated if short and to the point;
♦ Mean, vulgar, bigoted or other offensive remarks will not be tolerated;
♦ Typing your messages in capitals is considered SHOUTING; and
♦ Don't pass along chain letters, make-money-fast messages.

If you are unsure whether a posting or action is proper run it past the listserv moderator.

Two sites to download information on the proper netiquette for listservs are: The Net: User Guidelines and Netiquette by Arlene H. Rinaldi rs6000.adm.fau.edu/rinaldi/netiquette.html and www.es.net/hypertext/listmgr/list-netiquette.html.

Newsgroup Netiquette - There are guidelines to follow when one participates in a newsgroup:

♦ Observe for a while before determining if you want to be a member;

♦ Read the FAQ's file for the newsgroup – generally will talk about advertisements;

♦ Check to see if someone answered a question before you answer it the same way;

♦ Spamming - advertisements to non-advertising groups is strictly prohibited;

♦ No sexist, racist or demeaning messages which is also called Flaming;

♦ If discussions are lengthy between 2 members, change to E-mail instead; and

♦ Keep responses to the point and of reasonable length.

Important Newsgroups that provide valuable information on "Netiquette" are news.announce.newusers, news.announce, microsoft.public.netiquette *and* Frequently Asked Questions (FAQ) from news.newusers.questions.

FAQ – stands for Frequently Asked Questions. These computer files contain basic information about the different components of the Internet, software or hardware. They provide a simple introduction to a topic.

Searching the Internet

In order to locate information on the web it is generally necessary to use on-line search engines such as Yahoo, Alta Vista, etc. One types in keywords and the on-line search engine searches its index of WWW pages and returns with appropriate hits. The returned number of web sites can be staggering but the search engines and methods of indexing are becoming more sophisticated which limit the number of hits or rank them according to the number of times the term is used on the site, etc.

Full Text Search Systems

Some of the more popular WWW Search Engines

- Yahoo – www.yahoo.com
- AltaVista - www.altavista.digital.com
- Lycos – www.lycos.cs.cmu.edu
- Infoseek – www.infoseek.com
- Excite - www.excite.com
- HotBot – www.hotbot.com
- EINet Galaxy – www.einet.net
- Northern Light – www.northernlight.com
- Open Text search engine – www.opentext.com
- Web Crawler - www.webcrawler.com
- Magellan search engine and Web site reviews – www.mckinley.com
- C|Net Shareware search engine – www.shareware.com

Legal, Business and Other Sites

The following Internet locations and sites are meant to provide a significant starting point for your legal and non-legal research. These sites are updated frequently and will have links to other WWW sites. Since new web sites come on-line on a daily basis pay close attention to announcements in legal computer magazines, newspapers and other publications.

URL's (Uniform Resource Locator) are the citation addresses on the Internet to locate legal and nonlegal resources. The most used URL is http:// that refers to World Wide Web Servers. For example the

WWW site for the American Bar Association is http://www.abanet.org. The http: prefix to all of the following sites has been omitted in the following site addresses since many web browsers today do not require this prefix.

However, how good is the information? Two web sites that provide a discussion in evaluating factual information on the web are Ten Cs For Evaluating Internet Resources (www.uwec.edu/admin/library/10cs.html) and Thinking Critically about World Wide Web Resources (www.library.ucla.edu/libraries/college/instruct/web/critical.htm).

Legal Listing Sites: There are number of "comprehensive" legal listing sites that display the location and provide a hyperlink directly to other legal sites containing significant legal materials or links to where the legal information can be found. Universities, bar associations, individual and commercial sites provide organized "legal lists" to other legal and non-legal sites. The quality of these sites depends on their ease of use, easy access, maintenance of the site, accuracy and when they are updated.

- American Law Sources On-Line – www.lawsource.com/also/
- Legal Information Institute at Cornell Law School - www.law.cornell.edu.
- American Bar Association – www.abanet.org.lawlink/home.html
- FindLaw: Internet Legal Resources – www.findlaw.com.
- FindLaw - LawCrawler – www.lawcrawler.com
- Internet Legal resource Guide – www.ilrg.com
- The Legal List – www.lcp.com
- Hieros Gamos is sponsored by Lex Mundi – www.hg.org .
- Indiana University School of Law – www.law.indiana.edu
- Federal Courts Case Law Finder - www.law.emory.edu/FEDCTS/

Selected Federal Sites:
- United States Code - www.law.house.gov/usc.htm
- US Constitution - info.rutgers.edu/Library/Reference/US/constitution
- Congressional Bills - www.house.gov/Legproc.html
- Code of Federal regulations -www.access.gpo.gov/nara/cfr/cfr-table-search.html
- Federal Rules of Civil Procedure -www.law.cornell.edu/rules/frcp/overview.htm
- Federal Rules of Evidence - www.law.cornell.edu/rules/fre/C101.html
- UCC –www.law.cornell.edu/ucc/ucc.table.html
- FedWorld - Scientific, technical, engineering and business related information from the federal government - www.fedworld.gov
- GPO Access - www.access.gpo.gov/su_docs
- Full Text state statutes and legislation on the Internet – www.prairienet.org/~scruffy/f.htm.

Expert Witnesses
- Compilation of sources for expert witnesses has been put together by the library association - www.nocall.org/experts.html
- The National Directory of Expert Witnesses - www.claims.com
- You can find medical experts who are also authors of medical articles by using the Medline abstract database - www.nlm.nih.gov/
- Expert Pages - www.expertpages.com/
- Legal Research Network ($99 per year) - www.witness.net/
- National Consultant Referrals - www.referrals.com/
- Findlaw - www.findlaw.com/13experts/index.html
- The International Directory of Expert Witnesses - www.expertwitness.com
- The SEAMLESS WEBsite - www.Seamless.com
- IDEX defense network (www.idex.com)Findlaw site - www.findlaw.com/13experts/index.html

Hypertext Brief
- www.shsl.com/internet/supcourt/brief.html

- www.fr.com

Legal Forms

- Legaldocs - www.legaldocs.com
- Findlaw Internet Legal Resources - www.findlaw.com/16forms/index.html
- Online Legal Forms - www.versalaw.com/versuslaw/forms/index.html
- Legal and Business Forms -www.geocities.com/capitolhill/1802/buslegal.html
- The 'Lectric Law Library's Law Practice Forms -www.lectlaw.com/forma.htm
- West's Legal Forms on CD-ROM - www.westgroup.com
- HotDocs - www.capsoft.com/index.html
- Informs from WordPerfect - www.corel.com

Periodicals

- Mediafinder includes 6200 hundred directories listing over ninety thousand periodicals (www.mediafinder.com/index.cfm).

Litigation Information

- National Law Journal - www.ljx.com/litigation/index.html
- National Law Journal articles - www.ljx.com/memos/fulltext.htm
- Jeff Flax's Home Page - rainbow.rmii.com/~jflax/

Medical Information.

- Jeff Flax's Medical Resources - shell.rmi.net/~jflax/jmf_med.htm
- Pharmaceutical Information Network - www.pharminfo.com
- Martindale's Health Science Guide lists medical dictionaries and medical texts - www-sci.lib.uci.edu/HSG/Medical.html#diction
- Various anatomy sites include The Digital Anatomist - www9.biostr.washington.edu/da.html - Human Anatomy Online - www.innerbody.com - and The Visible Human Project - www.nlm.nih.gov/research/visible/visible_human.html
- Locate physicians through the American Medical Association - www.ama-assn.org/ - and medical journal abstracts using Medline - www.nlm.nih.gov/

Court Reporters

- www.verbatimreporters.com/ncra/reporter/assoc.html

Legal Software Reviews

- Law Office Computing – www.lawofficecomputing.com
- Law Technology Product News - www.ljextra.com/ltpn
- American Bar Association - mwww.abanet.org/lawmart/software.html

Internet Legal Information

- The Internet Lawyer - www.internetlawyer.com
- Legal ethics – www.legalethics.com
- Consumer law page –www.colson.com/lawonweb.htm
- Nonlawyer practicing law – www.nolo.com.catalog/index.html

News Services

- Sign up and get news via e-mail - www.infobeat.com
- Internet Sleuth searches several news databases simultaneously (http://isleuth.com/).
- Newslink provides links to online newspapers, magazines and radio/TV - www.newslink.org/menu.html
- For a site with newspaper and magazine links to more than six thousand sites (http://pppp.net/links/news/NA.html/).
- PRNewswire's Company News On Call provides free access to hundreds of public and private news releases (www.prnewswire.com/).

- AudioNet provides audio versions of news events (www.audionet.com) or sign up and get news via e-mail at www.infobeat.com.

Travel and Weather Information

- NOAA site - www.nws.noaa.gov/climate.shtml - provides old weather data including climatic and historical data records.
- TravelWeb - www.travelweb.com
- Airline tickets – www.iecc.com/airline
- Maps for any part of the country or city. - www.mapquest.com
- Internet travel Network - www.itn.net/cgi/get?itn/about:Mj6pqbb6qyg
- Travel Discounts - www.traveldiscounts.com/discount/airlines/airindex.html
- Maps and directions - www.city.net and www.zip2.com

Financial & Business

- Disclosure – financial and business information on companies -www.disclosure.com
- American Association of Individual Investors - www.aaii.com
- Portfolio Trackers – Yahoo – my.yahoo.com; Reuters Moneynet – www.moneynet.com; and Microsoft Investor – investor.msn.com.
- Wall Street Journal - www.wsj.com
- For government SEC Filings visit - www.sec.gov/
- Private companies' information sites include Dun & Bradstreet that provides business reports for a fee - www.dnb.com/. Hoover's On-line provides free access to search for information on over 9,000 companies - www.hoovers.com/. Dun & Bradstreet provides information free of charge for over 100,000 companies -www.companiesonline.com.
- To locate information on over 1100 associations visit Associations Online (www.ipl.org/ref/AON/).

Finding People, Attorneys and E-mail Addresses

- Yahoo People Search - locates people by name or address - www.yahoo.com/search/people
- Bigfoot - www.Bigfoot.com
- Internet white pages - Four11 - www.four11.com
- American Directory Assistance – www.abii.com
- Infospace – www.infospace.com
- E-mail Finder - www.iaf.net
- WhoWhere? - www.whowhere.com
- BigBook - www.bigbook.com
- BigYellow - www.bigyellow.com
- Locate an attorney - West Group- www.westpub.com
- LookupUSA - www.lookupusa.com
- GTE Superpages: Yellow pages - www.superpages.gte.net
- ON"VILLAGE - www.worldpages.com
- WhoWhere – www.companies.whowhere.com

- Worldwide Phone book - www.super.de/phone/
- Yellow Pages - s17.bigyellow.com/
- Switchboard - www.switchboard.com/

Finding a Job.

- The SEAMless WEBsite - www.seamless.com/jobs/index.html.
- Doug Hume's Home Page - www.voicenet.com/~dhumes/
- National Law Employment Center - www.lawjobs.com
- Careerpath – classifieds from numerous newspapers - www.careerpath.com

Business Sites

- U.S. Postal service zip codes and postage rates - www.usps.gov
- Federal Express - Provides real-time information on where your package is , who signed for it and if it was delivered - www.fedex.com/track_it.html
- Site allows searching of the domain name database to discover U.S. companies registration - internic.net/rs-internic.html
- Time magazine - www.pathfinder.com
- Dun & Bradstreet - provides business reports for a fee - www.dbisna.com/dbis/dnbhome.htm
- Hoover's On-line - - free access to search for information on over 9,000 companies - www.hoovers.com
- Securities and Exchange Commission - SEC filings from 1994 forward - www.sec.gov
- Companies online – enter the name of a company and this site tells you about it. - www.companiesOnline.com
- Inc. Magazine – lists small fast growing companies – www.inc.com.
- Yellow pages – lists companies - www.bigyellow.com
- QuoteCom Home Page - provides daily quotes on stocks, options, commodity futures, mutual funds and bonds among other financial data. - www.quote.com
- Edgar database of corporate information - www.sec.gov/edgarhp.htm. Search for, review text and download zipped files of SEC documents - www.worthnet.com/www/seczip/index.htm

Software and Hardware:
- Shareware - www.shareware.com;
- Computer software reviews and shareware - www.stroud.com
- Computers - www.dell.com; www.gateway.com
- Collection of windows software - www.tucows.com

Other Sites:
- Electronic Frontier Foundation – www.eff.org
- Bookstores - www.amazon.com;
- Clothes – Lands End – www.landsend.com; L.L. Bean – www.llbean.com; REI – www.rei.com;
- Auctions – www.ebay.com; www.netauction.com; www.uce.com.
- E-mail reminder service - www.neverforget.com
- Dilbert - www.unitedmedia.com/comics/dilbert
- Coupons for grocery stores, products, restaurants, etc. - www.hotcoupons.com

Software and Hardware for the Internet

Browsers

To use each of the separate Internet components – e-mail, file transfer, newsgroup, etc. – a specific type of software is required to access their functionality. These different software packages are generally provided from an ISP. However, software developers have begun to integrate into one-software package these different Internet functions for users. The most notable examples of this trend are the Netscape Communicator™ (www.netscape.com) and Internet Explorer™ programs (www.microsoft.com).

Sets out below are different Internet functions and the two most popular software programs, there different modules and other standalone products.

Internet Function	Purpose	Netscape Communicator Professional	Microsoft Internet Explorer	Other products
Browser	View WWW Pages	Navigator	Internet Explorer	Mosaic
E-mail	Send and receive e-mail	Messenger	Outlook Express	Eudora
Newsgroup reader	Reads messages from newsgroups		Outlook Express	Free Agent, WinVZ
Discussion Workgroups	Discussion areas	Messenger	NetMeeting	
Meeting Scheduler	Set meetings with others	Calendar	None	
Calendar	Calendar	Calendar	None	
Meetings (audio and text)	Voice, communication, use whiteboard to draw on, send files to, live participants, and use application sharing to demonstrate use of program.	Conference	NetMeeting	
Video	Video format	None	NetShow	See discussion under video software
WWW page editor	Edit WWW pages for publication	Composer	FrontPage Express	See discussion under Web Authoring tools
On-line Shopping	Manage shipping addresses, credit card numbers for on-line shopping	None	Wallet	
Push Technology	Pushes information to the web user	Netcaster	Internet Explorer 4.0	
Multimedia Client	Receives streaming multimedia data	None	NetShow	

Cost	For entire package	Free Evaluation Download www.netscape.com. Cost – generally around $70.	Free download www.microsoft.com

Other Internet Software

Plug-ins. Plug-ins are computer programs that plug-in to Netscape™ or Internet Explorer™ that enable you to handle new kinds of information. Some useful plug-in programs are @ttend (wwwlegalspan.net) that allows you to attend CLE courses and depositions online real-time; Realplayer™ – (www.realaudio.com) plays sound files as you download them and iChat™ (www.ichat.com) that allows you to participate in chat groups on the web. Plug-ins for a variety of Internet software can be found at TUCOWS (www.tucows.com); Consummate Winsock Applications Page (www.cws.internet.com); and the Netscape™ site (www.home.netscape.com).

Broadcasting – PUSH Technology. The WWW has been a tremendous success utilizing PULL technology. PULL technology is the ability of a user to search the web and then PULL information off of web sites. Now, PUSH technology is being utilized to save the user time searching the web. Instead of information being sought out by the user the information is PUSHED to the user.

The Wall Street Journal stated that "The transformation of the Web into a broadcast (push) medium could be the biggest shift in information technology since, well, the Web itself". This type of software will provide easy access, notification and delivery of personalized information on the Internet or Intranet to a user. Customizable channels of multimedia content can be sent to clients, customers or employees. Subscribers select what information they want from a Web site or other data source and, when changes occur, they are notified and view multimedia content right inside their browser or other application. This software allows the user to select the information one wishes to receive at their desktop as opposed to being bombarded with e-mail or taking the time to search the web.

These programs can provide network news via the Internet and also has the capability to allow users to broadcast corporate or law firm developments news over Intranets. Over the Internet news, stock prices, weather, sports and more can be displayed on the viewer's desktop. Employee benefits, results of latest cases in the office, new personnel, etc can all be broadcast over an Intranet. This creates a new way of communication with one's employees or clients.

There are a number of features one should consider in deciding which "push" program to choose. Does it deliver all kinds of content, software or data or is it limited to web-based material? Does it let you control the timing of when content is sent, when played, and how often displayed? Does it let the user personalize the content that is received? Does it let you notify your users that information has arrived? Does it allow you to maintain your privacy while receiving very targeted information? Some of the different broadcasting programs utilizing the new PUSH technology are:

- PointCast™ - www.pointcast.com.
- Marimba™ – www. marimba.com
- BackWeb™ – www.backweb.com
- Netdelivery™ – www.netdelivery.com
- Freeloader™ – www.freeloader.com.
- Intermind Communicator™. - www.intermind.com
- Caravelle's Transceive™ – www.caravelle.com

Fax Software for the Internet. This software allows the user to fax over the Internet thus eliminating long distance phone bills. It works in conjunction with word processing programs. FAXfree™ (www.tacsystems.com).

Publishing Tools for HTML documents. WWW pages are compiled using HTML programming language. The basic language is relatively easy and straightforward to use in preparing HTML pages for publication. However, many programs have HTML conversion capability built into their program to make publication of HTML documents easy. The latest releases from Corel and Microsoft show a major shift to allowing a user to easily convert different applications to HTML for Internets or Intranets. For example Microsoft Office 98™ includes a word processing, presentation, spreadsheet and a database application. All of the applications permit the user to convert the document, database, etc. in an HTML format for instant publication to the WWW.

There are other specialized programs to assist in publishing documents. PubNetics™ allows the user to format small or large documents into an HTML format for Web publication. It has special features that automatically sets up hyperlinks based on a rule based indexer. For example you can have it create a table of contents and then the program will automatically link to areas of a deposition, etc. (www.pubnetics.com/). See also Trellix™ (www.trellix.com).

Web Authoring Tools. There are a variety of programs available to assist in creating, developing and maintaining a web site. Some software considerations:
- Price and Platform compatibility;
- Features: Search and replace, spell checker, edit HTML tags, validate remote links, validate internal links, and publish to web site;
- HTML extensions; tables, frames, font size, font color;
- Interactivity: image map editor, client side image maps, form fields, forms handler, Java applets, and database queries; and
- Other: page templates, clip art, image editor.

Some products to consider:
- Microsoft FrontPage™ and Frontpage Express™ – www.microsoft.com/frontpage/
- Backstage Internet Studio 2.0™ – Macromedia Corp. – www.macromedia.com
- Netscape Composer™, part of Netscape Communicator™ – www.netscape.com
- Claris Home Page 2.0™ – Claris Corporation – www.claris.com
- Corel Web Designer 1.1™ – Corel Corp. – www.corel.com
- Hotmetal Pro 3.0™ – SoftQuad, Inc. – www.softquad.com

Bookmarking WWW sites, images, video, etc. MeltingPoint™ (www.docuwork.com/) is an Internet research manager for attorneys and law librarians. It permits you to bookmark and organize Web information you find valuable. It cross-references Web information to your own matters, issues, witnesses and precedents.

Audio. Audio clips can be placed on web sites for instant listening or for downloading and listening to at a later time. Now you can listen to your favorite news, music, and sports sites, just like with a car radio. The audio can be a live broadcast or on-demand. See Realaudio™ (www.Realaudio.com); Iwave™ - VocalTec, Inc. (www.vocaltec.com/) and Progressive Networks™ (www.real.com).

Video. Video can either be downloaded or played real-time over the Internet. Generally video is downloaded in an AVI format and then played on the user's computer. However, streaming video allows one to see the video as it's downloading to your machine. While a bigger bandwidth is preferable all you need is a 28,800 modem and a free software plugin. Several products are available to play video on your computer or to view it real-time. @ttend - LegalSpan Corporation (www.legalspan.net) ; Vivo Active - www.vivo.com/; VDOLive - www.vdolive.com/; and RealVideo – www.real.com; NetShow (www.microsoft.com).

Internet Phone and Voice Mail. Internet Phone offers unlimited long distance and international conversations for the cost of an Internet connection. The quality is not as clear as a regular phone but improves with connection speeds. To allow both parties to talk at once you must have a full duplex sound card. Other features include voice mail, whiteboarding and document sharing and cross-platform capabilities. Internet Voice Mail is a software program that lets you send voice mail over the Internet for free to anyone with an email address. Internet Voice Mail works like your email program - just enter a person's email address, record a message, and send it off. You can even add text or attach files. The person to whom you are sending a message to can hear your voice for just the cost of your Internet connection. VocalTec, Inc. - www.vocaltec.com/; Iphone - www.Pulver.com..

Remote Control of Computers. Timbuktu allows you to control computers remotely using the Internet. (www.netopia.com).

The LegalSpan Network (www.legalspan.com)

DepoCast

Save the expense, time and hassle spent traveling to observe depositions. Now you can @ttend without ever leaving your desk. Read the transcript, hear clear audio and watch the deponent on video in *real-time* from *virtually* anywhere Internet connections are available. DepoCast makes it easy and inexpensive to be there!

inSession (with Speaker Central)

Obtain continuing education and credits from the convenience of your office or comfort of your home with a standard Internet connection. @ttend both live and prerecorded seminars provided by legal associations, firms, corporations and national speakers including Michael Arkfeld, Kathy Shimpock and Gail Thackeray.

The Digital Practice (with Author Central)

Adapt to a world of electronic communications and an evolving digital legal system. From basic concepts to advanced applications, *The Digital Practice* is designed to improve your law practice today and secure its transition into the 21st century.

CourtCast

You and your clients can view important court proceedings in real-time from participating courtrooms across the country. In addition, those courts handling high-profile cases may use the LegalSpan network to provide public access to news reporters or others.

ExpoCast

Eliminate the hassle, footwork and expense of traveling to trade shows to learn about the latest products and services available to the legal profession. LegalSpan lets you @ttend its free virtual expo that provides product demonstrations, sales literature and training sessions.

Internet Hardware

Sharing Internet Access. If you only have one telephone line you can share the Internet access with three computers. A system called WebShare enables three computers to have simultaneous shared access to the web. Protec Microsystems (www.protec.ca/product/product.htm).

Web cameras. Web cameras are cameras that snap pictures that can be uploaded instantly and viewed with a web browser. They can take color images and put them on self-contained web servers at a rate of one frame per second. Anyone with a browser can see the images. Microplex (www.microplex.com); Axis Communications (www.axisinc.com); CU-SeeMe™ (www.wpine.com/Products/CU-SeeMe/ com); and Quickcam™ (www.connectix.com/ com).

WebTV. WebTV combines the benefits of the Internet web with the television set. It provides for Internet access using a television set. It features an e-mail connection, search engine and access to the WWW. All that is required is a television and a telephone line. Access is provided by the WebTV Network for unlimited access for approximately $20 a month and a $100 connector. (www.webtv.com)

Windows 98™ contains some technology breakthroughs that marry the mediums of TV and personal computing. In particular WebTV® for Windows enables your PC to receive television programs and special data transmissions. Among the benefits: Internet connections "over the air," without a phone line or monthly connection charges from an Internet service provider.

All you need is:

- Windows 98™
- A TV antenna or cable connection
- A Windows 98™–compatible TV tuner board.

Once you're set up, you can:

- Watch TV on your PC monitor. View a TV program full screen, or in an on-screen window while you're working in any Windows-based application.
- Enhance your viewing with interactive TV programs. More and more, TV program producers are coding interactive elements into their broadcasts to broaden the viewing experience. You may, for instance, be able to enter a chat room and talk with other viewers of the same program; send e-mail to an actor in the show; get information on characters; play along with a game show; buy products online; access supplementary information through links to Web sites.
- Receive multimedia files and software upgrades "over the air" with support for WaveTop technology. Data is piggybacked onto the TV signals of Public Broadcasting Service shows available to 99 percent of U.S. TV households. Many program providers are sending information in this way, including CBS Sportsline, PBS online, The Weather Channel, Time, Entertainment Weekly, Money, Fortune, and Sports Illustrated for Kids.

Choosing a Web Site Provider to Host and/or to Build Your Web Site

If you intend to have an ISP host and/or build your site there are several important considerations:

- *References and reputation in the community.* How many web sites have they successfully completed? Determine whether they completed them on time and on budget. Do a credit reference check. Make sure they actually did the work that they are taking credit.
- *Who are the members of their team?* Are the members actual employees or are they free lancers who are brought together for this project? How many other projects have they completed together?
- *Are they responsive?* If you have problems with your site how quickly do they respond to your calls? Do they have a knowledgeable support department? Are they familiar with latest technology advancements on the Internet? Is their support available 7 days a week 24 hours a day?
- *Pricing.* Do they bill by the hour or by the page of development. How do they break down their costs? Generally status reports on how many people visited your site are free.
- *Total bandwidth of provider – Speed of the ISP's inbound line.* The ISP must maintain sufficient inbound connection to handle the access calls into your web site. Know exactly what network connection your ISP has to the Internet! This will determine whether your ISP can handle peak load periods and potential outages. Determine if the speed is actually existing or is in the planning stage.
- *Maintenance.* Negotiate a maintenance program for your site before you develop your site. Will the ISP check for dead links, file transfer problems, etc.
- *Total server space.* What is the amount of server space provided? How much does additional space cost?
- *E-mail server.* Is an e-mail server included as part of the price? How many e-mail accounts are available for employees? Do they have autoresponder, forwarder and mailing list capability?
- *Domain name registration.* Is this included in the web site development?
- *Listserv setup.* How much does it cost to set up a listserv? What are the monthly charges?
- *Telnet access.* Does telnet access cost additional?

- *Extensions.* Does the site support realaudio, realvideo, and Microsoft FrontPage extensions?

Building Your Web Site

It is becoming increasingly popular to have your own WWW home site because clients and potential clients have access to it from anywhere in the world at anytime. If you build a web page will anyone visit it? Maybe. Internet users will access your web page if it provides them value and meets their continuing needs. For example, if you have hypertext links to all of the legal caselaw and statute databases throughout the world one can be assured that a great number of people will visit your site. If you are an authority on the impact of the 1st amendment on the Internet and provide updated materials on the subject then a more select group will visit your site. For two references see *The Lawyer's Guide to Marketing on the Internet* – Gregory Siskind and Timothy Moses and *The Lawyer's Guide to Creating Web Pages* – Kenneth Johnson published by the ABA. (www.abanet.org).

Your web site is a reflection of your firm and yourself. Consider it a firm brochure or other promotional literature. It reflects what clients, potential clients and other lawyers will think about your firm. It reflects the same as when a client visits your offices and how your staff treats him. If you are going to have a presence on the web invest the necessary money and involvement in creating the web site to reflect your firm image. Remember people visiting your site will come away with an important first impression of your firm - make it count.

To construct a web site you need:
1. A domain address;
2. An Internet service provider (ISP);
3. A web server; and
4. Web site pages.

1. A Domain Address. A domain address is the address on the web that identifies your web site. The address www.venerable.com is the WWW address for the Venerable Law Firm. A domain name can be obtained by your ISP or by yourself. There is an initial fee of $100 and an annual recurring fee of $50 to maintain your domain name. Make a list of several names in case one is already taken. It is suggested that your ISP get the name for you and save you the hassle of contacting and maintaining the name.

If you wish to obtain your own name it is necessary to go to InterNIC, the entity that manages the Internet domain addresses. They can be contacted at http://rs.internic.net or by telephone at 703-742-4777. At http://rs.internic.net/rs-internic.html one can search the list of domain names to determine which ones are available and then complete the registration on-line or download a form to fill out. If doing it on-line you need the hostname and net address of your ISP. After completing the form and mailing it InterNIC will notify you of the acceptance of the name.

Your own domain name also provides a permanent e-mail address for you. Even if you move to a different provider the domain name is yours and you do not have to change the address for other people sending you e-mail or listserv mailings. It also provides a permanent location for your law firm or other commercial activities.

2. Internet Service Provider. See the prior part discussing *Considerations for Choosing an ISP* to host your web site.

3. Web Server. The web server is generally provided by your ISP host and is the location where your web site and pages will reside. Most ISP's generally provide a full range of web hosting services.

4. Web Site. A WWW site is the entryway by clients and potential clients into your firm. It will provide them an impression of your firm and may impact their decision whether to retain your firm. For this reason it is essential that the construction and marketing of your site and pages always focus on your intended audience – your present and potential clients. Before developing your site plan determine your target audience. The type of audience will impact the architecture, graphics, type of content, types of services and production plan for your site. If you were attracting corporate executives in need of merger services then the site would be different then if your audiences were primarily immigration clients.

The uniqueness of WWW pages lies in their multimedia graphical format and the ability to use hypertext linking in the design. HTML or HyperText Markup Language is the standard programming language used to construct web sites to that enables software such as Netscape and Internet Explorer to view your constructed site. Hypertext WWW pages are interactive, automatically taking you to the exact information you want. This information can be in any format or be part of other applications.

Constructing Web Pages. The HTML programming language is "free" and does not require specific software to purchase before constructing a home page. However, there are a variety of software packages available for sale and some free that make it easier to construct your home page.

Web pages are composed of plain ASCII text so a simple text editor will enable one to compose a web page. A web page is generally composed of a head and body element. The head element generally contains the title information, author and other information, which enable indexers and search engines to locate the page. If composing a page remember that the head element is important for other users to locate your web page. Use common reflective terms for your page that are generally used in the industry. If you were designing a page for your law firm it should contain information reflective of the type of law that you practice and not just your law firm's name.

The body element generally contains the textual body of the page. It can contain a number of formatting options and most importantly embedded images or hyperlinks to other documents or web sites. Tags tell the browser the part of the web page that has been accessed. All tags are enclosed in angle brackets(<>). There are three basic styles used in web documents:

- Logical style elements which breaks the document into paragraphs, quotes and so on.
- Physical style elements enable the coder to use bold, underline, italic and other physical styles in your document.
- Content style elements provide the capability to enrich your web document by linking your document to graphics, lists and other items.

The following book on HTML provides important information if you decide to program your own site.
HTML Primer (www.ncsa.uiuc.edu/General/Internet/WWW/HTMLPrimer.html).

An HTML editor works like a word processor but provides the additional feature of converting the document into an HTML document ready for WWW publication. Available software range from freeware to packages costing around $100. See the list of products above under the *Web Authoring Software* part.

Construction of the Web Site: In-house or outsourcing

One of the difficult questions to address is whether to construct your web site in-house or hire a third party to build it. There has been a proliferation of self-help articles for lawyers on how to construct your own web site. The literature generally touts the ease of use of HTML programming and how over a weekend a professional site can be constructed. This is simply not the case. The actual construction of a web site even with web programming software is not easy. In order to build a site you need to understand HTML programming, the different graphic image formats, how to scan images, the FTP protocol with the ISP you have contracted with to host your web site and a myriad of other issues. Lawyers are experts in the practice of law and may find they have to invest hundreds of hours in constructing a web site. This does not mean that a firm on a daily basis should not do the maintenance of a web site by publishing new material, etc. However, unless the firm is willing to hire an employee to spend a substantial amount of time on the project you should seriously consider hiring a third party to construct the site. For a Directory of Legal Web Developers go to www.internetlawyer.com.

Whether you construct and maintain the site in-house or contract out all or part of the construction one needs to consider the following issues:

- Determine how often the site should be updated.

- ▪ Determine whether the webmaster or someone else is responsible for ongoing development, maintenance and security issues. Consider the time necessary and whether a partner, associate, paralegal or other staff person would be the best choice. Oversight of the web site can be by a firm employee or committee
- ▪ Any agreements with 3rd parties need to address the issue of the ownership of the intellectual property rights in the site. Other considerations include the standards for completion and maintenance of the site.
- • Potential liability for lawsuits – do you have insurance in place?

Building Your Web Site – Content and Appearance

The claims are coming fast and furious about your need to market on the web, "one personal injury firm picked up two new clients within a week after their home page was launched", "one corporate law firm picked up enough business to pay for its site" and so on. Do you need a presence on the web? Yes, for several reasons but approach your involvement and investment with caution. It is very difficult to quantify the actual number of visitors to a site within a week's time and the reason you were visited. We know that there are millions of users but do they actually connect to your site and if so for what reason is not entirely clear.

The ideal web site is one with substantively useful content that attracts repeat visitors and becomes known as the "expert" in a particular specialty area.

Your WWW site can be the hub of communications with your clients. Be sure and include e-mail, telephone and other firm information. The capabilities of the WWW are being updated and will one day offer full motion interactive video with sound. In essence one will dial you up through the web for dynamic one-on-one communication.

There are many present communication methods to solidify your relationship with your clients. Today we can send e-mail to clients, authors of legal articles or to anyone. Along with files we have the capability to "open" select environments or Extranets for your clients for file libraries, discussion forums, questions and surveys and a host of other applications. Don't forget your clients are also constructing web pages for a presence of there own on the WWW. Don't forget newsgroups. If your clients and potential clients engage in discussions with others in specific newsgroups be sure you participate.

Suggested do's and don'ts.

- ♦ **Create a distinctive, consistent professional look to your web site.**
- ♦ **Give value to your targeted potential clients for visiting your home page.** For example, a number of sites have firm newsletters, caselaw commentaries, analysis of legal news, and practice guides that provide existing clients with legal knowledge of an area of interest to them. If your client is concerned about premise liability because of a number of properties they own provide articles of interest to this group of clients. Not only will existing clients appreciate the value of such materials but also other potential clients will definitely visit your site. Maybe you want to provide hypertext links to many other areas on the web involving premises liability issues such as insurance, pending legislation and so forth. Firm materials

should be downloadable such as newsletters, brochures, questionnaires, etc at your site. Give away the basic law to the clients. The essence of the Internet is the capability to publish and provide the beginnings of a dynamic relationship with people or companies.

♦ **All materials such as newsletters must be updated at reasonable intervals.** Provide resources that are not easily accessible. Frequently Asked Questions (FAQs) about a particular area of the law such as automobile accidents would be useful to someone who was just in an automobile accident. The content will convey the firm's image. Use a last update notice on site.

- Clients can also use FAQ's on your web site for review. For example, law firms can provide basic information about a Chapter VII bankruptcy. If the FAQ is good it provides a very unobtrusive way of marketing your firm since potential clients and others will be referred to your firm to view the FAQ. See The Bankruptcy Law Finder – www.agin.com/lawfind/

♦ **Hypertext links must be checked to ensure that the connected site is still in operation.**
♦ **Minimize graphics it slows down the navigating.**
♦ **Ensure a text only alternative.**
♦ **Links to other sites for your clients can keep them returning to your site.** Some examples include government agencies, other organizations that may offer useful information to your clients, link to your client's sites, other related professionals, unpublished decisions, new regulations, agency memos, etc.
♦ **Material should be written in a conversational rather than a "legalese" method.**
♦ **Determine how to distinguish yourself from other firms and attorneys.** Tell what you do; do not over emphasize who you are.
♦ **Firm Content.** Provide a service description, resumes and other credentials of your firm.
♦ **Photos of firm.** Provide exterior and interior photos of the firm.
♦ **Contact Information.** Provide a lawyer biography, picture and e-mail addresses, phone number, address, etc. Consider an audio or video of the attorney on the site.
♦ **Representative clients.** List clients represented by your firm.
♦ **Location.** Provide branch office locations and directions to firm.
♦ **Encryption information.** Set forth where public keys for the firm's lawyers can be located.
♦ **ISP.** Make sure your site is on a ISP server that can handle the traffic of your site and other popular sites.
♦ **Guestbooks, Consultation/ Intake forms and initial consultation fees may be effective.**
♦ **Place recruitment information on the site.**
♦ **Date your pages.**
♦ **Search engine.** Consider a search engine that will enable a user to search your whole site immediately.
♦ **Make your site browser friendly.** Ensure that Netscape, Internet Explorer, Mosaic, CompuServe, America Online, Netcomm browsers all view your site appropriately. Also, allow for users who want to use a text-based mode
♦ **Review the WWW pages of other law firms.**
  ♦ Bricker & Eckler Law Firm - www.Bricker.com
  ♦ Venable Law Firm- www.venable.com/
  ♦ Free legal opinions - www.Cooley.com
  ♦ Audio hello - www.Seamless.com/rcl/
  ♦ The Virtual Law Firm - www.tvlf.com/
  ♦ Moye, Gile, O'Keefe, Vermeire & Gorrell - www.mgovg.com
  ♦ Pepper & Corazzini - www.commlaw.com
  ♦ Real estate - www.aloha.com/~rekimoto/eeh.html
  ♦ Jeffrey Kuester – www.Kuesterlaw.com/
  ♦ The Tax Prophet - www.taxprophet.com
  ♦ Muchmore and Wallwork - www.mmww.com

Marketing Your Web Site

How are clients and potential clients going to find your site? Register with search engines. Visit the search engines sites and register under headings such as "getting listed" or "submitting a listing". A simpler way is to visit Submit-It (www.submit-it.com). This service submits your web page to all the major search engines at once. Another site to consider is www.sitepromoter.com.

Another way to promote your site is through other sites that will register your site under a special category such as tax attorneys, environmental law and so on.

Other ways to market your site:

- Have your site address on business cards, stationary and brochures, fax cover sheets and other office materials.
- Participate in newsgroups, listservs, and other conferencing and add your web site on your signature file.
- Ask others to include a link to your site.
- Key words such as firm name and specialty area should be near the beginning of site so search engines can find it.
- At your site have visitors sign up for your newsletter.
- Create an Internet e-mail mailing list of clients and potential clients for newsletters that focus on useful information. In the newsletter list your site and note that the newsletters are archived on the site.

Presentations can be made to clients and others on the Internet, Intranet or Extranet. You can create a central repository of presentations which can be accessible on-line or for downloading. Remote access would allow one to download the presentation from any location. Microsoft PowerPoint software allows the user to save the presentation to an HTML ready format to publish on your site or for subsequent downloading.

Ethics and the Internet

Visit www.legalethics.com for excellent discussions regarding WWW ethical considerations concerning:
- restrictions on advertising;
- E-mail;
- Newsgroup;
- and Unauthorized Practice of Law.

Security on the WEB

One of the major concerns of the Internet is security. Internet security generally refers to the issue of someone accessing your computer system through the Internet and thus having access to your firm's data or web site or intercepting e-mail transmissions. This is of special concern to the legal profession since one of our ethical obligations is to maintain our client's confidences. However, there are numerous software tools available on the Internet to enhance the security.

Firewalls are "electronic fences" that keep unauthorized users out of your LAN. Firewalls can range from packet screening router configurations to multiple firewall servers' in-between your LAN and the Internet. The more secure firewalls are the less convenient they are for authorized users to use the system. Auditing tools to determine if illegal tampering has occurred should be in place. Test your firewall at regular intervals to check for leaks.

Cookies are a special message put on your computer by a web site when you visit their site. The purpose of the cookie is to make your next visit to the same site go smoother. For example if you order a book from an online bookstore your credit card number may be stored on a cookie on your computer. So the next time you go to that site the number automatically appears when you order an item. The problem is if someone else uses your computer then they might charge things on your computer.

Public key encryption is a method of encoding or encrypting your e-mail messages to prevent unauthorized users from reading them. It is based on each user having two encryption keys. The sender has a private and public key. The sender encrypts the message with his private key and then sends it to another user to unencrypt his message with a public key. The most popular encryption program is PGP™ (Pretty Good Privacy). Some distributors of Internet products are Network Associate (www.nai.com). A non-commercial version of PGP is available at web.mit.edu/network/pgp.html. Also consider RSA Data Security Public Key Crytosystem™ (www.rsa.com). For answers to your frequently asked questions on cryptography see www.rsa.com/rsalabs/newfaq/.

A book on the subject entitled *Protect your Privacy on the Internet* by Bryan Pfeffenberger is available from John Wiley & Sons or by ordering it from www.amazon.com.

For recent discussions and information on security, access the following web sites:

- National Computer Security Association - www.ncsa.com; and
- Law Journal Extra - www.ljx.com

Newsgroups on security issues.

- comp.security.announce
- comp.admin.policy

Intranets and Extranets

An Intranet is a group of Internet services, such as Web pages, that are only accessible within an organization. For a discussion on Intranets and Extranets see *Chapter 3, Networking and Group Computing.*

Conclusion

The Internet has been and will continually be compared to the evolution of America through the construction of railroads and the highways. As America grew the nation's cities and towns were connected by first the railroad and then by the highways. Commerce and people moved using these main forms of transportation. Towns that were not connected to these main transportation arteries died out or their population significantly decreased.

> Transport of the mails, transport of the human voice, transport of flickering pictures—in this century as in others our highest accomplishments still have the single aim of bringing men together. Antoine de Saint-Exupéry (1900–1944), French aviator, writer. *Wind, Sand, and Stars*, ch. 3 (published in *Terre des Hommes,* 1939).

Information, people and goods traveled along these physical routes. What impact will the Internet have upon these traditional transportation methods? Firms that are not connected to the Internet will have a difficult time competing and connecting to their clients.

The social considerations of this vast array of people communicating from across the world on any subject are revolutionary. Many of us remember the "iron curtain" that precluded communication between the East and the West. This curtain could never exist in today's technological society. It would be pierced by countless communications between people on both sides of the curtain. Censored disclosure of information to people would be nonexistent. With this constant and far reaching communication instantaneously between people of the world what will be the result?

This page has been intentionally left blank

Chapter 5

Management and Personnel Technology Considerations

Persons grouped around a fire or candle for warmth or light are less able to pursue independent thoughts, or even tasks, than people supplied with electric light. In the same way, the social and educational patterns latent in automation are those of self-employment and artistic autonomy.

- Marshall McLuhan

Introduction

The message in the last several years has been to buy computers, software and network them together and, somehow, they will mysteriously provide you with a competitive edge. This message hasn't lived up to our expectations. Why? More computers do not, necessarily, equal greater strength. The old adage of "strength in numbers" does not apply to the acquisition of computers. e sales pitch implied that all you had to do was buy the product. The problem is that they did not sell you the "lawyering process" and "firm process" with the computer. The lawyering process is within you. That lawyer process has to be applied towards the software and hardware on a professional level. It requires a new chemistry of thought. You have to look inward to apply the process to the computerization of your practice. The capabilities of the hardware and software are present today. What is required from you is an open, inquiring mind and a desire to apply this technology.

The focus of this section will be the how to's of implementing technology and a technology culture in the firm. The prior sections on infrastructure and telecommunications explored the many issues affecting software, hardware, networking and the Internet. All of these sections need to operate in harmony to realize the huge potential for the "virtual law firm" that may one day be a reality for your organization.

Engineering and Re-engineering Technology in the Law Office

The effective engineering of technology in a firm is a dynamic and ongoing process. To engineer or re-engineer requires a commitment from all levels of your organization. This commitment must be from an organizational and technical perspective. It is imperative that the leadership of your firm addresses the radical technology changes that are occurring. It is critical to the competitive health of a firm or organization.

This section applies to a solo practitioner as well as to a larger firm. It is vitally important that a legal practitioner has a plan for the integration of technology. If you fail to plan then your practice or firm will always be trying to stay competitive and plan for the future without any objectives. The section is partially entitled re-engineering technology because after numerous discussions with firms it is apparent that original technology plans have lost support or the plan was not broad enough to incorporate some of the new technology breakthroughs and applications. With the rapid change in technology it is essential that the re-engineering process occur on a constant basis.

> *It is change, continuing change, inevitable change, that is the dominant factor in society today. No sensible decision can be made any longer without taking into account not only the world as it is, but the world as it will be.... This, in turn, means that our statesmen, our businessmen, our everyman must take on a science fictional way of thinking.*
> **- Isaac Asimov**

Legal practitioners must adopt a new science fictional way of thinking. We are living through a major transitional period where information is literally at our fingertips. Whether it be legislative materials, judicial decisions or data from agencies, information is being accessed and exchanged at revolutionary rates. Many standalone and group computing applications are gaining a valuable foothold in law firms across the country. Case management systems, the Internet, document assembly, full text retrieval, imaging and trial presentation systems are but a few of the applications for which a legal practitioner needs to plan. To ensure a better practice you must have synergy between technology, processes and people. The implementation of these systems does not happen by happenstance but requires leadership and a commitment from management.

Committed Management Support and Involvement

To revitalize the technology plan in your firm the managers and leaders of your organization must embrace a technology vision and support a technology culture. The firm's leaders must understand and take action to reflect and implement firm technology strategic objectives. If the leaders do not understand or are opposed or noncommittal to integrating technology into your organization, then the allocation of available resources – money, training and people - will not get a priority. Without equipment, software and training small automation pockets or islands may develop but no firmwide implementation of automation will take place.

> Fred Bartlit, Jr., Esq. of Bartlit Beck Herman Palenchar & Scott in Chicago, Ill. says the firm's culture must support technology. His firm gives strong recognition to partners, associates and others who discover and are able to present technology legal applications. Whether it be "Dave the Database Wizard" or "Mary the Macro Queen" these individuals are acknowledged and compensated for their expertise. They become the seed of firmwide implementation of technology efficient applications. They are constantly challenged to present new and better technology applications. Fred himself uses full text, databases, graphics and a host of other applications reasoning that to lead a firm requires that one must know more about these applications than the other members of his firm.

One of the keys to adopting technology in the firm is to gain firm leadership support. Leadership support can be gained in a number of ways. If the "technology idea" can originate from your leader then it will have a much stronger chance of success. If your manager has a close friend who has enacted technology and whom opinion he trusts this may be the best avenue. If management can attend an outside seminar or presentation as a team on how technology is used it may be one of the best methods to take a serious look at technology. Another way is to host a technology seminar in-house. Besides being eligible for CLE approval it gives the firm members and leaders the opportunity to ask specific questions of the state of technology and the industry trends from a respected expert.

> Probably the two most important ingredients for successfully implementing law firm technology are leadership and training. The first comes from the top; if the leaders of the firm do not lead the way to technology, the rest of the firm will struggle needlessly and probably unsuccessfully, only partially achieving the benefits technology has to offer. Similarly, if everyone in the firm is not properly trained, then the technology investment will not be fully realized. *Reality Today, A Prototype of the Law Firm of the Future,* Nicholas Wallwork, Muchmore and Wallwork, P.C. (www.mmww.com).

Management Barriers to Implementing Technology

As you implement technology one can run into obstacles to implementing technology in your firm. Some of the common problems are discussed below.

Technology Disconnect - Among businesses there is a commonly used phrase called "technology disconnect". As applied to law firms it refers to the gap between the managing partners who make the bottom line decisions for the firm and the technologists who make the major technology recommendations to the firm that may cost thousands, tens of thousands, hundreds of thousands, or millions of dollars. I hear many stories from the "technologists" that the firm does not support their efforts. But is it surprising in light of some of the past technological solutions that were sold to law firms and failed to become reality?

However, technology today is mature enough and generally standard enough to make reasonable future decisions, but the disconnect may still lie between the managing partners and the technologists or now more popularly called the Chief Information Officer (CIO). The managing partner does not understand the technology and the CIO, unless he or she is an attorney and/or partner, does not understand the business of the law firm. The managing partner usually does not see his job as understanding the technology let alone implementing it. The CIO does not understand the practice of law and remains focused on installing the technology but not the applications or teaching the applications that will benefit the firm. The solution is for both the managing partner to take a greater interest in technology and the CIO to take a larger role in understanding the business of the firm. The foundation of the old must be preserved with the calculated implementation of new technology investments.

The managing partner(s) will have to be fluent in broad technology concepts so that they can communicate intelligently with the CIO about the value of such concepts to the firm. It is important for the CIO's to demystify the technology to the lawyers and others in the firm. This can be accomplished by scheduling speakers, training sessions, keeping resource material available, and so on. The managing partners must be willing to understand the technology and bridge the gap between their bottom line roles and the implementation of new technologies. Lawyers who did not grow up in the computer era run law firms. They do not understand their power, capability and applications. Their resistance to the incorporation of digital information into the firm will spell the end for these firms.

Be careful what you wish for - you may get what you wish! One situation to be wary of is where the leaders accept that technology is important and see the implementation as buying some hardware and software and without training the firm will somehow be automated. They generally will "tell" the committee, Chief Information Officer (CIO) or technology advocate what to do. A very difficult situation is involved here. Generally they are the authority in the firm but do not understand technology and generally are too busy to spend the time understanding it. Education, if the leader takes the time, unfortunately may be the only solution.

Computer Literacy - A recent survey showed that 51% of the top executives in the United States are computer illiterate. They rely heavily on their management team for advice for technology purchases. The main reasons for computer illiteracy are that computer knowledge and skills are considered a low priority, executives are intimidated by computers and they resist change. They may be the naysayers who will not support your efforts to enact your firm's strategic plan. Their negative comments and actions can cause a rift and much worse a nonadoption of technology in the firm that may eventually cause its downfall.

Technology Department Resistance - Strangely enough your own technologists may be against implementing new applications and maybe for good reason. Does your firm support their department with sufficient resources? What happened the last time that they implemented a new technology? Did you hold them responsible for glitches? Did you reward them for their long hours and worry about the implementation of the technology?

One sign of their hesitancy is shown in meetings where they point to a 3 year implementation period for applications that could realistically be up and running within 6 months. Others are reluctant to move to client/server technology because it decentralizes their control over the computers. Be aware of the technologist who does not want to change. They are content in the DOS environment, using outdated technology and see change as more work. However, change for change sake is not good – the benefits must be demonstrated.

Capital Investment and Billable Hour Concerns - Most law firms are not capital intensive. The money that is earned by the firm is distributed to its members. The firm did not have to set aside or consider the thousands or tens of thousands of dollars that are necessary to implement or upgrade existing technology. It is difficult to convince one of the senior partners to invest substantial money in new software, hardware and training when he may be retiring in a few years. Also, beware of the impulsive enthusiasm where the partners have not committed for the long term.

Do not ever underestimate the impact of the billable hour on a technology plan. In simple terms it would be more profitable for a firm if each attorney practiced law with a quill pen and lawbooks. The lawyer could charge by the hour, incur no secretarial expenses and manually research the law. The lawyer would make more profit then by automating. In fact if one invests in technology to get the work done faster then the firm will lose revenue by investing in the technology and by decreasing the number of billable hours that one could charge their client. This is a short sighted view that does not consider your client's need for low cost efficient services, value based billing and being able to handle more matters in a shorter period of time.

Once you understand the obstacles to implementation sound practical approaches can be developed to overcome any objections. However, a word of caution, some law firms will not change. They have old cultures, cumbersome structures and politics. They will give only lip service to needed reengineering and quiet the unrest by investing in some technology. Unfortunately, if a firm's management is unwilling to adopt technology then they will be discarded like the typewriter.

Selecting and Retaining a Technology Consultant

The fast paced changes in the information technology revolution can be overwhelming and intimidating. Technology selections may determine the success or failure of your firm. Sounds dramatic but we only need to look to the recent past and look at mainframes, Wang and Apple computers systems to make us tread cautiously through this revolution. Failure to make the right selections can mean that hardware and software purchases may have to be discarded. It is imperative that important technology changes such as the Internet and Intranets be incorporated into your present and future planning efforts. Your firm does not have to be on the *bleeding edge* of these technology efforts but should be on the *cutting edge* to maintain your competitive edge.

That is why I strongly suggest that a "consultant" should always be part of your technology planning efforts. However, competent knowledgeable legal consultants are difficult to locate. They should be independent and not tied financially or through other forms of remuneration to specific hardware or software vendors. All to often I have heard "independent" consultants tout the utility of specific software packages even though they were obtaining a commission or other form of incentive from the software company to sell their products. Also, be aware of vendors offering "unbiased" advice as to the ideal setup for your law office. Many vendors do not understand the "business" of the legal profession and provide solutions tailored for other type of businesses.

Many firms "appoint" a partner, associate or staff person such as a paralegal to be the 'computer person" in their organization. Whenever technology questions, decisions or research arise this person handles them on behalf of the firm. Unfortunately, the world of technology is moving at such a rapid rate in all areas that it is difficult if not impossible for the in-house person to stay abreast of the latest technology advancements and then choose the right solution for your firm.

You also need to realize that an attorney and other professional legal staff's mission are to provide legal services to their client. It is not to how to best connect to the Internet or which document assembly package is the best. There is a tradeoff for using the services of your professional staff to research and determine the best technology solution for your firm. Always consider that a lawyer or paralegal bill at a certain amount. Will the in-house person selected arrive at an accurate technology answer within a short time? Will it actually cost more for the in-house person to understand the technology then to bring in a consultant? The final decision, customization and maintenance can be done in-house but do not replace the function of a technology consultant with a skilled legal advocate.

I suggest that firms use consultants in conjunction with there in-house computer staff to arrive at the best technology solution for their practice area. A legal consultant should be used when considering a:
- major hardware or software system change;
- office relocation or addition;
- merger of firms;
- annual or semi-annual needs assessment;
- addition of numerous lawyers; and
- any other event which significantly impacts your information technology system.

A *legal* technology consultant's job is to understand the hardware and software applications used in the legal industry. There are several reasons why one should retain the services of a reasonably priced competent legal technology consultant. They are able to:
- Keep abreast of the latest product releases and the trends in the legal industry as well as in the general computer industry;
- Bring knowledge gained from other jobs to your firm to enhance your efficiency and effectiveness;
- Provide presentation of latest technological changes;
- They may be able to provide a link to the best prices in town;
- Can provide annual or semi-annual assessment of your needs; and

- Can grow along with your technological growth.

Selecting a consultant

The process of selecting a consultant should focus on a number of important factors. A consultant should:

- Understand your legal practice;
- Have the personality, temperament and people skills to get along with firm members;
- Have substantial prior experience working with law firms;
- Have great communication skills. Be able to use simple language to communicate about technology issues so that you understand the concepts. Beware of consultants that talk mumble jumble;
- Be stable and professional;
- Be available for fast response;
- Always maintains a solution oriented approach;
- Charge a reasonable fee for services. Consultants charge generally from $75 to $200 an hour.
- Check out his or her references. Ask for the contact person *for his last five jobs*, not just the references he provides you;
- Have the required technical skills for the particular project; and
- Have the required legal applications knowledge for the project.

Agreement with consultant

In order to prevent an unpleasant experience consider using the following contractual clauses and methods to ensure a favorable result:

- Set forth in writing the responsibilities and duties you wish the consultant to assume? Set forth the proposed services and deliverables (reports, deadlines, benchmarks). Incorporate proposals into the contract.
- Set forth in writing the project's anticipated cost? Does the consultant bill by the project or by the hour? When is payment due and how should it be made? Save a final payment until the project is completed and accepted. Consider dividing the project into pieces so the cost will be based on the individual subprojects completed. Provide an early notification method if the consultant feels that there will be a cost or time overrun on the project. Request a written explanation why such an overrun may occur.
- Reserve the right to terminate at any time paying for services received. Set forth the name if you want a particular consultant. Do not permit the consultant to enter into contracts on your behalf.
- Delineate the lines of authority in writing. Do not allow the consultant to obtain approval from another member of the firm on a project or extension of a project without your approval.
- Disclose and discuss the firm's legal goals.
- Discuss the methodology of how price quotes will be obtained. Be sure to compare apples to apples.
- Discuss strategies on quality of products, lowest prices, staff training, implementation strategies, installation of products, conversion of old documents or data to the new format and testing.

Consultants can provide tremendous value for the money and can guide you through the information revolution. Take time in your selection process. They can save a tremendous amount of aggravation and free you to practice law and not technology.

Technology Implementation

Lawyers are in the information and knowledge business. As a lawyer, one must use available information sources, and with one's expertise, experience and honed skills, translate this information into a quality work

---

product. Providing this knowledge to your client in a timely fashion that fairly measures the values of the services to the client is very important.

Technology is advancing and meeting the information and knowledge needs of the legal profession. Cellular and video phones, word processors, faxes, modems, wide and local area networks, notebook computers, the Internet and CD-ROM informational disks are but a few of those advancements. These technologies are not integrated into the legal practitioner's practice by happenstance. It requires thoughtful planning and integration into a firm. The application of the technology process is not easy - it must be learned, practiced, and upgraded. Think in terms of information technology tools and the people that can activate those tools for your cases. Think in terms of your client's needs and how the application of technology can meet those needs. Every law firm must have a strategic plan and a structure to carry out this plan.

CyberDavid Rocks Goliath

In the Bible, David took a major risk that would not have looked good in strategy meetings. A cybercorp newcomer needs less raw heroism than that exhibited by the biblical hero; it can use new ideas to exploit an old company's weaknesses. It can use newer technology, virtual mechanisms, and electronic marketing. Because of its size, it can build a cozier relationship with customers. David can win in many corporate situations because Goliath is loaded down with baggage of an earlier era.

Old corporations often have old cultures, inappropriate to the mercurial cybercorp age. They have cumbersome structures and politics. Their computers are snarled up in spaghetti-like software that is murder to change. They pay lip service to reengineering themselves but make only mechanical changes within the present structure-when that structure ought to be scrapped.

Today's technology makes possible virtual space and virtual operations. A small company does not need expensive offices; some employees can work at home. Key players may live in different cities but be linked electronically. A small company can be a virtual company.
- James Martin, *The Wired Society*

For solo practitioners, small firms and large firms the opportunities for automation are immense. Solos and small firms can effectively compete with larger firms using automation. The downside is that generally they do not have the expertise to automate. It is essential these lawyers remember that there are many resources to assist in the automation efforts. For example, the American Bar Association and in particular the Law Practice Management Division are publishing many technology books and newsletters written by lawyers and others explaining technology solutions. State and local bar associations are providing CLE and other training. Seek out friends and attorneys who are technology minded and share information and your vision of the future.

To successfully implement technology in the firm you must strategically plan its integration into your firm. Strategic planning is never static - it is always dynamic, changing and ongoing. The following are considerations and steps that you may want to incorporate into your implementation efforts.

The Technology Decision-Maker. Appoint someone who is responsible for the ultimate decisions regarding technology in your firm. That person should not be a dictator, but instead be open, curious, intelligent, and have a technology vision. It will be necessary for that person to understand technology concepts and legal applications. It will always be easy to criticize the decisions of this person because of the fast paced changes occurring in the technology area. However, as long as the person uses due diligence in researching, understanding and applying the collective knowledge of the group then that is all that one can ask. Also be aware of the self-anointed attorney technologist or consultant who have not kept up with the technological changes, who sell a particular piece of software or who crusade for one particular pet application.

Technology Committee. A technology committee can be a formal and informal link as an organization adopts technology as part of their integrated strategic plan. The committee is important to facilitate and support the integration of technology. Presentations at office meetings can be sponsored or co-sponsored by the technology committee. Lines of authority need to be defined between committee and administrative staff. The chairperson of committee should be a person with a practical technology approach. The chair should be able to communicate the benefits and be the bridge between the technology and non-technology employees. It may be necessary to outsource part of the technical work, as an attorney's time constraints may not permit him or her to keep abreast of the changing technology market place. The committee can be a benefit as well as a hindrance if they refuse to listen to new ideas and technologies.

Within your organization there will be the controllers, followers, adopters and naysayers. The controllers will see this as something they want to take over or control. If they have an experienced background with law and technology they are invaluable assets. If they want to control just to control then your organization may be severely handicapped if they choose solutions which are not appropriate or to costly. The followers will follow the lead of the management and will adjust to the new technology. The adopters will readily accept the new technology and will assist in the implementation and making it successful. The naysayers are the group that can undermine a successful implementation. There are a whole host of covert and overt reasons why they will be against the project. Unfortunately, it is necessary to minimize their influence or convince them of the merits of the project.

Do not neglect minor technology issues in the firm. Have the technology needs of the branch offices been adequately considered? Branch offices need to be included in the entire process. It is unfair to exclude them based on the distant from the office or smaller size. Seriously consider videoconferencing or other communication means to include them in the meetings.

On the committee place key decision-makers, experts and people impacted by the decisions that are made. Technical people as well as legal professionals should be on the committee. How are people who are resistance against change going to commit to the mission and objectives of the firm? What type and when should the entire law firm be included in the planning? Communicate with all members of the staff - have them become stakeholders and buy into the solutions. Plan big, start small, and change the course if you need. Include all staff - attorneys, paralegals, support staff - on your planning committee. They are all stakeholders and will be impacted by your technology choices. Make sure partners and others are in agreement and accountable for the direction.

Understanding Computer Concepts and Legal Applications. Determine available and emerging technologies and how they apply to your practice. Assess what other law firms are doing or not doing. Ensure that the members understand computer concepts and how they apply in a conceptual sense to legal applications. List the different automation functions that are being considered: advanced word processing; time and billing, databases, and so on. Determine what functions you want to automate. It is unnecessary that one becomes a technologist but one must understand what is meant by document assembly, full text, the Internet and so on. Information and understanding must be acquired before one can formulate a vision. Have a vision of what you want your firm to look like in 1, 5, 10, 15 years. Will it be a "virtual" firm? What do your clients want in that same time span? Do they want to share development of your technology plan with you? What is the technology direction and focus of the firm? The key leaders must visualize the future of the practice of law in your firm. Your team must be agreement on the direction and focus of the firm.

Technology Agenda and Strategic Objectives. Formulate a technology agenda and objectives of what areas of automation will be developed. Part of the agenda statement should be "to use technology and management innovation to maintain a position of leadership in the legal community." Another goal would be to include the provision of quality legal services for your client at a fair fee. Identify and focus on the lawyer's needs and provide the technology to assist them. For example how can technology assist them in managing their billable days. Will a calendar and docketing system provide the control over their caseload to assist them? What do our clients want - do we become partners with them in integrating the practice of law and their business by technology? Do we share case management systems, automated document assembly systems, databases and so forth? Prepare a one, five and ten year plan realizing that changes will be necessary.

Re-engineering Law Office Processes. As you begin to analyze the law office and litigation functions you will soon discover that one may have to consider changing the workflow and business processes to meet your automation goals. For example since the docketing and scheduling and timekeeping software will be on the computer should the staff member who is part of the law firm section or litigation team handle all of these duties or do you still route docketing matters to the docketing clerk. A very good book to read is Reengineering the Corporation by Michael Hammer and James Champy. It provides a insightful look at reinventing business processes. If you will be using paperless images on a case should the documents be imaged when they arrive at the doorstep or should the attorney determine if they should be placed in the imaging database? Should the scanning be outsourced or should the firm invest in the equipment and training to do it in-house? Should we hire a new person while we are doing this? There are many questions that must be asked as you re-engineer your law office processes and workflow.

Job titles and duties of employees will change as we use computers more and more in the practice of law. For example, the WWW and other databases are filled with valuable case information that has be uncovered. Internet specialists will become an integral part of the law firm structure. Also, evidence specialists will be hired to locate, categorize, and computerize witness facts, document information and controlling other discovery materials in an electronic method.

The Virtual Law Office. More and more people are telecommuting from home or branch offices, as we become more interconnected. Workers are finding fewer distractions while working away from the office. As this trend continues specific strategies should be considered since office space and other resources may be decreased depending upon your firm's approach to this work schedule.

Great attention should be planned for the integration of technology into the design of law offices. Consideration will have to be given to what, where, and how technology will be integrated. Computers, video conferencing, voice and data communications networks, and security devices all have to be planned for in setting up and designing your office at home or at work. Individual law offices will decrease in size and technology conference centers will become larger to meet with clients, conduct depositions, and electronically handle your client's business. A little forethought ahead of time will drastically cut remodeling needs prompted by integration of technology.

Plan of Action – Technology Life Cycle. The following System Development Life Cycle discloses the technology issues that need to be considered during different phases of the implementation process.

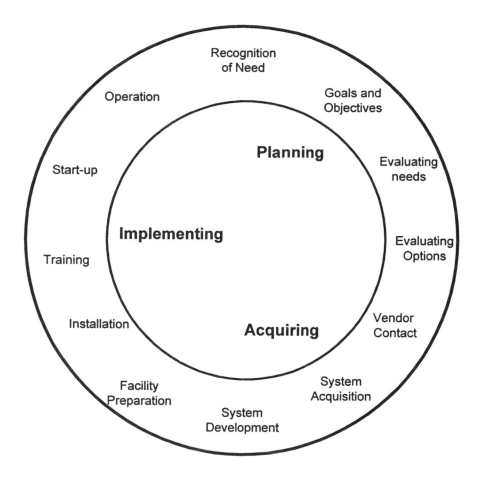

Source: Planning, Acquiring, And Implementing Court Automation, National Center for State Courts and State Justice Institute (1993).

In regards to a particular case there may be additional implementation factors to consider. For example, what is the size of our firm, nature and size of case, time constraints of litigation, number and location of parties involved, client interest, cost savings, and size of budget. Compare it to the manual handling of indexing and imaging of documents. Consider the possibility of early settlement, number of witnesses and number of documents. What is the capacity of the firm's hardware and software?

If you are soliciting services through a systems integrator for hardware, software, networking and other services it is suggested that a Request for Proposal (RFP) be developed. An RFP if properly prepared will enable one to obtain similar competing bids from vendors. Software and hardware prices are constantly changing and the vendors generally keep track of these changes and pass the savings along to you.

Creating a Technology Minded Legal Culture. Reward employees - attorneys and support staff - who brings and assists in the implementation of new technology advances. Foster an environment of efficiency and forward thinking on the use of technology. Let your clients know that you are using the technology and that the firm's staff is committed to being efficient in the handling of their matters. Encourage employees to take risks and then compliment them even if the course of technology action was not successful. Keep asking the question as to whether your firm employees are taking advantage of the latest and most cost effective advances for your clients.

Support the technology change by providing education. Classes, books, periodicals, audiovisual and other aids should be available. Keep current with PC Magazine, Law Office Computing, Wired and other publications. Network through professional organizations, hire technical experts and support the risk takers.

Team Implementation. Successful implementation of technology requires a team effort. Participants must include representatives from the partners, associates, paralegals, secretaries and members of the information management department. You must realize that automating even one application such as timekeeping impacts all the members of your firm. If they are left out of the planning for implementation process it could seriously hinder your success. They must commit to the technology vision and objectives. They will become the focal point of your implementation plans.

Take time to build a team for implementing projects. Have buy-in from all levels of employees. Communication, teamwork and patience should guide your actions. For each new legal application - E-mail, document assembly, etc. - what is the strategy and timeline for implementing it? Consider a pilot program for each application. Remember that people will use technology if it is easy to use, convenient, and provides real value in their life. Implement effective quick solutions that work. Don't hesitate to praise and give recognition to firm employees on adapting to the new technology.

Focus on benefits not the failures since they will also occur as the new system is implemented. Identify problems that stand in the way of automation. Set objectives for solving the problem. Lawyers generally do not absorb new

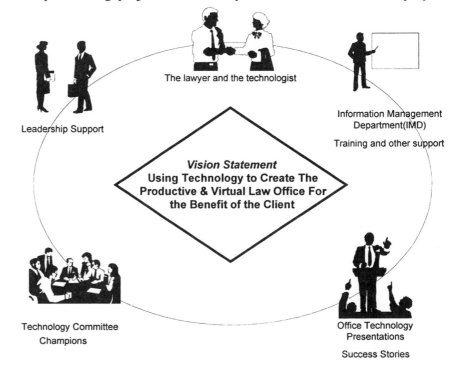

The lawyer and the technologist

Information Management Department(IMD)

Training and other support

Leadership Support

**Vision Statement
Using Technology to Create The
Productive & Virtual Law Office For
the Benefit of the Client**

Technology Committee
Champions

Office Technology
Presentations

Success Stories

training in a classroom environment and may feel embarrassed by their lack of knowledge in the computer area. Training should be available on an individual interactive method. Identify software and hardware products that meet your needs. Make sure that objectives and decisions are set and that there are available resources to implement this direction. Keep leaders and employees advised of progress. Measure the progress in Return on Technology Investment (ROTI) and in other intangible ways.

One source of office unity is to prepare and present an office technology seminar using in-house lawyers and support staff as speakers. The employees become increasingly committed and learn in the process. Everyone benefits, the presenters as well as the audience. Cover the computer concepts as well as the legal applications. One major consideration is whether these employees are credited in some manner for working on office technology projects. Recognize their value as they try to provide a positive motivational learning experience for their fellow staff members. Presentation questionnaires should be distributed to understand the effectiveness of their efforts.

Use outside speakers and locate lawyers or other legal professionals that use the software or hardware. Monthly presentations will keep the employees focused on technology applications. However, focus on computer concepts and practical lawyering applications. If you present only theory the audience will quickly tire of the presentations. Show them immediate value and ease of use. Recruit the computer novice to present. The other employees will say that if that person can do it they also can. Outside speakers, consultants and vendors can be a good source for presentations. However, ask ahead what the message is that they will be presenting. Contrary messages to your organization can be damaging. National and local technology seminars provide good content material for presentations and a list of potential speakers. Always follow up after the presentation and report back to the staff if any action is taken.

Technology Budget – Hardware, Software and Staff. There are a number of major components when constructing a budget for technology which include:
- Hardware and Software,
- Technical support,
- Data management,
- Application development, and
- Training.

Sufficient IS personnel should be available to assist the legal professional in completing their work. Fifteen years ago few lawyers used computers so few IS people were needed. Now we see lawyers using computers on the road, at home and at other locations. Lawyers need to be lawyers and not computer technicians. Approximately 10 years ago one IS person was needed for every 50 users. Recently we have seen ratios of 1 IS person for every 20-25 users. In addition we see secretaries and others filling part of the IT need. In any case computer software experts should be available to lawyers for any software they are using to assist them to complete there work and ultimately maximize the profit for the firm.

Consider leasing as a viable alternative to buying for the following reasons. It:
- Ensures against technological obsolescence by providing for upgrading,
- Preserves cash flow, and
- May provide income tax advantages on the monthly lease payments (confer with your accountant).
  There are many manufacturers including Dell and Gateway who have reputable leasing programs.

Training & Competency Testing. Studies have shown that software users need proper training or they will spend up to four times as much time learning it on their own. Training will cut down on time away from lawyering, time to learn the software and the time you are using it incorrectly. Training should always simulate real-life scenarios.

There are those that are computer comfortable, those willing to learn and those that are technophobic - which is having a fear of technology. A recent survey by Michelle Wei and MCI confirmed that only 10 to 15% enjoy technology, 50-60% are hesitant/prove it (show me if the bugs are worked out) and 30-40% are downright resistant. In sum, 85% of the population are hesitant or opposed to technology - www.ocpapsych.com.com\wei.htm.

The training needs of each will differ and it is important to use different techniques for different members of the firm. However, if they are intimidated or feel dumb and are forced to use it their job performance will actually decline. They will become more technophobic then before.

Don't forget to access the needs of your audience. Do they need basic Windows training, intermediate or more advanced training, etc? Focus on the value provided to the legal professional. They will appreciate the training if it is directly beneficial to their duties. Marginal applications with little value to the firm should not be implemented.

Some training points to consider:

- Computers are not cold alien creatures. They are merely machines that have hardware and software. One does not have to be a computer scientist to run a computer as attested to by the fact that many kids today are comfortable in front of a keyboard and monitor.

- Computers share many common characteristics. Almost all PC's are operating on DOS or Windows 95/98 software, except for a small percentage of the market operating on Macintosh. The software, especially Windows 95/98 share similar commands and protocols which enables users to transfer their training from one program to other programs.

- Courses, books, magazine articles, newspapers and TV programs are dedicated to teaching the novice to the advanced user about computers. Use them as much as possible.

- Finally and most importantly, the professional in the legal industry are generally some of the brightest people in the world. Attorneys have all graduated from law school and have passed a bar exam. Computers are organizational tools that can be mastered by them.

- Finally, relax and enjoy the adventure of learning about the instrument what will impact our society for the next several hundred years.

There are many different types of training available:

- *On-line CLE and other software training* – We are starting to see an emergence of Internet sites offering on-line video, audio and text tutorials on legal technology training and substantive CLE programs. For example, LegalSpan (www.legalspan.net) provides real-time or archived CLE "inSession" programs over the Internet using a regular phone line. Using the @ttend software one can also view and receive depositions, trade show information and live court proceedings from the following LegalSpan broadcasting modules:

  - DepoCast - broadcasts of live depositions over a secure connection allowing corporate counsel, co-counsel, expert witnesses and other appropriate parties to receive the court reporter's real-time transcript and video/audio feeds;
  - ExpoCast – a virtual trade show where broadcasts include demonstrations and training sessions for legal products and services; and
  - CourtCast – broadcasts of live legal proceedings from courtrooms.

This technology has many uses and provides the capability for a practitioner, law firm or company to broadcast with limited interaction any meeting, deposition, legal proceeding or CLE program. Corporate counsel could broadcast to several outside counsels at the same time; law firms can broadcast to branch offices; and state bar committees and sections can broadcast to remote members.

The proliferation of real-time and archived Internet CLE programs delivering content in audio, text and video and allowing discussions with other participants will proliferate over the next several years. This paradigm shift will include undergraduate and graduate courses, national and state legal conferences, advocacy courses and all types of legal training that will be available to you at your desktop. For a list of on-line CLE courses visit the FindLaw Internet Legal Resources WWW site. (www.findlaw.com/07cle/index.html).

- *Third Party Books, Tapes and CD-ROMS* – There are many training materials available for general off the shelf software in computer stores and magazines. For example Viagrafix provides video training for a wide variety of software, including most popular software packages. Video training allows you to learn by watching TV or using their CD-ROM interactive series. Video Training Services – Viagrafix, 800-842-4723. (www.viagrafix.com).

- *Hands-on Instructor Training* – Most people seem to prefer instructor-led training where the instructor can respond to specific questions from the legal professional because that is how they are used to learning. Costs range from $75 up to $150 per student. Instructors should be course certified by the manufacturer. Instructor training can be on-site if you have the equipment or at a local community college, CompUSA or any location with the proper setup. The phone book yellow pages will disclose a list of vendors.

- *Software Tutorial Programs* – Many software programs have excellent self-tutorial programs that should be used since they come with the programs.

- *Self-Directed Training* - Many software packages now have videotape training tapes or CD-ROMS where one-on-one instruction can be used for those that prefer this method or who geographically cannot attend hands on training.

- *Office Presentations* - Presentations by known experts is a low cost method of providing training to employees. Their profession is the training of computer users. The time and cost of creating a training session in-house should be balanced against the hiring of the presentation by outside experts.

- *24 hour help desk.* Someone should be designated the 24-hour help person(s) who can be contacted whenever someone has a problem using the computers.

- *Intranet help desk.* If your firm has implemented an Intranet then authoring self-help and self-fixing software is available. Commonly called call-avoidance software a user accesses a prebuilt database of solutions for common or unusual firm wide computer or non-computer problems or procedures. In some cases the software can actually fix problems on the PC. Maintaining the content and ensuring that the information is accurate is important but should be offset against the time saved in answering person-to-person questions. Web self help sources include: Advantage kbs: (www.akbs.com); Inference: (www.inference.com); ServiceSoft: (www.servicesoft.com) and SystemSoft (www.systemsoft.com).

- *Conferences and Seminars* – Many states and national organizations put on technology seminars where actual users of technology will detail their use of software and technology centers are available to see demonstrations of software and hardware.

- *Individual training sessions.* Some attorneys prefer this method with an understanding personal trainer. They will not be embarrassed by their lack of knowledge and can learn at their own pace.

- *Group training.* This type of training is good for disclosure and understanding of overall computer concepts and applications. For example, if the firm is implementing timekeeping then the concept, application and required use by all employees can be explained in an initial presentation.

- *Customized computer training programs* - Lotus ScreenCam97 (www.lotus.com) is a multimedia screen and sound capture utility. It allows you to create, edit and distribute PC movies via e-mail, the WWW and Intranets. This program enables you to record your screen activity, including pull down menus, scrolling, highlighting, and file opening and closing. Simultaneously, ScreenCam can record your voice while you narrate. This enables you to create personalized training tools that you can share across your network. It allows for unlimited distribution of a ScreenCam player that can be downloaded off the web free of charge. This enables a user to view your movie. Another program to consider is *Dan Bricklin's demo-it* (www.pparadise.com). This full featured demonstration builder for Windows provides easy to use demonstration building features including interactive options for the user.

A small investment in software training will pay big dividends in both productivity and employee morale. With so many training options available there is no reason why you cannot take full advantage of your software investment.

Competency Testing. Some firms are starting to require certain levels of technology competence. Just as there are technology competency requirements for a variety of other jobs the legal profession will begin mandating them as the need for efficiency grows. Determine on what computer literacy level the attorney is. Does she or he have any training using computers, if so build on that competency level. Outside training vendors will identify your needs and provide an estimate to use for budgetary purposes. The implementation of technology requires that all team members reach a certain level of proficiency with a computer. There should be minimum levels of core competency for lawyers in the use of technology. The standards or basic hands on knowledge should include the following:

- Office Management Systems – an understanding of the philosophy and commands needed to operate group computing software such as GroupWise, time keeping systems such as Timeslips and work product filing systems such as PC DOCS.

- Case Management Systems – contact and docketing systems such as Amicus Attorney, Microsoft Outlook, or Lotus Organizer.

- Litigation Databases – information systems to locate, edit and produce reports of case data. Programs include Concordance, Summation or Microsoft Access.

- Graphics – the creation of simple graphics and slideshow using programs such as Microsoft PowerPoint and Visio.

- Communication Programs – connecting to the office remotely, sending files, and searching on the Internet.

- Document Assembly – basic assembling of a document using a word processor and HotDocs or other assembly software.

- Full Text search and Retrieval – to locate witness information in deposition, interviews or other full text documents.

The competency standards for a firm will change as applications change. However, commitment by all in the firm will be greatly increased with the imposition of competency standards.

Return on Investment. Measure, report the results and start evaluating again. Has our original agenda and objectives been achieved? Why or why not? Has their been an advancement in software development for say voice recognition? Will it now meet our objectives in a cost-effective manner? It is vitally important to start the process again.

The advancements to integrate into your practice must be planned for and implemented on a firmwide basis. This requires a constant reassessment of the technological advancements. For example some important goals for your firm may be to increase and promote communication with your clients, increase productivity using document assembly software or increase effectiveness in litigation by investing in multimedia presentation software and hardware. It is necessary to attempt to measure the benefits if implementing technology into your firm. It is not sufficient to say that the new technology will improve this or eliminate that. Instead technology expenditures should be linked to a strategic plan where certain goals and measurable benefits are set forth.

A cost benefit analysis may be difficult to quantify but efforts should be made to create a causal connection between the expenditure and the benefits. For example if laptop computers are purchased will this result in more billable hours? If desktop systems are installed in and attorney's home will the attorney self-train himself and bill more hours? Does a remote connection to the attorney's home provide more billable hours since they will not have to commute? At a system wide level will the use of computers decrease the number of support staff needed?

Keep track to determine if your firm has met its goals, timelines, and project dates. The staff should be advised as to the benefit obtained from the use of technology.

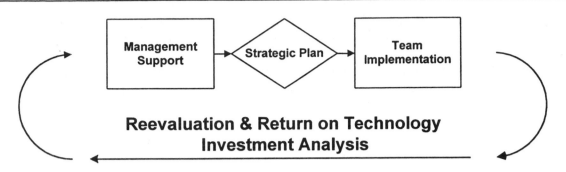

The important point is to ensure that the functions you automate bring real value to the firm. The technology investment in dollars will be significant both in training and the actual hardware and software investment. This investment should be tied to a return of investment measured in client retention, client attraction, efficiency, cost savings, lowering of overhead costs, competitive advantage in cases and so on. Focus on measuring, if possible, the Return on Technology Investment (ROTI). This should encompass productivity gains, expense reduction and recovery of costs. If you can show that a contract was prepared in minutes instead of hours then this is a significant productivity gain. If the electronic transfer of contracts and other documents can reduce express mail charges then track these charges. There is software and hardware technology available to track the costs of faxes, copying, printing and telephone charges to the client. Track not only the tangible benefits but also the subjective benefit of clients supporting your technology efforts.

Conclusion

Unfortunately the technology revolution did not occur 40 or 50 years ago because the law firm managers would have grown up with technology. Instead, lawyers and managers are struggling to understand and implement value oriented technology solutions. Those that are not because of computer literacy, billable hour or whatever reason are subjecting their firm to risk of downsizing or closing their doors.

With perseverance and the assistance of a consultant a firm can change its technology culture and ride the wave of this technology revolution. However, it requires the commitment of the firm's leaders, allocation of sufficient resources and team implementation. The return on investment can provide both tangible and intangible benefits. It is difficult to change and implement this new technology but the survival of your firm may be at stake.

This Page Intentionally Left Blank

Chapter 6

Computer Concepts and Legal Applications

Introduction

Applying technology to the practice of law requires that one have a basic understanding of computer concepts before one can apply them to the lawyering process. In this section basic computer concepts will be defined and illustrated. Discussions will focus on the primary components of these concepts as well as a general discussion of their application to legal functions. The next sections will apply these concepts in greater detail to a variety of legal applications that can be used in your firm.

For example, once you understand the concept of "full text" then by using "full text" software you will discover that one can locate information in an electronic deposition or trial transcript within seconds. You will also discover that any firm or case information which is in a "full text" format such as office policies, work product, interrogatories, interviews and so on can also be searched in seconds.

> The purpose of this book is not to find and recommend the "best" software for a particular computer concept. It would be a huge undertaking to locate, acquire, test and recommend the best software because of the number of products, upgrades, and new product releases. A few "leading" products will be referred to but the resources section of this book contains the names and addresses of testing facilities, magazines and books that focus upon specific software product selection.

The key is understanding the concept and then applying the concept to specific lawyering functions that provide value to your firm.

Whether it is an outliner to set up a blueprint of your case or graphics for presentation of your trial themes all computer concepts have a place within the practice of law. Unfortunately there is not a "killer" software program that incorporates all of these concepts. Instead, there are many "standalone" products that can fill your needs. However, the "integration" of these packages to work together has taken a major step forward with the introduction of OLE, DDE and more recently HTML language used in Intranets, Extranets and the Internet. There is a significant trend of these standalone packages "integrating" with other standalone packages. For example we are seeing case management programs "integrate" with litigation support software and with billing and accounting software.

Converting computer data from one usable format to another.

Compatibility of software formats is necessary not only to share data within your applications, but with other attorneys or the court, etc. You need to know how to convert data from one usable format to another. Conversion issues can arise in using a file from one version of a word processing program to a different version of the same word processing program. Issues can also arise from converting word processing information into spreadsheet, database or graphics presentation data.

Some suggested methods or tips for solving or preventing conversion problems include:

❑ *Software conversion.* A popular conversion software to convert data from one format to another format is Data Junction software (www.datajunction.com).
❑ *Questions for users.* When getting a file from a colleague or others one needs to ask from what type of computer and platform did the file come from. Also you need to know is the file from a word processor, spreadsheet, database, etc., what brand and version of software is being used, can it be converted to ASCII, and who is the person to contact if problems arise?
❑ *Disk Labeling.* Label the platform (Macintosh or PC), file format and application program (word processing, database, graphic, etc.), and program version on the transfer disk;
❑ *Client and co-counsel compatibility.* Determine early on in the process the platform and application compatibility of your client or co-counsel.
❑ *File extensions.* Extensions on a file may provide the information to convert a file so label the disk accordingly. For example .WP, .WP5, .DOC disclose that it is a word processing file; .WK1, .WK3, .XLS

are spreadsheet files; .DB, .DBF, .DTF, .MDB are database extensions; and .PCX, .TIF, .BMP, .WPG are extensions for graphics. There are many other extensions.

❑ *Automatic conversions.* Many applications automatically convert dissimilar file formats into usable data. For example Microsoft Word automatically converts WordPerfect files into Word documents.

❑ *File Format Save Features.* Most popular applications allow the user to SAVE the document in one of a number of popular formats that the end user will be using.

❑ *Exporting and importing technique.* Exporting data to a special format to be IMPORTED into another program may be a solution. Determine the importing, exporting capability of your software.

❑ *ASCII conversion.* Most data can be stripped down or SAVED to basic ASCII text for importing or conversion into a different file format. The file extensions are usually .TXT or .ASC.

❑ *Data Length.* Moving data from a word processor into a database or spreadsheet may require the data be shortened for a field or cell.

Converting data for use by different application programs will present special problems. As the different programs" integrate" using DDE and other shared data protocols then the difficulty of reusing data will substantially lesson.

Computer Concepts and Legal Applications

The following computer concepts will be discussed along with their relationship to specific legal applications. The continuing focus will be upon the relationship of these concepts to the practice of law.

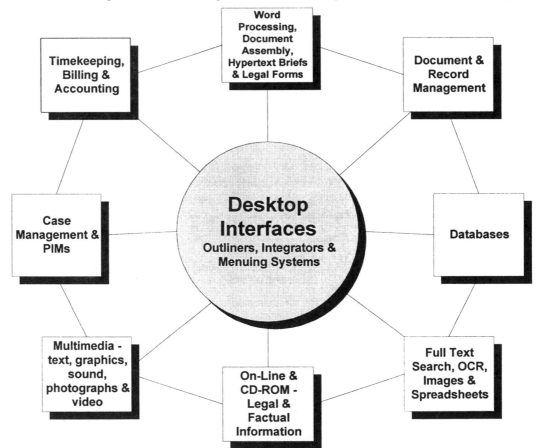

Applying these concepts to your cases will provide the instant control over the factual and legal information on behalf of your client.

Desktop Interfaces - Outliners, Integrators and Menuing Systems

Since there is no comprehensive software product to handle all of the above functions there is a need to tie together the different software applications in order to access case information. Some of the approaches to handle this problem have been to use a desktop interface, outliner, integrator or menuing system. For example most recently we have seen Windows 95/98™ desktop interfaces link to case or office information.

These interfaces sometimes have been called an "attorney's workstation" or "attorney's desktop" to reflect in some way how an attorney practices law. They have been developed to interface, launch or access the different legal tasks in a hopefully understandable method for the legal professional. Generally on the same computer screen one can access the firm's administrative functions as well as access specific case information. For example, a menuing system may have an icon that you configure to launch into the firm's billing program and word processor.

The *desktop interface* has moved from a DOS menuing system to a Windows menuing system to an Internet browser type of interface. With the strong emergence of the Internet and Intranets the web browser desktop metaphor is beginning to become the desktop of choice as reflected in Windows 98™. From the desktop browser you can launch applications such as a word processor, spreadsheet, etc. and at the same time connect to different parts of the world or your local LAN using the web interface.

Many of these programs enable the user to "customize" the interface to reflect the individual practice and preferences of the user. For example, Windows 95/98™ as a menuing system is taking more of a functional work approach as opposed to a software product approach. Instead of clicking on an icon to open Microsoft Word™ one is able to set up a legal document as an icon. By clicking on the icon it will enable you to go directly into the legal document. This approach is long overdue and reflects the way one works on a case.

Outliners are one of the best front-end tools for lawyers to use as an interface to the substance of one's case or other law office functions. Outliners inherently reflect the way lawyers think. In any case we have a set number of tasks and other matters that have to be accomplished. Whether it is incorporating a company or representing our client in a personal injury case a plan of action needs to be developed. An outliner or similar interface can provide this function as well as the capability to customize the links that will permit one to access different information sources for your case.

Outlining programs are extremely useful in organizing your case. An outliner is what the name implies. It enables one to create an outline of any or all of your case. Whether you are

```
Corel WordPerfect - C:\MyFiles\Smith vs XYZ Corp (unmodified)
File  Edit  View  Insert  Format  Tools  Window  Help

I.    Smith vs XYZ Corporation
      A.   Pleadings
           1.   Complaint Filed 4-65-97
           2.   Answer filed 5-3-97
           3.   Interrogatories submitted - 6-9-97
           4.   Interrogatories Answered - 8-15-97
      B.   Witnesses
           1.   Plaintiffs witnesses
                a.   Fred Smith
                b.   Mary Smith
                c.   Joe Seetall
                d.   Frank Obser4ver
           2.   Defendant's witnesses
                a.   Bill Hightower, President of XYZ
                b.   Mary Woods, secretary
      C.   Exhibits
           1.   Accident report
           2.   Lost earnings statement
           3.   Medical records
           4.   Property loss report
```

involved in commercial transactions, litigation or any specialty the outliner can be your case notebook. An outliner screen is blank when initially accessed and enables the user to customize it for his or her case. After typing in the main case management components such as Legal Issues or Witnesses then one can create subheadings for these areas in the outlining program. After creating subheadings these can be collapsed and expanded depending on which part of the case you are working on. If you create a Witness main heading then all of the witnesses can be the next level subheading and then these subheadings can be reorganized at the touch of a key. It is not necessary to cut and paste, but merely move the witness notes, which can include direct and cross-examination notes, to the new location. Many attorneys rave about the benefits of outlining programs because they function like a lawyer "thinks". It enables them to "outline" their case in the same fashion as a case or trial notebook.

Other outliner features include the capability to move blocks or headlines quickly for a different arrangement of your key points. Generally, outliners include word processing features such as line wrapping, adjustable margins, indents, line spacing, clipboard functions, spell checker, search and replace features, and so on. Second, you can use the search feature to locate a specific witness name and address or the date a particular court order was entered. The search feature permits you to locate any information in the outline in seconds. If you have a question about a proposed direct examination of a witness, a simple search will locate this information immediately.

> **Idea Generators and Brainstorming Software**
> Have you ever been stuck on how to approach a particular problem or issue in a case? If so software is available that has a computerized idea bank or thesaurus. The software assists you in looking at alternatives to a given problem. Idea Fisher (www.ideafisher.com) and Idea Generator (www.ideagenerator.com) by Gerald Nierechy who wrote the book *The Art of Creative Thinking*.

Some additional legal applications of an outlining program are to organize appellate arguments, set up the question areas for direct and cross examination, set forth the legal issues that need to be researched, to do lists or a list of exhibits of your case with a listing of any evidentiary issues for the document. Since it is created by the user it can be used for any legal application which requires an organizational approach. Outliners can be found in word processing programs and more recently are finding their way into litigation support programs such as Summation™. Below is an example of using the Summation™ outlining program. This outliner also permits one to view video depositions and other multimedia information from the outliner.

Integrators and menuing systems perform similar functions as an outliner but integrate the different application programs primarily using icons to represent different programs or functions. For example, an integration program may have an ICON for Witness A's testimony. After pressing the ICON a small word processing window may open giving you the capacity to view the testimony. Another ICON may launch Microsoft Excel™ to access a spreadsheet to determine damages in your case.

Outliners, integrators and menuing systems will continue to gain in utility as they begin to permit the legal professional to organize his/her work in any manner they choose.

Contrasted with Word Processing, Databases and Full Text Search & Retrieval Programs.

There are inherent limitations with outliners depending upon the program you choose. Outliners are not powerful word processors. They have built in outlining functions which enable you to easily manipulate main and subheadings of your outline. Outliners generally cannot function effectively with depositions or other

---

transcripts. Part of the reason for this is the very nature of outliners is to "outline" information. They are not designed to process large text documents. They may not accept a large text file and are unable to "index" the data that is accepted, which results in slow searches. Nor do they effectively act as databases except in smaller cases. Databases generally separate discrete segments of information in documents for document, witness, or issue indexing. A variety of reports can then be created from these abstracts including chronology reports. An outliner does not have this capability.

Case Management and Personal Information Managers (PIMs)

Many of the procedural and administrative functions of the practice of law can be easily organized and automated using case management and PIMs software. These include functions such as timekeeping, docketing, calendar, address books and others. The two main categories of software to handle these tasks are case management and personal information management (PIM) software. There is no clear line of demarcation between these two categories of software. Many functions are contained in both types of software and this trend of "integration" will continue, as their objective is to manage case, procedural and administrative legal information together.

Case Management Software. Case management software manages case information. It is generally thought of as managing the procedural and administrative and not the litigation part of your cases. It is intended to be an integrated collection of functions that work together to manage the tasks involved in the practice of law. For example, the user can track court due dates and identify cases that are nearing time limitations. Case management is intended to eliminate many of the repetitive input tasks inherent in case management processes. For example information such as a client's name should be able to be shared with a word processor and other programs.

> One approach to case management is to use generic project management software. Though not tailored specific to the legal industry it contains many powerful project or case management features. Microsoft Project™ for Windows. (www.microsoft.com).

Case management software programs are different and do not all contain the same functions. The key is focusing upon the functions that are most important to you and the selection of software that meets your needs.

Shown are screen examples of case management software called Amicus Attorney™.

Some case management functions to consider are:

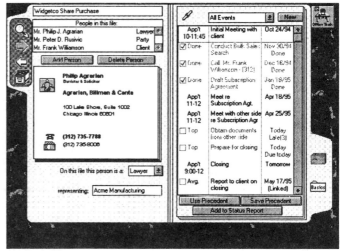

- Case information tracking capability – Does it track by case #, name, client, date opened, or present status?
- Document assembly – Does it "integrate" easily with your word processor program to create form documents?
- Timekeeper – Does it automatically keep track of the time spent on cases?
- Customized reports – Does it allow for reports to be created for your specific needs?
- Accounting – Is there an accounting module?
- Case document management – Will it index and manage case documents?

- Calendar or schedule – Does it automatically calculate court dates in conjunction with court rules of your jurisdiction?
- Ease of integration with 3rd party software – Does it actually "integrate" with 3rd party software or just export data to the other application?
- Can you customize the interface screens?
- Ease of use – Is it intuitive and user friendly?
- Technology up-to-date – Does it keep up with the latest technologies such as Windows 98 or Intranets?
- Docketing capabilities – Does it automatically calculate court dates?
- Conflict checks – Does it have the capability to perform conflict checks?
- Name and address book – Does it have an integrated address book that can be searched and also integrated with your word processor?
- Online help – Is the on-line help easy to use and comprehensive?
- Technical Support – Is there an 800 number and are the support personnel knowledgeable about their product?
- Import and Export capability – Can data be easily imported and exported to other programs?

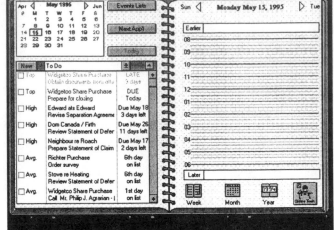

Personal Information Manager (PIM). A Personal Information Manager program is designed to organize case and personal information. Information such as names, phone numbers, addresses, calendar and court dates, to do lists, time and billing information and a variety of other information can be organized and accessed in these programs. PIM programs can be generic programs like Microsoft Outlook™ or legal specific programs such as Amicus Attorney™ designed for lawyers to manage case or transaction information, calendar and docketing, contact management, time and billing, etc. The PIM one selects should have the capability to share information easily with your favorite word processing program in order to eliminate re-entering common case data for pleadings, correspondence and other legal materials. Below is a screen shot from Microsoft Outlook™.

A quality PIMs program should have the following features:
- Calendar, Appointments, To-do list or Task Manager;
- Calendar reminders;
- Contact address and phone directory; and
- To do lists and prioritization.

Other features available on some PIM programs include:
- Docketing screen (Project and tasks screen);
- Time entries and timer;
- Client contact and case manager;
- Reminders, case activity checks;
- Outliner;
- Notes and attachments;
- Different view formats;
- Telephone dialing and call tracking;
- Ticklers and alarms;

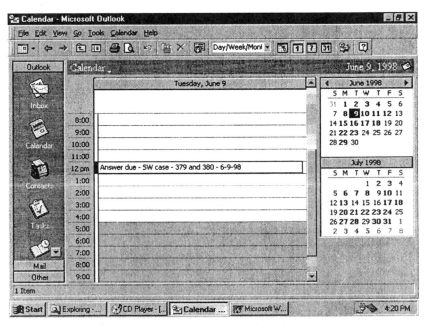

- Import and Export capability;
- Bring forward capability;
- Group calendaring capacity;
- Security features; and
- Database creation.

> **Electronic Post-It Notes**
> Automating your case will not force you to give up your post-it notes. They are now available in an electronic form to be attached to all of your applications. Post-It Software Notes – www.mmm.com

Products: Some case management and PIMs software to consider include Amicus Attorney™ (www.amicus.ca/); Time Matters for Windows™ (www.timematters.com); Microsoft Outlook™ (www.microsoft.com); GroupWise™ (www.novell.com); 21st Century Lawyer™ (www.21stcenturylawyer.com/); Goldmine™ (www.goldminesw.com/); Maximizer™ – (www.maximizer.com); Case Master III™ (hwww.stilegal.com/); Act!™ - Symantec (www.symantec.com/); ProLaw™ (www.prolaw.com); Pins and

> Vendors usually refer to case tasks performed by a legal professional as front office functions such as recording billable time or case management. Back office functions refers to tasks such as accounting, bookkeeping, ledger and billing reports.

Needles™ (www.needpins.com); Lotus Organizer ™ (www.lotus.com); LawBase™ Case Management System 6.0 (www.synaptec1.com/); Abacus (www.abacuslaw.com); and Compulaw™ (www.compulaw.com).

Timekeeping, Billing and Accounting

One important ingredient of a successful law firm is to have accurate contemporaneous tracking of billable time, subsequent invoices to your clients and an up-to-date accounting of your revenues and expenses. Time and billing software is being used extensively in law firms to track the time spent on cases and the resultant invoices to clients. Using this type of software can save countless hours of manual timekeeping and the preparation of invoices

The Timeslips Navigator - with its icon button menu bar and color-coded feature maps - allows you to quickly access commands and program functions. This innovative breakthrough of interface design takes ease-of-use to an even higher level.

since many of the tasks have been automated.

Accounting software automates the basic accounting functions of a firm. These include the general trust ledger, reconciliation, disbursements and so on. One question to ask is whether the timekeeping, billing and accounting programs are integrated or compatible with other law office software. Many of the products have incorporated additional law office function features such as accounting (general ledger, accounts payable, etc.), case management which includes docketing, conflict checking and calendaring functions.

Features and products. Depending on which software one purchases it may contain the following features:

- Time entry from desktop;
- Track time and expenses;
- Customized billing statements;
- Handle multiple cases;
- Provide an audit history;

- Analyze the financial trends of firm;
    - YTD figures,
    - Flat fee performance trends - profit or loss, and

- Summary reports by client and lawyer;
- Built in timers to record phone calls and other legal tasks
- Case budget for money spent and money available;
- Security access codes;
- Remote access;

- Conflict avoidance;
- General ledger & financial reports;
- Accounts payable and check writing;
- Mailing label generator;
- Spell Checker;
- Default entry fields;
- Customizable database fields; and
- Report capability

Products: Some of the available legal specific products include Timeslips™ (www.timeslips.com/); Tabs III ™(www.stilegal.com/); Amicus Attorney™ (www.amicus.ca/); Time Matters™ (www.timematters.com); PCLaw Jr.™ (www.pclaw.com); and Juris™ (www.juris.com/). More generic products includeQuicken™ and Quickbooks™ (www.quicken.com); and Carpe Diem™ (www.pscorp.com/). One unique product to move the information electronically to your corporate clients is Pro/Fee Electronic Billing Management software (info@dchcorp.com).

Word Processing, Hypertext Briefs, Legal Forms, and Document Assembly

The processing of words will continue to provide the most significant amount of use of computers in the legal profession. Our profession is built on the preparation of pleadings, letters, corporate papers and so on. We write, argue and settle cases using verbal and written words. It is indeed unusual the law office that has not incorporated the use of word processing into a large part of there everyday use. The volumes of materials discussing how to use a word processing program in the legal profession will not be duplicated here. The focus will be upon the advanced features of word processors as well as the integration capabilities with other software programs.

It is important to realize that the word processor is just that a word processor. It is extremely time consuming to enter data and generally does not save a significant amount of time in preparing repetitive clauses or documents unless you use its advanced features or link it to other computer application programs, most notably, a document assembly program. In this section we will examine advanced time saving features of word processors such as AutoText and focus closely upon the critical and important interface of word processors with a full-featured document assembly program.

Advanced Features - Word Processors

The two most popular word processors are Microsoft Word™ (www.microsoft.com) and WordPerfect ™ (www.corel.com). The following features are generally available in these two packages but may be identified by different names.

Macro. A macro is a recorded series of commands, mouse clicks or keystrokes that "playback" within a word processor, spreadsheet or other application automating repetitive tasks. They can add standard blocks of text and format documents to standard law firm formats. They can connect the word processor to other applications such as a case or document management system and database program. Creating macros is relatively easy in most applications and usually just requires one to turn on a recorder, go through the keystrokes, save, and name the macro. It can be played again and again by clicking on an icon to which it has been assigned or by pressing a preassigned keyboard command. Macros are generally written for tasks that are repetitive or tedious. There are many legal user macro groups that oftentimes share macros that they have created.

Revisions. The revision feature will show where text or graphics have been added, deleted or moved. The recipients of your legal documents can comment on, change or add to the document and you can view those alterations. Changes by various authors can be tracked to show who made the requested changes. Also, documents routed to other parties can be protected from permanent change until final decisions are made. Reviewers can add annotations without changing the content of the documents. This feature is very important when a document needs to be revised by a number of people. It saves significant time in eliminating the need to redraft copies and rechecking the entire document each time a new draft is prepared and routed to the various parties. Another program for comparing different versions is Comparite™, which is bundled with Cite Rite II™ and Full Authority™ and developed by Jurisoft (www.jurisoft.com).

AutoText. AutoText enables you to reuse text and graphics by clicking a button or typing a few keystrokes. For example if you type in the name of an AutoText entry say the word *Michael* and press the AutoText button then the AutoText stored for the word will appear. In this instance the AutoText stored could be the name and address for the person.

Michael R. Arkfeld
126 East AnyWay Lane
Phoenix, Arizona 85282.

This feature has many uses in the practice of law. It would be easy to set up form interrogatories using this feature by identifying key interrogatory questions by subject or event categories. For example, one could type in "Name" and click on the AutoText button and the interrogatory question of "State your name and any other names, including nicknames, that you have been known by over the past 10 years." would automatically appear. Another popular use is to set up boilerplate contractual clauses that would automatically produce a clause that has been previously typed in. It automates previous work by typing in a few keystrokes.

Formatting. Within word processors formatting text means changing the font, size, spacing and other character features. This is usually done on a per word basis. Advances in word processing permit you to now format paragraphs and entire documents to a predefined standard. After completing the document you then apply an auto-formatting tool to apply the desired pleading, memo, appellate brief format or other format of your choice.

Templates. A template is a blueprint for your routine documents. It can contain the fonts, formatting, AutoText entries, AutoCorrect entries, styles, and macros for the specific document of your choice. It can also be linked directly to a database to retrieve data important to the document. For example, you could have a client template document that would automatically fill out the client information, terms, etc. and format it onto your letterhead stationary. You also could fill out certain database records and have the database automatically execute a routine in the word processor to prepare a complaint. Templates combined with a powerful database can systematize most of your routine legal document work.

Mail Merge. The mail merge feature is misnamed and should be named Data Merge. The reason is that the "mail merge" feature enables you not only to merge names and addresses but any other data into any document of your choice. For example, if you set up a database to control deposition notice time, dates, locations and so forth that "data" can be "merged" with a Notice of Deposition document automatically to produce notices to the parties involved.

The mail merge function is an extremely valuable tool for the law firm. A partial list of documents created with the merge function could include: initial client letter, complaint, answer, interrogatories, request for production, reports to clients, enlargement of time notices to the court, firm revenue reports and so on.

Wizards. Wizards, experts, and coaches are features in programs that fulfill a request to make software programs user friendly. Wizards take you step by step through the process of creating many types of documents. For example one wizard aptly termed the PLEADING WIZARD in Microsoft Word takes you through the process of creating a pleading including numbered lines, correct caption, and so on. It reduces to a few minutes the steps necessary to create a pleading in a case. Once you save the results of your wizard as a template and set up a mail merge from a database you immediately have the beginning of a powerful document assembly system. Other document types that can be created with wizards include tables, calendars, faxes, resumes, newsletters and memos.

Other powerful features of your more powerful word processors include:

- Outlining;
- Envelope Addressing;
- Grammar Correction;
- Master Document Organizer for briefs and other long documents;
- Automate Table of Contents & Authorities creator;
- Undo/redo commands;
- Bullets and numbering;
- Extensive label and envelope print options;
- Customized toolbars;
- Drag and drop text;
- Spell Checker;
- Bookmarks For Documents;
- Annotating, Revising And Routing Documents By e-mail;
- Sound Embedding;
- AutoCorrect - automatically corrects commonly spelled words in your documents;
- Embedding OLE objects such as graphs, clipart, etc.; and
- Field insertions for automatically inserting dates, time, etc.

> If you have a need to create an index for a large document consider Indexicon™ software (www.iconovex.com). It automates the tedious task of indexing large documents.

The word processor is obviously an important tool in our profession. When it is combined with other applications and advanced word-processing tools it becomes increasingly valuable.

Contrast word processors with database programs

Word processors are not database programs. They are unable to structure a set of data, sort it, export it and create relational tables. Many firms try to control their document data information using word processors. The use of document information once entered in a word processing document is very limited. Use a database if you are attempting to control structured information from your litigation documents, document assemble legal materials or generate database reports.

Hypertext Briefs

Word processors now offer a feature to create hypertext HTML documents. HTML documents permit a user to click on a word, phrase or symbol that is linked to other information. After clicking on the word or other symbol you are immediately taken to this other information such as a case, etc.

After converting a word

> One of the first HTML hypertext briefs was filed in a federal case by the firm of Fish & Richardson, P.C. The CD-ROM brief was hypertext and linked to provide easy and immediate access to all reference material including cases, statutes, trial transcripts, patent office documents and video depositions. To receive a copy visit Fish and Richardson at www.fr.com. Another hypertext brief can be found at www.shsl.com/internet/supcourt/brief.html

processing document HTML it can then be read by Internet browsers. For example in several cases attorneys have filed hypertext briefs. In these briefs links are highlighted to indicate when more information is available. A cited case could be highlighted and then when you click on the highlighted portion it jumps to the actual case for the reader to view. One could also link exhibits, treatises, deposition pages or video, and any other text, graphics, sound or video. The defacto software used to create and present hypertext briefs is Adobe Acrobat™. (www.adobe.com). For example, by clicking on the case name <u>Borah, In re</u> it jumps to the case. This hypertext brief was created by inData Corporation (www.indatacorp.com).

Legal Forms

Be aware that there are hundreds of electronic legal forms available that may meet the needs of your practice. These legal forms can be copied to your word processor. Basic as well as advanced forms for virtually every practice area are available. Alternative clauses are available for different factual situations. Some forms even contain links to applicable laws, checklists, statutes and caselaw. Some sites to visit include: Legaldocs™ (www.legaldocs.com); Findlaw Internet Legal Resources (www.findlaw.com/16forms/index.html); Online Legal Forms (www.versalaw.com/versuslaw/forms/index.html); Legal and Business Forms (www.geocities.com/capitolhill/1802/buslegal.html); The 'Lectric Law Library's Law Practice Forms (www.lectlaw.com/forma.htm); West's Legal Forms™ on CD-ROM (www.westgroup.com); HotDocs™ (www.capsoft.com/index.html); and Informs™ from WordPerfect (www.corel.com).

Document Assembly Systems

In the practice of law the capability to automatically assemble documents can significantly impact profitability. Document assembly is a system designed to assemble documents automatically. If you prepare wills and trusts, corporate papers, litigation pleadings, retainer agreements, letters, or any area of law, you will benefit by setting up a document assembly system for your specific area. By automating document assembly you can reduce the need and wait for support staff to type and proofread documents. Time restraints no longer prevent documents from being completed.

Document assembly systems are systems designed to take variable or clause information from a user and generate completed or nearly completed legal documents. Variable are words, short phrases, data or numbers that change from one document to another. The names of parties to a contract, the payment amounts, completion dates and so on are examples of variables that change for each contract. Also clauses or alternative paragraphs can be inserted in a document the same as variables.

Document assembly systems are generally menu-driven, question and answer systems that guide the user through the document assembly project. Some systems simply request the user to fill in the blanks and that data will be inserted in the proper place in the document. Some systems can manipulate the data by performing calculations or formatting it in a specific way. Clauses and the user's own forms or templates can generally be added depending upon the features of the program. Document assembly systems are available for a wide range of law specialties – wills and trusts, litigation, contracts, incorporations, collections, evictions, partnerships among others.

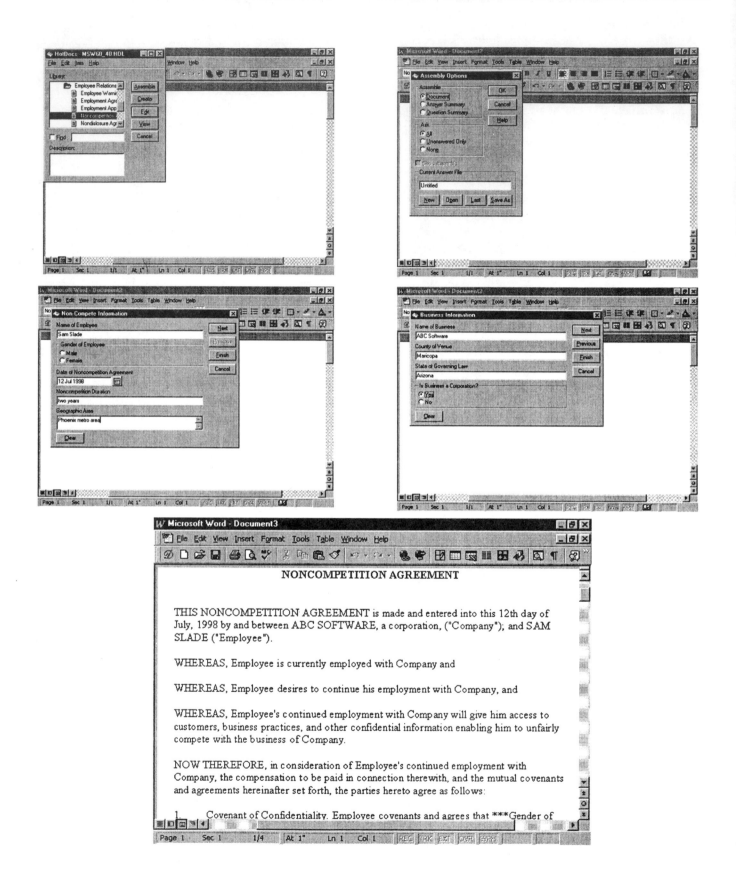

A recent feature to look for is the capability to fill in preprinted forms using a computer. As if using a typewriter a legal professional can fill in the forms on a computer. These preprinted forms can then be printed. The user can define the fields and can save the answers for use in drafting similar documents.

Implementing a document system is much easier with the new software on the market but certain steps should be followed:

1. Determine the specific practice area that you wish to automate. If your firm practices in several areas you may want to choose a small practice area to implement the initial document assembly system. If you have only one or two practitioners in the area it will be easier to agree upon the forms and clauses that will be automated.

2. Identity the process, documents to be automated and the shared common parts of the documents such as headings, client information and other identical information. The automation of your practice area will require a review of the present manual workflow process to identify the most efficient way to streamline the workflow. Also important is to assemble all documents and determine their interrelationship with each other. This will be important in later determining the collection of variable information and the order of collection. Also, identify the users of the systems to properly design the interface.

3. Choose your software package. Focus on what type of functions you wish to perform. Some of the software and forms available may be more appropriate for general practice as opposed to the attorney who has his own set of forms and wants to automate those. Determine how well the software handles an attorney's own forms and clauses. Another consideration is the ease of installation, setup, and user interface. Does the software provide case management functions along with the document assembly features?

4. Prepare a final version of the documents and begin scripting. Make sure you have final forms of documents since subsequent changes will impact other related documents. Scripting or setting up the conditions of a document depends upon the complexity of the document. This is tedious but important since it impacts the variable information entered, the conditions and final assembly of the documents.

5. Create and design the user interface screens that will be used to obtain information from users. Depending upon the software one chooses you can create user friendly but powerful interface screens. The user screens do not have to follow the document layout but can be tailored to how the information is accumulated or the thought processes of the user. It may be useful to develop written questionnaires for users if the information is not being entered directly into the computer.

6. Test and retest the document assembly system. Be sure and test the system before releasing it to the users. Input many different factual scenarios to check out the accuracy of the variable, scripting and the formatting.

7. Implement training and help systems. Set up individual and group training. Provide the opportunity for a resource person to help new legal professionals use the system.

Document assembly systems for your practice area are an effective way to automate the assembly of documents in your practice area and remain competitive with other lawyers and nonlawyers. Many states are unable to control the unauthorized practice of law and "document preparers" are continuing to provide legal services. One way to effectively compete in this area is with document assembly software. If the client or someone other than the attorney would enter the data into the database the attorney can then give final approval to the assembled document.

Many document assembly systems are set up for specific legal practice areas. They are set up to enable users to access specific forms and other materials for specific practice areas. In some instances they are set up to run with your favorite word processor and enable you to automatically assemble pleadings. They are usually jurisdiction specific enabling the users to know, for example, that a form personal injury complaint in New York has been reviewed by qualified New York attorneys who have conformed it to the local and

> One of the first seminal document assembly systems was designed and implemented by Charles Pear for automating conveyancing documents for the sale and financing of residential properties. This system resulted in obtaining new business, substantial new billings and much better service for their clients. Law Practice Management Magazine, Nov/Dec 1993.

statewide rules. Instead of using general "forms" which you need to customize to your jurisdiction these are already customized with applicable forms for your jurisdiction.

These document assembly or practice systems may contain:
- Checklists;
- Discovery;
- Form letters;
- Fee agreements;
- Pleadings;
- Motions;
- Pretrial Forms; and
- Jury Instructions.

Some of the practice systems available are medical malpractice, personal injury, products liability, aviation, bankruptcy, federal civil practice forms, jury instructions, California Civil Practice Forms, and Illinois, Louisiana, Massachusetts, Michigan, Minnesota, Missouri practice and jury forms. Since these desktop practice systems are being released on a monthly basis it is important to contact legal publishers for the desktop systems available for your jurisdiction.

In order of use the ABA 1997 Small Law Firm Technology Survey found that: estates, wills & trusts; real estate; family law; civil litigation (plaintiff); corporate/business, personal injury, and bankruptcy document assembly systems are used the most.

Expert Practice Systems. An expert system is an intelligent computer program that uses data and inference systems to solve legal problems, which otherwise would require significant human intervention. They are decision and advice oriented and differs from document assembly systems in providing a high level of advice based on logic as opposed to just relying on variables or clauses. Expert systems require a significant amount of time and money to develop. The resulting system can lower the per case cost and become a firm asset that remains.

Products: Capsoft Development Corp. document assembly products include the popular HotDocs™, HotDocs Pro™ and CAPS Author™. (www.capsoft.com). HotDocs™ is a document assembly and form automation package that can be purchased along with over 1000 general practitioner forms and templates or federal forms that can be used or modified. CAPS Author™ is the higher end document assembly software that can link to external databases, distribute automated documents using run-time modules, and other features.

ExperText (www.expertext.com) has a product for managing and assembling forms called FormBank™. It uses an automatic teller machine metaphor to deposit and withdraw forms for use by users. WinDraft™ (www.lawtech.com/windraft/) is a document assembly engine that works as an add-in to both Microsoft Word™ and WordPerfect™ and is built on the Microsoft Access™ database engine. Also, check with legal publishers such as West Group (www.westgroup.com) and Lexis (www.lexis.com) for document assembly substantive systems.

Integration of word processing with a document assembly database program.

There are two primary approaches for document assembly. One can use macros or internal word processing programming to assemble documents or one can integrate with "database" programs and merge data from the database into the word processing documents. Database programs such as HotDocs™ are created specially for document assembly. Other generic database programs such as Microsoft Access can merge data with Microsoft Word.

Many firms use a database to track case and client information. This same database can be "merged" with word processing documents to prepare mailings for clients, pleadings, etc. This prevents wasteful duplicative entries and ensures accuracy from a master database.

Generally, there is a master or template document that is joined with a database program where specific case data is stored. After the specific case data is entered, the database will automatically insert the data into the master or template documents and "assemble" the documents. It is not necessary to locate a "form" that was previously created and go through the document word by word and tailor it for the case you are working on.

Instead, the data is automatically inserted into the proper documents in the proper location without cutting or pasting. Complex, lengthy documents can be assembled in literally seconds after the key data is entered.

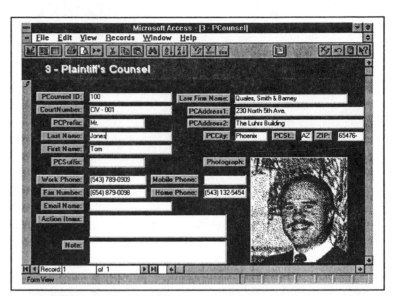

- This database was created in Microsoft Access™. The data on the Access screen will be merged into the template in Microsoft Word.

- This template form is in Microsoft Word. The data from the database will be automatically inserted in the fields located on the form. This form was created by following specific "wizard" questions.

- To merge the data one has to click on a button and it will create the document as shown. This 'template" can be used and reused for all of your pleadings in a case or different cases. The data in the database is linked into the word processor to enable one to reuse the data over and over without re-entering the information.

Document and Record Management System

Say the word document and record management to 10 different people and you will get 10 different definitions. Th reason for this is the words have come to hold many different meanings as we attempt to control physical and electronic documents in the workplace. Also, many vendors define their software as document and record management software even though they may only offer a few of the modules for a "comprehensive" management system.

Suffice it to say that the whole industry of document and record management is in a state of change. Additional features and pricing changes sometimes occur on a daily or ad hoc basis as vendors and customers try to figure out the best product solution and cost structure. Some of the common characteristics of a "comprehensive" document and record a management system will include:

- Storage of different document formats in a central depository (computer files, imaging, faxes, audio, video, e-mail, etc.)
- A Windows and web based interface;
- Controlling computer files such as word processing, etc.
- Controlling access to documents through security passwords, etc.;
- Maintaining a history of changes;
- Retention schedule;
- Archiving of old documents and restoration of documents as one needs them;
- Searching for documents by document profiles or other indexing and through full text searching;
- Labeling for paper files;
- Scanning and viewing of images of paper documents;
- Receiving, sending and indexing faxes;
- Accessing documents through a LAN, WAN or Internet;
- Providing for a customizable database such as SQl or Microsoft Access as a front end;
- Bar code tracking of paper files and documents;
- Sorting profile data of documents – such as author, client, etc. ;
- Publishing documents to an Extranet or Intranet for consumption by hundreds of workers;

- Routing documents through workflow systems;
- Marking up documents;
- Three–tiered systems; and
- Y2K Compliant.

The reality of case and record management is that generally you will be controlling both paper and "paperless" information in your case. Much has been written of moving from a "paper" to a "paperless" office and litigation system and in spite of slow progress many firms hold to the goal. Part of the reason for the slow growth is that most software packages focus on control of the digital electronic format of the information but pay no attention to controlling and indexing the paper in your cases that is not converted to a digital format. The documents in the law office of today are on a mix of media such as paper, images, microfiche, etc. To solve this problem-integrated document record systems that control the paper and paperless information in your case need to be used.

For example, Smeadlink™ is an integrated document management software product that allows users to select from modules to meet their current needs while preparing them for the next generation of document management solutions. Smeadlink™ users index, manage, use, and maintain documents, regardless of the storage media, in one software application.

Smeadlink™ is built around the Librarian which is the user interface and control center for all Smeadlink modules. All system functions are performed from this screen with the click of a mouse.

Librarian's tabset and tabs visual metaphor is appealing and intuitive for the end user. It allows users to quickly switch to any system component. Librarian allows users to search for documents using a variety of search tools. Once a record is identified, users engage the viewer to display images, faxes, PC documents, e-mail, etc. Librarian is built around Microsoft Access™ permitting the end user to customize databases for their particular needs.

The other modules include:

- Imaging. Imaging is typically used for litigation documents, correspondence, internal documents and any other law firm or court document that needs to be available on-line. After scanning the indexed document users can search for documents using Librarian, and once a document is identified, users select the record and engage the document viewer.
- Fax Manager. It receives, stores, and displays faxes, and then can index and route the document to the end user. This allows users to filter out non-record material prior to inclusion in the document system. Fax Manager also allows users to fax document images directly from Librarian with the click of a mouse.
- Bar Code Tracking. It provides tools for efficiently managing the storage and use of hard copy documents (paper and microfilm) in law firms and in courts and they also can be used for inventory control. Using bar code technologies allows users to quickly perform check-in/check-out functions in record centers and libraries. No more lost or misplaced files. The current location of a document can be easily determined, and the document transaction history is displayed on the same screen.
- On-Demand Coded Labels provides the ability to produce color or black and white labels as needed that match the database record exactly. This module is ideal for creating customizable case file labels for case record centers, central file areas, or by the attorney's support staff. It can be used to create new labels or match labels already in use. Labels can include readable text, bar codes, and color-coded indexing bands.

- PC Files allows users to index and retrieve documents created on a PC in the document management system. The work product of lawyers can be shared or retrieved instantly.
- Workflow automates paper and paperless workflow in an office or court. The workflow of most cases is predictable and can result in significant timesaving if cases are not bottlenecked at some person's desk.
- Archive Manager selectively archives electronic case files and other storage materials based on retention schedules.

Controlling Workproduct and other Computer Files.

One of the key assets of a firm is its legal work product. However, the amount of documents produced by a firm is immense and so a particular challenge exists as to how to easily save and categorize these documents in order to retrieve them with little effort. Once this is solved legal professionals are better able to serve their clients in a timely and efficient manner.

There are generally three methods of managing work product on your computer:

1. If you have a word processor than set up simple directory names and label documents in a meaningful way. So if you wish to locate the contract in the Groenen case then it should be in a subdirectory named /Groenen and the filename, if limited to 8 characters, can be Contract.fin standing for "final contract". Windows 95/98™ now supports long file names so one could label the document as "Final contract on the Groenen case. The important thing is to establish a consistent, uniform and easily understood classification method for all members of the office to easily use to label and locate documents. Classification methods can be based on the case, chronology, and/or categories such as contracts, forms, legal research, etc.

   In the new word processing programs built in document management features have made it much easier by to mange documents. They are called summary fields or properties of documents and are similar to a card catalog system. These properties or summaries can then be searched to locate particular documents.

2. The second option is to use a full text retrieval package to locate your documents. A full text package is able to search for the specific words in a document and bring back "hits" on where the document is located. The section on Full Text Search and Retrieval covers this topic extensively. However, you should be aware that Windows 95/98™ provide for the capability to full text search your entire hard drive or specific directories for specific words. Under the Start menu, click on FIND, and you could search for the word Groenen and all documents containing that word would le listed for further review. However, it is slow because the words have not been indexed.

3. The third option is to invest in specific products designed for document management. There are a number of products that are "integrated" and provide document management, imaging, full text and other record management capabilities. However the "robustness" of the individual components will depend upon the particular suite of products integrated. These document management systems typically create a library type index card for each document. Searches can be performed on the index card. Name, date, author, topic and version database fields can track a document. They can launch documents, implement record retention policies, and also secure access to certain documents.

Features & Products.

Some of the features to consider include:

- Version control;
- Archiving and restoration;
- Documents can be removed from network, worked on and then returned;
- Extent documents can be integrated with word processor;
- Control access to files, security, document distribution;

- Ease of use;
- Grouping documents;
- Ease of installation and maintenance;
- Management of word processing, spreadsheets, images, and e-mail formats;
- Groupware integration;
- Automatic document creation;
- Networked based;
- Database can collect information such as document profile, author, long document name, client, matter, typist, dates, comments, etc.;
- Indexing of the full text of the document; and
- Search capability by client matter, author, Boolean, keyword and full text searches

Products. Some record and document management products to consider include: Smeadlink™ (www.smead.com); FileNet™ (www.filenet.com); PC DOCS Open™ (www.pcdocs.com); Lava Systems™ (www.lavasys.com); and Worldox™(www.worldox.com).

Databases

Law firms maintain vital case and office information in databases. There are many legal applications for databases in the practice of law. To name a few, databases can be created for case document information, witness lists, employee lists, marketing information, brief banks, exhibit lists, work product information and conflict information. In databases you can keep all your data in one place where it is easy to find when you need it. Updating information is easy and when you need to summarize information you can create professionally looking reports such as an exhibit or witness list.

A database is similar to a common address book. As you place last names in your address book then when you need to locate a person by their last name you go to the "H" section or whatever section which begins with the first letter of their last name. However, what do you do if you remember the first name of the person but not the last name? In a manual system you literally would have to look at each name to see if the name "David" is part of the name. A computerized database would solve this problem since you would merely search the first name of the database for the name "David" and retrieve all records of persons with this first name. In seconds you could get your answer.

The primary components of a database are the table where the information is kept, the form where information is entered and the most important part the report that summarizes the data entered into the records.

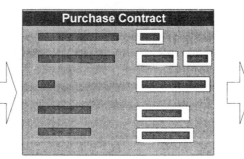

| A table keeps all the information about a single subject, for example, documents, in one place. | A form makes it easy to enter and review information about documents. | A report makes it easy to summarize and print information about the documents. |

Definition

In computer terminology, a database is simply a collection of mutually related data or information stored in computer record fields.

They are organized collections of information similar to index cards, phone books, manual trial notebooks or file cabinets of documents. Under either an electronic or manual system one has to input document or other information on paper or into a computer to later access, retrieve, and analyze the information. The immense advantage of a database is the retrieval time of databases is generally measured in seconds and not minutes, hours, or sometimes days. Also, once you enter information into these fields, you can use the SAME data in these fields repeatedly for other software applications and different reports.

A database management system (DBMS) is a set of features of the software that lets you manage the data in the database. This generally includes the ability to select records, delete, add, sort and so forth. The great benefit of databases is that they allow one to produce reports that lets you easily track and locate the data you are interested in.

> Database can be confusing when vendors and others talk about a "full text' database or an "image" database as compared to a "document" database. Technically a full text document can be considered as part of a database but this book will refer to these three concepts as separate and a database will be referred to as a document database or any structured database that captures discrete fields of information.

> A seminal study conducted by Price Waterhouse demonstrated the immense value of a properly constructed database. In this study a team of paralegals was instructed to locate in a document population of 10,000 documents a certain author who wrote on a particular subject. It took 67 hours for the paralegals manually to search through the documents to find 15 of the actual 20 documents that pertained to the author and subject. Using a database it took 4 seconds to find all 20 documents that pertained to this author and subject matter. The 10,000 documents had to be coded first, but the same coding has to be done if you are manually managing the documents. Once coded you can continue to do searches that take seconds instead of hours.

Components of a Database File

Even though databases have been used in the legal field for several years there is no uniformity in the terms to describe database components nor do all database programs have similar major features. Generally, the primary components to a database file are:

- *Database or Case File*

The computer records associated with one case are often referred to as a "database" or "case file" in most programs. These terms are often used interchangeably in database software programs and literature. On the right is an example of a case file containing a database in the Summation™ program.

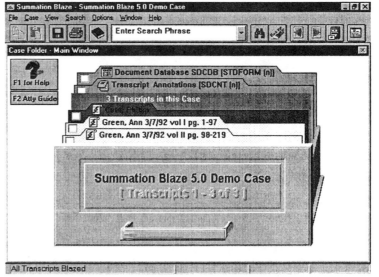

- *Tables*

Databases are based on tables. Tables contain the structured information that comprises your database. In some programs there can be one or multiple tables for a case. Tables are broken up into rows and columns. Each row represents a database record. Each column contains the mutually related data from different cases. Each item or cell in the row is called a field. A field is a "single item" of information.

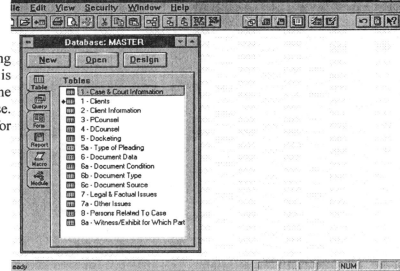

Tables form the underlying foundation of all databases. Once the data is entered it is stored in the database table. One can create many tables for a particular case. This screen is an example of many tables for a single database.

Form

A computer form is the data entry screen that contains a collection of fields. They can be custom designed for your case needs and design preference. Each name on the form is a field. Collection of these fields makes up a computer form. After each field name, information relating to that field can be entered. Once entered the data is stored in the underlying table. The form is the interface between the table and the data entry. For example, when a database is created in Microsoft Access™ a common field could be Document Type. This field would be part of the table. This same field would be placed on a FORM for data entry purposes. When data is entered on the form the data is actually being inserted into the underlying table for storage.

It is important that the database program software have the capability to create as many FORMS as you need within a single database file. Thus, within a document control application, you could create another form, such as the personal information about persons connected with the documents. Then, you would be able to add data to both forms to be stored in a single underlying table. After information is entered into these different forms, searches can be conducted into both forms simultaneously in the same or different fields to retrieve specific information or records.

This capability to create more than one form in a case file offers immense power to the creative user. Multiple forms make entry of data easy, since well defined forms can be created to collect specific information depending upon the information in your case.

- *Record*

A record is a filled-in form. The correct terminology would be to retrieve a record (not a form). Before any information is added, the screen is called a form. Once information is entered into a particular field on a form and saved the form is called a record.

*   *Field*

The field on a form is the location on the computer screen where specific information is entered and stored. All of us have had the task of completing paper forms that request specific information. For example, a request for your name would be included on a driver's license application form. On a computer screen, the location for your name is labeled a field.

After you enter information into these field areas, you can retrieve these records for on-screen or printed reports. For example, in a document application database, a field may be called DOC # that means Document Number. After entering document numbers into this field in multiple forms then, you can print a report of these document numbers along with information from other fields about the documents.

Field Properties

Generally, most software programs provide the capability to limit and define what information can be entered into a specific field in a computer form. These are called field properties, definitions, or elements depending upon the program. They control the entry of information into the field. These are important because it prevents you from entering the wrong information in the wrong field. The computer will retrieve and sort your information based on what has been entered into a particular field. If the information you enter into a field is accurate, then the reports generated from this information will also be accurate.

The following are examples of field definitions that may be assignable to define what information can be entered into a particular field on your computer form. For example, in the document date field only dates can be entered in this field. If you attempt to enter a dollar amount or text in this field, the computer will not accept it. Field definitions or properties capabilities will differ as to which database program one purchases.

*   *Data Type:*

The first attribute that may be definable for a field is the Data Type. Some of the data types that you can define a field to accept are alpha/numeric (A1000-A0010), numeric numbers (003,056), numeric range (34-56), dates (09/02/89, 3/13/77, 4/2/90), real numbers with a decimal point, text (Witness Jones will testify that the car ran the red light.), notes (some programs limit the amount of text), time (defined by hours, minutes, and AM or PM), or dollar amounts ($20.00). In addition to these main types some programs are capable of precluding or permitting other kinds of data from being entered.

*   *Data Entry Width:*

For each field that you create, you can also decide the data width of the field. The data width is the number of characters or lines that can be assigned for a particular field. In some programs, the maximum data width depends on the data type. For the data type DATE, the maximum length is 8 characters in some programs so 04/10/89 as a date is permissible.

*   *Unique Values or No Duplicates Allowed:*

The third field property that is generally available is to assign to a field the capability to provide unique values to data. This prevents duplicates from being entered into particular fields in your form. In a document control case, it is important that different document numbers are given to different documents. For example, if you enter Z0001 in the DCNO field and save the record, you should not be able to enter this same number in another record in the same case. On the other hand, the document date field would allow duplicates since the date of a document may be the same for different documents.

- *Validation Codes:*

When you create fields, some database programs give you the option of programming what information will be permitted to be entered into those fields such as name, issue codes, etc. This is called validation control. Some programs have Lookup Tables that are a sophisticated way to speed data entry and to validate information that is entered in certain fields. For instance, you can program the computer to accept only certain names of individuals, document types, or legal issue codes in fields. This feature is important to ensure accuracy in the entry of data in these fields. Suppose that you program the computer to accept only the last names of Jones and Smith in the NAMC (Name Code) field. Then, if you attempt to enter the last name of McCoy, the computer will not accept that last name since it is not a valid name for that field.

The importance of this field definition shows up later when you retrieve the names of individuals for sorting and reports. If you misspell the last name and type S-M-Y-T-H when you enter the data, instead of S-M-I-T-H, then when you search for the word "SMITH" the computer will retrieve all records that are connected with "SMITH," and will not retrieve the "SMYTH" record. Assigning validation control to a field prevents this problem. This will prevent the computer from accepting a name spelled S-M-Y-T-H if it has not been previously programmed to do so.

- *Required Field:*

The fifth definition of a field that you may be permitted to assign is required entry in a field. Essentially, this means that you are required to enter data into this field. Otherwise, the computer will not save the record. For example, you should consider making the document date field a required field. The reason for requiring the date field to be filled out is to ensure that the document record appears in the correct date location for a chronological report of your documents. If a document does not have a document date on it, then estimate the date if your program permits it.

- *Multi-Entry:*

Another field property one is permitted to control and define is called a multi-entry attribute. Technically, the multi-entry definition allows you to add multiple entries or indexes to a particular field that can later be searched as individual entries. In practical language, this means that if you have a field designated a legal issue code field such as ISSC then you can enter multiple legal issue codes into this field. For example, you can enter the legal issue codes - contract, breach, defective, and warranty - into the ISSC multi-entry field of one computer record. You can then subsequently search the ISSC field for the legal issue code "breach," and it will retrieve this record and all other records where "breach" is in the multi-entry field.

This gives you the capability to provide multiple indexing of information by using the multi-entry definition. This is an extremely important feature in the practice of law. For instance, you might have the legal issue code "contract" entered in this field in twenty document records. In addition, you may have entered the legal issue code "breach" into fifteen of those SAME records in this same field. The twenty document records also may have a field labeled SUMM, for summary of the document. When you search for the code word "breach," it will retrieve only fifteen of the records, instead of twenty. You can then review the document summary for these 15 records. If you search for the legal issue code "contract," it will retrieve all twenty records. Instead of having to create thirty-five database records you can use multiple indexing and create only 20 records.

Flatfile and Relational Databases

Flatfile databases consist of one table. This table cannot be "related" to other database tables. Flatfile databases can be effectively used in legal applications but are limited in their flexibility and power.

In a relational database information is organized into multiple tables. The tables are divided into rows and columns. A collection of tables is defined as a relational database if you are able to link them together using a field common for each separate table.

Relational databases and can be linked together to provide relationships for case management or law office management purposes. A relational database stores information in a collection of tables - each table storing information about one subject. For example, you may want to combine information from a Documents table with a Witnesses table to create a report showing which documents are connected to which witness. The two tables share one type of information in the case, the document number, but otherwise maintain unique data. Storing data in related tables is very efficient because you store a fact just once which makes retrieval and updating of the information faster.

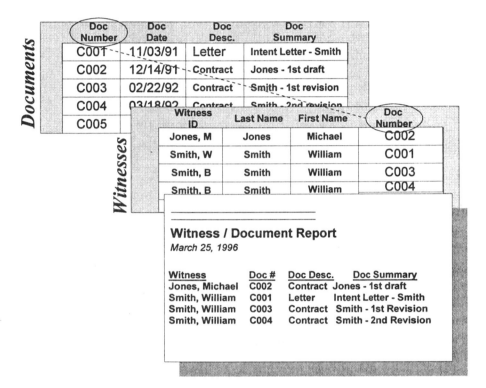

Modifying a Database

You may discover that in a particular case, another field needs to be added to your database to give you control over other information, or that you wish to change the elements of a field. For example, the date the documents were received by your client from the opposing party may be important information to capture on all of your documents. If so, then you should be able to modify the predefined control application form by inserting a field anywhere on the form to capture this information. Ensure that the software you chose permits a database to be subsequently modified.

> **CAUTION:** *If you delete a field or shorten the length of a field which has data entered, you may lose the information in that field. It is obviously best to modify the field elements before you begin to enter data into the forms.*

Database Report Generators

Database software should have a powerful report generator that permits you to create a variety of reports to view on screen, in written form, or save to a computer disk. The primary value of any database that you use is what reports you can generate using the data that you have entered. If you create a case file and enter a large amount of data information, but are unable to generate usable final reports, then for all practical purposes the information in your computer is worthless

Database Features and Products:

Databases can be as simple or as complex as you want them to be. They can have a few fields on a form to capture critical document information or they can be so advanced that they control your word processor in preparing certain documents on specific dates. It is important that whatever database you choose that it contain sophisticated features for future growth. Some features that you may want to consider:

- Fields can be user defined and are not fixed;
- Fields – text fields should have no less than 1500 word capability;
- How difficult is it to define the fields and forms?
- Indexing Ability - increases the speed of your searches;
- Fields - capability to add, delete, or modify during use;
- Support from software vendor;
- Multi-user capability a must;
- Batch entry available;
- Conversion or importing and exporting of data availability;
- Security features;
- Field definable by type of data;
- Vocabulary list or pull down lookup table availability;
- Global search and replace;
- Default entries;
- "Ditto" your previous database record;
- Searches should be easy to formulate and execute;
- Sorting on any field;
- Exploded searches - searches and reports based on multi-indexed fields are returned in one   report for each separate index;
- Multiple field searching - can search multiple fields at the same time;
- Ease of use;
- Can you create customized reports for your needs? Are reports easy to construct and does it have the capability to extract the valuable information you need?
- Are the databases and reports reusable for other similar cases?

  Products. Some database products to consider include Summation™ (www.summation.com); Smeadlink ™(www.smead.com); Microsoft Access™ (www.microsoft.com); Paradox™ (www.corel.com); Concordance™ by Dataflight Systems (www.dataflight.com); and Filemaker Pro™ (www.filemaker.com).

Database Applications for the Practice of Law

Databases have several important uses in the management of your case and law firm administrative matters. Databases can control in a structured manner case and law office information. Once stored the information can be retrieved, organized, placed in report or chart format, chart format, and used and reused in any manner that is important to you and your firm.

Litigation Management. Organization and retrieval of facts, documents, and their relation to the issues and witnesses of a case, can become a major headache for trial attorneys and can take valuable time away from developing proper strategies for trial preparation and presentation. Many attorneys voice their concerns over their factual material and repeatedly say that, "We need a system to index evidence. . . We need a system to produce a chronological report of the important evidence in this case . . .We need a system to list the trial exhibits in an upcoming case . . . We need a system to disclose which documents witness Smith is linked."

One widely used solution relating to their concerns is creating computer databases to control and organize documents, persons connected with documents and the legal issues that pertain to those documents. The purpose is to establish a computerized and controlled central collection of evidence and documents relevant to the case.

Will creation of databases linked to electronic images produce a better quality and less expensive product for the benefit of the trial lawyer and client? The old manual methods are too time-consuming, inefficient, and costly for adequate case preparation. No amount of clerks can find the answer in several thousand documents in a timely, meaningful way.

The law school teaching methodology of analyzing cases by identifying the legal elements and factual propositions of a case, and then identifying the witness testimony and documents that are connected to those legal elements can now be transferred to a computer. Your work product and analysis can be preserved and the reliance upon the human memory can be decreased. As the facts and documents of a case grow, your ability to handle complex litigation with minimal resources will increase.

Databases are not intended to serve merely as substitute storage for the massive volume of documentary data, but to manage the documents and have quick access to valuable information during any phase of litigation. Having this information available in this format will give you the capability to quickly locate, update, cross-reference, and reprint the document information in your case. Your valuable time then can be spent in analyzing your case for factual patterns that support your legal position.

Document Control Database.

One of the most widely used applications for databases is to control document information in your cases. Once you enter the dates of documents in the document date field, you can then retrieve all documents connected to a specific date or prepare a chronological date report of all the documents in the database. This information is extremely important in order for you to "analyze" the significant facts relevant to a case. For example, below is a chronology report referencing contract documents in a particular case.

Document List

16-Sep-95

DOC DATE	TYPE	DESC	DOC #
3/4/76	Medical Records	Plaintiff's records	100001
3/5/76	Medical Records	Medical Records of the plaintiff's second accident	10220
3/24/86	Manuals	Map handdrawn	##-trx001116
9/2/86	Manual	Table of Content - Rotary effect	Rotary
11/19/86	Other	Traffic Accident Report	##-trx001145
3/5/87	Manual	Automobile Dynamics Manual	Flip01
4/7/88	Manuals	Crawler Skid Shovel Manual	DROTT
5/4/88	Time Records	Plaintiff's time records for 1986, 1987, and 1988.	101
4/5/89	Statement	Witness Statement	##-trx001146

After properly structuring a document database, the following reports can be easily generated to assist in the administration and case management of your cases:

Discovery

- Were particular documents disclosed to opposing counsel and when?
- Which documents are protected from disclosure because of privileged or confidential communication?
- Are there any missing pages or illegible parts of documents that were produced?
- Which documents should be disclosed to the opposing parties' request to produce that pertains to the contract and modifications thereto?
- Chronological reports of the dates of the documents.
- Documents sorted by document type such as doctor's orders, lab records and so on.

Depositions

- Locate all documents that are connected in any way to a witness who will be deposed.
- Locate any person who has testified concerning a certain document.
- Which documents do I need a foundation that can be provided in a particular deposition?

Motions

- Which documents are available to support a motion for summary judgment contending that the defendant did not control the actions of an independent contractor?
- Which documents are available to support pretrial memorandum on whether the plaintiff breached his contractual obligation to pay for the products as delivered?

Trial

- List documents in support of major legal and factual contentions for one's opening statement.
- Generate lists of which witness will introduce specific documents, chronological list of all documents, author/addressee listing and opposing counsel's list of document exhibits
- Obtain a list of documents connected to each witness for direct or cross-examination.

Other uses of databases include:

- Correspondence, Pleadings and Docket case tracking;
- Marketing - mailing lists, prospects names, client information, lawyer biographies, marketing activities, referral sources, revenue information by client, marketing plans, activities and results;
- Conflict of interest checking; and
- Coding a jury database prior to and during trial enables you to assist in selecting jurors.

> **Myth:** Most attorneys believe databases are most useful during trial in that they will be able to mysteriously produce a key document to impeach a witness during trial. In reality, their greatest use is pretrial.

Database Link to Full Text Document Information

Databases are created to structure information into specific fields for later retrieval. If you conduct a search on the DATE field of a document abstract database then the dates of documents will be returned. Structured databases produce accurate reports. However, how does one "integrate" or "link" information from a full text document like a deposition with a database?

The structure of information in a "full text" document is radically different than the highly structured fields in a database. In order to link or transfer key full text information from a full text document to a database field some programs permit one to cut a passage from a full text document like a deposition and embed it into selected fields in your database.

These programs are designed to also transfer the name, volume number and page and line numbers from where the testimony was taken from the deposition. This would enable you to clip the key testimony from depositions for subsequent witness or factual proposition issue coding. The coding can also be done in the full text program itself for subsequent searches. Simultaneous searches can then be conducted over both the database and full text documents.

Another method is not to clip excerpts from the full text document but to search the entire full text document and database simultaneously. For example, if a particular witness in his deposition refers to ten of the document records in a database, then coding the deposition full text to the particular document database records will result in retrieval of both the full text and database records. If different witnesses testify concerning a particular document, then that testimony can also be coded and reviewed at the same time to discern inconsistencies, admissions, or damaging material. This is especially useful for pretrial preparation, negotiations, preparation of witnesses for depositions, and trial itself.

MYTH - Loading documents into a computer as "full text" documents is a panacea that obviates the need to develop a coding system and the cost of coding documents. Full text conversion alone cannot be substituted for a coded system.

Image Link To Database

Software now enables you to link an exact image of your important documents to document database records. They are then available for instant viewing at the touch of a key. If you have a question about a document at a deposition, or if you want to review the document while preparing a motion for summary judgment, then at the touch of a key, the document can appear on your screen for review and analysis. Imaging software also enables you to print an exact copy of that imaged document instantaneously.

Imaging enables you to zoom in on a portion of the image, flip the image from top to bottom, mirror the image, and change the brightness, contrast, sharpness, or linearization of the image. With the rapid decrease in imaging cost and the technological breakthrough with CD-ROM writers, imaging the documents in a case has become a cost-effective and time-saving feature.

The key to connecting an image to a database record is to "link" the image to the database record. An image is an electronic

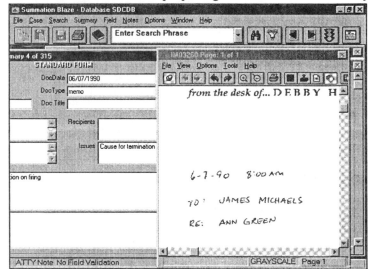

snapshot of a document. The words on the image cannot be searched since they are not in a full text format. Therefore, you have to connect the image to the database and then search the database for the image you want to view. Generally, one has to manually link the image to each database record and then the viewing of the image is always available. Systems have been developed to automate this process by saving the image by a filename which is subsequently downloaded into a database field. This downloading creates the "link" necessary for the viewing of the document which saves countless hours of data entry and linking. *See also, Chapter 7, Integrating Images With Your Database.*

Database Contrasted with Word Processing. You may have created a document, legal, or witness index with references to specific factual information with a word processing program. If any of the information changed in that index, then it was necessary to go back into the word processing program, add the necessary information, rearrange columns and locations of information, change numbering, etc.

This is not necessary if you use a database program. In a database, once you have entered information in a particular field in a record and you subsequently change that information or add new records, then the computer will automatically retrieve, resort, and REPRINT a report reflecting the changes in your case. This capability to reuse the SAME data for many purposes also applies to other fields in your computer database records, such as document number, document condition, persons connected with specific documents, legal issues, etc. This capability has saved law firms countless hours and one of the major reasons why they continue to use databases.

Conclusion

Database Advantages:

- Consistent objective coding will provide you accurate issue, witness, chronological and document information reports.
- Nonstandardization of terms is not a problem since the coder is reviewing and coding the relevant legal issues, objective data, witness references and document information. Retrieval of full text information is limited by the lack of uniformity of terms for witnesses, events, etc.
- It is generally less expensive to code, image and link the document to the database record for instant viewing then to convert and cross reference a paper document to full text.

Limitations:

- With a database the document population would have to be recoded for new legal issues or reference to a new factual proposition.
- Errors in database coding can occur where a search of full text materials will be accurate for the specific query that is made.

The reasonable combined use of databases, full text and images will provide the attorney with the best electronic control of his case at a reasonable cost. The database coded fields will ensure that any individual or issue connected to the case will be consistently coded, that dates will be accurately placed and in a retrievable format, and critical case objective data will be captured. Images of documents of these coded databases can be linked to a database record for instant retrieval.

Full Text Search & Retrieval & Optical Character Recognition (OCR)

Full text search and retrieval systems enable one to search for any word in a "full text" format stored on a computer disk and then go to that exact location. For example, if a lawyer were searching for the term "fired" in a deposition the software would immediately find the term every time it was used in the document. You can then view the word in each part of the deposition where the word is found. *See also Chapter 7, Deposition and Trial Testimony.*

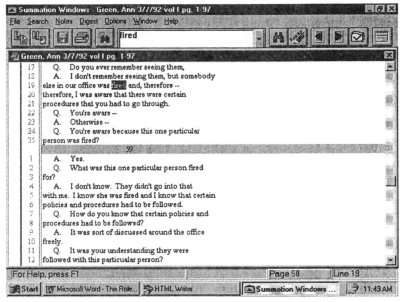

The next screen is an another example of using full text to search for factual information. The search was for the word "bronco".

A substantial amount of the factual and legal information that is important in a case is in a "full text" format.

Generally, a document is in a full text format if it is in an ASCII format. ASCII is a format that most computer programs recognize for transferring data between programs. Essentially any document produced in a word processor is in a "full text" or ASCII format. Once in an ASCII format it can be imported and searched in a full text program. The most noteworthy example is the deposition of a witness. Other examples of full text documents include trial transcripts, witness interviews, expert reports, e-mail and interrogatories, federal and state Rules of Civil Procedure, Criminal Procedure, Evidence and Appellate Procedure.

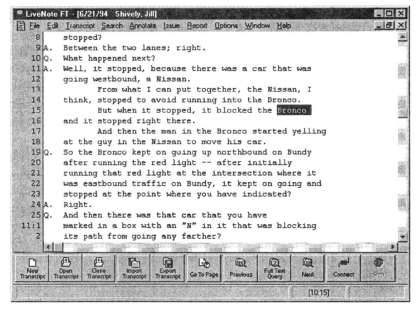

There are many full text search engines. For example, if a brief is typed into your computer the "full text" search feature of your word processing program can search and locate any word in that brief. In Windows 95/98™ Microsoft has incorporated a full text search engine labeled FIND to search for words on your hard drive and locate the computer files where the words are located. Summation™ includes a legal specific full text search engine.

All full text programs are not created equal. There are many different modules and intelligent search features that are not included in all full texts search and retrieval programs. For example, full text search modules in word processing programs are not tailored for the legal industry. They do not maintain the integrity of the page and line number in deposition programs and do not transfer the page and line numbers. If you want to clip and attach significant testimony concerning jurisdiction for a motion for summary judgment, it is mandatory that the deposition title, volume, page and line number be retained for your attached exhibit. Some full text programs retain this information while others like word processing programs do not retain this information when the testimony is printed.

Full Text Applications for the Legal Field

Some more powerful full text legal applications include:

- Quickly retrieving important testimony of any witness;
- Making summaries of depositions as you read the deposition on the screen, capturing any text in notes, and retrieving those annotations for powerful reports in a page, subject, or chronological format;
- Identifying and sorting testimony by user selected issues or subjects, i.e., subjects such as work history or educational background;
- Organizing all information witness Smith said concerning witness Jones and comparing it against other testimony given by witness Smith or Jones in other depositions or cases;
- Organizing all the favorable and unfavorable admissions in the case;
- Identifying and sorting events in chronological order;
- Organizing all material that supports filing a motion for summary judgment;
- Tracking testimony from multiple parties or experts about a particular issue or exhibit; and
- Pinpointing damaging testimony.

> Legal specific full text programs set their files up as "cases", "casefiles" or "databases" that equate to one of your cases. The use of the term "database" is confusing here since in computer language it generally describes a specific computer application of isolating specific factual information in designated fields. However, some software companies define all material that is searched in a full text program as a "database". Technically, it is a "database" of "full text documents". This is to be contrasted with a "database" where structured fields are created in which to store discrete identifiable information. With the risk of confusing the issue further, some litigators will create a document abstract database and then import the database into a "full text" program for search and retrieval purposes. For our purposes full text will mean a document that contains numerous paragraphs and is not contained in a database field.

Components of Full Text Programs

Below are the primary components of full text programs:

- *Case File* - A case file is a term that refers to the master file where all of the documents in a single case reside. A case file can be the name of a case, Smith vs. Jones, or the name of a specific legal area, Federal Rules of Court, Brief Bank, etc.
- *Document/Transcript* - A document is a complete unit of information within a case file, such as a deposition, witness interview, court transcript, motion, court rules, or procedures. Documents must first be copied to the computer's hard drive and then added to a case file before they can be accessed.

Note: Some software programs, such as DiscoveryZX, are provided "free" but require a proprietary format before the program will view the deposition or other full text document. The court reporter will charge you $25.00 to $35.00 each time a document is converted into this proprietary format. Therefore, anytime full text documents such as witness interviews, depositions, trial transcripts are to be imported into ZX you have to pay a conversion fee.

❏ *Search Mode* - Provides the capability depending on the sophistication of the software to search for individual words using Boolean search techniques, natural language or a number of the other search features described below.

❏ *Database Integration* - Some full text programs integrate a database module with the full text module. Generally, both modules can be searched simultaneously.

❏ *Voice annotation* – Some software programs enable you to insert voice annotations that other members of your litigation team listen to when reviewing the deposition or other full text material.

❏ *Indexing.* Indexing refers to the conversion by the computer of a document into a word index. The index is a list of words of the document which have been "indexed" according to which document they are in, page location and line location. Indexing significantly speeds up subsequent searches of full text software since the words have already been indexed and "located". This makes a difference if one is searching a large number of documents or a large document. If the documents are not indexed then the computer literally searches each line of a document for matches to your search query.

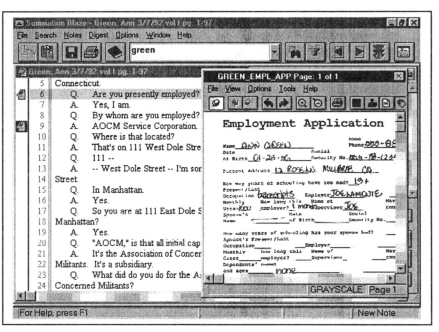

❏ *Portability.* An important capability of full text software is its portability. By simply transferring your documents to a computer, you can take your entire case with you anywhere you go. Convenient print commands permit you to print reports that summarize your notes and other information for use with your trial notebook, further increasing its portability.

❏ *Image Integration* - Some programs combine all three modules - full text, database, and image linking. The images can either be linked to a database record or to full text information.

❏ *Outliner.* Some programs like Summation™ have a built in outliner module along with its database, imaging and full text modules. Excerpts from the full text can be dragged and dropped into the outliner.

❏ *Attachments* – This enables the user to attach for viewing other ASCII, word processing, image, video or computer files to selected parts of the

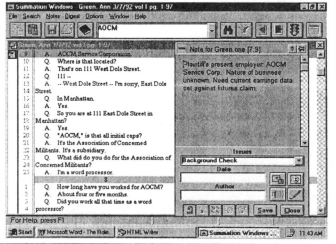

transcript. These materials can be viewed by executing a keystroke command or icon.

❏ *Display Mode* – This is generally the main screen for full text programs. The screen on the right is the display mode for a deposition in Summation™. It is here that you view the full text of a document and any enhancements imbedded in the text of the document. Once you are in the display mode, you can move instantly to any page of the full text document through a variety of commands, such as moving down one page, skipping to a specific page number, or scrolling the screen through several lines of text. While in display mode, you can generally add enhancements to the text, i.e., notes, issue codes, cross-references, or markers.

Enhancements

Some programs enable one to add enhancements like notes, cross-references, date references, issue codes, or markers within the full text document. Subsequent searches and reports can then be prepared based upon retrieval of these enhancements. You can imbed in the full text of a document, enhancements to summarize areas of interest and importance. These belie one of the most powerful features of full text programs because, when using these enhancements, you can place any information you want anywhere in the full text, retrieving it later for quick reference or reports. In most programs an enhancement will not actually become part of the full text, but "attached" to the text. Thus, while searching the document, you can exclude or include your enhancements in the search. The following is a detailed description of enhancements generally available in full text programs:

Note (Annotation) - A note is an extended comment imbedded within the full text of a document. Notes can contain dates, names, follow up codes and so on. Use notes to make comments that are far too lengthy for issue codes. A note can be searched for keywords along with the full text.

Cross-reference - A cross-reference is a word or words imbedded within text that permit you to connect particular words or full text throughout the selected documents. It is used to clarify ambiguous relationships. For instance, if you want to cross-reference witness Jones with his title, vice-president, his first name Frank, or the pronoun "him" everywhere they appear in a deposition, place a cross-reference code such as Jones wherever vice-president, Frank, or him occurs to create a cross-reference between the words. This link - between Jones, vice-president, Frank, and him - can then be searched and retrieved while viewing a full text document or for printed reports with the search request Jones.

Issue Code - An issue or factual code can be embedded in the full text document. For example, you could enter the issue code Damages in the full text to indicate a passage dealing with a financial loss. You can then search and retrieve all issue codes entitled Damages that were entered in the full text. Factual information in your full text documents located near the code Damages will be available for immediate on screen review or printing. If you use multiple issue codes, an issue code report can be generated in alphabetical order.

Marker - A marker is used to mark an entire page for future reference. You can use a marker to mark pages as a reference tag for important concepts or information. You can use it as a quick tag for admissions to use for summary judgment or you could

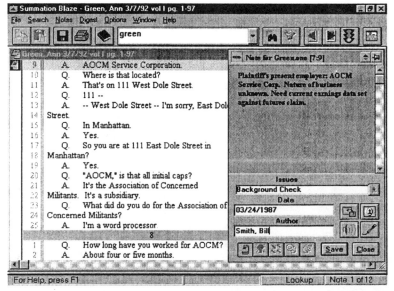

use it to mark testimony taken during a deposition or trial if real-rime reporting is being used.

Hypertext Links - A hypertext link is the capability to link together any two separate sources of digital information and then jump to the secondary source whenever necessary. If a witness talks about Exhibit 1 you can link and highlight the words Exhibit 1 and then immediately jump to an image of the exhibit. Some full text programs like e-transcipt™ (www.pubnetics.com) are set up using an HTML hypertext format.

Full Text Searches

By searching a full text document for important words or phrases you can gather useful and pertinent information about your case for reports. This area is where the greatest search advancements are being made. A variety of word searches are at your disposal, such as synonym searches, proximity searches, phrase searches, and wildcard searches. The searching of documents using full text in the practice of law is extremely important. Equally important is the ability to increase the precision of your search so that the number of return "hits" is manageable.

Recall and Precision. The goal of full text searching is to retrieve the information in your case that is relevant. In full text parlance this is referred to as recall and precision. Recall means to retrieve all information that is connected that *could* be useful. Precision relates only to those documents that *are* useful.

These two concepts are inversely related. As the precision of your search increases the recall of the number of documents decreases. If your request is too precise then only one or two documents will be recalled. For example if I search for "car" then I would "recall" all references to car regardless of which witness discusses a car. However, if I search for "corvette" then the search is more precise and the number of occurrences would be significantly lower. The problem with too precise of a search is that if the "corvette" is referred to as a "car" by a witness then you will not locate that particular reference if you only search for "corvette".

Every search feature of full text systems supports recall or precision. For example, how close key words are grouped in a document would increase precision but decrease recall. Wildcard searches would increase recall but decrease precision. The importance of this concept is that if your search is too broad then the number of documents recalled will take a long time to review whereas if your precision is reasonable then the number of "relevant hits" will be manageable. Recall and cross-referencing the text with keywords can strengthen precision. For example, some full text software offers you the ability to add synonyms. When you are conducting a search the synonyms would automatically be included in the search.

> "Regardless of the size of the library, no human will browse more than 20 documents to find what they are looking for." Paul Nelso, VP of Excalibur Technologies.

Searches. Below are a number of different search concepts and features that assist in your full text searches. Be aware that they are not part of all full text software products on the market.

- *Boolean Searches*. Boolean searches refers to a search for information using "AND", "OR" and "NOT" commands. For example, if you want to search a number of different documents such as depositions and witness interviews for the terms "driving' and "beer" then the search term would be "driving AND beer". If a document contained these two terms then it would be a "hit" and retrieve the document and the location where the terms are located. The more terms you include in the search with AND such as "driving AND beer AND night AND juvenile" then the narrower the search.

    If you wish to include more documents then use the OR command. In this example any documents containing "beer" *or* "driving" would be returned. This obviously enlarges the number of documents that will be located.

    If you wish to exclude documents then you need to use the word NOT. For example, if the important information involves driving and beer but that will return unneeded documents involving a prior boat accident involving beer and driving then the search phrase (beer AND driving) NOT "prior boat accident" would return only the relevant documents. A quote around the words "prior boat accident" generally directs the computer to locate these three words together. Unfortunately, there is no standard full text engine or command structure followed by all full text developers. Though many use the standard Boolean search format they will change how to formulate search requests. For example some developers require that combinations of words such as General Motors be in parenthesis or quotes while others do not require this. The software manual for a particular software product needs to be consulted for the appropriate search syntax to use.

- **Single Word Search** - Type in a single word for which you are searching. For example, if you type in the word "fired" all occurrences of this word in the full text will be located.

- **Wildcard Search** - The wildcard symbol (*) can be used with any search to retrieve different conjugations of the same word. Using an asterisk means that any word ending or beginning with the specified letters will be retrieved. For example, use the search request *tion to retrieve all words ending in *tion* or *auto* to retrieve all words containing the letters *auto*. For instance, if you type in the search phrase *process*, it would locate the words process, reprocess, processor, processing, etc.

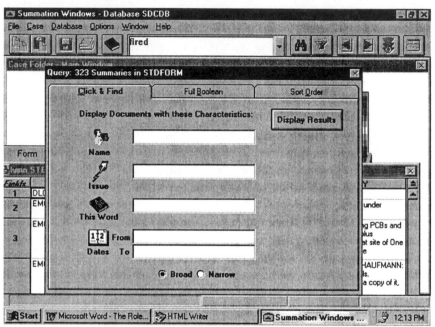

Advanced Search Features. The following are advanced search features available with some software programs. As you will discover the emphasis is on a sort of "artificial intelligence" built into the program.

- **soundalikes** - is a method whereby the computer will take a word and produce a list of words which "sound" similar. For example, searching soundalikes for the word "confident" would yield confidential, confidence, etc. It will use the consonants of the main word and will retrieve soundalike words.

- **Phrase Search** - The search phrase "General Motors" would locate text where the words are side by side.

- **Synonym Search** - Many programs allow you to search for synonyms. For example, if car and automobile are used in the document then when one searches for car then all occurrences of car and automobile would be retrieved.

- **Proximity Search** - To retrieve a word only when it occurs within a specific number of lines or words of another word, use a proximity search. For instance, to retrieve all instances in which car occurs within 3 lines of the word accident, type in the appropriate search command such as car /3 accident.

- **Combined Word Searching** - Combined word searches are used to combine synonym, proximity, and/or Boolean searches. For example, you can search and locate all words beginning with *auto*, but not the word *automatic*, and also get hits for the word car.

- **Similar document searching** - finds all documents that are similar to the primary document. For example, if you locate a particularly important document then the computer would analyze the document for keywords, location of words and concepts within the document, the number of times they appear and so on to compare with the other documents. Then other similar documents would be retrieved for your viewing.

- **Fuzzy searching** - locates words that closely match the spelling of the primary word. Many of the popular word processor packages have this capability when you do a spell check. It will retrieve similarly spelled words and suggest possible replacements. For example if the primary word is *liability* then the location of the words *libility, liable, lability* should be brought to the reader's attention. Fuzzy searching can be particularly useful when locating materials that have been OCR'd. (Optical

Character Recognition converted). When converting documents to full text using OCR software the errors that occur include leaving out or misspelling letters in words. Fuzzy searching will retrieve close spellings of those words for review. The sophistication of fuzzy searching varies from product to product.

- **Statistical Searching** - is where other words are retrieved that are statistically related to your primary word. Statistical association of words to other words is accomplished at the time the document is "indexed'. When a document is imported into the full text software the program produces a index of all the words and their relationship to other words. When you "expand" your search of the primary word it will retrieve all documents where "other" words are statistically related to the primary word even though the primary word is not in the document. When the primary search term is not in the document then documents that you would have not been able to locate because they do not contain the primary word will be retrieved.

- **Conceptual, Thesaurus, or Related Searching** - provides other words that are similar or close meaning to the primary word. There can be shades of different meanings to the similar words. Example would be the ability to search for the word "car" and hits returned would include locations of "auto" or "vehicle" automatically. Some full text software comes with a thesaurus or you can purchase a thesaurus that is related to the subject matter of your case. Some permit you to add or create a thesaurus for your case. However, this can be quite time consuming.

- **Topical searching** - enables you to search documents by topics and subtopics relevant to your case. You can provide weighted relevance to the different topic outline to retrieve only those documents that pertain to the topics and the precision will be determined by the weight given to the topic. This can especially useful if you know and can define the various topic outline - implying that you know the contents of your document set - in order to retrieve the documents based upon the weight you give to the various topics and subtopics.

Traditional search engines are based within the context of alphanumeric data and provide little help for locating information in visual data such as an image or picture. Software is now available to match photographs, video clips, trademark, fingerprint images or any other type of visual image. Excalibur Visual RetrievalWare – www.excalib.com

Topical searching offers an advantage if you specialize in a particular area of law and the terms as applied to a group of documents remains the same.

- **Weighted Relevance Searching** - will sort and retrieve documents according to the "weight" given to the documents. The weight given to documents will depend on the weighted criteria of the software program. Some programs will give statistical weight to the number of times the primary search terms are found in a given document and their proximity to each other. The purpose is to retrieve the most "relevant' documents first for your review. In comparison a topical search would return the documents where *you* provide the emphasis given to a topic - whereas the weighted relevance would return the documents where the terms are located most frequently and in proximity to each other. Natural language programs are using weighted relevance as they group words and return the relevance of the terms in close proximity.

- **Adaptive Pattern Recognition** - This system *indexes every letter* on every page. It learns and remembers binary patterns found in the text. When you conduct a search it conducts the search based on discrete patterns in the text. For example, if you search for asbestos then even if the word is spelled asbest~~ or abestos then the algorithm will find enough patterns to locate these hits. This technology has proven especially useful with documents that have been OCR'ed and have not been cleaned up after conversion. If one searches for the word "beer" then any word that matches those characters will be retrieved. In adaptive pattern recognition if the term is spelled be~r because of an untranslate due to a problem with an OCR conversion then the word would still be found based on the pattern recognition technology.

- **Associative retrieval** - where certain terms appear frequently near the terms you are searching then these may provide clues for further searching using the new associative words.

- **Natural Language or Non-Boolean retrieval** - instead of using and/or connectors you prepare your search request in ordinary language and the computer automatically converts it into algorithms. Depending on the software it can be extremely beneficial and enables you to retrieve exact information quickly and accurately.

If judiciously used with a clear understanding of its strengths and its weaknesses full text search programs are a valuable tool. An individual familiar with the vocabulary of a case can increase the retrieval of key information tenfold. Full text search advances are important to the location of information but the sharp persevering inquisitive mind of a researcher cannot be overstated.

Reports. Generating reports that condense and simplify huge volumes of data in full text documents will prove invaluable in your case preparation and trial. Using the report functions of full text programs can save countless hours of summarization and preparation.

Report options should enable the viewer to view, print or export custom reports to other software applications such as WordPerfect™, Word™, etc. Reports should be able to be created for individual files, issues, dates or keywords in notes.

Some full text reports along with the features are:

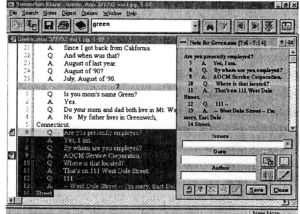

- *Digest* - This report allows you to capture manually a portion of text from within a document and send it to a computer file or print it out on a report. This is useful for digesting large documents by copying only the necessary and important information to the report. Advanced full text programs will automatically transfer the deposition name, volume number and page and line number to the digest, word processor or database form. This report is especially useful and time saving when you are combining all the testimony of witnesses to support a motion for summary judgment on a particular element of your case. Also, when preparing your trial notebook for direct or cross examination you can "cut" only the important testimony from a deposition and insert it into your trial notebook with all page and line numbers intact.

- *Vocabulary Listing* - This report will provide a compiete or partial list of any words contained within a document or case file. If you want, this report also can provide the number and location of each occurrence of a word.   Words such as asbestos, earnings and speed can be printed out with document, page, and line locations for easy reference to your full text documents. Such reports will increase your understanding of what the key terms are that are being used in the case. With this knowledge one can then prepare search phrases that are more precise.
- *Surrounding Text Report* - This report is similar to the above report, except those full text programs will automatically print the text surrounding a word. The number of lines before and after the word is generally user defined.
- *Enhancement Report* - This report will give you a quick and complete summary of the enhancements to your case. It can also generate a report of enhancements that occur followed by a list of the document locations in which they occur. Note that the enhancements can be ordered alphanumerically depending on the program. See prior part on *Enhancements*.
- *Date Summary* - This generates a report of your enhancements in a chronological format. If the time sequence is important such as in a malpractice case or contract negotiations then a chronological report can be generated based on the user imputed dates for certain events testified to in the deposition or in other documents.
- *Occurrences* - A useful feature in some full text programs is a display of all the occurrences of a search request. The occurrence display will show all occurrences of the master word by both page and line number.

Full Text Features and Products. Some full text features to consider:
- Indexing capability;
- Advanced searching capabilities;
- Report formats;
- Adding enhancements and annotations;
- Exporting reports or files to other program formats;
- Searches in both text and annotation (and database if available) simultaneously;
- Vendor history and cost of product;
- Ease of use and installation difficulty;
- Can existing collection of full text documents be imported?
- Is it scalable?
- Text synchronization with video;
- Cross - referencing links to sound, images and video;
- Voice annotation capability;
- OCR capability;
- Accepts standard ASCII documents without conversion to proprietary format;
- Training program and manuals and technical assistance; and
- Security.

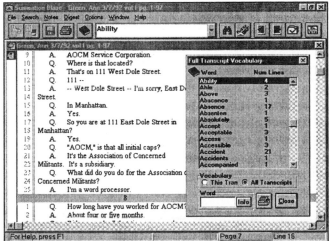

Products: Text retrieval software can either be generic (horizontal consumer market) or legal specific (vertical legal market). Generic software is usually less expensive and will perform full text searches very well. Legal specific full text packages are generally more expensive and are customized for use in the legal profession. Customized features include maintaining the name, volume, page and line number integrity in the full text program itself. What this means is that if you "digest" specific passages of text into a file that it will format the text with accurate name, volume, page and line numbers. This is extremely useful and efficient for attaching testimony to motions for summary judgments, etc. Other "legal specific" features include inserting enhancements such as notes, legal issue coding, dates, image attachments and cross-referencing. Subsequent searches can include the text, notes, cross-references and other enhancements. Reports are also generally customized for legal specific needs.

Legal specific full text software include Summation™ (www.summation.com) which includes an integrated full text, database, outliner and imaging program; LiveNote™ (www.livenote.com) which includes real-time and full text modules and e-transcript™. (www.pubnetics.com) which is a full text module..

Some generic full text packages are ZyIndex (www.zylab.nl/); ConText™ by Oracle (www.oracle.com); Folio Views™ (www.folio.com); Ipso Facto™ (203-726-1911); ISYS™ (www.isysdev.com); Fulcrum™ (www.fulcrum.com); Topic™ by Verity (www.verity.com); BRS/Search™ (www.dataware.com); Excalibur/EFS™ (www.excalib.com); and askSam™ (www.asksam.com);

OCR - Optical Character Recognition - Converting Documents to Full Text

OCR is software that can convert the letters or numbers that appear on a page to a bit mapped image and then into computer readable text known as ASCII. OCR software analyses the dots or pixels on a bitmap page and tries to figure out which dots are an "A" shape, which are in a "8" shape or other graphical shape. It than compares the character to its library of pattern templates. If there is enough of a match, it sends the ASCII equivalent of that character to the output file. The conversion of these dots into individuals letters will then form words. These words can then be searched

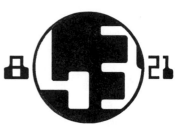

using full text software. OCR software will work well with typed pages but not as good with boxes, lines, or handwriting on the document.

A two step process is involved in converting paper into full text. First, the paper is "scanned" using a scanner that converts the paper into a digital bitmap image or a collection of black and white dots. Then OCR software reads and then converts the represented dots into alphabetic letters or numbers. Then the converted full text is loaded into a full text program for searching. Images do not have to be converted immediately but instead can be converted later if the information becomes important as a coder reviews the document.

OCR is gr~at, but how can I correct err~rs ~n the conver~~on to a f~ll text docu~e~nt?

The major issue in the conversion process is CONVERSION ACCURACY and COST. Depending on the type and format of the written documents, the conversion rate for documents can easily fluctuate between 70% to 99%. This means that only 70% to 99% of the document was accurately converted into full text. The problem is that the converted document has misspellings and unintelligible characters. The number of mistakes depends on the quality of the original paper document and the OCR software. If it is a first generation photocopy and clear type like a deposition then the conversion rate can be quite good - 95-99% range. If the 3rd or 4th generation photocopied paper has lines, smudges, handwriting etc. the general rule of thumb is that the conversion rate will end up to be 50-80% accurate. The accuracy conversion rate is improving and with the use of spell checkers and ICR, Intelligent Character Recognition, the conversion rate should increase over the next few years.

OCR software vendors claim they are 99.8% accurate but this only applies to laser printer pages that are with perfect, easy to recognize text. Generally pages are skewed, dog-eared, faded, faxed and have letters that touch, columns, shading, etc. What do errors cost to clean up?

- 10 seconds to repair an error;
- 60 errors in a page that that has been 97% accurately converted;
- 10 minutes to repair the page;
- Typist $24/ hour (including benefits) = $4.00 per page to clean up. (Many service bureaus charge $1.00 to $2.00 to clean up a page that has been OCR'd.);
- 100 Page document may cost as much as $400 to repair.

One technique used by many firms is to OCR important documents and not clean them up. Even if the conversion rate is 70% you still get hits on 70% of the recognized text. One can also purchase sophisticated full text software features such as adaptive pattern or fuzzy searching to locate words which have not been accurately OCR'ed but which will be located because of the similarity with similar words. In addition firms will use an abstracted database along with full text searching.

OCR Features and Products. Some important OCR software features to consider:

- *Formatting* - should allow you to recognize tabs, margins, boldfacing, underlining, italics, different fonts and varying font sizes.
- *Fonts* – should be able to recognize letters and numbers by font type. This increases the accuracy.
- *Preprocessing* – De-skewing is the ability of OCR software to recognize and compensate for paper that has been improperly scanned in. It should also be able to recognize and delete boxes from forms.
- *Zoning and forms control* – allows you to define an unlimited number of "zones" areas from which characters are used to create, index or populate a database. You draw boxes around these areas you define as zones. Zones are stored as templates.
- *Foreign language* – recognizes foreign languages.
- *Character files* - allow you to choose "numerical only" or "alpha only" so it won't confuse a "5" with an "S".
- *Image file formats* - Should allow you to convert common and uncommon image formats such as TIFF, G3, G4, PCX, GIF, Bitmap and more.
- *Output File Format* - The translation output file should be able to be saved in a word processing, spreadsheet, database or ASCII format.
- *Spell Checker and Context Check* – The software should offer suggestions from a spell check type directory for unrecognized words. Also check on letters or numbers in context so an "I" in a word won't be mistakenly recognized as a "1". Software should allow you to build supplement dictionaries of name and technical words germane to the case you are working on.
- *Type Size* - Can recognize characters as small as 4-point or as large as 72-point. Newspapers have 72-point headlines. Directories have a lot of 4-point type.
- *Control* – should allow you to control the scan dots per inch, # of pages to scan, and scan now and OCR the documents later on. Other considerations are whether you can OCR multiple pages and save all pages as a single file or as separate files. Can it scan a double-sided page and keep the pages in order?

Some products to consider: OmniPage™ by Caere (www.caere.com); TextBridge™ by Xerox (www.xerox.com); TypeReader™ by Expervision (www.expervision.com) and Summation™ (www.summation.com).

> ***Word Wand™ Scanner*** - This handheld scanner looks like a highlighter but actually scans and OCR's text and imports it into your word processor. The 6" X 1" X 1" scanner plugs into the parallel port and scans written text and imports it into your word processor where your cursor is located. Perfect for capturing quotes form written opinions and other written documents. (www.wordwand.com)

Full Text Compared to Images

Images are an "electronic snapshot" of a paper document. It is important to note that images CANNOT be searched using full text software. The words on an imaged document are not in a "full text" or ASCII formats. They are merely dots on a bitmap digital image. To locate a document image the image must be linked with an index or database. The database is searched and after the database record is located the attached image can be viewed. The cost of an image is approximately 10 cents or less per page. Converting a document to full text requires OCR software and if "cleanup" is desired the cost generally increases from $.50 to $2.00 per page. Images generally take approximately 50 K of storage for each page. This is to be contrasted with full text where a 400 word one page letter only occupies 3 K of space since only the words are digitized and not the whole page.

Limitations of Full Text

Full text conversion of your material is not the complete answer to controlling factual information in your cases. One of the main limitations to full text searching is language. The language used to describe any event is too variable. An event, person or concept can be described in a number of ways with different words. I can refer to a person as John Smith, husband, manager, friend, owner, debtor and so on. Words are inartfully used without standards among people. Another example is the use of medical terms among the lawyers, physicians and others in a case. Was it a broken arm, fractured arm, or comminuted fracture? Dates also pose a problem since a May 15, 1990 date will be missed if listed as 5/15/90.

Full text software still lacks sorting and precision in managing text in a structured manner. Full text software references text but does not manage it. Full text lacks the structure and precision of a database.

Should You Convert Documents to Full Text?

In a typical lawsuit, you will obtain written discovery from opposing counsel. These can be answers to interrogatories, tax returns, corporate documents, and any other written documents pursuant to a Request for Production or other discovery mechanism. After one receives this material, a decision has to be made whether to convert these written documents to ASCII full text, so that you can search these materials with a full text software program. Besides the cost of conversion, which may be substantial, one issue that has to be addressed is whether full text conversion will meet your needs to control the document information in a case.

There is one school of thought that all of the documents in a case should be converted to full text no matter what the cost. They will argue that this meets their needs for document control and that no database coding is needed. They will contend that full text searches will locate the evidence they'll need in a case. However, as discussed above there are severe limitation is locating information in a full text only environment. For example, will a search for "Mr. Kowoski" in 1000 documents that have been converted to full text, find all the relevant documents? Probably not, because Mr.

> A classic study revealed that a full text search failed to retrieve a significant number of full text material that was relevant to a case. The classic study commonly referred to as the Blair and Maron Report is actually named "An Evaluation of Retrieval Effectiveness for a Full-Text Document Retrieval System." authored by David Blair and Professor M.E. Maron. (Communications of the ACM, March, 1985, 28:3)
>
> The paper was based upon the massive Bay Area Rapid Transit (BART) accident case where a computerized train failed to stop at the end of a line and crashed through the wall and into the parking lot. The resulting lawsuits reached the amount of 250 million dollars. In the case there were 350,000 documents that were relevant to the case. One of the law firms "full texted" all the documents and reasoned that with the right search you could find anything. The startling conclusion was that the software retrieved only 20% of the relevant documents out of 350,000 documents on-line!

Kowoski may be referred to as a "manager", "Frank", "sales manager," or any number of other references other than his last name.

To counter the problem some attorneys resort to abstracting or coding the complete document collection, depending on the size of the document collection. This also had its inherent limitation because someone would have to decide the proper coding, certain codes may be missed or the coder might be inexperienced or inattentive when valuable documents were being reviewed.

Many of today's experts recommend that you use a combination of full text and indexing. They suggest that you full text the important documents in your case and code the other documents. If part of the abstracted documents becomes relevant later on then those can be OCR'ed and then added to your document collection. Also, with the recent plummeting scanning costs to "image" a document and the immense storage capabilities of CD-ROM the actual attached image of the document can be attached to either the abstracted document database or to the OCR version. The image itself can be converted to full text at any time.

Full Text Compared to Database Abstracts

Some factors to consider:

- Searches - In full text they are made against the complete text of the document - so there is no chance of not locating the specific information because of coding errors.

- Searches - In databases searches are made against the coding that is connected to the document. Abstracted coding may not have identified all the key words, concepts, issues, or persons connected to the case. In fact complete documents may be missing.

- Subjective coding - Aside from objective coding - date, author, etc. - the subjectiveness of the document coding is reduced by using full text searches since you have no one who is deciding upon the relevance and interpretation of documents and their relation to the case.

- Breadth of material - In full text once you have the document in full text you have the complete document always to search whereas in an abstracted database you only have the coded material.

- Use of Different Terms. In full text the use of different terms for the same subject or event results in fewer "hits" of the relevant information. This problem is solved by database abstracting since consistent terms will be used throughout the coding process.
- Costs. Depending upon the condition of the documents conversion of paper to full text and cleaning the documents up will cost more than the objective coding of a document and the attachment of an image. However, this will depend on the type of documents, etc.

Chapter 7 provides further legal application techniques for full text documents and techniques on how to effectively manage these types of documents.

Imaged Documents

Imaging is a technology that stores documents as electronic photographs in a computer system. These digitized computer files of documents are known as images. An imaging system consists of a computer, scanner, document management software, storage device, workstations, and printers. A page is sent through a scanner and "scanned". When scanned the document is converted into a "bitmap"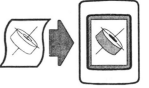

image. The bitmap is composed of tiny dots represented by dpi (dots per inch). It is then stored on a computer disk. After checking for quality the image is indexed for later retrieval since the image itself cannot be search. However, if the image is scanned using OCR software the words on a document are converted to ASCII machine-readable text that can be subsequently edited or searched like a word processing file.

This image can be displayed on workstations eliminating the need to retrieve the paper document. The documents can be retrieved in seconds and several people can use the image simultaneously at different locations and routed to different members of the law office. Space for paper storage is reduced, security is increased and original documents are never lost or damaged. Images can also be instantly printed.

Document imaging systems enable a law firm to manage and control the documents in a case by maintaining images of the documents in the computer. Key information of the document is indexed to identify the document for later retrieval. For cases the images can be viewed chronologically, by witness or by legal issue - it depends on how you indexed the document.

There are three primary uses of imaging:
- Litigation support; (see further discussion in Section 7)
- Archiving old files; and as a
- General filing system.

Imaging Process

Scanners are used to capture the image of a document or graphic into a computer. Also, with a scanner you can scan a piece of paper and later one can use OCR software to convert the words on the paper to ASCII readable text. This text can be imported into your word processing for changes such as a brief or interrogatories. Scanners have been significantly reduced in price. A high quality scanner can be purchased for $150 -  $300. Scanners can either be small wand like tools that can scan a few lines at a time or a 90 page per minute high-end machine. One of the primary differences in scanners is the resolution scanning capability and whether it is in color or black and white.

Format. The de facto standard for a document image is TIFF (Tagged Image File Format) which is also the standard for fax machines. A TIFF image can be altered and changed by simple computer graphics programs.

Scanning or Input. Imaging begins with scanning and converting documents into bit mapped images consisting of millions of light and dark pixels or dots. Most scanning software enable you to choose the resolution at which you want to scan the document. Resolution of a document is measured in dpi or dots per inch. The resolution you select depends on how sharp you want the image to be. The higher the dpi the sharper the image and the more storage it takes. For this reason most documents are scanned at 200 dpi unless they are needed for presentation purposes like in court then they are scanned in at least 300 dpi.

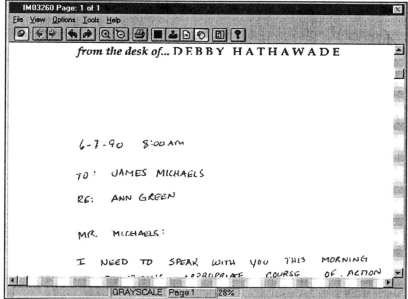

Storage and Retrieval. Images can be stored on floppies, hard drives, optical disks or on CD-ROM. The primary storage device is CD-ROM and is the major reason why imaging was not popular prior to the CD-ROM revolution is that there was no low cost storage media available to handle the large amounts of storage required for images. Per image it requires approximately 20,000 - to 50,000 bytes of space so 50 - 100 images will require approximately 1 to 5 megabytes of storage. A CD-ROM can hold up to 15,000 document pages depending on the density of the document and the dpi the document is scanned.

Images are generally retrieved using a CD-ROM player. CD-ROM players are built to hold one, 4, 6, or hundreds of CD-ROM Disks. The larger players are referred to as jukeboxes since they resemble the old jukeboxes that played records.

Output. Images can either be viewed on your monitor or printed out. Generally after searching a database the multiple records and images linked to the records are printed for trial books or witness kits, etc.

Integration and linking to full text or databases. An image is a piece of electronic paper. Like actual paper it cannot be searched for specific words like full text documents. For this reason your imaged documented must be LINKED to an index, database, or full text document. Then when you want to retrieve the document locate in your database the abstract of the record and the image will be linked to that record. The image can then be retrieved for viewing.

Benefits and Costs of Imaging System

The decision whether to digitize the documents in your case will turn on a number of factors listed below. It is suggested that the digitization of the documents in your case first be done on a small or test case to understand the benefits and pitfalls of these different methods of digitally organizing your case

Image vs. Paper Comparison

	Imaging	Paper
WORKFLOW FACTORS		
Accessibility	Instant Electronic access	Slow and inefficient
Multiple Party Access	Multiple party access available	Limited access when needed by multiple parties - depends on # of copies and location.
Concurrent Access	Concurrent user access available	Depends on number of paper copies.
Lost or misplaced files	Cannot be lost or misfiled. Caution: You can misindex a document then it would be difficult to locate	Misfiled and out of file problems
Environmental Impact	Environmentally helpful - requires CD-ROM or other storage media.	Trees and processing costs.
Indexing	Required	Required
Security of Stored Documents	Depends on the user's computer accessibility	Depends on paper procedures and location

Witness Review of Documents	Can easily "blowback" or print copies.	Need to copy documents.
Remote Access	Available using CD-ROM, Internet or modem accessibility. Viewing images may be slow depending on bandwidth connection.	Available if paper copies are at remote location.
COST FACTORS		
Storage Cost	Low	High
Labor and Access Cost	Low	High
Cost per Image	10 cents + per page. The cost will vary depending upon the quality and condition of the documents to be scanned	N/A
Cost to Copy	$100 per CD-ROM disk - up to 15,000 images or pages on disk.	8 cents + per page
Cost to Print	8 cents + per page	8 cents + per page
Shipping Costs	Low	High
Disaster Recovery Cost	Low - copy of images can be stored off-line.	Another copy of paper must be stored off site.
Software Cost	Free+. Some service firms are giving away image display software and are focusing on the profits generated from scanning your paper to create images.	None
Cost of Equipment	Use present computers, monitors. network and CD-ROM readers. CD-ROM readers cost $150+. May need to upgrade printer speeds and monitor size.	Paper, three ring binders, file cabinets & bookcases

The Sierra Club Legal Defense Fund calculated that California courts receive at least "293, 776,455 sheets of 20-pound bond a year - 1,470 tons of paper" ABA Journal/October 1992. Switching to imaged documents would not only save trees but the resources necessary to process the paper.

Features and Products

Image retrieval software enables the user to display, manipulate, print hard copies as well as perform a host of other functions.

- *Image Movement Features.* Most image programs give you the capacity to manipulate the images in a variety of ways. Enlarge - by moving a pointer over a specific area you can enlarge that area for review. Rotate - if you want to rotate the document 360 degrees then rotation tools will permit this.
- *OCR Conversion* - once the document is an image you can block out parts of the document to permit OCR conversion and then transfer the converted text for full text searching into a database or full text program.

- *Highlighting.* You can use a marking device like a mouse or a light pen to highlight the text. These tools generally include yellow blocking features or marking in red, blue, green, etc.
- *Notes.* If you wish to add a note to the document then you can add personal notes about the document for later searching and retrieval.
- *Printing.* You can flag the documents that you want printed as you review them and then batch print them.
- *Page Functions* - Provides the capability to page through a document or GO TO a specific page.
- *Redaction.* More sophisticated programs permit the ability to black out or redact certain portions of the document because it is privileged or work product. When printed the redaction covers up the blacked out portion.

Some considerations in selecting an imaging system include:

- Scalability as your imaging system grows;
- How many documents will be imaged?
- Does it use standard TIFF format or is the format proprietary?
- Is it going to be networked?
- Is there a need for a CD-ROM jukebox and will it be compatible with your imaging software?
- Does it provide for OCR capability?
- Also see scanners and storage devices in Section 2, Hardware and Software.

Some products to consider ScanRevolution™ (www.indatacorp.com) Smeadlink™ (www.smead.com); LaserFiche™ (www.laserfiche.com); Watermark™ (www.filenet.com); and Opticon™ (www.dataflight.com).

Encryption of Images

Encryption is the process of encrypting an image to prevent it from being later altered. Most image formats were created and are used by the publishing industry. The images in this format are easily alterable in paintbrush programs. The publishing industry needs to be able to ALTER the image for advertising purposes and so forth. The problem in our profession is that the document image we use should never have the capability of being altered or it may present problems in having this image or document admitted into court.

ISII Standard. One encryption standard is use today is the ISII standard. ISII stands for International Standards for Image Identification. ISII format represents a means whereby scanned document images can be traced back to the point of origin by use of a uniquely assigned 31 character alphanumeric id. The format of an ISII Descriptor number code which is on every image is:

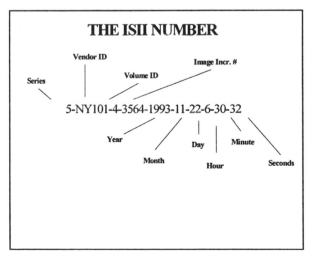

BP	Field name	Content
01	Series	Number
02-06	Vendor ID	Number
07-12	Volume ID	Number
13-17	Image Incr.#	Number
18-21	Year from 1-9999	Digits
22-23	Month from 1-12	Digits
24-25	Day from 1-31	Digits
26-27	Hour 0-23	Digits
28-29	Minute - 0-59	Digits
30-31	Seconds 0-59	Digits

Comparison of ISII and Tiff/PCX

ISII	Tiff/PCX
1. Secured	1. Unsecured
2. Audit Trail	2. No Audit Trail
3. Unique ID #	3. No Unique #
4. One Format	4. TIFF - 30 Formats
5. Organized	5. Unorganized
6. Unlimited Integration	6. Limited Integration
7. Made for CD-ROM & Legal Document Management	7. Made for Publishing

On-line and CD-ROM - Legal and Factual information Databases

Introduction

Robert Berring, Professor of Law, University of California, Berkeley School of Law, has recognized a changing legal and factual research paradigm:

> "I believe that we are in the middle of a shift, a generational change really, in the way people use information. On one side of the divide are people who primarily use books as their source of information and who view printed information as the only valid form of information.
>
> On the other side are people who see information as divorced from its format. Be it on a page, on a terminal or in some other electric form, information is information.
>
> This shift is especially important in the field of law because law is so centered on its research process."

Professor Berring believes the paradigm shift is occurring because of "overload". "There is simply too much stuff. One hundred and twenty thousand cases entering into our system every year, two million sections of statutes enacted throughout the country - there is simply too large an amount available for any individual to intelligently sort through."

Traditionally lawyers have used books, books, and more books to research the "law". This time consuming task of locating materials in musty, dusty libraries was oftentimes considered a badge of honor, especially when you were able to locate the "case". The major paradigm shift in legal research occurred approximately 15 years ago with the introduction of the "on-line" legal research databases. These subscription on-line services such as Westlaw, Lexis and LOIS can locate a list of cases from anywhere in the country in seconds. What use to take days and hours has now been reduced to seconds.
The downside is the per minute cost, fixed location, and necessity to rely upon the phone line, modem, and other necessary equipment. It has not been economically feasible to spend hours viewing a terminal analyzing the cases because of the $3.00 to $4.00 costs per minute to be on-line. This is changing with free Internet legal sites and CD-ROM availability.

Lawyers in all areas of their practice need information and more information. Concise and relevant information can assist you in all phases of the legal process. From drafting a contract pre-lawsuit analysis, drafting pleadings, filing briefs/motions, discovery, and trial and post trial research information is needed

Below are examples of questions that could be answered using free or fee based on-line sources and CD-ROM disks that are currently available:

Product Liability
- Get the financial profile of a manufacturer and/or parent company named in your product liability suit.
- Search the literature to locate any discussions of a product in question regarding warnings or performance concerns.
- Acquire documentation of the standards and specifications for a type of product to determine if the manufacturer was in compliance.

Medical Malpractice
- Determine if a failed surgical procedure performed on a client was appropriate for his condition.
- Learn the long-term psychological ramifications for a client who has been paralyzed or permanently injured.
- Obtain documentation regarding the side effects of drugs prescribed for your client.
- Search medical literature to determine if a course of treatment or level of care were outside of established norms.
- What are the latest medical articles on lung cancer?

Business
- Search for trademark infringement.
- Create a financial profile of a company, credit history, corporate affiliations, etc.
- Obtain copies of newspapers that contain references to an individual, product or business entity.
- What government contract provisions are mandatory in all Department of Transportation contracts?
- What is needed to prepare an agreement in conformity with the Uniform Commercial Code to sell 500,000 yards of cloth to a clothing manufacturer?
- Did Dimension Cable Corporation make a profit in 1991?
- What is the Dun & Bradstreet's rating for XYZ Corporation?
- Did ABC Corporation have a copyright on their research documents?
- What federal statutes are applicable to a defendant's proposed stock offering?
- What legal publications have discussed the venue requirements of a corporation incorporated in Delaware, but doing mail order business in other states?
- What federal regulations apply to the use of a new pesticide?

Court Rules
- Will the affidavit of the plaintiff's attorney create a genuine issue of fact to preclude a motion for summary judgment?
- What are the complaint pleading requirements for a case in the California courts?
- What are the applicable Rules of Procedure for litigation in Texas?

Litigation
- What is the personal income data for the juror's county in Omaha, Nebraska?
- What interrogatories should be sent on a wrongful death case?

General
- What effect would a Chapter 11 filing by the plaintiff have on a particular case?
- What tax consequences occur if a defendant settles with the plaintiff?

"We always made the library very important. It kind of represented the intellectual capital or the knowledge bank of law and it was very important to express that, . . . I think today that information is ubiquitous. We get it everywhere. So, the significance of the library as a repository of information is less of an importance." - Doug Zucker, Gensler Associates, Law Office Designers

- How many lawyers and what are their areas of expertise, in the law firm of Frank and Howard in Houston, Texas?

Law Firm Information Sources

Within any legal organization there are generally three information hierarchies: on-line databases, CD-ROM, and printed materials. Traditionally print material has been the main source of information. However, with the phenomenal emergence of the Internet and proliferation of CD-ROMs law firm information sources have changed dramatically in the last few years.

On-line legal databases have been available since the 1980's but legal publishers' high prices kept most practitioners away from these services other than to perform initial case listing research. Today in some respects, practitioners continue to use books since they are not being charged by the minute. Recently, with the advent of the Internet and CD-ROM, prices of electronic access to caselaw and written materials has changed considerably. This has required legal organizations to rethink what type and combination of legal materials will comprise their libraries – electronic and/or print. The available sources include on-line databases, CD-ROM and printed material.

On-line Databases

On-line databases are any information stored in computers located anywhere in the world that can be accessed through the use of another computer. When you call into the database you are "on-line". On-line databases are available in both the legal and nonlegal area. With the emergence of the Internet on-line databases have grown in use and popularity. For example, the Arizona Legislature has made available for FREE on the Internet the Arizona Revised Statutes and Constitution. These statutes can be searched by using a full text search engine on-line and then downloading or printing the material you want. This site also offers session Laws (chapters), Bills (Printed and Engrossed versions), Adopted Amendments, Calendars (Caucus, COW, Third reading, etc.), Committee Agendas and Bill overview (Status of Bill). The site address is www.azleg.state.az.us/. This is but one of thousands of legal Internet WWW sites where valuable legal and nonlegal information can be found.

Legal Database Services. The three largest on-line fee legal database services are LOIS (www.loislaw.com), Westlaw, and Lexis-Nexis. We think of these three services as being primarily law related. However, they have greatly expanded their secondary legal and non-legal resource materials. Lexis-Nexis provides on-line extensive information on cases, statutes, SEC filings, bill tracking, medical databases, law reviews, patents, jury verdicts among many other databases.

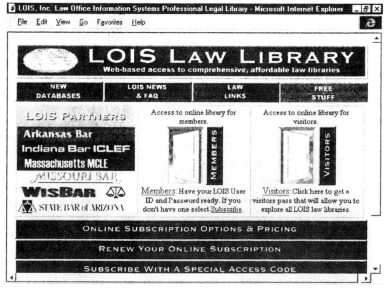

Westlaw now offers jurisdictional materials, news and information, practice area materials, texts and periodicals.

Westlaw has several hundred additional database files available by their addition of Dialog. They also have added the materials from the Dow-Jones News Retrieval databases providing access to several hundred newspapers and other valuable material on-line. (www.westgroup.com).

LOIS offers CLE material from many of the state bars from across the country in addition to primary law, statutes, court rules, etc. (www.pita.com).

Some factors to consider when using on-line services:
- Per minute charges;
- Free;
- Monthly subscriptions;
- Considerations for choosing a particular database;
- Content – what meets your needs; and
- Access speed.

Search engines for legal information. There are thousands of informational databases available on-line. These databases contain valuable information for your cases. Whether it is a commercial, domestic relations, child support, products liability, environmental toxic tort case legal and factual information for your case is available. Some of these on-line databases are free to search to your heart's content. Others cost hundreds of dollars per hour to search which place a premium on efficient search techniques.

However, there is no common "search engine" that is available to search all of these databases. Some valuable on-line databases are coupled with full text search engines that are difficult to use because of outdated command structures.

The first generation, and still used today, are the Boolean logic, and structured commands search engines that are difficult for the end user. Newer search engines employing techniques such as natural language, relevance or word frequency ranking and automatic thesaurus features are now being used by many databases. For example, Personal Librarian was the first commercial application to offer natural language. Users can formulate their query in a natural language sentence structure. Thus, the search phrase " I need information about the responsibility of a rescuer of distressed property" will be sufficient as a search query. It then ranks the documents according to relevance. Relevance depends upon how many times a word occurs in a document, the documents length and other factors. They can be used for CD-ROM or on-line services.

Search Engines for the WWW. There are several full text search engine WWW sites on the Internet to assist you in locating specific factual or legal information from any of the thousands of WWW pages. Many of these search sites have "indexed" the web sites to provide quick results to your search requests. They are essential to locating legal and nonlegal information if you do not already have the web address or URL. The most popular search engine sites include:

- Yahoo! (www.yahoo.com) organizes sites by category and allows for full text searching and
- Alta Vista (*www.altavista.digital.com*) catalogs individual web pages and is one of the faster search engines on the Internet.

- Other search engines include Excite (*www.excite.com*); Infoseek (ww.infoseek.com); Magellan (*www.magellan.mckinley.com*); and Lycos (*www.lycos.com*).

> For an excellent book on business research consider the *Business Research Handbook: Methods and Sources for Lawyers and Business Professionals* by Kathy Shimpock. Aspen Law & Business, 1 vol. looseleaf (updated twice a year). Call 1-800-638-8437 or order it from www.amazon.com.

Excellent sources for how to search on-line databases are the law librarians at law schools or at law firms in the community. The law librarians association is taking aggressive steps not to be left behind with the paperless changeover and could emerge as the future "information brokers" of the computer revolution.

Internet Sites

See *Chapter 4, Internet and Telecommunications* for a listing of WWW Internet search engines and legal and nonlegal sites for the legal practitioner.

CD-ROM

The cost of buying and storing written legal material is immense and firms will seek alternatives to maintaining their own vast libraries. One of those alternatives is CD-ROM technology. CD-ROM technology enables you to focus on a select group of materials for a fixed fee with no time limit.

All of us have had that queasy feeling while searching on-line database services that charge by the minute whether you are efficiently locating the information you need. It is similar to hiring a taxicab for the first time in a strange, unfamiliar city. As you are being driven to your location, you wonder if the driver might be lost, especially as the money meter continues to climb as time passes by. The CD-ROM solution solves this problem by providing unlimited access for one fixed cost to specialized databases.

A CD-ROM library combines the power of personal computers with the traditional research techniques to provide an efficient, cost-effective way to perform topical research. You acquire the speed and

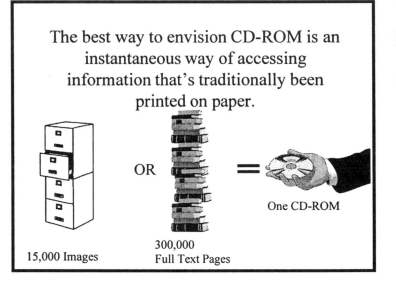

The best way to envision CD-ROM is an instantaneous way of accessing information that's traditionally been printed on paper.

15,000 Images   OR   300,000 Full Text Pages   =   One CD-ROM

convenience of computerized research with the fixed cost and the simplicity of books. Features include project management functions such as timekeepers for billing purposes and specific case notebooks. Some software vendor's libraries typically include case law, digests, statutes and regulations, treatise work, and other related materials. Information is organized into books. You can browse each book a line at a time, flip from page to page, or jump between references. Samplings of some areas in which CD-ROM's are currently available are:

- State Case and Statutory Law,
- Federal Civil Practice,
- Federal Securities,
- Government Contract,
- Federal Taxation,
- Shepherd's, and
- Bankruptcy.

The type of information from various CD-ROMs publishers is extensive. For example for litigation two useful CD's are:

- Michie's TrialSearch which provides on-line over 75,000 transcript pages from instructive trials on opening statements, summations, examinations, introduction of evidence, making and overcoming objections and preserve issues for appeal (www.michie.com); and

- Human Anatomy, Radiologic Anatomy, and Microscopic Anatomy CD-ROMs from the American Medical Association. Price: each $79 (www.ama-assn.org/).

> CD-ROM - (Compact Disk with Read Only Memory) has a storage capacity of approximately 300,000 typed pages. With this immense capacity, a comprehensive collection of legal case and reference materials, magazines, and statistical information can easily fit on just a few compact disks. The information on these disks can be accessed through most personal computers using a CD-ROM disk drive or through a CD-ROM drive attached to a network. The Digital Versatile Disc (DVD) is replacing the traditional CD-ROM.
>
> The DVD is the next-generation optical disk standard that has already been introduced. It has a storage capacity of 2.5 GB and above. It will store at least 90 minutes of video. The storage can potentially be increased to 18 GB since the new standard allows for double sided and double layered storage. It is designed to be backward compatible, which will enable current CD-ROM's to be played. DVD (Digital Versatile Disk) technology will find its way into legal in 1998.

We will continue to see a proliferation of customized legal materials for the specialty areas in law. For example, if your practice consists of personal injury law, corporate, tax, and so on specialized CD-ROM databases are available.

CD-ROM disks are not limited to just the legal field but all information areas. Newspaper and magazines on CD-ROM can be checked for background on clients, expert witnesses, corporations, and communities. Corporate information is available on annual statements, officers, product areas, and so forth. Scientific and technical information databases, trademark, patent, and product information and review are available. These are just a few areas of the literally thousands of CD-ROM disks available today with vast amounts of information on these disks.

The Internet will displace CD-ROM's to some extent but the use of CD-ROM for legal research has entered a tremendous growth rate. Most, if not all, states have their case law and statutes available on CD-ROM. The proliferation of CD-ROM titles from many publishers and the fall of prices for CD-ROM readers have been the driving forces. For example, the United States Code is available on CD-ROM disk from the United States Government for the astounding low price of $35.00.

The CD-ROM electronic format for legal materials is available from a number of publishers. It is unusual if any substantial body of legal materials used by practitioners is not available on a CD-ROM. One source for a directory of CD-ROM materials is Directory of Law Related CD-ROMs. This CD-ROM directory provides the following information in all areas of law, legislation, and regulation. It provides the title, publisher, data provider, distributor, search software, format, compatible drives, minimum equipment specifications, networks, site licenses, languages, print equivalent, coverage dates, updates, number of disks, description of contents and toll free support numbers. Added in 1995 is a list of citations to publications that have reviewed the particular CD-ROM. This directory is updated 3 times a year. It is available through Infosources Publishing (www.infosourcespub.com/).

The following is a review of the features and benefits of using CD-ROM legal research technology:

- Speed - Most CD-ROM readers access information within approximately the same speed as a hard drive. A whole library of publications can be searched quickly.

- Up-to-date - There are two ways the material on the disk is kept current. First, updated disks are periodically sent. Second, you may be provided access to on-line update databases that supplement information on the CD-ROM disk.

- Comprehensive Research - In addition to traditional print search techniques you can also perform electronic word searches to find relevant documents. You formulate these searches in the same manner you would with other on-line services - searching for words, phrases, or key numbers. Word searches helps you find information you wouldn't find using a printed index.
- Automatic Cross-referenced to Other Documents - The search term searches all references on the disk. This enables you to jump from one related document to another instantaneously. In essence, this will follow your thought process through the entire range of pertinent research sources. For example, it can take you from a citation to the full text of a case or from a code section to related regulations. It can also take you from a case to a list of Shepherd's citations.
- Fixed Cost - There is usually an initial purchase or lease cost plus a monthly subscription rate. You can research as often and as long as you like and sometimes access on-line updates at no additional charge. Research costs for one or ten of your cases remains the same. You can search, locate, read, and analyze without worrying about each passing minute.
- Little Training - It offers you the familiarity of traditional electronic research. Traditional commands or similar on-line service's commands are generally available so you don't have to "learn" a new program.
- Space Savings - The extraordinary compactness of the library (5 1/4 inch disks) saves expensive shelf space.
- Location Convenience - The convenience and efficiency of having it at your desk or in your briefcase are immeasurable. CD-ROM readers can be purchased as part of a notebook computers which allows you to take legal authorities with you wherever you go.
- Electronic Notebook and Bookmark - CD-ROM's enable you to capture information from a disk and add your own notes, then copy it all to your favorite word processing program. Some programs have the capability to automatically keep track of all your time and research for every project.
- Computer and Software Needs – A low end 486 with a Windows configuration is all that is generally needed.
- Cut and Paste. You can cut the entire opinion or parts of it and paste it into your word processor for citation to the court.
- Case Print Format - some publishers allow the user to print the case in the traditional two column written format like in the federal and state reporter

Some of the publishers of CD-ROM's include:
- Law Office Information Systems (LOIS) (www.pita.com).
- Lexis-Nexis and Michie (www.lexis-nexis.com).
- Westlaw (www.westgroup.com).
- Shepard's/McGraw Hill (www.bender.com).
- Matthew Bender (www.bender.com).

The cost of jurisdictional CD-ROM's differs from jurisdiction to jurisdiction depending upon the competition. However, when considering the cost the following factors should be addressed:
- Ease of Use;
- Searching Power;
- Plain language search engines;
- Network Support
- Pricing and licensing issues;
- Integration with hard copy systems;
- Integration with on-line systems; and

- Updates.

Information Brokers. Over the next several years we will see the emergence of "information brokers" who will be experts in the location of information over the information on-line highway. These cottage industries in their "virtual" offices will be as commonplace as paralegals in law firms. Not only will litigators have associates, investigators, paralegals, computer technicians, but an "on-line" information broker will become part of the litigation team. Due to the huge volume and number of on-line databases available it will be wise in terms of saving time and money to hire a professional on-line service searcher.

Spreadsheets

Spreadsheet application programs provide the user with the immense capability to perform simple and complex mathematical calculations. The data is generally arranged in a table of numbers in rows and columns. They have long been used in business and were one of the first applications that started the use of personal computers in business. The primary reason is that in spreadsheets you can change one number of your business calculations and it can automatically change all the rest of the numbers. This is important in a business or legal "what if scenario" or other financial calculations. Spreadsheet packages have excellent text, data and charting formatting capabilities that rival table functions in word processing packages and graphics packages.

For example, you can use a spreadsheet to calculate a structured settlement offer to determine the present day value of the money that needs to be invested. If the amount per year or per month increases or decreases during your negotiations then a new amount can be instantly calculated. Spreadsheets can be used to calculate what if scenarios involving your case and keep control of the damage and administrative case costs of litigation. Graphs can be easily prepared showing the different settlement positions of the parties.

Legal Applications. In the practice of law spreadsheets can be used to calculate::

- Personal injury - lost wages, past and future medical damages, structured settlements, loss of enjoyment of life, pain and suffering; and negotiation settlement "what if" scenarios
- Litigation Support Costs - abstracting, coding, imaging, conversion to full text, paralegal, associate, and partner costs, and task oriented billing ;
- Domestic Relations - child support, property division, and alimony payments; and
- Real estate - Closing statements, truth in lending statements, and mortgage payment, loan calculations and amortization schedules.

Some products to consider include; Microsoft Excel (www.microsoft.com); Lotus 123 (www.lotus.com); and Quattro Pro (www.corel.com). Specialized calculation packages to consider include Personal Injury Economist, Wrongful Death Economist, Wrongful Termination Economist and Structured Settlements Economist. Advocate Software (www.advocatesoftware.com).

Multimedia - Text, Graphics, Sound, Photographs & Video

We are increasingly being asked to present our cases – motions, briefs and oral arguments – in a multimedia format.

Multimedia is both a technology and communications concept. As a technology concept multimedia is explained in the sense of using text, sound, graphics, video, and animations to persuade.

Integration. The integration of multimedia - text, sound, graphics, animation, digital video and Interactivity into a presentation is one of the objectives of digitizing your information. A respected multimedia-authoring tool is Macromedia Director (www.macromedia.com) which enables one to create presentation, educational CD's, simulations reference materials and more. Various file formats can be imported and VCR's, CD-ROM players and a variety of different equipment can be controlled with this program.

Multimedia is taking the various forms of media - sound, text, graphics, video and animations - and presenting various combinations of the above to persuade a trier of fact as to your client's position.

As a communications concept, which is more important then multimedia as a technology concept, the digitization of information for use in multimedia provides a new and dynamic method of presenting your case to the trier of fact. Only in the last 10 years have we been able to digitize and present our case information in this new and dynamic way.

Always remember that visual aids can reinforce the points of your argument but you are center stage. These are visual aids; you are not a human aid.

See also Chapter 8, Using Multimedia in Legal Proceedings.

Graphic Presentations

Graphics software enables one to give a visual impression to the viewer by a picture. The verbal and visual presentation of a concept, relationship or event reinforces it in the viewer's mind. A variety of graphical programs are available to assist in the creation of visual pictures.

Most common of the presentation graphical programs are the ones that enable one to create bullet slides, bar graphs, pie charts, timelines, organization charts and a host of other graphical depictions which provides the viewer with a visual impression by pictures and data. Another type of graphics software are design programs commonly called CAD, Computer Aided Design, programs to design the interior of a home, manufacturing plant, roads, etc. Finally, there are paint programs such as Microsoft Paintbrush that enables you to draw freehand the picture of your choice using a mouse or other pointing device.

Some common presentation graphics programs would include Microsoft PowerPoint and Harvard Graphics. This software is easy to use out of the box and provides a number of user friendly features including tutorials, predefined graphic templates, and clip art. They offer a good basic set of drawing and annotation tools. They provide the capability of creating bullet slides, graphs and use of clip art to explain your client's legal position. They generally come with a "screenshow" feature that enables one to arrange the created slides in whatever order is best suited for the presentation. These programs enable one to create multimedia presentations using graphics, sound, text, animations and even live video inserted as OLE objects.

Often, special "niche" graphics software can provide valuable assistance in your cases. Two such niche packages are VISIO™ (www.viso.com) and ABC FlowCharter™ (www.micrografx.com/flowcharter/). VISIO™ is a graphics program that is complementary to general presentation graphic programs such as Microsoft PowerPoint™ and enables the user to create specific relationship "type" charts that can then easily be used with a general graphics application program. The program provides numerous stencils to assist in depicting "relationships" important in your cases.

For example, below VISIO™ was used to visually depict concurrent ownership of three corporations by the same key family members in different corporate positions. The family members had Korean names that were confusing if one tried to pronounce them since they were very similar sounding. However, when depicted in a graphical representation it provided a clear depiction of the interrelationship of the parties.

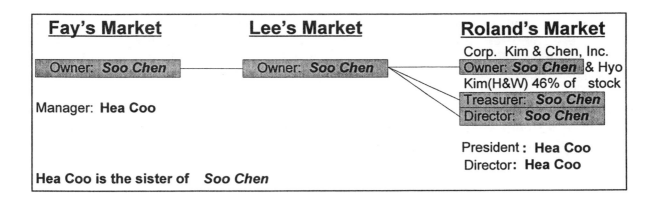

The following diagram was prepared in 5 minutes using Visio™ software.

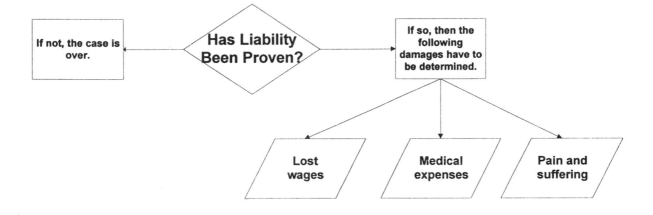

Master slides and templates. One the easiest and quickest way to design a presentation is to use the prepackaged presentations that are part of most presentation programs. These prepackaged templates contain master slides, speaker notes, outlines and handouts. They have the heading and bullet items already in place only requiring one to insert the applicable text. The color scheme chosen generally follows all of the rules for contrast, letter size and so forth. In fact, some are tailored for different types of businesses or professions.

Slides. Slides are generally the building blocks of your presentation. A series of slides will form a presentation. The slides main points should support the speaker's comments. Slides are not intended to reflect all the words of the presenter. As you create a visual ask whether each visual supports your main theme or message. Clip art, flow charts and graphs can add significantly to the understanding and communication of your message.

Use comparisons, analogies or examples for the trier of fact to better understand the message. Be succinct with the words on the slide. Use the following checklist on your slides:

- Six by six rule - No more than six lines of type per slide and no more than six words per line;
- You should be able to can read a non-projected transparency or computer slide from 6 feet away. A 35-mm slide should be able to be read at arm's length;
- The smaller the group - the fewer the visuals.
- There should only be one message per slide;
- Seven items per slide - lines, blocks, clip art; etc.; and
- Complex material should be shown sequentially.

Font and Type Size. The choosing of the type is the most important part of your presentation because 60-80% of your presentation is in text. Legibility is the key. Remember that fonts are designed to carry a message not to draw attention to themselves.

There are thousands of typefaces that come in variations such as bold, italic and different sizes. Different types of emphasis can be obtained by using italics, bold or different colored fonts. The Helvetica styles work the best since they are simple and clean. Use only one to two fonts per presentation. Be consistent in the use of fonts, sizes and weights. The size of the font is referred to as points with the greater the number the larger the font. The 16 to 18 point type is preferred since it can generally be read from anywhere in the room.

Colors. Colors can add immediate interest and impact to your presentation. Studies have shown that colors in presentations can accelerate learning, retention, willingness to read, increase action, highlight information and reflect favorably on the speaker. Colors must be used wisely.

- Warm colors such as yellow, red and orange portray intensity and movement. They symbolize fear, excitement passion or speed. They advance toward the audience. They are good for lettering and to highlight, poor for backgrounds. They are also good for motivating an audience.
- Cool colors such as green and blue are associated with water, meadows and harmony. They signify solidarity, dependability, security, calm, credibility and a conservative approach to information. Examples are Big Blue for IBM and blue uniforms for policemen. Green may be more effective with presentations requiring feedback. Blue is best used for backgrounds. This color retreats from the audience and is often used for background colors.
- Black as a background is perceived as final. It is often used for emphasis when displaying financial data.
- Backgrounds - if one is going to change a background color it will assist the listener if you first go to a color like gray to neutralize the effect on the audience.
- Graduated color backgrounds are pleasing and professional looking

Contrast. Contrast refers to the color of your background and the other lettering and objects on your slide. The best contrasts are colors that are complementary on the color wheel. For example with a blue background choose yellow or orange lettering. It is important to create high contrast slides. Contrast of colors allows your message to be read at any distance. The contrast of the colors you choose may be more important then color itself. For example yellow and white type against a blue background is easy to read

Clip Art. There are two primary formats for clip art.
- *Bit-mapped (raster) images* are recorded pixel by pixel. Tiff and PCX are the most common bit-mapped formats. They can be imported into presentations. They cannot be enlarged nor shrunk without losing some of the resolution.
- *Vector images* are composed of a set of computer instructions that redraws the pictures depending upon what size you want. They can be enlarged or shrunken without losing detail. It cannot match the detail or realistic look of bitmap images. EPS, CGM and WMF are standardized vector formats.

There is a variety of low cost clip art available on the market. (ww.corel.com).

Graphics should add structure, emphasis or organization and not merely decoration to your slides. They will distract from your message if not clearly linked to the subject. They can be very visually appealing.

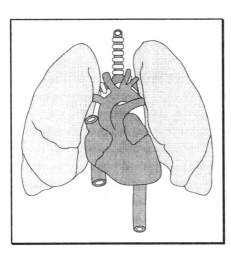

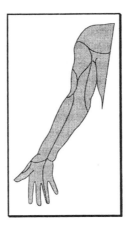

Graphics- Pie Charts, etc.

Charts generally have a specific purpose:

- Pie chart - To show the parts of a whole;
- Bar chart - to compare several elements against each other;
- Stacked bar chart - To compare several elements over time;
- Line chart -to show changes over time where there are many increments of time and many changes; and
- Line, bar or dot chart - shows relationship or congruent trends between elements.

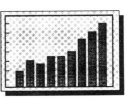

Transitions or Builds. The term builds refers to presenting your information in stages to keep the audiences attention. Emphasize key points with color builds. Dimming back the prior point ensures they will focus on your points and it will control the eye movements of your audience. A word of caution is to be consistent with the same transition throughout the presentation. Otherwise the audience will be distracted by the various transitions that are employed.

Output. After completing your slide presentation how do you display it to your audience? There are numerous output media and the proper one depends on a number of factors. The output can be transferred to 35-mm slides, black and white overheads, color overheads and slide show presentations. See Section 8 for a detailed discussion of output options.

Medical Illustrations. A.D.A.M - the acronym stands for Animated Dissection of Anatomy for Medicine stores intricate color illustrations of all organs and systems of the body. By a simple point and click method one can explore how various parts of the body are linked together or create specialized illustrations. For example, one can paint onto any part of the body first, second or third degree burns. The program also contains detailed animation sequences showing how standard surgical operations proceed. The program was originally developed for medical instruction and is now is used in over half the medical schools in the country. The CD-ROM contains superbly rendered color images, animations of the human anatomy as well as common injuries, radiology and histology. Output can be to color printers, video, black and white or saved in a file. A.D.A.M. Software, Inc. (www.adam.com.) (800-755-2326).

Slide Show Presentations. They are beginning to be used frequently in legal proceedings in opening, closing and examination of witnesses. Slides can be embedded with sounds or linked to other applications such as animations and so forth. Some presentation systems have runtime versions that enable you to copy and give away the presentation to run without the underlying software. Other features in presentation software include outliners, hyperlinking, autobuilds and linking video. The various output devices for this type of presentation is covered in Chapter 8.

Audio

The power of sound should not be overlooked in your presentations. Sound can stir an immediate emotional response. To use sound it is necessary to have a soundcard or the "hardware" built into the motherboard or computer chip. Most soundcards enable one to record, playback and edit sound. The sound converter on your card will change analog sound to a digital format. These are commonly labeled as WAV files and require a significant amount of storage. MIDI stands for the Musical Instrument Digital Interface. Sound cards that include MIDI enable you to play back a musical performance right on the computer.

Photographs

Digitized Photos - There are three methods of having photographs digitized for use in a computer presentation or for insertion in a pleading. Paper photos can be scanned in, a digital camera can be used and photos can be downloaded into your computer or a regular roll of film can be sent to a film developer for digitized processing.

Paper photos can be scanned into a computer and then used in a trial presentation program or in a number of low cost presentation programs. All that is needed is a scanner and scanning software. The quality of the scanned photo will depend upon the scanning equipment and the software. Many firms outsource the scanning of photos to service bureaus. The cost varies depending upon the size of the photo and resolution quality needed. One inexpensive way to scan photos is to use the EasyPhoto™ (www.easyphoto.com) reader that enables you to take a standard size photo and scan it through a 5" x 7" box that attaches to your computer. It is available from various outlets for a low price.

Recently, low cost digital cameras have been introduced that enable anyone to take pictures and download them immediately into a camera in a digitized format. The cost of $5,000 per camera for quality color digital photos has dropped to approximately $400 per camera. Photo image editing software such as Photo-Shop™ or CorelDraw™ (www.corel.com) enables the user to touch up or manipulate the image. Within minutes one can snap a picture, download it into a computer, print it and present it in a legal proceeding. Special consideration should be paid to the resolution quality compared to a traditional camera and storage space required on a computer.

Video

Video can add power and have a significant impact upon the trier of fact. To be able to impeach a witness with a prior videotaped deposition can literally win a case for you.

> MPEG stands for Motion Picture Experts Group. This ISO standard provides for a uniform format for video compression standard. This standard requires "hardware" support. The new Direct TV uses a form of MPEG. MPEG2 is a proposed ISO standard that allows for higher resolution motion video compression.

The easiest method of capturing and displaying video is with a VCR. The major problem with accessing and viewing video on computers has been fitting the huge video files on storage medium like a hard disk or CD-ROM and playing them back fast enough to achieve a smooth playback on the screen. However, this has been solved with significant advances with the new CD-ROM format called DVD. DVD is able to play back a feature length movie on a DVD reader.

Check out real-time streaming video over the Internet using @ttend™ (www.legalspan.net). It delivers full motion video, depending on your bandwidth, using a scaleable compression that adjusts the image quality.

One common application of video is the digitization of deposition videotapes. When depositions of a witness are recorded on videotape they can be digitized onto a CD-ROM disk for playback. CD-ROM enables the user to instantaneously access any part of the deposition in a non-linear fashion. One can immediately jump to different parts of the video without fast forwarding. To locate specific testimony the tape is linked to the full text transcript that is called video

> An inexpensive method of capturing frames off a video is a product called Snappy video grabber. Snappy enables you with a mouse click to capture a frame off video and then use it in a graphics presentation like PowerPoint. It plugs into your parallel port and connects to a VCR, TV, camcorder cable or any other video source for under $200. It should be part of your multimedia arsenal. (www.snappy.com).

synchronization. Line link or a time stamp link can link it to the full text using either a line that is part of the full text transcript and the video. It is much better to plan the synchronization prior to depositions being held to ensure the synchronization result intended. Costs for conversion are approximately $300 per tape for digitization to a CD-ROM not linked to a deposition and up to $450 per tape when synchronized to the lines of a deposition transcript. See DepositionDirector™ at inData (www.indata.com).

Conclusion

We have covered the primary computer concepts and have discussed in some detail many of their applications to the practice of law. The changes have been immense and will continue to be for the next several years. In the next section we explore more closely how to apply these concepts to legal applications.

This Page Intentionally Left Blank

Chapter 7

Managing Litigation Information Using Technology

Facts can't be recounted; much less twice over, and far less still by different persons. I've already drummed that thoroughly into your head. What happens is that your wretched memory remembers the words and forgets what's behind them.

- Augusto Roa Bastos

Introduction

The practice of law requires a lawyer to continuously organize and control the administrative, legal and factual information of cases. Case files are opened, billing accounts are set up and preliminary plans of action are developed to resolve cases on behalf of clients. If a complaint or answer is filed then the lawyer's focus is to control and present the information to convince the factfinders of the merits of a client's case.

However, case and litigation management is a constantly changing interactive process. Legal issues change, witness's testimony can take on added importance depending on how issues change, pleadings impact pretrial motions, trial exhibits are affected by information in interrogatories, calendaring and trial dates affect settlement positioning and changes in the law can overturn the best laid plans. During this case process it is imperative that a lawyer is able to easily control these changing conditions efficiently so as to be able to present their client's case in the strongest and best possible light in settlement negotiations or trial.

The management of the ever-growing amount of digital and paper information poses a major challenge as reflected in the following report:

- Business and government agencies generate 900 million pages of information each day, including 76,000,000 letters and 21,000,000 other documents;
- Approximately 1.3 trillion paper documents are stored in the U.S. and companies estimate they have access to only about 10% of their paper based systems;
- Creating and moving paper based information accounts for up to 10% of corporate gross revenues;.
- The information workforce is increasing and now stands at 54% of total employment; and
- The amount of digital information in offices is doubling every three years.

  Linda Myers-Tierny, " An introduction to Text Management, " Office Computing Report, Vol. 14, No.10.

Paper and record-keeping demands on businesses and law firms have produced a dramatic impact on litigation. From simple to complex cases attorneys are struggling to handle and master paper and digital handling problems.

The following sections will focus on how one can best control various paper and digital materials understanding that the options are dictated by a number of factors such as time and expense.

Manual Control of Case Information

Traditionally lawyers use tools such as pens, paper, typewriters, file cabinets, file folders, expandos and notebooks to manage their case materials. For example, as we review documents we write in a case or trial notebook relevant information in a legal, witness, issue or chronology section. When an issue changed we manually copy the information into a new issue section. With depositions we color code issues with colored paperclips or with stickums for particular issues. If one dropped out we are faced with going through the whole deposition to locate the spot where it came from.

"In considering the issue of cost control, one myth should be dispelled immediately. I often hear lawyers who have not worked on a complex case discussing whether a new case will 'justify the cost" of a computer. They believe that using a computer greatly increases the cost of the document work. Nothing could be further from the truth. Ninety percent of an information system will be identical whether or not a computer is used . . . the use of the computer adds a small cost at the start of the litigation that will be recouped over time by decreasing the cost of retrieving information." - Madden, Litigation Magazine, **1978.**

Documents have always presented accessibility and retrieval problems. Many 3-ring notebooks are put together to assist in the location and indexing of case information. They are routinely pulled apart to copy a document for witness review, preparation for a summary judgment or as an exhibit for a deposition or trial. Oftentimes the original is lost or a 4th or 5th generation copy becomes illegible. If more than one legal professional is working on the case the document we need always seems to be checked out. Small armies of lawyers, associates and legal assistants have been put together to accommodate some of these large cases. From revenue perspective large paper cases generate mini-fortunes for firms that bill by the hour and use the manual method of organizing their cases. Manually controlling case information requires a significant amount of personnel time and has proven to be quite costly.

Manually controlling paper is also drudgery and is not what the practice of law is about. It does not measure the "worth" of a lawyer but oftentimes measures how much paper he or she has shuffled. The goal should be to spend more time using information and less time looking for it.

Digital Control of Case Information

Digitally controlling case information means obtaining case information in a digital format like e-mail or converting paper and other analog information into a digital format and then using computers to store, access, retrieve, organize, print and send information. Digital Information can be in a data, sound, graphics, text, or video format.

Benefits.

The primary benefits to convert and control information digitally is:

- *Storage capacity* - Computers can store a voluminous amount of facts and law. One CD-ROM disk (640 mg) can hold 300,000 pages of full text information or 15,000 document 'imaged" pages. The drastic reduction of hard drive prices ($199 for 3 gigabytes) makes it inexpensive to store data in your computer. A DVD disk holds at a minimum 4.2 gigabytes of information or 2,100,000 full text pages, 105,000 images or 90 minutes of full motion video.

- *Search, retrieve and review* – Documents, depositions, trial transcripts, case law and other case materials can be searched and information retrieved in *seconds*. Document indexes can be searched and images of documents viewed instantly. Real-time translation of testimony can permit you to view the testimony of a witness on a computer within seconds in a deposition or trial. The Internet now permits us to send real-time the text, audio and video of a witness in a deposition or trial over a regular phone line.

- *Organization* - Legal and factual information can be coded and organized for witness, chronological, and legal issue reports. This information can be easily reorganized as the issues and factual information in your case changes. Calendaring and docketing information can be organized and accessed easily.

- *Analyze* - Factual and legal information can be grouped for case analysis. One can trace the different witnesses' involvement with a set of documents or events. One can instantly review the different witnesses' accounts of an accident or commercial transaction that pertains to a specific legal or factual issue.

- *Reports* - A variety of reports can be instantly generated such as witness, chronological, legal or factual proposition summaries. Witness kits can be easily prepared.

- *Collaboration* – Digital information can be easily shared in a group computing environment where participants are located anywhere in the world.

- *Portability* – Document images, depositions, and all case materials can be easily taken with you or provided to co-counsel at a low cost and quickly.

- *Presentation* – Exhibits involving graphs or documents can be effectively presented to jurors and changed on the fly as your case progresses. Significant time can be saved presenting your case in a digital format.

Why Litigation Support? *The Sky is the Limit*

Every area of computer automation has its philosophers, practitioners who look beyond the obvious into the whys and wherefores of their particular bailiwicks. Typically, these people see vast implications where others see only hardware and software.

Two such seers in the area of litigation support are Walter Bithell, of Holland and Hart in Boise, Idaho, and Sam Guiberson, of Guiberson Associates in Houston. Both are litigators with the experience and insight to shed light on what, for many, is murky territory indeed.

"If you look at it as just a system for filing documents, it's really a waste," Bithell says. "But that's the way a lot of lawyers use it. Instead it should be used as a way of getting a handle on documents so that we can think our way through them. It allows a lawyer to pick up on fact patterns, and that's really what litigation is all about."

Guiberson adds that the marketplace has tended to create unrealistic expectations about computers. "It's far too simplistic for lawyers who have not done this work to think that all they need to do to catch up with the trend is to go out and buy something off the shelf," he states. The truth is that there is no shelf upon which the really decisive skills can be found. Those skills are more organizational and process-oriented, and they aren't for sale out there. It's acquired through experience.

When practitioners realize that litigation support is simply an adjunct to their thinking process - albeit a very powerful one - then Bithell and Guiberson are in agreement - the sky is the limit.

"Once you input the information into your system, you can just sit there and generate all sorts of interesting areas to explore," states Bithell.

"You can say, for example, 'I wonder what was going on here in June . . . I wonder when the first letter was sent that prompted party number one to respond this way . . . I wonder when the first time this subject comes up in any of the documentation . . . I wonder if it was ever discussed at a board meeting . . . and so on.' It's a great way to highlight factual patterns that could be crucial to your case."

Guiberson uses a visual metaphor to describe what litigation support can do. "As we move along the paper trail, what we have studied becomes more remote and what we have looked at most recently becomes more present in our minds, even though that may not be representative of the merits of the particular case.

But what computers do is put you in the center of a paper sphere where every document and every piece of data is equally accessible to your intellectual process. That way, you're no longer victimized by your immediate recollection. You can postulate or consider relationships that are far broader than those based on what you read yesterday or what you forgot last month. This brings about a big change in the way you approach evidence and investigate facts."

Bithell and Guiberson agree that it also tends to change the competitive rules of law practice itself. " Litigation support is a great equalizer," Bithell says. " It opens up a whole series of options to small and medium-sized firms that they didn't have before."

According to Guiberson, the changes wrought by this technology are nothing short of revolutionary. "The necessity of building large organizations to supply expertise and analysis for large lawsuits may be a thing of the past," he says. "Now the kind of organization that is capable of taking on major litigation is much, much smaller - albeit better trained - than it had to be before."

- Steve Keeva, ABA Journal

What is Information Technology (IT) Management?

IT is any hardware or software that assists in the management and control of the case or litigation process. Any hardware or software that supports the management of calendaring, docketing, preparation of pleadings, searching depositions or any of the myriad's of litigation processes is IT. Word processing, databases, full text software or trial presentation software and hardware are all considered IT.

> Complex litigation can be a costly, tedious and time-consuming drain on the litigants and their lawyers. But automated litigation support can help solve these problems . . . . .Nobody benefits if legal staff spend hundreds of hours chasing paper. If all of this time is billed, the client pays too much. If the firm writes some of it off, then the firm is losing money. -- Clifford Shnier

Objective of IT

The objective of IT is to be able to control case materials in a digital format that replicates and improves upon the lawyering methodology that has been successful in your practice. IT software should be viewed from the perspective of how is it going to help to control the administrative, factual, or legal information in your case. How can it assist me in getting better control of the witness testimony, medical information or other factual information in my case? Can the software be integrated into my total digital management of my case? Will it work with my existing software? For example, if I obtain new imaging software will it integrate with my existing applications? All of these decisions are not separate and distinct but must be viewed toward creating a cohesive and comprehensive digital case notebook.

At the heart of your case are the causes of action, legal issues and factual propositions that you must ultimately prove to prevail. The development of your legal cause of action, legal element, factual proposition, witness and other coding or organization scheme is central to creation of your electronic trial notebook. This organization methodology forms the foundation for your case and is the glue that binds all of your factual and legal information together. To have the factual information available for all stages of your case such as discovery, voir dire, opening statement and closing argument of your case requires a comprehensive approach to the use of automation through the full litigation process. For that reason all software and hardware should support the management and control of the core legal issues and factual propositions of your case.

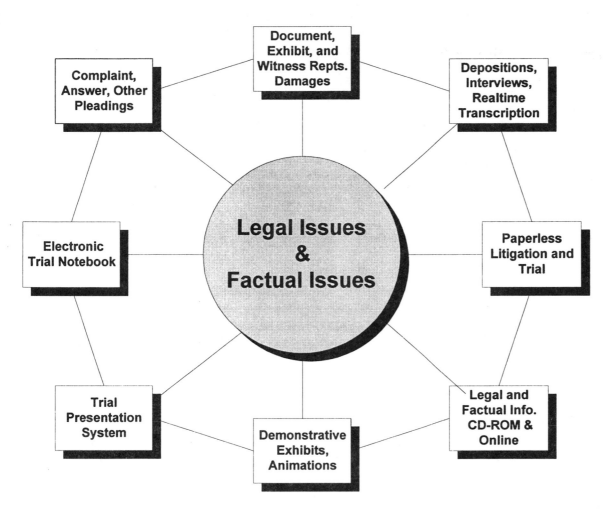

IT Obstacles.

Applying technology to the practice of law has not been easy for several reasons.

- *Development of IT has not generally replicated the practice of law.* The practice of law requires us as advocates to investigate a set of facts and apply those facts to established precedent and statute. In some instances we are called upon to argue the case before various legal tribunals. However, this can be become complex as we are asked to apply and present those sets of facts in a variety of ways. From discussions with opposing counsel, to legal arguments before a judge and opening statements before a jury the facts and law of your client's case must be presented in the most effective and efficient way. Those developing IT software have not generally replicated the litigation process. Instead the interface design has been left to technicians who do not understand the practice of law.
- *Factual information comes from a variety of sources in different formats.* We collect facts from documents executed in the past, interrogatories, witness interviews, experts, depositions, request for production, request for admissions and so on. Once collected we need to isolate the critical facts in those applications and organize them for witness preparations, opening statements, summary judgments and so forth. Organization of these facts implies that on-screen or written reports can be generated setting forth the facts as they relate to a particular witness or legal issue. However, few software programs address the integrated need to use databases, full text, graphics and images in a connected manner to provide single comprehensive analysis and reports.

For example, does one enhance a witness's testimony in a full text program and then generate a report unique to that software and then generate a database report, in a different program, concerning documents relevant to the same witness and run another report? Will an imaging program connect not only to a database but to a full text software program? Using software for legal purposes is not an easy task but it can be done with amazing results.

IT Goals

There are several goals of using IT software and hardware:

- *Becoming an advocate and not a paper shuffler.* Having the information in a computer will enable you to practice law - and not spend your time organizing the paper in your case no matter how large it is. You will spend your time being an advocate and weigh the strategies instead of being a paper shuffler.

- *Workproduct is Preserved.* One major problem in most law offices today is that when the facts of a case are reviewed for motion preparation, investigations, or discovery proceedings, the analysis of those facts is not recorded in a method that can be reused later for additional proceedings. All too often we immerse ourselves in a case to respond to a motion or answer a discovery request, and then walk away from the case. We fail to record and forget many important work product insights we gleamed in the case. When this information is in a computer, in a controllable manner, then refreshing your memory with the legal elements, factual propositions, and the information that support your position, is easy and available for your further use. All of us have been in a situation where the lead attorney or paralegal who is in charge of a case, leaves the organization or is reassigned. Obviously, the control over the case suffers. The person who was in charge was very familiar with the legal and factual basis of the case. When that person is taken off the case, the multitude of details and any legal and factual analysis of the case usually leaves with the person. The solution lies in requiring that important data and work product of a case be entered into the computer. This can be done without a substantial investment in additional resources or time. When this information is in a computer, in a controllable manner, then refreshing your memory with the legal elements, factual propositions, and the information that support your position is easy and available for your further use.

- *Controlling the legal and factual information in your case.* Normally, when your client approaches you about handling a case, he presents you with a set of facts and requests that certain action is taken. Your client's case will generally progress into an expanding set of facts that will fit into one or more legal theories. Unfortunately, the legal theory at the outset is subject to change as more facts are collected. The known facts are constantly rearranged to present your client's case in the best possible light. As the multitude of facts and documents grow, it becomes harder and more time consuming to rearrange these facts into different legal categories. Computer software can solve this problem by using an integrated electronic database, full text retrieval, and linked graphic images system. This system will allow you to rearrange these facts with a minimum of effort. Software can provide immediate access to these facts, whether they are in documents, depositions, or interviews with witnesses, etc. Instead of depending upon the human memory, the facts can be instantly accessed through computer software. In effect, this allows you to focus on the analysis and presentation of your client's case. You will discover that after storing these facts in a computer, it is much easier to rearrange and reorder them for a more effective presentation of your case.

The following sections are designed to begin addressing these IT issues from a case management and litigation perspective and apply various computer concepts to control case material and performing other pretrial tasks. They will focus on the control of information contained in legal materials such as:

1. Interrogatories;
2. Request for admissions;
3. Informal interviews;
4. Depositions;
5. Expert reports;

6. Request for production - documents;
7. Investigative information;
8. Legal research;
9. Client materials; and
10. Other materials.

These techniques are meant to be generic and apply to a variety of
in DOS or Windows, the lawyering process still needs to be analyzed and
make it easier, but one still needs to understand the computer concepts in
will benefit you, the practitioner.

So, let's explore some ways that one might connect and organize t
mind that the capability of the particular software will dictate some of the o

Implementing IT

Case Litigation Workflow

As you transition from a paper litigation practice to a paper and an
electronic "paperless" case and litigation practice the flow of the work within
your office will change. Instead of having a clerk log in and file a paper copy
of a pleading it may be received as a "digital" copy by modem or it may be
scanned and indexed by your clerk for later retrieval. This will necessitate a
refocusing on the "workflow" within your firm. Workflow has been defined
as the "sequence of activities that are performed with business processes".
Workflow analysis requires one to focus on the tasks to perform the work
associated with the processing of factual and legal materials in your case. In
a typical law office lawyers are supported by a variety of ancient and cutting
edge services - couriers, phones, E-mail, videoconferencing, etc. The
purpose of these services is to support the detailed and diverse flow of
information in the office. Transforming or reengineering an office requires a
reexamination of the workflow process in the office. Such a workflow

reexamination will enable you to optimally utilize the old services and to bridge them with the new services.

As we transition into an electronic workplace the "group" will be increasingly involved in the work
product because of the ease of enabling other people to be involved in the process. Software called "groupware"
is focusing upon this phenomenon of having group members having immediate access to the information and
immediate input. This will require further workflow analysis for the routing and the processing of the litigation
work. Electronic lawyering within a law firm must be visualized as you process information. Just as the
assembly line factory process revolutionized the manufacturing process computer technology will revolutionize
the workflow process in litigation.

To assist in capturing the workflow process there is a new group of software called *workflow software*.
It provides software tools to depict tracking of the process, icons to represent people, places, or things, time and
cost analysis, and other features to assist in the determination of the most efficient and productive workflow. It
assists in restructuring workflow processes and provides the users the ability to delete wasteful steps in the
workflow process.

Graphical workflow software also allows managers to represent and review litigation processes at a high
level of abstraction. They break apart processes and depict litigation or other business processes using maps or
other graphical aids. They also can depict the resources needed to run these processes. Because they are
graphical you can use them to teach and discuss.

of the litigation process will depend upon you and your work processes. The following is

...eting with client. At this meeting the general description of the case is described. Certain events, ...ses and document information is collected to begin to understand the case. The ...t is interviewed if they are a part of the case or have a general understanding of the ...atter. The size of the case in terms of size of the document population, number of depositions to take, etc. is discussed. A preliminary course of conduct is decided upon and the necessary resources and budget to handle the case are discussed.

- *Involvement of litigation team.* The attorneys, paralegal and other members of the team are assembled and a case briefing is provided.
- *Determining level of IT.* The extent of IT is determined based upon the requirements for the particular case. Existing hardware and software resources are inventoried and additional needs are determined. Discussions are held to determine if integrated software is needed or whether only a database program is needed for the case. A budget should be developed and approved by the client.
- *Setting up case management software.* A decision is made as to managing the overall strategy of the case by using software designed to incorporate docketing, case action plan, timekeeping and contact information.
- *Setting up an IT case/trial notebook.* A determination is made as to the cause of action, legal issues and propositions and some of the themes of the case. The initial coding for connecting factual information to the legal issues is discussed.
- *Accumulating client material.* Paper documents, computer ASCII files and any other client materials are accumulated.
- *Loading and Inputting case information into computer.* All full text ASCII material should be loaded into the computer. Initial design of the case database and document bibliographic indexing should be discussed. Consideration should be given to adding issue fields and other subjective coding fields to the database or full text indexing software. Enhancements in the form of note tags, document summaries or event summaries can be completed and added to the full text materials. Standardization of legal and non-legal terms should be decided.
- *Initial discovery or disclosure from opposing party.* The initial disclosure of the opposing party's materials will raise issues in terms of using IT such as images and full text to manage the information.
- *Legal and factual issue reformulation.* The legal and factual issues should be reformulated after reviewing the opposing party's case materials. Special attention should be paid to your client's strengths and weaknesses, legal theories, damage components and possible insurance coverage.
- *Visual Aid Plan.* Preliminary visual aids should be developed to reflect the themes of your case. They can be used to explain your position to your client, witnesses and for any pretrial proceedings with the court.
- *Document management.* The relevant documents should be coded. As new case material is accumulated they should be added to the existing database. A determination should be made to code the documents in-house or outsource them to a service bureau. Bibliographic indexing and imaging can be outsourced to a service bureau. If it is to be done in-house determine the availability of existing resources and timelines. Assign responsibilities for IT supervision providing IT training if needed. Determine if the material should be converted to full text.
- *Initial Investigative Stage.* A variety of reports should be generated to provide an analysis of the case up to this time. A chronology of initial events, timeline, important words and phrases, issue codes and specific time limited chronology reports should be run and analyzed to assess the strengths and weaknesses of your client's case.
- *Depositions.* In setting up the first round of depositions prepare witness kits from your existing database. Prior to the deposition run database reports on the witness for author, recipient, person mentioned, copied and so forth. Sort by date, name, and issue if coded. Analyze for questions, patterns, etc. Tag documents and print if imaged or pull the documents. Prepare an outline of questions for witness, dates and role for deposition. Determine if real-time transcription should be used for the depositions. Should the video be

sent real-time to your expert witness or others who live out-of-state? After taking the depositions review, annotate and generate case issue and chronology reports on the key elements of the case. Formulate follow-up questions for witnesses and prepare deposition digests to support pretrial motions. Chronology of key testimony and documents and key deposition excerpts should be prepared for analysis. Flag areas where a witness has changed his testimony or position on issues or events.

- ▪ *Case Evaluation.* After the first set of depositions evaluate the strength and weaknesses of your case again for your prospects in trial or to pursue settlement. Run database and full text reports by cause of actions, elements and supporting evidence.

The workflow of your case may differ but this gives you an idea of how to use IT in the preparation of your case for trial.

Preliminary Considerations

Case Commencement and Involvement of Litigation Team

The commencement of a case provides an important opportunity to plan your case strategy before the case takes on a life of its own. Whether you are answering a complaint or filing the lawsuit the beginning of a lawsuit initiates a host of deadlines, discovery analysis and disclosure. Some states like Arizona have mandatory disclosure rules and fast track court dates which increases the pressure to efficiently plan your case with other members of your litigation team.

Case strategy must involve all members of the litigation team and law office personnel. In any lawsuit the litigation team must commit to the same goals and objectives. They must be aware of the strategy of the case and the responsibility of different team members. Their focus must be on a favorable outcome to the litigation on behalf of their client. All members of the team are important including the senior attorneys, associates, co-counsel, legal assistants, secretaries, clerks, coding clerks, imaging support staff, computer technicians, and outside support personnel such as animation companies and all others.

From the outset there should be a consensus what the case is generally about, the themes of the case, causes of actions, and the legal and factual propositions needed to prove your and the opposing sides of the case. Case management plans should be set forth with specific dates and task assignments. Failure to do so can easily lead to a loss of control of the case and negotiation leverage on behalf of your client.

When you decide to automate the litigation the team has to understand, accept, and commit to the use of the technology or otherwise it will not be successful. The benefits of automating should be shown to them to assist them in their assignments as well as the overall objectives of the case. You must show them the benefits of creating a document abstract showing the connection of a witness to all the documents in a case and the ability to retrieve that document list immediately for a deposition. Provision of some sort has to be made for team members that will not accept the technology applications.

The responsibilities of the individual team members must be clearly stated. For example, who is responsible for setting up the codes on a case? Who determines the themes to be presented to the trier of fact? Who is responsible for imaging the documents and for the quality control? Does the legal assistant do the subjective coding or the associate? The timetable for certain automation tasks must be included in the overall timetable for other parts of the litigation such as depositions, requests for discovery and so on. For example, if a deposition of a key witness is held and the document database is not completed then in the deposition the attorney may miss examining the witness about some key documents.

These case management issues will take on added importance as we transition into case groupware solutions. Groupware will enable the case members to access the factual and work product of the team electronically.

Determine Specific Case Hardware, Software and IT Personnel Requirements.

At the outset it is important to determine as concisely as possible your hardware, software and IT personnel requirements for your case. There are many factors that will influence the design of your IT system for a particular case. If you fail to adequately assess your needs then the project can be a disaster that will not please your client who may have funded your IT efforts.

Litigation software and hardware is reusable. Once purchased, most software can be used with many cases simultaneously. A $2,000 investment in an integrated document database, full text, and imaging software will cost only $200 per case if used for 10 cases and $20 per case if used for 100 cases. The cost actually decreases the more you use it.

In regards to a particular case, the extent and type of automation depends upon the following factors:

- Nature and size of case;
- Time constraints of litigation;
- Number and location of parties involved;
- Client interest;
- Budget;
- Possibility of early settlement;
- Number of witnesses and documents;
- Hardware requirements;
- Software costs; and
- Personnel needed on case.

Specific hardware and software considerations are included in Chapter 2. A beginning checklist to assess your needs would include:

Software:

- Databases;
- Full text search and retrieval;
- Spreadsheet;
- Real-time transcription and video;
- Imaging;
- Outliners;
- Graphics;
- Networked capable applications;
- E-mail;
- Backup software and hardware;
- Telephony;
- WWW Browsers;
- Integrated software suites;
- Group computing software;
- Trial presentation software;
- Case Management or Personal Information Management (PIM) software;
- Document assembly or expert practice systems;
- Document management system for workproduct, pleadings, etc.; and
- CD-ROM case law or other legal materials.

Hardware:

- Computer availability – standalone or network;
- Operating system – DOS, Windows 3.X or Windows 95/98 or other environment;
- Processor speed of computers;
- RAM in the computer;
- CD-ROM Players and jukeboxes;
- Speakers and sound card;
- Scanners;
- Digital cameras;
- Optical drives;
- Bernoulli drives;
- Surge protectors;
- Zip and Jaz drives;
- Monitors – size and resolution quality;
- Printers & Plotters;
- Communication modems;
- Video capability; and
- Notebook computers and features.

Network:

- Network operating software;
- Network applications;
- Network bandwidth and speed;
- Bandwidth connection to the Internet;
- Intranet; and
- Extranets.

Personnel:

- Lead attorney supervision;
- IT consultant;
- Case IT manager;
- Computer technical specialists;
- In-house trainers and on-call help desk;
- Coders – if coding in being done in-house;
- Attorneys and paralegals to do subjective coding, run reports, etc.;
- Graphic person for visual aids;
- Presentation software specialist; and
- Others.

Determine Existing Hardware, Software and Personnel Resources. Within your organization check to determine what hardware and software is available to assist you in automating your cases. Many times software has been purchased and was used on a certain case and now sits unused on the shelf. If it is an older version an upgrade may be very inexpensive.

Delegation and Assignment of IT Tasks and Workflow

One of the difficult transitional areas for legal professionals is the reassignment of workflow processes as we change from a "paper" to a "paperless" case system. Digital control of case information presents new methods and skills that are obviously not present in a paper or analog system. A paper system required documents, folders, expandos, filing cabinets, etc. A "paperless" system requires ASCII disks, OCR software, a scanner, database design, etc. Below is a beginning checklist of tasks that need to be assigned for a digital case management system. Many of the areas discussed and covered in other parts of the book such as Hardware and Software in Chapter 2. The following section is designed to start the process of assigning these areas to the lead attorney, associate, paralegal, computer support staff or others.

MANAGING LITIGATION INFORMATION (See chapter 7)	
Outliners (See chapter 6)	
- Initial outline/trial notebook of case	Attorney
- Review of outline for suggested changes	Support staff
- Updating case outline	Attorney or support staff
- Connecting to other digital information – full text depositions, etc.	Support staff
- Training on how to use software	Support staff
Database – for document control and other applications. (See Chapter 6 & 7)	
- Legal needs assessment (what will the database be used for – document information, witness information, etc.?). What information should be collected? What reports are needed?	Attorney
- Design of the database(s)	Support staff
- Testing the database	Support staff
- Designing and printing reports	Support staff
- Approval of database design and reports	Attorney
- Formatting existing computer data for importing into database	Support staff
- Formulate legal and factual issues, witness and other codes.	
- Develop document and image numbering system	Attorney and support staff
- Inputting objective data into database	Support staff
- Inputting subjective data into database	Attorney
- Editing database	Attorney/Support staff
- Periodic printing of reports	Support staff
- Backup computer data	Support staff
- Training on how to use database	Support staff
Images – to attach a digital copy of a document to a database record for viewing on the computer screen. (See chapter 6 & &)	
- Determine needs assessment of why documents will be imaged and attached to database record.	Attorney and support staff
- Select imaging software depending on case needs	Support staff
- Determine who will do initial scanning of documents – in-house or outsourcing.	Attorney
- Accumulate client and opposing party documents	
- Scan documents and convert to images.	
- Attaching image to database record	Vendor or Support staff
- Training on imaging software	Support staff
Full Text – to search depositions or other litigation material by individual words. (See Chapter 6 & 7)	
- Select full text software after needs and comparison study. Carefully consider advanced search features. Attorney for legal needs assessment, Support staff for comparison of products and hardware needs.	Attorney/Support Needs
- Set up case file	Support staff
- Determine computer format that full text material needs to be in.	Support staff

- Determine if images will be linked to full text materials	Attorney
- Determine if video depositions will be taken to ensure accurate synchronization with full text	Attorney
- Contact court reporter to provide copy of depositions and exhibits (if you are having them attached as images) in specified format. Also, contact court reporter to set up video dispositions.	Support staff
- Link images to specific transcript passage	Support staff
- Determine if you want to convert paper documents using OCR into full text data.	Attorney
- Convert selected documents into full text data	Support staff or outsource
- Import full text depositions and other material into full text software program	Support staff or outsource
- Train attorney and others on software program	Support staff
- Design reports for on-screen review or printing	Support staff with attorney legal analysis needs
- Review and code deposition by issue, witness or other codes	Attorney and/or support staff
- Search depositions for specific testimony from witnesses for impeachment, etc.	Attorney
- Compile and review reports for case analysis	Attorney
- Print out reports on a periodic basis	Support staff
Real-time Transcription of Testimony – instant translation onto a computer screen of a witnesses testimony. (See Chapter 7)	
- Determine if you want to use real-time reporting. Explore the benefits of using real-time technology.	Attorney/Support staff
- Formulate best strategy to use in deposition. Is opposing counsel cooperative? Should you use it without notice to the opposing counsel?	Attorney
- Do you wish transmission to a remote location such as your office, expert witnesses' office and so on? If so, does court reporter have proper communication setup?	Attorney
- Select a certified real-time reporter	Support staff
- Select and purchase real-time software and train litigation team.	Support staff
- Select hardware equipment needed for the deposition.	Support staff
- Install and test system with court reporter two weeks before deposition	Support staff
- Train attorney on use of real-time software	Support staff
- Using real-time during the deposition. Have a specific strategy as to who will be using the real-time computer and their objectives.	Attorney

Digital Case Management/Trial Notebook

Both a case management plan and a trial notebook should be set up for your cases. The case management plan generally will handle the non-litigation information such as billing, docketing and so forth. The trial notebook will contain the litigation information such as document abstracts, legal issues and witnesses. Both are essential to the effective control of your case.

The purpose of a digital case/trial notebook is to provide ready electronic access to the non-litigative and litigative facts and law of your case. It should literally be your command post to locate and retrieve the relevant information in your case.

Setting up a Case Management System

Case management is one of the most important yet often overlooked aspect of a lawsuit. When a new case comes into an office a flurry of activity surrounds the case. A case file is opened, billing arrangements are set up, address books are filled with the client's information, conflict checks are performed, then a complaint or an answer is filed then generally the case will be put away. Usually until the court or the opposing party prompts us the case will grow old in the file cabinet.

A variety of questions will arise about a case. What is the case deadlines? When should discovery start? Should I interview the witnesses now? These questions can be addressed by automating a case management plan and following it. The practice of law is a business. A case management plan is important for all of your cases. It should include a plan of action tied to dates of when certain legal or discovery events will be completed. Such a plan will assist in ensuring that the case is being properly prosecuted and will prevent the situation of always having to put out fires.

Case management systems generally control the non-litigative aspects of your cases and focus on calendaring/docket, personal and firmwide scheduling, conflict checking, case accounting, time and billing, and tracking daily case activity. These important law firm functions will reduce your malpractice exposure while at the same time provide automated case action plans. The newer versions are incorporating essential integration features that enable the user to customize the interface screens and to easily link with their favorite word processor such as Microsoft Word or WordPerfect and other case management software such as PC-DOCS.

To create case management plans many attorneys use case management software or **Personal Information Manager Systems** (PIMs). These systems have generated substantial development over the last few years. They generally consist of a calendaring system, address file, and other personal information tools for your practice. They can be developed to provide a case action plan for your cases.

See Chapter 6 for further discussions on Case Management Software and Personal Information Managers.

Setting up a Digital Trial Notebook

Just think about it. Your case is set for trial tomorrow and your electronic trial notebook is ready.

- The jury selection process will be enhanced with your jury evaluation software that has the personality traits and other relevant data of a cross section of individuals that will compare voting propensities against the answers of your potential jurors.
- Your exhibits, graphics, video and other material for your opening statement is on a CD-ROM for easy access and presentation.
- Your direct and cross examination outlines are linked directly to the underlying supporting data such as text and videotaped depositions, expert reports, documents and case material. Access to these materials is at the touch of a key. You use a light pen to draw on the exhibits to point out the major points you want to make to the jury.
- Legal authorities are on your CD-ROM disk with an open telephone line to one of the legal publishers or the Internet for location of other legal and factual material as needed.
- The court reporter is providing a real-time text and video feed back to your computer and over the telephone line to your expert in his office located 500 miles away since he will not be testifying for another week.
- Legal motions are substantially prepared needing only testimony for the motion for directed verdict or other motions which will be taken from the court reporter's live testimony feed into your computer.
- Bullet charts supplement your closing argument and other materials prepared during trial and easily integrated into your prepared arguments.
- The jury instructions are modified in your computer and "published" to the jurors by use of the monitors in the courtroom.

Farfetched? No, these technologies are available today and used to varying degrees during trials. But what is still eluding the legal profession is the ultimate "integrator" of these hardware and software technologies so that the litigator has one simple but powerful entry and linking of his legal and factual materials in his trial notebook.

A digital trial notebook should duplicate electronically the primary function of the written, manual case notebook. It should be your electronic paralegal designed to provide direct access to the correspondence, pleadings, documents, facts, and law of your cases. It should be a customizable system that lawyers immediately recognize and can identify as the approach they use when preparing a case. It provides you the command post to access your case's facts, documents and law instantaneously using your favorite software programs.

The digital trial notebook should enable you to custom organize your case in a simple, yet flexible manner. It should provide direct access to specific case information in any Windows or DOS software application. So at the click of your mouse you should launch from the theory of your case into your favorite software programs to the essential information about your case.

Organizing litigation information involves all computer application programs word processing, spreadsheets, databases (legal and factual), images, full text, video, presentation tools and other programs such as a PIMs. Not only does one use all these programs but it is then necessary to thread and chain together the legal and factual issues with the witnesses testimony to enable the user to prepare for direct, cross and other aspects of the litigation process.

Many a software company has tried and many have failed trying to provide the "ultimate" litigation trial notebook attempting to be everything to everyone. Usually they provide one or more of the different computer applications such as full text and imaging but neglect the critical connecting links with other 3rd party programs such as a database or outliner. So, what is the answer? What should a digital trial notebook be?

A digital trial notebook should give one the capability to automatically access the specific case information in all other software applications. It should record your keystrokes or pathnames of the other programs so that you can automatically launch into other Windows programs saving valuable time. Whether it is a form document, deposition, or access to trial exhibits one mouse click should provide you direct access to this valuable information. Such software should be able to be used in ANY area of law that you practice to replicate the "lawyering process". Whether it be tort, corporate, business transactions, domestic relations, criminal, and so on.

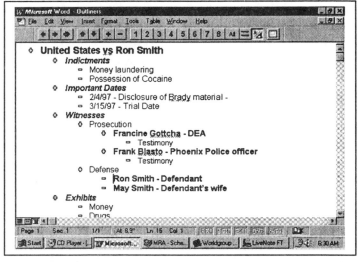

Outliners & Integrators. One solution to the front end of a trial notebook is to use an outliner or integrator as the interface of the electronic trial notebook to the substance of your case. This should provide the necessary links and interface to the computer applications that you will use to automate the legal processes of your case.

In outlining software programs, this is accomplished by "collapsing" and "expanding" subsections of your outline. If you need to rearrange the order of your witnesses because of travel problems or the changing nature of the case, then the sub-outlines of your case can be moved by the touch of a key. It is not necessary to cut and paste, but merely move the witness notes, which can include direct and cross-examination, to the new location. Many attorneys rave about the benefits of outlining programs because they work like a lawyer "thinks". It enables you to "outline" your case in the same fashion as a trial notebook.

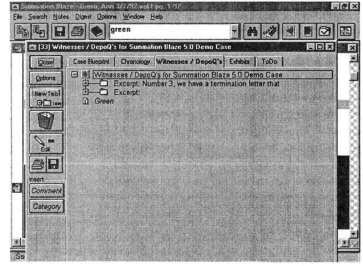

Integrators perform similar functions as an outliner but integrate the different application programs primarily using icons to represent different programs or functions. For example, an integration program may have an ICON for Witness A's testimony. After pressing the ICON a small word processing window may open giving you the capacity to enter to review or enter testimony data. Another ICON may represent launching Microsoft Excel to determine damages in your case.

However, one major pitfall of many front-end integration programs is mandating to the attorney how to set up his trial notebook. They "tell" the attorney how to set up his notebook by designing the software interface to reflect the designer's belief on how the notebook should look. The fallacy in their approach is that all attorneys approach and organize their notebooks differently. The front end user interface for the attorney must enable him to easily design the interface himself. Some outlining programs and integrators are starting to permit you this capability but we are a significant way from achieving this goal.

Using HTML to create a Digital Trial Notebook. One recent major development that holds substantial promise for the front-end integration protocol is the use of HTML programming language. HTML or Hypertext Markup Language is used extensively in the World Wide Web pages of the Internet. It basically enables the user to create a text document and link a word, letter, image or video to another document, application, video etc. As your Internet trial notebook is developed one can link a phrase such as "Deposition of Jane Smith" to her actual deposition or a description such as "Photos of plaintiff in the hospital" to actual scanned in photos of the plaintiff.

HTML is one of the most programmed languages in the world today. The standard is relatively open and major corporations such as Microsoft and Sun Microsystems are rushing to upgrade the programming language to be able to link and show video, sound, graphics and other multimedia information. This bolds extremely well for the legal profession since our legal and factual information is in all forms - video, text, graphics, and so on. It is not difficult to conceive that a browser such a Internet Explorer™ or Netscape™ would be the front end "outliner" tool with links to both your "Intranet" and "Internet."

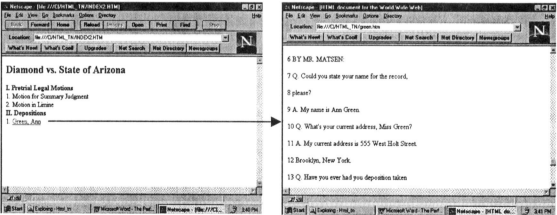

and access all the case information on your network but also would have links to information anywhere in the world on the Internet. Above is an example of an HTML trial notebook with a hypertext link to the deposition of Ann Green.

One could "construct" a trial notebook on your laptop with appropriate links to other case information.

IT Choices – outliners, document assembly, databases, full text, images, spreadsheets, real-time, and presentation.

In Section 6 we discussed extensively the definition, features and limitations of databases, full text, images and other software. In this section we will discuss the philosophy, techniques and actual applications of using IT software in a case. The following is a summary of some of the computer tools available to assist in controlling case information in a digital format. Understand the strengths and weaknesses of these tools as you decide how to best control your case information.

Outliners
- **Strengths**: Provides for the outlines of your case broken down by categories and subcategorizes. Suboutlines can be collapsed and expanded. Can provide links with other programs such as full text, databases, etc.
- **Limitations:** Does not permit large full text documents to be imported nor the abstracting of document data for sorting, reports and so on.
- **Software:** $100+
- **Primary Legal Application:** Outline the legal and factual strategy of your case. Acts as your command post or blueprint for your case.

Document Assembly
- **Strengths**: Combines word processing and database for quick assembly of legal documents. Case data can be reused.
- **Limitations:** Depending on software choice and level of document assembly setup can be difficult. Requires setup using compatible word processor and database such as HotDocs or Microsoft Access.
- **Software:** $50+
- **Primary Legal Application:** Quick assembly of letters, pleadings, motions, status reports and other documents requiring the merging of a word processing document and specific information contained in a database.

Full Text
- **Strengths**: Text can be searched for individual words or phrases
- **Limitations:** Standardized terms in documents are oftentimes not used requiring indexing, cross referencing or thesaurus building.
- **Software:** $200+
- **Paper Conversion to ASCII text:** Minimum $1.00 per page which includes error correction.
- **Primary Legal Application:** Depositions, trial transcripts, other legal materials in an ASCII format such as witness interviews or work product.

Databases
- **Strengths**: Document information can be abstracted, indexed and the results sorted by chronology; witness, legal or factual issues or document type, etc.
- **Limitations:** Database can be word searched. Setup may be difficult depending on choice of software.
- **Software:** $100+
- **Database Design:** Can be reused for other cases. depends whether in-house or outsourced.
- **Data Entry:** Objective coding is priced at per field of information entered. Subjective coding usually done in-house.
- **Primary Legal Application:** Used to capture specific data off of documents such as author, recipient, persons mentioned, legal issues, type of documents for chronology, witness or legal issue reports.

Images
- **Strengths**: Exact digital copy of documents can be stored in computer.
- **Limitations:** Individual words on documents cannot be searched. Must be indexed or linked to database record to locate documents.
- **Software:** Free +
- **Scanning:** 10 cents per page and up.
- **Primary Legal Application:** Documents can be instantly viewed on-line and used for in-court presentation.

Spreadsheets

- **Strengths**: Performs simple or high level math calculations using built in formulas.
- **Limitations:** If used for data other than numbers such as names and addresses the data is not as easy to sort and share with other applications such as a word processor.
- **Software:** $100+
- **Primary Legal Application:** Damage and other mathematical calculations.

Real-time Transcription Of Text and Video

- **Strengths**: Provides instant translation of testimony for review, impeachment or use during deposition or trial. Testimony and video can be sent to anyone in the world during trial or deposition such as your expert who may be located in another city over a regular phone line on the Internet.
- **Limitations:** Need videographer and highly skilled reporter who may charge a premium.
- **Software:** Free +
- **Primary Legal Application:** Depositions, trials and other legal proceedings.

Presentation

- **Strengths:** Depending on the software it provides the user the capability to create and present exhibits for the courtroom. Exhibits can be enlarged, drawn on and set side by side for comparison. Captures the jurors attention, fosters understanding and saves time.
- **Limitations:** may require the services of outside vendors to assist in preparing.
- **Software:** $100+
- **Primary Legal Applications:** Presentation for clients, settlement conferences or courtroom.

Integrated IT Software. There is no particular software package that performs all of the organizational tasks that are needed for a comprehensive electronic trial notebook. These tasks include an overall plan, document indexes, witness indexes, correspondence and deposition management, interrogatory control, production of documents control, admissions, pretrial orders, substantive motion preparation, opening statements, closing arguments, and so on. However, with the selective use of outliners, document assembly, databases, full text retrieval, and imaging software, valuable solutions are available.

The integration of different software applications - word processing, databases, spreadsheets, full text and so on - that enable one to link and share vital case information is vitally important. This sharing of information between programs is essential for multitasking and the practice of law. The use of OLE, DDE and the seamless integration of software such as the Microsoft Office Suite provide significant productivity gains and control over the facts of your case. The challenge with software is to take the best of the different software packages and link and integrate them together to form a powerful "digital case notebook".

On the market are some integrated litigation support programs that combine some or all of the following modules: transcript management (full text), document control (databases), case plan (outliner); document pictures (images) and a single search engine. They allow for simultaneous searching of all information collected together. Other additional features of some integrated programs include in court presentation functions and legal authority databases. For example, Summation has an integrated database, full text, outliner and imaging module while LiveNote has integrated full text and real-time modules.

Some "integrated" products to consider Summation™ (www.summation.com) (database, full text, imaging, and outliner); DepositionDirector™ – synchronizes video and text, trial presentation system, real-time video broadcasting for depositions and trials.) (www.indatacorp.com) (Summation and inData have integrated their software to work together); Smeadlink™ (www.smead.com) (database, imaging, labels, document management software, fax manager, etc.); 21st Century Lawyer™ (case calendar, and database) (www.21stcenturylawyer.com); and LiveNote™ (full text and real-time) (www.livenote.com);

Focusing on Cause of Actions, Legal Elements, Factual Propositions, Name and Other Codes.

The development of a cause of action, legal element, factual proposition and name coding system offers a significant advantage in creating your electronic case notebook. This coding can form the foundation for your case and the glue that binds all of your factual and legal information together. The organization of your case revolves around legal, factual, witness and other procedural issues. Creation of legal, factual, etc. codes to link key information is not difficult and is a process we engage in on a daily basis with our cases in a manual method. Your work product and analysis can be preserved and the reliance upon the human memory can be decreased. As the facts and documents of a case grow, your ability to handle complex litigation with minimal resources will increase. Below is a database record showing issue, authors and other coding fields.

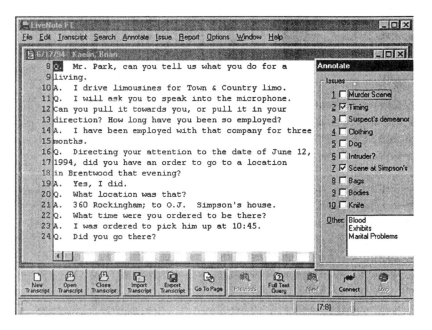

To begin creating an effective manual or digital trial notebook one must determine what legal principles and factual propositions you will have to establish in court in order to convince the trier of fact that your client should prevail. Initially, a review of the applicable legal authorities is important in assessing your client's legal position. The law school teaching methodology of analyzing cases by identifying the legal elements and factual propositions of a case and then identifying the witness testimony and documents that are connected to those legal elements can now be transferred to a computer. After discerning the elements of the causes of action and defenses that apply, it is necessary to obtain the evidence to establish for the court that your position is the correct one. When the court prepares to write their decision, or a jury is instructed as to the law of the case, they will have to determine whether the legal elements of your cause of action have been proved with sufficient factual evidence. These are very time-consuming functions but can be made much easier by using computer applications.

The examples that follow will assist in setting up the computer coding system for the legal elements and factual propositions of your case. Once this is completed and your factual information is coded under one or more elements, you will always have available a summary of your case that will be invaluable for negotiations, your opening statement, closing argument, preparation of your witnesses for trial or deposition, etc. The coding process will develop links or chains between your evidence so that important factual information can always be grouped or reported together for your use.

The legal issues connected to a case are obviously very important. Whatever factual information is collected, it must be connected to the *legal issues* that it relates.

For instance, if a contract document pertains to three different legal issues, then the factual information entered into the computer about that specific document can be connected to all three issues by the use of multi-entries in one record. The purpose and value of this type of field is that it will later permit you to search any of these issue codes, such as "nonpayment" and then generate a written report giving a description and summary of each document as it relates to the "nonpayment" issue code. You can do this for each issue code that you enter. This will give you control over what documents support the legal elements or factual propositions that you will have to prove in court in order to prevail in your case. Below is a Summation document database abstract of a letter that has been coded with the issues OSHA and Health Dept. There is a variety of other coded information directed at the legal and factual issues of the case.

Creating Legal Issue Codes. Aside from a brief description of the legal elements, your emphasis should be placed on concise formulation of the factual propositions of your elements so that the factual information you develop can be properly coded and indexed.

Below are two case examples where the legal elements and factual propositions have been coded. DO NOT USE BOTH SYSTEMS AT THE SAME TIME. In these examples the legal elements and factual propositions have been coded using a letter code and a word code. If your factual evidence is coded with these codes then anytime an issue arises about the "non-payment of the money" then the critical evidence will already have been coded and a report can be run to retrieve locations and type of evidence that support or not support your factual propositions. This way you will always be in control of the legal and factual analysis of your case.

Generic Form - Legal and Factual Proposition

Letter Codes	Word Codes
A = Cause of Action	_____ = Cause of Action
B = Legal Element	_____ = Legal Element
B1 = Factual Proposition	_____ = Factual Proposition
B2 = Factual Proposition	_____ = Factual Proposition
C = Legal Element	_____ = Legal Element
C1 = Factual Proposition	_____ = Factual Proposition
C2 = Factual Proposition	_____ = Factual Proposition
C3 = Factual Proposition	_____ = Factual proposition

Contract Cause of Action

Letter Codes	Word Codes	Legal Element or Factual Proposition
A	Contract	Contract Cause of Action
B	Duty	Duty to perform contract requirements
C	Breach	Breach of contract terms
C1	Non-Payment	XYZ Company failed to pay for last six month's supply
C2	Acceptance	XYZ Corporation accepted the widgets
D	Damages	Damages - Contract price of goods

Negligence Cause of Action

Letter Codes	Word Codes	Legal Element or Factual Proposition
A	Cause-in-fact	Causation-in-Fact element
B	Duty	Duty of care element
C	Breach	Breach of duty element
C1	Improper Lookout	The bus driver did not maintain a proper lookout
C2	Failure to Yield	The bus driver failed to yield making a left hand turn
D	Proximate Cause	Proximate cause element
E	Damages	Damages element
E1	Property	Damages - property
E2	Lost Earnings	Damages - lost earnings

Name Code List. A name code list should be developed to connect case information to different people. Name lists can be short, abbreviated name codes or letter/number codes. Do not mix the two coding systems. As you're reviewing your case materials for the first time, you will be able, generally, to compile a substantial names list which you can use for linking case information to people connected to the case. Some of these people will later be deposed and/or called as witnesses at trial. It is very important that whatever factual information is collected is connected with the person or persons to whom it relates for preparation of witness kits, etc.

For instance, if a contract document refers to three different persons, then the factual information that you enter into the computer about that document can be indexed or connected to all three persons by the use of multi-entries in the one record. Later, you can retrieve this record for deposition or trial reports by searching for any one of the three persons or the document itself.

You can either assign specific codes to each of the persons connected with a case or use their last name. If you have two people with the same last name, then use the first letter of their first name also.

Examples:

   A. Name Codes

Short Code	Full Name
Anderson, M	Anderson, Mike
Anderson, J	Anderson, Jane
Danmouth	Danmouth, Frank
Zuchowski	Zuchowski, Bill

B. Alphanumeric Codes

Short Code	Full Name
W0001	Anderson, Mike
W0002	Anderson, Jane
W0030	Danmouth, Frank
W0140	Zuchowski, Bill

With some database software programs data entry quality control is ensured by validation features that precludes entry of a name into the computer unless it has been previously authorized by someone who has validation control over the names. This ensures that whoever is entering the data in the computer does not enter an unauthorized or a misspelled name. Computers generally search for the EXACT spelling of names or other case information so it is important to correctly enter name and other case information.

Other Codes. Besides issue and name codes you may want to develop simplified coding system for other matters that arise in your case. Codes for a variety of categories can be entered to retrieve records for specific purposes. For example, you may decide to use a code such as PD to mean that further investigation or follow-up on a case is needed. The same coding technique can be used for interrogatories (Interr), request to produce (RTP), etc.

Code Sorting. Generally, in database programs, the computer will always read and sort the first column first. It gives priority to numbers in ascending order, then it will give priority to letters in ascending order for your first column. For example, if you have the number 1, number 2, and letters A and B in the first column of four document numbers, the report will come back with the document numbered 1 first, 2 second, A third, and B fourth.

Below is an example how one software program will sort the following document numbers. Always keep in mind that it first reads the first column of each number, and then will proceed to the second column of each number for sorting and sub-sorting of the document number.

Sorting Order

.001
0001
001
002
1
10
101
A1
B11
C01

It is best to test your coding system on the software program so the sorting will be acceptable for your later reports.

Approaches to Connecting the Legal and Factual information in Your Case

After obtaining or converting your case information to an electronic format the key is the ability to organize and connect the information for a variety of legal uses. The information should be organized in a method to enable one to immediately retrieve legal and factual information for a summary judgment, witness deposition preparation, opening statement, closing argument and so forth. The linkage or methodology to connect this information is key to the electronic control of your case. Some suggested methods to connect and organize your information are:

Coding. One of the primary ways to connect information in your case is through the use of codes. Codes can be developed to reflect the legal, factual, witness and other issues in your case. Once you isolate specific case information then that information can be coded and, therefore, CONNECTED to a factual or legal issue. For example, if a party in his interrogatory answers says that improper speed is an issue because he saw the defendant traveling at a high rate of speed then that factual information should be coded with an improper speed code and a witness code. If two other witnesses are also going to testify about improper speed then that specific factual information should be linked to the witnesses and the legal issue wherever it is located. If the factual information is in interrogatories, depositions or any other source then the codes will "chain" the information together for valuable reports. Reports can then be generated based upon the codes, requesting all factual information about improper speed and which witnesses will testify about this important factual issue. Herein lies the secret to the organization of your case.

Below are three documents that are connected to the legal, name and other information in your case. The critical "linking" information can be entered into a database and expanded reports can be instantly generated. As the case grows additional new documents can be abstracted and new reports generated.

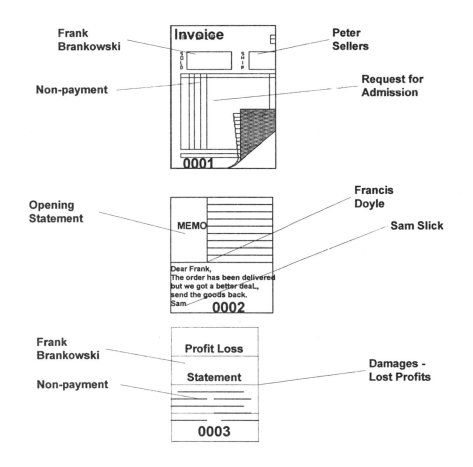

After coding these three documents in a database the following reports can be instantly generated and then updated as new information is entered.

Witness Report

Witness	Doc. #	Doc. Type	Doc. Description	Notes
Brankowski, Frank	0001	Invoice	Invoice for widgets	Authenticate
	0003	Financial Statement	Profit/Loss Statement for 3rd Q.	Ask Frank about Marginalia
Doyle, Francis	0002	Memo	Discloses reason for breach of contract	Present as image to jury
Sellers, Peter	0001	Invoice	Invoice for widgets	Authenticate
Slick, Sam	0002	Memo	Discloses reason for breach of contract	Present as image to jury

Legal Issues Report

Legal Issues	Doc. #	Doc Type	Doc Descrip.	Notes
Damages - Lost Profits	0003	Financial Statement	Profit/Loss Statement for 3rd Q.	Ask Frank about Marginalia
Non-Payment	0001	Invoice	Invoice for widgets	Authenticate
	0003	Financial Statement	Profit/Loss Statement for 3rd Q.	Ask Frank about Marginalia

Other Issues - Procedural Report

Other Issues	Doc. #	Doc Type	Doc Descrip.	Notes
Opening Statement	0002	Memo	Discloses reason for breach of contract	Present as image to jury
Request for Admission	0001	Invoice	Invoice for widgets	Authenticate

However, the difficulty with coding is that all software does not support the coding and reporting process. Whether it is database, full text, imaging or outliners codes should be inserted to enable the user to group and link this information. After linking the ideal situation is to be able to view on-screen or print legal and witness reports, in the order desired by the user, of the connected information.

Complete Full Text and Database Search. One solution used by some practitioners to the non-connectability of different software packages is to print electronic reports of the different formats - full text, databases, outliners and so forth and then import them into a sophisticated full text program for searching purposes. This has been used successfully in a number of cases.

Cut and Paste. In this method one would cut important legal and factual information and paste it into a designated section of a "trial notebook". If you intend to cross-examine the defendant about the speed of his vehicle then any reference to the speed by him or any other witness in a deposition, interrogatory, request for admission or police report is cut and pasted into a special section of your trial notebook. For example, if you are setting up your trial notebook in a word processor then one would paste this information under a section entitled DEFENDANT - CROSS, IMPROPER SPEED. Although This reflects the digital way of using a scissors to cut and paste into a trial notebook.

This method requires that the same factual information be repasted under other factual or legal areas where the facts are relevant such as in your OPENING STATEMENT or CLOSING ARGUMENT section and so on. If the legal issues change then material will have to be repasted depending upon the new categories.

IT Management of Specific Case Materials

The goal in the development of an IT management system is to control all the case information in your case. In order to achieve that goal you need to integrate a variety of different programs to your specific needs. Pretrial information control requires the application and integration of the computer concepts that were discussed in Section 6.

As we discuss the different ways to control this information in a digital manner one has to always consider the alternative traditional manner of controlling these same materials. For example, if you do not use a full text program to locate and reference information in your deposition do you continue to use colored stickers to issue code your deposition? The point is that there still is the necessity to manually control the information in your case if electronic methods are not implemented.

The following sections will focus on the different electronic methods of controlling the factual and legal information in your case. The critical issue is how to organize and control actual case information from whatever source it is derived. The following discovery information has to be organized and controlled for your case:

1) Interrogatories - answers;
2) Request for admissions - answers;
3) Expert reports disclosed;
4) Request for production - documents produced;
5) Depositions;
6) Informal interviews;
7) Investigative information;
8) Legal research;
9) Client materials; and
10) Other materials

The purpose of converting your documents into an electronic format is to be able to access, organize and provide reports for analysis. The goal of converting and enhancing the discovery material is to provide the following reports:

1. Witness kits;
2. Issue binders;
3. Chronological;
4. Deposition exhibit;
5. Trial exhibit;
6. Subject files;
7. Correspondence;
8. Follow-up;
9. Opening statements;
10. Direct and cross examination outlines, and
11. Closing arguments.

Documents

The process of producing or receiving documents poses several legal and factual electronic information issues. There are specific steps and decisions that have to be made to ensure that the digital organization of this material in completed in a low cost but effective manner. The primary electronic tool for capturing the majority of information off of these documents will be by entering data into a database. Secondary tools to be used will be creating images of the documents to link to the database record and the use of OCR to convert the paper into digital searchable full text. *For a review of databases, full text and imaging see Chapter 6.*

Screen Documents. At the outset, it is important to screen all pertinent documents as to their relevance to the case. Whether documents are relevant to a case will be determined by the applicable causes of action and legal and factual propositions that you need to prove. The relevancy of documents should become apparent after discussions with the litigation team.

> *It costs a few cents to screen a document but one to several dollars to code a document. Also, weed out unnecessary duplicates prior to inputting.*

Documents, which are highly relevant, should be abstracted. Those documents that also need to go to a specialist or expert should be flagged for forwarding to the appropriate person.

It is important for you to determine which documents will be key, marginal, or irrelevant to your case. Obviously, you do not want to abstract or input data into your computer on irrelevant documents since it would be a waste of time and your client's money.

Documents which have marginal value may develop a higher priority as a case progresses. Though you may decide initially not to enter data from these records into the computer, you may want to enter a record that summarizes all of these marginal documents so that you know that they're available at a later time. Also, it will give the attorney who is reviewing your written report, information that there are other documents that maybe relevant to their case and which they may utilize as they are developing their theories and strategies. Also, the attorney will have instant access to these marginal documents if they have been imaged in.

During the initial review of your client's documents you will need to determine the type of storage and the number of "copies' to make. The type of possible storage would include:

- Paper and
- Imaging.

Usually a control and working set of the documents will be reproduced. The sets can either be in a paper format or imaged. A control set would be an exact duplicate of the set provided by the client and would be set aside after being bates coded. A working set would be another duplicate copy but a set that would be used for witness review, preparation for summary judgment and so forth. Depending upon your choice the documents can be disclosed to the opposing party either in a paper or digital format. Originals should be stored in a safe location, copies should be used for coding.

Client's Documents and Request for Production. This initial review of your client's documents will determine whether they are responsive, whether they are useful (to whom?) and whether they are privileged. This will lead to four possible categories for your documents:

1. Not responsive and not useful;
2. Not responsive but useful;
3. Responsive and privileged; or
4. Responsive and not privileged.

- *Not responsive and not Useful.* A control copy of these documents should be maintained but not a working copy since they are neither useful nor responsive.

- *Not Responsive but Useful.* A review of the documents may disclose documents that are useful to opposing counsel or to your client. There may or may not be a requirement to disclose but a lawyer will have to have a control set and a working set. These documents should be indexed.

- Responsive and Privileged. It is very important to label immediately documents that are privileged. It should be noted on the document as well as in the database. Some firms are so careful regarding the inadvertent disclosure of these documents that a second database is created for the sole purpose of identifying and controlling privileged documents. During the indexing the basis of the privilege should be noted. A control set and working set should be created for the litigation.

- Responsive and not Privileged. Once the responsive and non-privileged documents are located then these should be disclosed to the opposing party. If it is a large production then the opposing party should review and tag the ones he wants to copy. Arrangements would have to be made for opposing counsel to inspect and copy or image the documents. The documents selected by opposing counsel should be noted by either numbering or renumbering the documents. Both a working and control copy of these documents should be created. These should be fully objectively and subjectively indexed. Some imaging programs enable one to redact privileged material on the image before the image is disclosed to the opposing party.

Document Reviewing Information. Some basic database information should be entered into your database upon determining the relevance of the documents. The information should include the following:

- Person's ID who reviewed the documents;
- Date Reviewed;
- Whether they were produced to other party; and if
- Not produced the reason.

Flag especially important (helpful or harmful) documents. All members of your litigation team should continually flag important documents for the following reasons:

- Disclosure to outside experts;
- Full Text conversion;
- Helpful;
- Harmful; and
- Whether they will be disclosed to opposing counsel.

This is a sample database screen capturing some of the information discussed above.

Other Party's Documents. When the other party discloses a copy of the documents to you a control set and working set should be immediately created. Depending upon their importance to the issues of your case these documents should be both imaged and objectively and subjectively indexed. Number all the documents that come through the door. This is done by using a sequential number stamp machine, computer generated labels or have a copying service copy them and have a number imprinted as part of the process. They should be easily retrievable by number. It is strongly suggested to number each page and not just each document.

Document Databases - Designing and Building. After screening the documents the design and building of the database are important steps since the final results of what data is entered is reflected in the reports that are generated. Control over the design and entry of information for your final reports is critical to a successful database application. For the design of a database to be successful, one should be able to locate key document data, documents that pertain to particular issues and witnesses, and any other data important to the theories of your case.

Creating customized database fields and forms will permit you to control the facts of your individual case, whether it is a medical malpractice, automobile, contract, wrongful termination, criminal case, or any other legal matter. Also, you can create fields and forms for law office management functions such as a phone directory, briefbank, and so forth.

Sometimes your information needs may change as the case progresses. This is often unavoidable because the issues of a case may change. In the event that you need to collect additional information about a case after you have started your application, some software database programs permit you to add or delete fields to a form even after you have added information to other database records. After adding additional fields to collect information, you can then generate new reports that include the new fields.

The lawyering process is required in designing your database. There is no software program that determines what data needs to be collected from a breach of contract case. The legal theory and factual propositions that need to be proved are the work product of the lawyer. Once these elements are identified, then the software can be "programmed" as to what information will be entered. Once entered the computer can retrieve and sort this information according to the legal theories that have been programmed by the designation of database fields, legal issue codes, and so on.

Below is an example of a Summation™ database design:

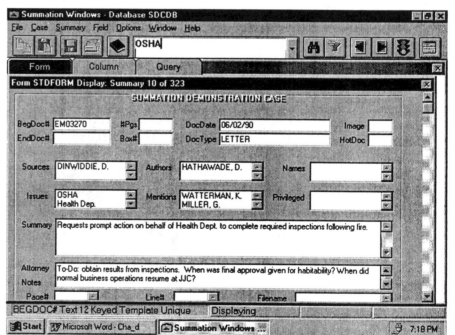

Rules of Thumb on Database Design. Building a good database can offer a real sense of accomplishment, but few outsiders realize this. Many computer enthusiasts, after having been asked to put together a simple database, have explored the outer reaches of the program and have become the unofficial "database programmer for the organization." If you start to proceed down this road, keep some of the following rules of thumb in mind:

- *Decide What You Want From Your Database.* Focus, focus, and focus on the end results. What kind of information do you want and how should it be organized? Base your design on your end results. Don't expect to get dependable data out of your applications if you don't build in a place for the right information at the beginning.
- *Design Your Database on Paper First.* Once you know what information you want to collect, plan how the data will be organized. Write all the different types of information that you will be collecting in your case. For example, one database form may contain information about the documents in your case, another the legal pleadings, another the personal information on all persons connected to the case and another form for an action plan on what steps you will take in preparing the case for trial. When planning reports keep in mind how the reports will look on the screen or on paper. Some programs only allow 80 columns and some monitors only display 24 lines at once.

- *Avoid Duplicity.* Do not collect the same data twice in different database records. You will save time and avoid data entry errors by only entering that data once.
- *Identify Each Record by a Unique Code.* Database management will be simpler if each record contains a field for a unique number - social security number, document number, witness ID code, etc. This will simplify searches.
- *Break Information into Smaller Fields.* Any information you want to use for searching and sorting should have its own field. For example, if you want to sort your document database by date and if you include the date information in a summary field, you will be unable to create a chronology report of the documents.
- *Allow Adequate Space for Each Field.* Be generous when assigning field lengths. Try to anticipate the longest possible entry for that field. For example it is suggested to allow at least 15 characters for first names, 20 characters for last names, 25 to 30 characters for addresses, two separate lines for addresses, city names should be 15 characters in length, state fields only have to be 2 characters, unless you have foreign addresses. If the field length is to short most database programs permit one to redefine the field length without losing any data.
- *Position the Most Important Information at the Top of the Form.* The information will usually be an ID number, document date, etc. when you are entering information into a document database form. In a witness information form the last name, first name, etc. will be the important information.
- *Make Data-Entry Forms Readable.* Forms that are clear and easy to read reduce data entry errors. Don't crowd fields. Spread them out on a page. Try to keep them in a vertical line to permit easy viewing of the fields.
- *Arrange Fields Logically on the Form.* If you will be entering data from documents, set up the form to reflect the data that will be entered in a logical manner. For example, the name of the document and its condition would be some of the first fields on a form.
- *Set Default Entries for Commonly Repeated Data.* Some programs enable you to set a default entry for certain fields, which can be overwritten if necessary. For example, many of the witnesses in a case may reside in the same city, like Phoenix. You can save data entry time by making Phoenix the default value for that field and the having the information already entered in the field when a new form appears.
- *Test Your Database Before You Use It.* Create 10 or 12 records and produce the reports that you need. This dry run should uncover any deficiencies. It is imperative that the lead attorneys sign off on the database design and reports that will be generated.

Document Database Sample Fields. The following are the properties assigned to different fields in a sample document control application. They contain legal and administrative considerations for various fields in a document control database. Also, some sample field properties are shown to give you an idea of there use. For reviews of field properties see *Section 6, Databases.* This will provide an understanding of some of the decisions that are required as you begin to design your own fields for your specific case. In any case you may decide to use five of the following fields or all of them depending upon budget, time, etc.

DCNO - Document Number

Legal/Administrative Overview:

- This should be a required entry field, meaning that a document number must be entered prior to saving the record.
- This may be the image filename that links the image to this record.
- For a further discussion on document ID numbers see Developing Document Control and Image Numbering Systems in the section that follows.

Caution: *In some programs, once you enter the document number and save a record, you cannot subsequently edit that document number. The only way to change a document number will be to delete the entire record while in the edit mode and reenter the data with a new document number.*

Field Properties:

1. Data Type - text
2. Data Width - 12 characters
3. Unique Value - Yes
4. Validation Control - No
5. Required Field - Yes
6. Multi-Entry Allowed - No

COND - Document Condition

Legal/Administrative Overview:
- In this field, enter the condition(s) of the document.
- Suggested objective coding for this field can be:

  1. Marginal - This notation will alert the reader to the fact that someone has written marginal notes on the document.
  2. Incomplete - This notation means that there are incomplete pages to this set of related documents.
  3. Illegible - This code means that the document or documents are partially illegible.
  4. OK - This code means that the condition of the document is acceptable.
- Multi-Entry should be allowed for this field.

Field Properties:

1. Data Type - Name
2. Data Width - 15 characters
3. Unique Value - No
4. Validation Control - No
5. Required Field - No
6. Multi-Entry Allowed - Yes

IMAG - Document Image Link

Legal/Administrative Overview:
- This field will permit you to enter information about whether a "graphic image" of your document is available for instant viewing.
- Information about a graphic image should be entered here if you have previously scanned in and linked a graphic image of a document to a record. For example, if the image of Contract #104 is linked to this record, type in the field identifier to link the image.
- You can generate a report of all documents available for "graphic image" viewing.

Field Properties:

1. Data Type - Alpha/Numeric
2. Data Width - 70 Characters
3. Unique Value - Yes
4. Validation Control - No
5. Field Required - No
6. Multi-Entry Allowed - No

DATE - Document Date

Legal/Administrative Overview:
- In this field, enter the date of the document.
- Acceptable date formats are generally MM/DD/YY or M/D/YY. Acceptable date formats for March 3, 1990 are 3/3/90 or 03/03/90.
- This is a required entry field, meaning that a date must be entered prior to saving the record.
- Estimate the date of document if no date appears on the document. This will assist you when preparing reports to have the summary of the document appear in at least the estimated year that it was prepared.
- Some programs permit unknown document dates to be estimated as 00/00/89. The 00 is the estimated month, 00 is the estimated day, and the 89 is the estimated year the document was prepared.
- If there are several dates on your document, be consistent from document to document. The date the document is executed or the date the last signature was placed on the document can be entered. Standardize this entry requirement prior to entering document dates in the application.

Field Properties:

1. Data Type - Date
2. Data Width - 9
3. Unique Value - No
4. Validation Control - No
5. Required Field - Yes
6. Multi-Entry Allowed - No

TYPE - Document Type

Legal/Administrative Overview:

- In this field, you will enter the type of documents. The type of documents will generally depend upon the kind of case that you are working on. For example, in a contract case, you may have documents that can be divided into the following categories:

    1. Contract Documents
    2. Correspondence
    3. Quarterly Financial Records
    4. Tenant Cash Receipts
    5. Modifications to Contract

Tip: *Prior to entering information into this field, separate out the different types of documents and standardize the entry names for these document types.*

Field Properties:

1. Data Type - Name
2. Data Width - 30 characters
3. Unique Value - No
4. Validation Control - No
5. Required Field - No
6. Multi-Entry Allowed - No

DESC - Document Description

Legal/Administrative Overview:

- In this field, enter a description and/or title of the document for identification purposes.

Field Properties:

1. Data Type - Text
2. Data Width - 2 lines displayed
3. Unique Value - No
4. Validation Control - No
5. Required Field - No
6. Multi-Entry Allowed - No

SUMM - Document Summary

Legal/Administrative Overview:

- Type in a concise, clear summary of the document. A natural inclination is to type in a lot of data concerning each document. It is better for retrieval and case analysis purposes to type in a short and concise summary of the document that meets the needs of the case. Otherwise, you are essentially duplicating the document by typing in a significant amount of data from the document which may not be needed. As you gain experience in abstracting or summarizing documents, this will become easier.

Field Properties:

1. Data Type - Text
2. Data Width - 4 lines displayed
3. Unique Value - No
4. Validation Control - No
5. Required Field - No
6. Multi-Entry Allowed - No

IMPO - Document Importance

Legal/Administrative Overview:

- The document importance field permits you to enter a code to designate the importance of the document. This will enable you to later retrieve documents according to the order of importance as they might relate to a given person connected to the case or a legal issue that concerns the case.
- Two suggested coding techniques are set out below to rate the importance of your documents.

1. Enter a numerical number to indicate its importance.

    10 - Highest Importance
    09
    08
    07
    06
    05
    04
    03
    02
    01 - Lowest Importance

Tip: *If you are going to use numerical values, always include a zero before the single digit number. This will ensure that the documents are retrieved and sorted in the appropriate order.*

2. Another technique would be to provide a word code for each document. For a particular document, you can give it the designation of HOT - Highest Importance, WARM - Luke Warm Importance, or COLD which is of lowest importance.

Field Properties:

1. Data Type - Text
2. Data Width - Four Characters
3. Unique Value - No
4. Validation Control - No
5. Required Field - No
6. Multi-Entry Allowed - No

NOTE - Notes

Legal/Administrative Overview:

- In the NOTE field, you will enter notes, investigative information, or comments regarding a document. You can enter data in which:
  - additional information needs to be located regarding this document;
  - requests for production of related documents should be filed;
  - interrogatories relating to the document need to be sent out; or
  - any other miscellaneous matter connected with the document needs to be   noted.
- The value of entering this information is that subsequently you can generate a written report based on this field and list the notes for follow-up work on the case. This same technique can be used for Request for Admissions, Request for Production, Investigations, and so forth.

Field Properties:

1. Data Type - Text
2. Data Width - 3 lines displayed
3. Unique Value - No
4. Validation Control - No
5. Required Field - No
6. Multi-Entry Allowed -No

NAMC - Names Connected with Documents

Legal/Administrative Overview:

- This field will record the names of persons who are connected with the documents.
- The name forms should be filled out while you are reviewing your documents for the first time. These forms are set up so that you can give an abbreviated name to the persons in the case or assign them an alpha/numerical code. Do not mix the two coding systems.
- Below is a suggested coding technique to indicate the relationship of individuals to a particular document:

A = Author
C = Persons copied with the document.
R = Recipient
M = Persons mentioned in document
= _____.

For example, if Smith was the author of a document, enter Smith-A or Smith(A) into the field area. After you enter the name of the person and his or her connection with the case, then you will be able to retrieve those records and create a report of who authored a particular document, who received copies, and so forth.

- Since this field has the capability of having multi-entry names, numerous names can be entered into this "field." After entering the names of the persons connected with the document, you will be able to search this field for any person who has been named in this field.
- To ensure that the only authorized issue codes are typed in and spelled correctly, the validation control feature is ON. This means that certain issue codes which have been previously authorized can only be entered into the computer.
- ALTERNATIVE METHOD: Some database designers prefer to create 3 or 4 fields for the names connected to a document. The fields are **AUTH** - Author; **MENT** - Persons Mentioned in the Document; **RECIP** - recipient or **ADDR** - Addressees. These separate fields can be searched separately or together to return all relevant documents pertaining to a witness.

Field Properties:

1. Data Type - Alpha/Numeric
2. Data Width - 17 characters
3. Unique Value - No
4. Validation Control - Yes
5. Required Entry - No
6. Multi-Entry Allowed - Yes.

ISSC - Legal Elements/Factual Propositions

Legal/Office Overview:

- In this field, you will enter the legal element and factual proposition codes for your case.
- This is an important field in your document control form since coding of this field will directly link a document to specific legal elements and/or factual propositions
- Setting up coding for the causes of action, legal elements, and factual propositions of your case has been explained in a prior section.
- To ensure that the only authorized issue codes are typed in and spelled correctly, utilize the validation control feature. This means that certain issue codes which have been previously authorized can only be entered into the computer.

Field Properties:

1. Data Type - Alpha/Numeric
2. Data Width - 17 characters
3. Unique Value - No
4. Validation Control - On
5. Required Entry - No
6. Multi-Entry Allowed - Yes, numerous codes can be entered into this field.

OTHC - Other Codes

Legal/Administrative Overview:

- In this field, codes for a variety of categories can be entered in order to later retrieve records for specific reports.
- Examples and forms in an upcoming section will assist you in setting up "other codes" for the OTHC field.
- For example, you may decide to use a code such as PD to mean that further investigation or follow-up on a case is needed. The investigative information will be entered in the NOTE field. After you enter the PD code in the OTHC field, you can retrieve those records and generate a report, with one column for the PD code and another column for the NOTE field.
- The same technique can be used for interrogatories, request to produce, etc.
- To ensure that only authorized OTHC codes are typed in and spelled correctly, the authority control feature is ON. This means that only certain OTHC codes which have been previously authorized can be entered into the computer.

Field Properties:

1. Data Type - Alpha/Numeric
2. Data Width - 17 Characters
3. Unique Value - No
4. Validation Control - Yes
5. Field Required - No
6. Multi-Entry Allowed - Yes

EVID-Evidentiary Issues Connected to Documents

Legal/Administrative Overview:

- In this field, you can enter information concerning the evidentiary issues or problems with a particular document. For example, if a handwritten document needs a foundation before it can be entered into evidence, you could enter information in this field that "witness Slade needs to identify document for foundational purposes." Later, when you are preparing an evidentiary report and want to know if there are any evidentiary document problems connected with the case, you can retrieve these records and generate a report that will summarize evidentiary problems for all documents in your case.

Tip: *If you have the same evidentiary issue for a number of documents, this is a good place to create a "macro" or a "lookup value" which will allow you at the touch of a key on your keyboard to reproduce a particular phrase or evidentiary sentence.*

Field Properties:

1. Data Type - Alpha/Numeric
2. Data Width - 70 Characters
3. Unique Value - No
4. Validation Control - No
5. Field Required - No
6. Multi-Entry Allowed - Yes

PRIV - Privileged/Confidential Information Connected to Documents

Legal/Administrative Overview:

- This field permits you to enter information regarding the privileged or confidential nature of the document. In this field, you would enter the nature of the privilege as it pertains to the document and then later generate a report of all documents that are not subject to discovery
- Some of the documents that you work with may be privileged or confidential and not subject to discovery by the opposing party. For example, if a document was prepared in "anticipation of litigation," this document can be considered "work product" and not subject to disclosure. Another document may be subject to an attorney-client "privilege" and not subject to discovery.

Tip: *This is another field where a "macro" may save you time in inputting certain key phrases.*

Field Properties:

1. Data Type - Alpha/Numeric
2. Data Width - 70 Characters
3. Unique Value - No
4. Validation Control - No
5. Field Required - No
6. Multi-Entry Allowed - Yes

HIST - Production History of Document

Legal/Administrative Overview:

- In this field, enter information relating to the disclosure or discovery of the document. Since most documents in a case are subject to discovery by the opposing party, it is important to maintain information, either when you received the document, or whether and when it was disclosed to the opposing party.
- Many times, due to the number of documents in a case, it is extremely difficult when a second or third request for production arises to determine whether or not particular documents have been previously disclosed, either through deposition, interrogatories, or other requests for production. To solve this problem, information about a particular document and its production history is entered here for future retrieval and report generation.
- It is suggested that standardized phrases are followed and used in this field. For example, for documents disclosed or received, you might enter:

  Provided to opposing party pursuant to Request for Production dated February 22, 1990.

  OR

  Received from opposing party pursuant to Request for Production of documents dated September 14, 1990
- Multi-Entry are permitted for repeated disclosure history or third party disclosure.
- To ensure that only authorized HIST codes are typed in and spelled correctly, the authority control feature is ON. This means that only certain HIST codes which have been previously authorized can be entered into the computer.

Tip: *A macro to standardize phrases or lookup table can be created to save a substantial amount of time in entering this information.*

Field Properties:

1. Data Type - Alpha/Numeric
2. Data Width - 70 Characters
3. Unique Value - No
4. Validation Control - Yes
5. Field Required - No
6. Multi-Entry Allowed - Yes

DEXH - Deposition Exhibit

Legal/Administrative Overview:

- This field will permit you to enter information establishing a particular document as an exhibit to a deposition. It is important to know whether testimony was provided by witnesses about the document.
- This field can be multi-entry so if a document is used as an exhibit in more than one deposition this information can be entered. Later, you can search this field for all documents as they relate to a particular witness and whether or not they were made exhibits to his/her deposition or to any other depositions.
- One of the most powerful features of some programs is the capability to link up the full text of a deposition of a witness directly to a document database abstract that was discussed in the deposition.
- You could also imbed cross-reference codes in the deposition, such as #008. Then you can immediately go to all cross-references relating to this document and what the witnesses testified regarding document #008 in their deposition.

Field Properties:

1. Data Type - Alpha/Numeric
2. Data Width - 70 Characters
3. Unique Value - No
4. Validation Control - No
5. Field Required - No
6. Multi-Entry Allowed - Yes

TEXH - Trial Exhibit

Legal/Administrative Overview:
- This field will permit you to enter information about a document as a future trial exhibit.
- For example, you might know that a purchase contract with a document number of 008 will be entered into evidence in trial. Before trial, you can enter information in this field indicating that it is "Plaintiff's Exhibit Number 1." Then, you can generate a report listing the document titles and a summary of those documents that will be used as exhibits in the trial.

Tip: *In order to sort this field in ascending exhibit order #, it may be necessary that you put in the number of the exhibit first to generate a chronological report of the exhibits. Thus, for a particular exhibit, you would enter:*
0001, Plaintiff's Exhibit #.

Field Properties:

1. Data Type - Alpha/Numeric
2. Data Width - 70 Characters
3. Unique Value - No
4. Validation Control - No
5. Field Required - No
6. Multi-Entry Allowed - Yes

FTXT - Document Full Text Link

Legal/Administrative Overview:
- If the full text of a document has been converted for use with this program and linked to a document control application record, enter information about the name and the type of full text document available for viewing. For example, if a significant contract document has been converted for searching and so forth, type in

"Contract 104 has been converted for full text searching" or a field describing that has been converted to full text.

- Later, you can retrieve all records pertaining to this field and generate a report showing all full text documents available for searching, viewing, and so forth.

Field Properties:

1. Data Type - Alpha/Numeric
2. Data Width - 70 Characters
3. Unique Value - No
4. Validation Control - No
5. Field Required - No
6. Multi-Entry Allowed - No

Indexing or Coding Your Documents. One key method of organizing and controlling the information in your cases is coding or abstracting the document information. **CODING or ABSTRACTING** means the determination and transfer of designated classes of information from each document onto a computer form that is designed for use in entering the selected information into the litigation support system. If you intend to image your documents indexing the documents is required because an image of a document cannot be searched. However, if the document had been converted to machine-readable text using OCR then the documents could be word searched.

The extent of indexing or coding depends on the usefulness of document. This will also determine whether certain documents should be converted to full text. There are two primary coding methods – bibliographic or objective coding and subjective coding.

Bibliographic Indexing (BI) or Objective Coding. In computer document control terminology, objective coding is coding that can be easily obtained from the face of a document. It does not require any "subjective" reasoning or thought process. Objective coding merely requires the recognition of certain fields of information such as the author, date, addressee, and the like. Approximately 16 pages can be objectively coded per hour. For example, objective coding of a document would include document number (or "Bates" number), document date, document type (if apparent), document title or description, the connection of persons with the document, such as author, addressee, persons mentioned, recipients, attachments, and exhibit numbers.

The most common coding of documents is bibliographic indexing (BI). BI is creating one database record for each document in a collection. Bibliographic indexing is increasing, as use of imaging becomes more popular and the need for document control increases.

BI should be used when:
- Imaging is going to be used;
- One has a large number of documents but are unsure of their relative importance;
- Budget considerations do not allow for a more detailed database; or when
- Paralegals or others will do further detailed or subjective coding in the office.

Subjective Coding. Subjective coding of a document involves determining the document's relevance to particular legal or factual issues and summarizing the document. This includes an understanding of the legal issues of the case and the application of those issues to the facts of the case. Often, legal technicians or paralegals are able to code this information for eventual review by the attorney in charge of the case. Approximately 8 document pages can be subjectively coded in an hour. Reading and understanding the text of the document, relevance, issue identification, summary, confidentiality code, comments, and whether to convert to full text are considered subjective coding. Codes are generally work product and not subject to discovery. However, codes used by your client in his business are probably discoverable and not protected by work-product. Since subjective coding is time-consuming and expensive ensure that only your critical documents are coded.

Are Your Database and Images Discoverable by Opposing Counsel?

It has long been thought that the document coding and imaging of your documents are protected under a attorney work product privilege. However, this belief is coming under attack as courts consider the discoverability of databases and images.

Opponents argue for the discoverability of bibliographic databases to assist them in managing and controlling their material discovered from opposing counsel. The owner of the database will argue that the database and images are the result of attorney's mental impressions, conclusions, opinions and legal theories. To argue such a position it is imperative that you take certain steps at the outset to protect your computerized data. For example:

- *Build a selective database.* If you choose to image and create a bibliographic index of *all* the documents in a case then it is difficult to argue that any attorney's theories are wrapped up in the complete computerization of the case materials. On the other hand if attorneys will consciously select documents that fit into your theories of the case and have those documents only databased and imaged then it a much stronger argument that they should be protected. If you turn over the computerized information the other side will know exactly your theory of the case. Judges do not generally understand databases and images and look upon them as clerical tasks and do not see the problem of turning over data to the opposing party. However, if it becomes an intimate part of your work product then a judge will be less likely to force you to disclose your data.

- *Enter into an agreement to share the cost of a database and imaging at the beginning of the case.* If you take the initiative at the outset to work out an arrangement to share the costs of a database and images then it is more difficult for the opposing party to plead undue burden or expense to the judge.

- *Review existing case law.* Decisions are handed down on a daily basis regarding the protection of databases. These will have a significant effect on how one sets up their database and imaging projects.

Developing Document Control and Image Numbering Systems. The document and imaging numbering or coding system for your application gives you control over the documents. If you are going to image documents the document database record number and the image record or file number can and should be the same number. A document and imaging numbering or coding system can be very simple or sophisticated depending upon your desires and the needs of a particular case. Below are three possible methods of coding your documents and images:

- *Numbering System Only* - You may decide to number your documents and images using a numerical system from A00001 through A10000. Thus, all the documents in the case would be given a number between A00001 and A10000. Your numbering system must always contain the same number of numerical and/or alphabetical digits. In some programs you must put zeros before the number up to the greatest number that you will be coding. For example, if you are coding up to the number A10000, then you must put in four zeros before the number one for your first document, i.e., your first document will have the number A00001. The computer reads the document number from left to right, so if you enter the number 12, it will be retrieved before the number 2 since it reads the first column of the document number first.

- *Numbering System by Document Type* - You might decide to set up a numerical coding system by document type. For example, in a contract case, the numbering system might be set up as follows:

A0001 - A0999 Contract #104 documents
A1000 - A1999 Contract #205 documents
A2000 - A2999 Financial records for ABC Company
A3000 - A3999 Cash receipts for widgets
A4000 - A4999 Open
A5000 - A5999 Pleadings and correspondence
A6000 - A6999 Documents obtained from Req. to Produce

- *Sophisticated Numbering System.* Many document-coding systems will utilize letters and numbers for a specific document to provide additional information about it. Below are some possibilities for a document coding system:

  a. The first letter or digit is the party that produced the document.

  > 1 = Plaintiff Adams
  > 2 = Defendant Smith
  > 3 = Non party Jones

  b. The second letter or digit is the location of the document.

  > A = Warehouse
  > B = File cabinet
  > C = Main office

  c. The third digit is the day it was produced.

  > 1 = Plaintiff's request to produce dated October 5th, 1981.
  > 2 = Defendant's request to produce dated November 16, 1981.

  d. The fourth alpha/number is the actual document number.

  > A001 = Contract #104

  For example, a document with the number 1A1A001 would mean the document was provided by Plaintiff Adams, is located in the warehouse, was received pursuant to Defendant's request to produce dated November 16, 1981, and the document number is A001.

Though it may seem complex, if you begin a coding system that you're comfortable with, you will discover after a short period of time that the codes can be easily remembered and you will not need a coding sheet each time that you code a document.

Coding Your Documents. It is suggested that a procedure and training manuals be developed to ensure that all the documents are coded in a consistent uniform method. A procedure manual will contain a description of the document processing that will take place and the order of the screening process. A training manual relates to a

> Tip: The Avery Pro Labeler program (www.avery.com) will automatically generate alphanumeric numbers or bar codes in serial number on attachable labels. Manually, you can obtain what is called a Bates stamper that automatically increases the number on the stamper each time it is stamped on a document. This will assist you in not having to either write the increasing numbers on the document or manually changing a stamper each time you place a number on a document. Outside service companies that copy or image your documents can customize document bar-coded numbers to meet your needs. Some photocopiers now automatically place a number on your documents as they are being copied. If possible attach a number along with a bar code. This will assist you later with in-court presentation or for pretrial retrieval purposes.

particular case and explains to the trainee HOW each step is to be performed and what is pertinent to the case.

Coding the documents can be accomplished by using either an "image" of the document or the "hard" copy. The advantage of imaging your documents is that the extent of the coding for the documents can be determined as the case progresses. With imaging, you can always retrieve the document since it is linked to a particular database record for instant viewing. For example, after a document has been provided limited objective coding and the document's importance has increased as the case progresses, then the document can be immediately accessed on your computer screen to do subjective coding.

"Hard" copies can be coded and then filed in 3-ring binders for later retrieval for viewing and further coding, if needed. Hard copies should be in a central location.

Coding Your Documents. There are a number of different methods for entering information into the computer from the documents. You can:

> Tip: Whatever coding system that you devise beforehand, make sure and test it out on the software program sorting and retrieval system since it will read the code numbers differently according to whether they are letters or numbers.

- Enter the field information directly from your documents into the computer.
- Reproduce an exact printed form of the computer form where someone can manually write in the information. After someone checks for accuracy, you can then enter it into the computer.

Tip: *One firm, when they are training support staff on the data to input, will take a replica of the computer document form and enlarge it several times as a teaching aide to explain the different fields of data entry.*

- Using dictation equipment, record the information to be entered into fields, and then have support staff enter the information into the database.
- Batch Entry – This is a method of entering document information in a certain format in a word processing program and batching it over or importing it into the database program. By this method, you can have a team of typists enter data quickly in a word processing program for importing into the database. The database "imports" the data into the database fields. This is a great time saver as it allows an experienced word processor to enter the data quickly. Batch entry, when done by teams of typists at multiple terminals is a very powerful and efficient way to enter data of either large or small quantities.

   The following are some other timesaving techniques for entering data into a database program.
   - *Duplicating Function.* Some programs enable you to press one key in a specific field to duplicate the information contained in the same field in a prior record. For example, if you typed in **ABC Purchase Contract** in the TYPE field of your prior document record, then, when you are at the TYPE field in a subsequent record, press the appropriate key and the TYPE will be duplicated in the second record automatically.
   - *Incremental Increases.* This feature will automatically increase the present document number by one from the previous document number. If you go to the **DCNO** field of your second document and press **the appropriate key**, the document number will automatically increase by 1.
   - *Field Entry Defaults.* This feature enables you to make the information in one or more fields appear in the document summary without retyping. To override, merely press the clear key or type over the information.
   - *System Date.* This feature permits you to place the current system date into a field with one keystroke.
   - *Lookup Tables.* This feature increases the speed of data entry and will ensure that words are not misspelled. At the press of a key, a lookup table will appear on the screen and will list, for example, the names of all relevant persons. Select the name or names of your choice, and by pressing the enter key, the name will be inserted into the appropriate field.
   - *Macros.* While adding information in the different fields of your computer form, you have the option of creating macros that you can activate any time. Macros are essentially the ability to combine several keystrokes into one "macro" keystroke. For example, if you were entering the

phrase "Code of Federal Regulations," you could save this phrase as a macro. Then you could press one keystroke to have this phrase automatically typed into the field of your choice in the same or different records. The macro would be saved for the future even after you exit from the program.

- *Field Properties.* For each field that you create, you have the capability to limit and define what information can be entered into that specific field. For example, you can designate a field a "date" field and only dates can be entered in the field.

Personnel Issues when Coding Your Documents. Many firms code their own documents instead of sending them out to service bureaus. If you decide to code your own documents here are some suggestions.

- Have a clerk enter in the objective coding for a document such as document number, date, type, and names connected with the document. A legal technician or paralegal could check the accuracy of this objective coding and subjectively code, i.e., summarize the document and put in issue codes that are relevant to the document. After this has been completed, an attorney reviews the original document and the entire coding.
- Coding personnel can include college or law school students. Have quality coders. Recent unemployed college graduates with a liberal arts degree are good candidates. Paralegals and junior lawyers can be expensive but are needed for subjective coding. Lawyers and other professionals are generally not good coders because they put to much detail in the records. Coders must have the ability to read a large number of documents, understand these documents, stay interested and locate objectively important facts. Labor costs make up a significant element of databases and should be calculated at the outset.
- A senior administrator can oversee the coding process with assistance from the lead attorney. Add an extra clerical employee if the coding process requires. Allocate sufficient number of coders for the job. Determine number of documents per hour and determine time to code collection.
- Train, train, and do further training to ensure consistency in the coding process. ACCURACY and UNIFORMITY are of paramount importance. Designate a quality control person and perform quality checks. Standardize terminology such as date, document types (usually no more than 20 types) and name formats.

All of us have heard of the term "garbage in - garbage out." It is important when entering data, that it is entered in the right field and correctly spelled. This is made much easier by properties assigned to fields that do not allow duplicates in certain fields and the validation control that only allows certain information to be entered. For example, only certain names can be chosen for the name field in a document control application, depending on which names have been previously authorized.

These are extremely important tasks and set procedures should be established for both objective and subjective issue coding. RE-CODING is very expensive. Consistency is the key. Run tests to determine if there are mistakes, and if so, retrain before you are to far into the project.

Other Coding Considerations. Other factors to consider for a successful BI coding project are the following:

- Will opposing counsel consent to sharing the cost of creating a bibliographic database and images connected thereto?
- Code directly into PC instead of on coding sheets, it reduces errors.
- Ensure quality control measures are in place including spell-checking fields, consistency of name and date insertions and appropriate Bates number.
- Define what a document is.
- Screen, screen, and screen the documents so that only relevant documents are chosen for BI. The per document cost may be low but the cost can increase rapidly depending on the volume of documents. Use file level indexing for less important documents.
- Add an issues field with 6-10 issue codes this will provide for some grouping by issues.
- Attachments can be handled in a field such as ATTACH: H - has, I – is, B – both or N – Neither and have 2 other fields to have the beginning page number and ending page number of the attached documents;
- Use BI for relevant documents and detailed subjective coding for critical documents.
- Security and access to the database is important to keep the confidentiality of the documents.

- Determine the timeline for the project.
- Who will be the contact person to the outside service bureau?
- What is the production schedule? Who is authorized to make changes to it?
- Client arguments – present the costs as being necessary because of the need to use up-to-date proven technology to control critical case information. The other side will be using the technology and request a denial in writing.

Retrieving Database Information for Editing and Reports. The capability of easily retrieving a select group of records from a database is the control that you need for litigation purposes. The software program you choose should give you this control by providing the capability to conduct a simultaneous comprehensive search and retrieval of your database records and full text documents for information critical to your case. It should enable you to conduct a search of each record by individual fields or multiple fields. Once these records have been retrieved, they are then available for on-screen viewing if images are attached, editing, and generating reports.

Software should enable you to search keyword, terms, etc., in each individual record and also search full text documents that are directly linked to the records for these same keyword or terms simultaneously. This includes concurrent searches of any cross-references, notes, or issue codes you may have imbedded in the full text documents.

Since the search feature is so powerful and critical to any database application, it is important that you become very familiar with this function and can search for and retrieve information with ease.

The purposes of searching for and retrieving records are:

1. To generate on-screen, printed reports, or reports saved to disk.
2. To retrieve records for editing purposes.
3. To retrieve records to view the information or for reviewing testimony from full text documents such as depositions.
4. To retrieve records that are linked to graphic images of documents so that you can view the graphic images of these documents on-screen or print them out.

This is an example of a database search using Microsoft Access.

The following are examples of information that can be retrieved by searching a full text and database information system. The sample database fields from which these searches will retrieve data are those discussed earlier in this section.

Document Database Application Searches

Single Field Searches
- Retrieve all document control records.

- Retrieve all document records where the documents are coded as being illegible or incomplete.
- Retrieve all records with document dates after July 1, 1986.
- Retrieve all records with a reference to "handwritten" in document type field.
- Retrieve all document records with a reference to the word "contract" in the description field.
- Retrieve all document records where a reference is made to the word "addendum" in the summary field.
- Retrieve all records where the document importance is rated as "HOT."
- Retrieve all document records with a reference to witness "Jones" in the note field.
- Retrieve all document records where "Jones" has been listed as a person connected to a document.
- Retrieve all document records where the word "defective" is an issue code in the ISSC field.
- Retrieve records where further follow-up or investigation has to be completed.
- Retrieve all document records where evidentiary problems have to be addressed as they relate to particular documents.
- Retrieve all document records showing which documents are privileged and confidential and not subject to disclosure.
- Retrieve all records that show a production history for a document.
- Retrieve all document records where the document has been used as an exhibit in a deposition.
- Retrieve all document records where a document has been used as an exhibit in witness Jones' deposition.
- Retrieve all document records that are going to be used as exhibits in trial.

Multiple Field Searches

- Retrieve all document records where a handwritten letter was described in the TYPE field dated after January 1, 1986.
- Retrieve all document records where witness Jones is connected with the document and which concerns the legal issue code "defective" in the ISSC field.
- Retrieve all document records which will be used as trial exhibits and with which witness Smith is connected.
- Retrieve all document records that concern further investigation or follow-up with witness Jones.

Database Searches with Full Text Documents

The following are examples of searches that can be conducted if a full text document is linked with your database.

- Retrieve all document records and full text documents for viewing regarding references to witness Jones.
- Retrieve all document records with the document number A109 and all cross-references to this document number in full text deposition or other full text documents

Note: *This search assumes that the A109 document number has already been imbedded in cross-reference codes in the full text deposition or other full text documents.*

Searches for Full Text Documents and Linked Graphic Images

- Retrieve all document records where there is a graphic image linked with the record.
- Retrieve all documents where there is a full text document linked to the database.

It is imperative that you become familiar with search phrases that can locate your document information after you enter the data. Herein lies the true power of a database for retrieving, viewing, editing and report generating of the information in your records.

Generating Reports on Database Information. Database software report generating features provide you with printed reports, on-screen reports, or reports saved to disk of your information for review and analysis. Database software should give you the capability to generate numerous reports in a variety of report formats.

The reports that you generate will generally be based upon records you have searched and retrieved using the search commands previously discussed in "Searching and Retrieving Records for Editing and Reports." Again, it is important that you become familiar with the search commands, so you can retrieve the records that meet your report needs.

After you have retrieved specific database records, you can generate reports in a variety of formats based on those records. Four sample reports that you could generate are listed below:

1. *Document Number Report* - Includes information about the document number, date of the document, type of document, and summary of the document.
2. *Chronological Document Report* - Includes information about the document date, document number, summary of the document, and the names of the persons and their connection to the document.
3. *Persons Connected with Document Report* - Includes information on the document number, persons connected to the document, document type, and document summary.
4. *Legal Issues Document Report* - Includes information on the legal issues, document date, and a summary of the document.

This is an example of a database and reports created using Microsoft Access.

These are a few of the reports that will be generated automatically by double clicking on the report name. The reports are all based on the design of your database and the data that is entered.

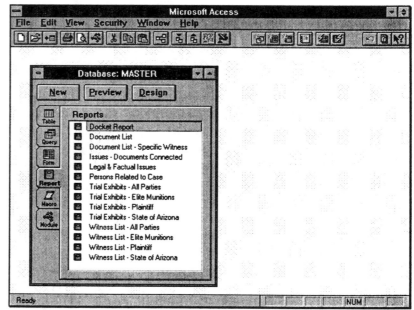

For example, the following trial exhibit report can be generated on-screen or printed in a few seconds since the underlying data was previously captured in the document data fields and the report was set up for automatic production.

Microsoft Access - [Report: Trial Exhibits - Elite Munitions]

File Edit View Format Window Help

16-Jan-95

Defendant - Elite Munitions

Exhibit For	TRIAL EXHIBIT NO.	DESCRIPTION
Defendant - Elite Munitions	D-E001	Crawler Skid Shovel Manual
Defendant - Elite Munitions	D-E002	Map handdrawn
Defendant - Elite Munitions	D-E003	Traffic Accident Report

Page: 1   Ready   NUM

Another report that can be easily generated is a chronological report. Once you enter the dates of documents in the document date field, you can then retrieve all documents connected to a specific date or prepare a chronological date report of all the documents in the database. This information is extremely important in order for you to "analyze" the significant facts relevant to a case.

Integrating Images with Your Database. One of the early and major considerations is to determine whether you should scan your documents so that you can electronically retrieve them later as "document images." An image is simply a photographic reproduction of a document stored on a CD-ROM or hard disk available for instant retrieval for viewing on a monitor. A single CD-ROM can hold up to 15,000 document pages depending upon the density of the pages and the resolution or dpi it is scanned. The image picture contains words, but you cannot search for individual words on the image. For this reason to locate an image you must index and link the document to a document index or database. The database can then be searched and the image retrieved since it is linked to a database record. However, if you use OCR software and convert the image to machine-readable text then the individual words can be searched.

Microsoft Access - [Report: Document List]

File Edit View Format Window Help

Document List

16-Jan-95

DOC DATE	TYPE	DESC	Image #
3/24/86	Maps	Map handdrawn	##-trx001116
9/2/86	Manual	Table of Content - Rotary effect	Rotary
11/19/86	Other	Traffic Accident Report	##-trx001145
3/5/87	Manual	Automobile Dynamics Manual	Flip01
4/7/88	Manuals	Crawler Skid Shovel Manual	DROTT
4/5/89	Statement	Witness Statement	##-trx001146

Page: 1   Ready   NUM

There are only two choices when faced with the task of managing documents. You can manually handle, organize and retrieve the paper. Paper has to be copied, documents have to pulled off shelves or out of boxes, files are misplaced or lost, storage is inconvenient and banker boxes are not easy for taking on the road. The other choice is to scan the documents as images or as machine-readable text using OCR software and control your information digitally.

There are several benefits for scanning your documents in order to digitally control the documents and other information in your cases:

- Instant access to your documents;
- Serves as a quick, informational source to defend against any early motions to dismiss or motions for summary judgment;
- Can be used to prepare for witness interviews and depositions;
- If you are the plaintiff in a case, you can acquire a significant preparation and organizational advantage by imaging all the relevant documents in your case at the outset. For those states, like Arizona, which have mandatory

> "Imaging technology has reached the point where a team can gain economic as well as strategic advantage by using imaging, even on cases with average number of documents." After analyzing the scanning, image retrieval, dedicated printer, coding, software, and training costs offset by savings in paper, space and personnel savings the it was more cost effective to use imaging technology. "You can reduce costs by using an image retrieval system and work more effectively . . . legal assistants and attorneys can spend less time on the tedious mechanics of maintaining paper sets of documents and getting their hands on copies of the documents they hope are of interest and more time on analysis and synthesis, the areas where the greatest gains can be found and the greatest value is created for the client's money." George Socha, litigation attorney with Halleland, Lewis Nilan Sipkins and Johnson, Costs and benefits of Image retrieval: A Case Study, Socha, Hennepin Lawyer, Jan.

disclosure rules, it would give an advantage to the plaintiff to quickly respond to court imposed disclosure rules;

- For a defendant, the rapid "imaging" of its documents by an outside service bureau or in-house would enable it to "catch up" to a plaintiff who had the luxury of months of preparing his case prior to filing his complaint;
- If multiple members of your litigation team, in-town or out-of-town, need simultaneous access to the documents, then CD-ROM imaging may be the answer. Once the documents have been captured to a CD-ROM disk, then a copy can be reproduced at a very low cost. Co-counsel or other members of your litigation team will always have access to the documents without the necessity of copying, shipping, and organizing the documents.
- The documents your expert needed could be easily printed or sent to him on disk and any additional ones could be quickly accessed and sent to him;
  - Automatic creation of witness and trial notebooks;
  - Easy redaction of privileged material;
  - Cost has dropped considerable. Using images has moved from the "special" case to within the financial reach of most law firms; and
  - Less personnel needed, reduction in storage costs, shipping costs decrease; and no loss or misplaced documents.

The decision to image your documents should be made at the outset to ensure that a proper link is set up between your database and imaging software program. Depending upon the imaging program images can be linked to any DOS or WINDOWS-based program. For example, if you are using Microsoft Access the image can be linked to a particular database record. Then when you search for and view the abstract of a record, the image can be viewed at the same time. Also, from this image, you could obtain information to put into your database record or block text, using OCR convert it to machine-readable text and transfer it into your database record. Below is an example of a document that has been abstracted and linked directly to an electronic reproduction of that document.

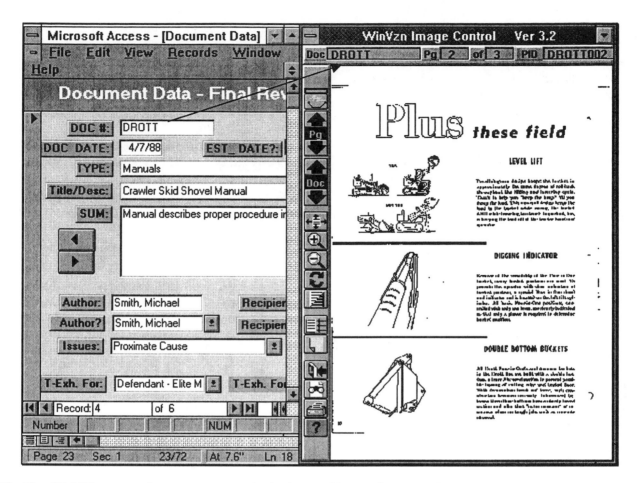

NOTE: The "link" between the two programs is the image filename" DROTT".

Hardware and Imaging Software. An image-enabled system can be set up easily with a personal computer, a CD-ROM player, a printer and software to operate it properly. Assuming you have a personal computer, CD-ROM player costs around $100 and the imaging software is free or available at a very low cost. One person obviously can only use this system at a time and CD's have to be manually changed if you have more then 15,000-document pages that can fit on one CD. However, it demonstrates how low cost it can be for an imaging system.

For multi users to have concurrent access you need a network and a multi CD-ROM player if you have more than 15,000 images.

Some imaging software products include ScanRevolution (www.indatcorp.com); Smeadlink (www.smead.com); InMagic Plus (www.inMagic.com); Summation (www.summation.com); and Opticon (www.dataflight.com).

Imaging Costs. The costs of scanning vary greatly from vendor to vendor. It is important to compare apples to apples when obtaining quotes from vendors. Some of the cost factors in an imaging project include:

- Hardware;
- Software;
- Per page scanning;
- Indexing;
- Personnel; and
- Training and Support.

Cost Comparison - Photocopy vs. Imaging Cost. The costs for scanning generally run approximately 15 cents a page. For the following cost comparison we are assuming the cost per page for scanning is 20 cents.

Document population - 10,000 pages
Image cost – 20 cents per page
Image Resolution – 200 dpi
Photocopy cost – 10 cents per page
Cost of the CD – Cost of the CD disk

Sets	Copy (10 cents per page)	Photocopy Total Cost	Image (20 cents per page)	Imaging Total cost	Savings
1st set	$1000	$1000	$2,000	$2,000	($1000)
2nd Set	$1000	$2000	$100	$2,100	($100)
3rd Set	$1000	$3000	$100	$2,200	$800
4th Set	$1000	$4000	$100	$2,300	$1,700

As you can see if multiple copies of documents are needed then imaging will cost less in the long run. This is besides the other significant benefits available if one scans their documents.

The following is a blank comparison sheet that one can use to begin the comparison of imaging your documents as opposed to leaving them in a paper format.

					Manual	Imaging		
1. Case size								
Number of boxes							boxes	
Average number of pages in each box							pages	
Average number of pages per document							pages	
Approximate time project to run							months	
Clerk/Secretary Billing time							per hr.	
Paralegal Billing Rate							per Hr.	
Attorney billing time							per hr.	
Cost of shipment of documents							per box	
2. Input Costs								
Time spent on review and preparation							minutes per box	
Cost of bates numbering							per page	
Cost of of bar coding							per page	
Photocopying cost							per page	
Firm time spent on photocopying							minutes per document	
Cost of scanning							per page	
Total docs to be objectively coded							percent	
Objective coding time per document							minutes	
Cost of Objective Coding								
Total docs to be subjectively coded							percent	
Subjective coding time per document							minutes	
Cost of Subjective Coding								
Total docs to be read by O.C.R.							percent	
Cost of O.C.R.							per page	
3. Retrieval and Storage Costs								
Floor space on one box of docs							sq. ft.	
Cost of storage space in firm							sq. ft. per year	
Cost of off/site/archive storage space							sq.ft. per month	
Total docs to be retrieved							percent	
							minutes per page	
							percent	
							percent	

Steps To Document Imaging. There are several important steps to ensure a successful and cost effective imaging project.

- *Document Collection & Selection.* Determine the document population? What types of documents are going to be imaged - maps, blueprints, medical records, corporate documents, etc. Which documents should I image and why? Should the clients, opposing party or third parties documents be imaged? Who is doing the initial indexing? Logging information such as document boxes and folders needs to be done? As a crude rule of thumb generally only 20 to 30% of documents are imaged. When doing the initial search pay close attention to what was reviewed, what was selected and the reason for not selecting certain materials. These decisions may be significant later on during discovery arguments. Should deposition and trial exhibits be imaged?

- *User Hardware and Software Requirements.* What type of software will I be using? Do I need additional hardware equipment? Who will be using the system? Will the firm be doing its own scanning? Can you choose the dpi rate the documents will be scanned? Is it a TIFF format or a proprietary format? Does it provide for redaction? Does it allow you to tag and group items for particular witnesses or issues? Does it allow you to rotate and zoom into the document? Will the imaging software link with popular database programs such as Microsoft Access or Paradox? Does it compress image files and to what extent will it support batch printing? Can you sort documents chronologically, witness or issue before printing?

- *Document Preparation Time.* Imaging documents means more then just feeding documents into a scanner. There is upfront time required to prepare your documents for scanning. The amount of time will depend upon the number and complexity of the documents. The function includes accepting and logging documents to be scanned, transportation, preparation of documents by category, delivering documents to a scanning station, removing them from scanning, and returning them. Attachments can be separated by blue pages and documents by yellow papers in your paper population.

- *Production Instructions.* Specific instructions should be provided to the scanning operators for various reasons.
  - For example, during your initial review of the documents you may determine that certain documents need to be sent to your consultant. Those documents can be electronically flagged and then routed to your expert after being imaged for his review.
  - Are their any time limitations?
  - At what dots per inch (DPI) will the documents be imaged? The greater the dots per inch the greater the clarity of the document Each page is approximately 30 kilobytes to 80 kilobytes with an average of 50 K per image. Images are normally scanned at 200 dpi but 300 dpi is sharper and better for subsequent OCR or trial presentation purposes
  - *Proprietary Image Format.* Will proprietary image format software be used?
  - *Tagging.* Will the images be tagged for beginning and the end of the document?
  - *Attachments.* Should attachments to documents be imaged as individual documents?
  - *OCR'ed.* Will imaged documents selected for OCR be converted during initial scanning?
  - *Project Dates.* Set the beginning and ending date of the imaging project.

- *Bar Code Labels* and *Automatic Image Numbering and Database Coding.* Bar code labels can be manually placed on your documents for coding and retrieval purposes. The bar code can contain a filename code that is read by the scanning software and becomes the filename for the document. These filenames can then be automatically imported into your database saving keystroke costs. The bar code can also include instructions to the computer to as to where the image is stored and what to do with when the image is retrieved. Then any time you want to retrieve the document just use a bar code reader to pass over the bar code and the document will appear on your computer screen.
  - If bar codes are not used some scanning software can also automatically assign a filename to a document that is being imaged. For example the name might be DEF1_001 which could stand for DEFendants production of documents, group - 1, document number 001. This coded filename then can also be automatically imported into a database and this number will become the document number, which eliminates a coding step. However, the number must also be placed on the paper document if you wish to retrieve it later.

- *Indexing time per document.* If you decide to index the documents by data entry some factors to consider include keystrokes per document, keystroke rate will depend on image quality, number of fields per documents, location of fields, location of information in documents to put into field, etc. Some language to include in your agreement would be:

- The documents will be coded over a ____ period of time.
- Document coding will begin on ____ and end on _____.
- The cost per document to code the agreed upon fields will be $_____.
- The average number of characters per document will be _____.

■ *Documents Per Batch* - There is no magic number of how many documents are in a batch but refers to the number of documents that is prepared for scanning at one time of your document population.

■ *Imaging Quality Control Checklists:*

- *Bar code Indexing.* If bar codes are used and are not properly read by the machine does it have built-in safeguards such as a beep to indicate additional time is needed to ensure the bar code is read?
- *Page Number Order.* Are page numbers in correct order?
- *Information Edge to Edge.* Is all the information contained within the image and does not run off the side?
- *Image Contrast.* Is the image too light, dark, etc.
- *Bates Numbering.* The Bates numbering must be on the page and legible.
- *Two-sided Originals.* Has the image of both sides of a two-sided original been imaged?
- *Checking Against Paper Copy.* Will images be checked page by page?
- *Skewed Images.* Are the images properly in position?
- *OCR.* If used the operators will have to verify the accuracy and quality of the characters converted.
- *Image Condition.* Do dirty marks, dark lines, smudges, etc. appear on the image?

Outsourcing. Outsourcing is a term used to describe hiring an outside service bureaus to scan, code or copy legal documents or perform other type of legal services. A whole service industry has been built up around the computerization of documents in the legal industry. Focus on the quality, reliability, service, experience, financial stability and price factors when selecting a provider.

When faced with a document-intensive case, your firm may want to consider hiring a litigation computer service company. They have the system and procedures, expertise and trained personnel to handle this work of converting documents to a digitized format. They should be signed to a confidentiality agreement and an agency relationship should be retained with the vendor to preserve work product immunities and the attorney-client privilege.

Two factors to consider in hiring an outside firm are concern over possible conflict of interest and loss of direct control over all levels of the support group. When a case changes it causes a change in the IT management due to a shift in the issues. Also, in certain legal cases where attorney's fees and a legal assistant's time are recoverable, a service vendor fees may not

Develop an overall strategy toward your IT project. Some factors that will impact your strategy are the size of the document population, available client dollars, discovery timelines. Check out the experience and financial stability of the service firm.

The decision to outsource as opposed to completing the work in-house depends on a number of factors:

- What resources - money, staff, supplies, equipment, and expertise - are available in-house?
- Who is going to run the litigation support area?
- What is the size of the case?
- Are you willing to make the training commitment?
- Can the case be processed within the time limits?
- Can the resources internally be kept busy on other cases after this case is over?
- If co-counsel is present what type of computer capabilities do they have?

- What is the comparison cost as proposed by outside vendors
- Can we divide the work between in-house and outside service bureau employees?
- And importantly, do you have the latest and most efficient hardware, software and expertise to do the job?

Selecting an Outside Service Bureau - It is important to have a clear understanding from the service bureau what your expectations are when you retain them to assist you in litigation management. Some suggestions:

- Prepare a Request for Proposal(RFP);
- Establish a timeline for the RFP proposal, publication, selection, negotiation and date of bid award. Determine if a prebid award conference is necessary to further explain the project. Do they need to have more information about the computing environment?
- The RFP should contain background information on the project, description of hr case, description of existing computing environment, description of procurement process, a needs analysis and implementation, description of an evaluation process, requirements definition, pricing, bidders references, format of responses.
- Number of pages and documents that need to scanned, numbered, coded, etc.
- How will they be prepared?
- Type of service - Objective and subjective coding, images, full text, time frame, vendor conflicts
- Are they helping the other side?
- Other factors –experience– how long has the vendor been in business? How long have they each service such as imaging, database, etc.?
- References, quality control procedures, staff resumes and experience, how long have they been with the company? Are permanent staff maintained or do they use temporary staff? Can they deliver remote site scanning services and can they image in a variety of formats and store the images on a variety of devices? Can the vendor meet the deadlines within the constraints of your case, security, facilities, and support.
  - Is the service a full service bureau? Can they handle imaging, coding, OCR conversion etc?

Deposition and Trial Testimony

There are five major areas where technology has been effectively used to manage deposition and trial testimony.

- Full Text Search and Retrieval with Electronic Exhibits;
- Video Depositions;
- Real-time Translation of Testimony;
- Real-time Broadcasting of Depositions Over the Internet; and
- Condensed Transcripts.

Full Text Search and Retrieval

Full text documents are those documents that have the "complete text" or "full text" of a document stored in a computer file. These documents can be word or phrase searched and you can instantly access the exact location of the words in the full text documents. Examples of full text documents include depositions and trial transcripts. However, essentially any document produced in a word processor is a "full text" document. Some other examples of full text documents that are accessible in a electronic file are witness interviews, reports, interrogatories, the Federal and State Rules of Civil Procedure, Criminal Procedure, Evidence, Appellate Procedure, and so forth.

Depositions of potential witnesses in your case are essential to adequately prepare for trial. They are generally taken for discovery purposes or for recording testimony. Just as important as taking the depositions is the accessibility and control of this testimony after the depositions are taken. Many lawyers manually attach color-coded stickers or clips to "code" the depositions in reference to liability and damage issues. However, since the middle 1980's, computer programs have been available which permit you to electronically "view" and "code" these depositions which gives you instantaneous access and control over this testimony. They are generally referred to as "full text search and retrieval" software.

Full Text Legal Applications. Some more powerful deposition computer applications include:
- Quickly retrieving important testimony of any witness;
- Making summaries of depositions as you read the deposition on the screen, capturing any text in notes, and retrieving those annotations for powerful reports in a page, subject, or chronological format;
- Identifying and sorting testimony by user selected issues or subjects, i.e., subjects such as work history or educational background;
- Organizing all information witness Smith said concerning witness Jones and comparing it against other testimony given by witness Smith or Jones in other depositions or cases;
- Organizing all the favorable and unfavorable admissions in the case;
- Identifying and sorting events in chronological order;
- Organizing all material that supports filing a motion for summary judgment;
- Storing large number of depositions on a computer;
- Tracking testimony from multiple parties or experts about a particular issue or exhibit; and
- Pinpointing damaging testimony.

ASCII Transcripts. Upon specific request from the court reporter, ASCII or full text copies of deposition and trial testimony are available in a machine-readable format. When setting up a deposition, ensure that your court reporter can provide a copy of the deposition in a computer-usable format. They generally will provide the "hard copy" for the standard fee and a computer-usable copy for $25.00 to $50.00. If you fail to obtain a copy at the time of the deposition and the reporter destroys her computer file, it will generally cost $1.00 PER PAGE to have the deposition converted to full text.

Images Attached to Depositions. Software is now available that provides instant access to images of exhibits for depositions on your computer. It allows exact images of your exhibits to be linked to testimony discussing the exhibit in your depositions for instant review.

For example, during a deposition, you may have a witness discuss her Employment Application and have it marked as Exhibit 1. Later, while reviewing the deposition testimony, you need to view Employment Application. Before, if you were reviewing the deposition on your computer, you had to retrieve the "hard copy" of the deposition and locate the exhibit in the back of the deposition to match it with the full text computerized testimony.

With imaging software the exhibit can be viewed on-screen with just a few keystrokes while you are viewing the full text deposition. All exhibits to depositions can be instantly viewed - handwritten statements, medical bills, income tax returns, medical

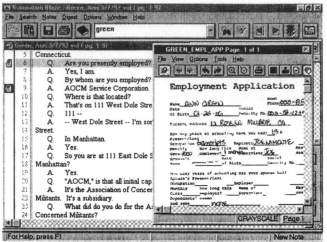

records, bills, and more. In another example, in a commercial litigation case, a particular witness in his deposition may testify concerning eight different commercial documents in a case. Now, using imaging software and your current text retrieval software, these commercial documents can be scanned into the computer and linked directly to wherever the witness testifies about the exhibits in the computerized deposition.

Preparing for Computerized Depositions - Standardization of Terms. When you know beforehand that depositions will be transferred to full text software, there are certain terms and phrases that should be standardized. By doing this, you will greatly simplify the process of searching and retrieving vital information from a full text document and will allow yourself to create more complete reports.

Some examples of areas to be standardized are:

- *Person's Names* - During depositions, people may refer to other people by various titles and names that they are familiar with, such as "my husband" or "Frank." It is important that the lawyers taking the deposition, as well as the person giving the deposition, refer to the same name at all times. If possible, also try to avoid the use of pronouns such as "he," "her," "him," "she," or "they" during depositions. Remember, every instance where a person is referred to in a deposition may be important, so having a standard title for each person will ensure that no information is lost in the cracks when subsequent searches are performed.

  For example, if Frank Smith is vice-president of company XYZ, you might want to refer to him as "Frank Smith." Therefore, friends of Mr. Smith should not call him "Frank" and employees should not refer to him as the "vice-president" during depositions.

- *Documents* - During a deposition, a witness may be called upon to identify various documents associated with a case. It is difficult to search and identify a document in a full text situation if the witness calls it a "contract" and the lawyers call it "Exhibit 10." It is, therefore, necessary to ensure that the same term or phrase is used throughout the deposition and any subsequent depositions refers to a single document or exhibit. In this case if you can refer to it as the "9th Street Map" or something more specific then exhibit.

  For instance, Map #3 of a traffic scene may be marked as Exhibit #1 for purposes of a deposition. The lawyers and witnesses of the case should refer to it solely as either "Map #3" or "Exhibit #1" for the deposition. Avoid calling it just a "map" or referring to it as "it" and you will greatly reduce your later coding of the full text document.

- *Issue Codes* - If you know beforehand what issues or topics will be discussed in a deposition, every effort should be made to refer to the same issue names throughout the deposition.

     For example, if an event deals with someone who failed to pay for widgets, one phrase referring to the event should be used throughout the deposition. If "Non-Payment" is used as the issue name, one should refrain from referring to this event as "Breach of Contract" or "Failure to Pay."

- *Medical Terminology* - During any deposition that deals with a medical condition or injury, a witness may refer to a condition by different terms than a doctor. It is obviously beneficial to have all deponents and attorneys' use the same terms throughout a deposition to save search and report time later on.

     For instance, a victim of a car accident may refer to a "broken arm," whereas another witness may refer to the victim's "fractured arm." One or the other is fine, just be consistent in the use of the term.

     Important: In the event that other names or terms are used, simply imbed a cross-reference code or note of the standard term to ensure retrieval.

Full Text Document Search Considerations. Before one retrieves documents for reports there are some important methods to increase the precision of the documents that you wish to retrieve.

- Understand the legal issues and factual propositions of your case and the source of the documents. This will provide you with a background of what documents are available and how they relate to your case.

- Limit your full text document population as much as possible. All documents in your full text document database should be relevant and important to your case. Marginal relevant documents should be coded into a database as a file of documents or as individual documents. If their value increase as the case progresses then additional electronic control can be implemented. If a large document population is needed separate the documents into smaller controllable groups. For example, if the documents can be separated by departments in a company then treat them as separate document populations. If the documents have an original organization try to keep them in that organizational structure.

- Standardize the witness names, liability terms and other commonly used informational terms in the case

- Review the vocabulary report of your full text document to determine what terms have been used and the number of times that they occur in your document. It may seem odd at first to review a vocabulary index of all the words in your case but it will give you significant insight on what and how many times certain words were used in your case. This will provide guidance for the patient and persevering researcher.

- Review the full text material and insert issue codes, cross-reference codes and notes or annotations reflecting the key points in your case. In effect, one is creating a mini "database" within a full text document to ensure increased accuracy for your searches. For example, in any location where if Mary Smith is referred to as the "mother" type in Smith, M. in the text itself or in a pop-up screen which some programs have to enter an enhancement. Then when you search for the term Smith, M. it will locate the area of the full text where she is referred to as the "mother".

- Legal documents such as depositions are much easier to search and have a larger number of relevant hits then nonlegal documents.

     Remember that computers are only a tool. They cannot replace the reasoned judgment of the attorney who is going to realize the impact of an evidentiary document.

Deposition Reports. Full text search software gives you not only the capability to locate specific words and phrases within an ASCII document, but there are valuable reports one can prepare using full text software.

Once a document has been converted for use within a full text program, it can be coded for reports. The reports traditionally associated with a deposition summary are:

- Witness/Issue Summary;
- Issue Category Summary; and
- Vocabulary.

In addition to these reports, there are a number of other reports that a full text program can generate that will be described in the next section.

Witness/Issue Summary Report

A Witness/Issue Summary Report is one of the most basic and common summarization methods used for depositions. The deposition is coded and summarized in the full text program using enhancements. After coding the deposition then a report can be printed like the one below setting forth the witness name, location in transcript where the testimony is located or the actual testimony can be inserted, summary of testimony and sorted by witness and issue code in page order. The Witness/Issue Summary Report would look like this:

Witness/Issue Summary Report

*Cota, Phillip: Page 8 Line 11

Concerns visitation of press site.

Issues: Background Check

*Cota, Phillip: Page 13 Line 18

Discusses prescription

Issues: Medical Record

*Cota, Phillip: Page 13 Line 20 to Page 13 Line 22

A.   I take six pills a day. One for high
21   blood pressure, I'm not sure what the other two
22   are. High cholesterol, but... Heart and sugar.

Issues: Medical Record

*Cota, Phillip: Page 16 Line 12 to Page 16 Line 17

"Cal OSHA section 4206 is clear on the
13   fact that the employer shall provide
14   and ensure the use of properly applied
15   and adjusted point-of-operation devices
16   or guards for every operation performed
17   on a power-operated press."

Issues: OSHA

*Green, Ann 3/7/92 vol I pg. 1-97: Page 7 Line 9

Plaintiff's present employer: AOCM Service Corp. Nature of business
unknown. Need current earnings data set against futures claim.

Issues: Background Check

*Green, Ann 3/7/92 vol I pg. 1-97: Page 54 Line 21

Green hesitant to discuss termination policies.

Issues: Background Check

*Green, Ann 3/7/92 vol I pg. 1-97: Page 62 Line 1 to Page 62 Line 7

States that Bill was on probation and that he told her this. Bill was a
questionable employee, but the reasons for his probation are not detailed.

Date: 04/19/1992
Issues: Background Check;Policies

*Green, Ann 3/7/92 vol I pg. 1-97: Page 62 Line 19

Bill Presley was fired in May or June, same time as pltff and just after
fire. Testimony indicates pltff thinks there may have been a connection.
Investigate circumstances surrounding this termination.

Date: 04/19/1992
Issues: Background Check;Policies;Rebuttal Citation

*Green, Ann 3/7/92 vol I pg. 1-97: Page 63 Line 2 to Page 63 Line 5

Do you know why Bill Presley was fired?
3   A.   I really don't know. I thought it might have had
4   something to do with the fire, but I still don't know, nobody
5   would say.

Issues: Timing;Fire Safety

*Green, Ann 3/7/92 vol I pg. 1-97: Page 64 Line 10

Pltff admits to not performing her duties & not calling fire dept.,
leading to term. for insubordination

Issues: Policies

Issue Category Summary

An issue category report is perhaps the most valuable summarization method available as it gives you a complete report of each topic (issue code) and any note associated with it for one or multiple depositions. Once again, it is generated almost exactly the same as the witness/issue summary report except that the report is printed in issue order as opposed to witness order. To continue the above coding examples, an alphabetical issue category summary report would appear like this:

Issue Category Summary

Background Check

*Issues:Background Check
Cota, Phillip: Page 8 Line 11

   Concerns visitation of press site.

*Issues:Background Check
Green, Ann 3/7/92 vol I pg. 1-97: Page 7 Line 9

   Plaintiff's present employer: AOCM Service Corp. Nature of business
   unknown. Need current earnings data set against futures claim.

*Issues:Background Check
Green, Ann 3/7/92 vol I pg. 1-97: Page 54 Line 21

   Green hesitant to discuss termination policies.

*Issues:Background Check;Policies
Date: 04/19/1992
Green, Ann 3/7/92 vol I pg. 1-97: Page 62 Line 1 to Page 62 Line 7

States that Bill was on probation and that he told her this. Bill was a questionable employee, but the reasons for his probation are not detailed.

*Issues:Background Check;Policies;Rebuttal Citation
Date: 04/19/1992
Green, Ann 3/7/92 vol I pg. 1-97: Page 62 Line 19

Bill Presley was fired in May or June, same time as pltff and just after fire. Testimony indicates pltff thinks there may have been a connection. Investigate circumstances surrounding this termination.

*Issues:Background Check;Rebuttal Citation
Green, Ann 3/7/92 vol I pg. 1-97: Page 64 Line 23

Green's opinion on Presley's firing

*Issues:Background Check;Fire Safety;OSHA
Green, Ann 3/7/92 vol II pg. 98-219: Page 140 Line 8

What are the guard's qualifications? Where did he get his information?

*Issues:Background Check
Green, Ann 3/7/92 vol II pg. 98-219: Page 142 Line 7

Potential cross-defendant: run asset check and determine limits of any subrogation clause.

*Issues:Background Check;Timing;Fire Safety
Green, Ann 3/7/92 vol II pg. 98-219: Page 196 Line 12 to Page 196 Line 20

A.   It was moving very quickly and I was scared.
13 Besides, Mr. Presley said he'd take care of it.
14 Also, I was scared. It seemed to come from nowhere.
15 It all happened so fast. I don't think that anyone could
16 have done beter under the circumstances.
17   Q.   Was anything else done by someone else?
18   A.   I don't know. Mr. Presley disappeared.
19   Q.   You don't know of anything else?
20   A.   I don't know of anything else. You might ask him.

Breach of Contract

*Issues:Breach of Contract;Policies
Green, Ann 3/7/92 vol I pg. 1-97: Page 70 Line 5 to Page 70 Line 7

Other than Lynn and Mary, has any
6 supervisor or management employee ever discussed the Joe
7 Jones's termination policies or procedures with you?

Fire Safety

*Issues:Timing;Fire Safety
Green, Ann 3/7/92 vol I pg. 1-97: Page 63 Line 2 to Page 63 Line 5

Do you know why Bill Presley was fired?
3   A.   I really don't know. I thought it might have had
4 something to do with the fire, but I still don't know, nobody
5 would say.

*Issues:OSHA;Health Dep.;Fire Safety
Date: 05/05/1992
Green, Ann 3/7/92 vol II pg. 98-219: Page 128 Line 20

Lynn Joy assured Green that it was safe to come back to work

*Issues:Background Check;Fire Safety;OSHA
Green, Ann 3/7/92 vol II pg. 98-219: Page 140 Line 8

What are the guard's qualifications? Where did he get his information?

*Issues:Background Check;Timing;Fire Safety
Green, Ann 3/7/92 vol II pg. 98-219: Page 196 Line 12 to Page 196 Line 20

A.   It was moving very quickly and I was scared.
13 Besides, Mr. Presley said he'd take care of it.
14 Also, I was scared. It seemed to come from nowhere.
15 It all happened so fast. I don't think that anyone could
16 have done beter under the circumstances.
17   Q.   Was anything else done by someone else?
18   A.   I don't know. Mr. Presley disappeared.
19   Q.   You don't know of anything else?
20   A.   I don't know of anything else. You might ask him.

Another report that can be printed without the enhancements but just the location of the issues would look like this:

Background Check

Cota, Phillip: Pg 8 Ln 11

Green, Ann 3/7/92 vol I pg. 1-97: Pg 7 Ln 9
Green, Ann 3/7/92 vol I pg. 1-97: Pg 54 Ln 21
Green, Ann 3/7/92 vol I pg. 1-97: Pg 62 Ln 1
Green, Ann 3/7/92 vol I pg. 1-97: Pg 62 Ln 19
Green, Ann 3/7/92 vol I pg. 1-97: Pg 64 Ln 23
Green, Ann 3/7/92 vol II pg. 98-219: Pg 140 Ln 8
Green, Ann 3/7/92 vol II pg. 98-219: Pg 142 Ln 7
Green, Ann 3/7/92 vol II pg. 98-219: Pg 196 Ln 12
Breach of Contract
Green, Ann 3/7/92 vol I pg. 1-97: Pg 70 Ln 5
Fire Safety
Green, Ann 3/7/92 vol I pg. 1-97: Pg 63 Ln 2
Green, Ann 3/7/92 vol II pg. 98-219: Pg 128 Ln 20
Green, Ann 3/7/92 vol II pg. 98-219: Pg 140 Ln 8
Green, Ann 3/7/92 vol II pg. 98-219: Pg 196 Ln 12
Health Dep.
Green, Ann 3/7/92 vol II pg. 98-219: Pg 128 Ln 20
Medical Record
Cota, Phillip: Pg 13 Ln 18
Cota, Phillip: Pg 13 Ln 20
Green, Ann 3/7/92 vol II pg. 98-219: Pg 134 Ln 23
OSHA
Cota, Phillip: Pg 16 Ln 12
Green, Ann 3/7/92 vol II pg. 98-219: Pg 128 Ln 20
Green, Ann 3/

On screen the report would look like this:

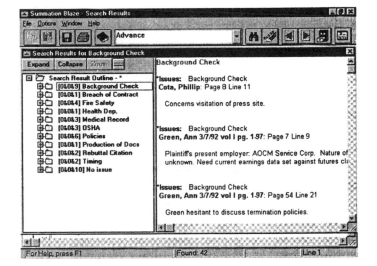

Other Summarization Methods

Only your intuitiveness and creativity limit the number and variety of reports a full text program should be able to generate. Listed below are a number of other reports that you may find useful:

Vocabulary Report. An on screen or printed report can be generated showing the location and surrounding text of a particular word. See above under Full Text Search Considerations for a discussion of this report.

Date Chronological Summary Report. This type of report can be especially useful for medical malpractice case or any case where dates or times of events are important. It includes a date in the text of an issue code.

Date Chronological Summary Report

EMPLOYMENT

Griffin, Gerald 1 vol 1 [17: 3]
09/01/67 Science teacher, Massena, New York school district.

Griffin, Gerald 1 vol 1 [17: 8]
01/02/70 Worked as outside claims adjuster for national insurance company in Barre, Vermont.

Griffin, Gerald 1 vol 1 [23: 7]
04/01/77 Started employment with Casey and Casey as a loss claims adjuster.

Griffin, Gerald 1 vol 2 [116:22]
05/01/77 Employed with Casey and Casey for one month prior to the issuance of the asbestos report.

Griffin, Gerald 1 vol 1 [23:20]
02/01/79 Promotion with Casey and Casey to assistant secretary.

Organize All Favorable and Unfavorable Admissions in a Case - Key testimony made by witnesses during a deposition can be extremely important for pretrial preparation of witnesses. To generate a summary of all favorable and unfavorable admissions in a case enter an issue code wherever an unfavorable or favorable admission occurs. Start each issue code and note with either the phrase "FAV-" or "UNFAV-." Use cut & paste to capture testimony within the context of the note.

Organize Material Relating to Motion for Summary Judgment - To generate a summary of all material relating to a motion for summary judgment in a case enter an issue code wherever any pertinent information occurs. Start each issue code and note with the phrase "SUMJG-."

Locate All References to Exhibits. Enter a cross-reference code wherever a reference occurs to an exhibit by a non-standard name. For example, suppose "Exhibit 1" refers to a "map" in a deposition. Then you would put the cross-reference code "Exhibit 1" where the word "map" occurs in the deposition.

Locate All References to a Witness. Enter a cross-reference or name code wherever a reference occurs to a specific witness by a non-standard name. For example, you would not put the cross-reference code "Smith" where "Bill Smith" occurs, but you would put "Smith" where "Bill" occurs without Smith.

Organizing Impeachment and Inconsistent Material. Testimony that is contrary to other testimony by that same witness can be vital during a trial to impeach or prove allegations of perjury or incompetence. To create and then make a report summarizing all the inconsistent and impeachment material enter an issue code wherever any pertinent quotes or information occurs. Start each issue code and note with the phrase "IMPEACH-."

Hourly Summary - Hourly summaries are often essential for cases dealing with medical issues.

Cut & Paste Summary - Using the Cut & Paste report, you can easily summarize an entire transcript by "cutting" portions of a text and "pasting" them to a trial notebook or other report.

Video Depositions

Recently there has been increased interest and use of videotaped depositions. A significant reason for this increase is their use in trials, whether it be the opening statement, during direct and cross examination, or in closing argument. With this being the age of the videotape and TV, you can imagine the stirring impact video depositions would have upon the court and jury. An article in the Maricopa Lawyer (Arizona) by Michael Hawkins emphasizes the impact of videotaped depositions.

Video Depositions Are Dramatically Different - Because They Are Drama

I have been doing trial work for the better part of two decades. While I have had some experience with videotaped depositions, it has been neither regular nor routine. The bulk of my experience, at least until recently, has been with the run-of-the-mill, standard deposition done in the comfort of one's own office...I recently participated in a lengthy trial in federal court in which nearly every witness was videotaped. The judge permitted extensive use of videotaped excerpts in opening statement, during direct and cross examination, and in closing argument. The adage that a picture is worth a thousand words is applicable and then some to video technology. To put it mildly I was astounded at the impact. That the video excerpts involved someone else's client was of no comfort....In short, preparation for the videotaped deposition is as different from the standard deposition as night from day. Failing to recognize this reality could result in dire and virtually irreparable consequences for your client.

- Michael Hawkins

Though more expensive, recording a deposition by video should be seriously considered in all your depositions. It encourages settlement for the following reasons:

- The parties stick to the issues and remain on task when the camera is rolling.
- Video demonstrates how your client or the opposing party will respond in court.
- The opposing party is aware that cuts from video depositions can be used at trial for video generation jurors.
- Turnaround time for video is generally quicker than for depositions.
- The accuracy of the deposition cannot be doubted.

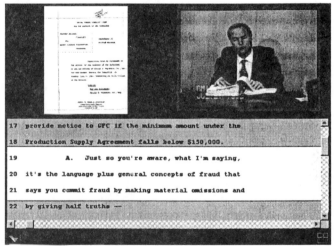

Cross-examination can be remarkably effective if the witness is impeached by a video image of himself making a contradictory statement. The preparation of your client for a videotaped deposition cannot be understated. The old rules of listen to the question, pause, and limit your answer just to the question, do not work in a videotaped deposition. "Don't volunteer an answer," and "You are not there to help the other side," may be the wrong advice. As the camera is rolling and your witness answers with short, evasive answers, the impact may come back to haunt him in trial.

Some suggestions for videotaped depositions:

1. Dress appropriately. Wear what you would for trial. There are reasons why newscasters wear certain colors on TV.
2. Look into the camera. This video may be shown to a judge or jury. If your eye movements are furtive and unfocused, then the trier of fact will give you little *credibility.*

3. Answers should be open and to the point. Do not attempt to evade answering the question if a simple effective explanation will do. To evade the answer and then to try and argue to a judge that the question was not the most artfully articulated may fall on deaf ears.

4. Since this may be shown in trial, prepare for it just like actual trial testimony. In a trial, the witness would not be eating or drinking coffee while testifying.

5. Take breaks often to stay fresh. Videotaped depositions can be extremely exhausting, just like a trial. Plan breaks often, if needed, and the reasons should be clearly stated on the record so it does not appear that it is being done for coaching purposes.

Synchronization of Digital Video and Text

The video of a witness can be synchronized with the text so that the text and video are always in alignment. Until recently the downside to video depositions was the time it took to review each deposition for the excerpts that you wanted since you literally had to sit through the entire deposition as it played on a VCR.

As the deposition or trial proceedings are recorded by the court reporter on videotape, a Computer Aided Transcription (CAT) system synchronizes the words with the video. After the deposition, an attorney can simply search for a relevant name, date, or phrase in a video

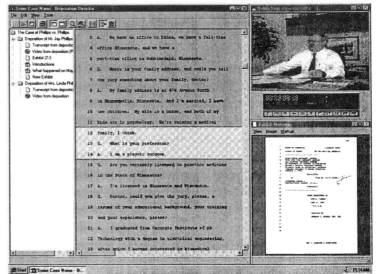

via a computer, and the computer will automatically go to the section of the video where the words were spoken. Thus, an attorney or judge can immediately retrieve both the text and video portions of the testimony for review. Then, certain excerpts of the video can be arranged for an opening statement, etc. One product that synchronizes video and text is DepositionDirector (www.indatacorp.com). *See also Section 8, Digital Visual Aids, Video.*

Real-time Translation of Testimony.

Real-time transcription is the capability of the court reporter to use a computer-assisted stenograph machine to have the testimony and/or video and audio of a witness appear on a computer monitor within

seconds from the time the words are spoken. Real-time translation of testimony is a computer application that has been under-utilized in the everyday practice of law. Its value in both trials and depositions should be seriously considered.

Real-time translation of textual testimony requires a highly skilled court reporter. Sometimes they request a premium rate for their services. Many court reporters are unwilling to do real-time translation because of the skill required. Since many cases are won or lost during depositions, it is surprising that more attorneys are not demanding that their depositions be conducted in real-time.

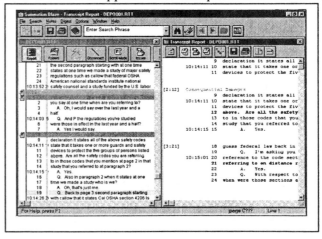

Real-time translation of a witness's testimony during a deposition or trial presents unique opportunities and pitfalls to the unsophisticated. Generally, a court reporter may have a computer available for you to use during the real-time transcription, however, under the Federal Rules of Civil Procedure, there is no such requirement.

Depending upon the specific software used during the real-time translation, the following features may be available:

- Review the testimony of a witness as he testifies;
- Search for prior testimony during the deposition;
- Add notes, cross-references, or issue codes during the deposition;
- Mark certain passages of testimony for later printing;
- A finished transcript is available in a short time after the deposition is completed.
- Transmit the testimony and video to remote locations such as your law office or expert's office through a modem and telephone line using the Internet.

Real-time software provides instant translation of witness testimony for viewing on a computer monitor for review, impeachment or use during deposition, trial or other legal proceedings. Products to consider are Summation (www.summation.com); Caseview (www.stenograph.com) and LiveNote (www.livenote.com):

Checklist - Deposition Real-time transcription of evidence

- **Determine if you want to use real-time reporting.** Explore the benefits of using real-time technology.. Reading back the testimony is eliminated; witness control is enhanced; witness testimony can be immediately printed out; hearing impaired litigants can now participate; testimony can be transmitted worldwide; examinations, motions and closing arguments are supported by actual witness testimony; and translation to other languages is enhanced
- **Determine if court reporter can translate testimony in real-time.** Transcription of live testimony to real-time cannot be done by all court reporters. Most court reporters do not write in real-time which result in many untranslates in the transcript that lessens the utility of the technology. It is relatively a recent technology in which most court reporters are not competent. The court reporting industry has a certifying process for certifying real-time reporters. Is there an extra charge for real-time reporting? Can you download or use the daily-uncertified transcript? Will the same court reporter be doing all the depositions? Is the court reporter or someone else available to ensure their equipment is correctly transmitting the testimony to your computer or to remote locations and to fix any problems?
- **Select and purchase real-time software and train litigation team.** Select real-time software that is non-proprietary, open, easy to use and can be connected to any of the different computer aided transcript (CAT) machines that court reporters use. The real-time industry has been hampered with software from vendors that only works with certain CAT systems forcing court reporters to upgrade and purchase certain CAT systems. In the last few years new non-proprietary real-time software has become available which works with any CAT system. Provide training to your staff on the software features and the strategy for capturing and controlling witness's testimony. If possible practice under actual conditions with a connection to a court reporter's machine. Software selection criteria should include whether the notes, cross-references, searches taken during the deposition can be saved and used in your full text program? Also, whether the real-time annotations can be linked to the final certified transcript or whether you have to re-enter the notes.
- **Select hardware equipment needed for the deposition.** To view and actually control the transcript testimony each person needs a computer, monitor and be connected to the court reporter's CAT system. Will you need to bring in a computer or does the court reporter have them installed? Do you have a backup system? If more than one person will be using the real-time do you have the necessary equipment to split the signal or transmit it to remote locations? Will showing the testimony be part of a deposition presentation? If so, how many monitors will I need?
- **Install and test system with court reporter two weeks before deposition.** Coordinate with the court reporter a time for all the parties to test their equipment in the deposition room. If sending testimonies to a remote location test the system. Can remote users transmit messages back to you in the deposition room

via the computer or e-mail system? Have a laptop or other computer configured and tested as a backup in case of problems.

- **Test two days before deposition.** Have the court reporter complete a final test of their equipment.
- **Using real-time during the deposition.** Have a specific strategy as to who will be using the real-time computer and their objectives. If you are alone in the deposition, have easy to use one keystroke commands available to mark important testimony. Don't forget to watch the non-verbal communications of the witness. Make sure witnesses excluded from the depositions do not view the real-time testimony. If alone, try to review testimony during breaks, while the witness is reviewing a document or any other time when your full attention is not required on the proceedings.

Two nationwide real-time court reporting firms are Southwest Reporters, Inc. (800-873-3376), and Barkley Reporting and Transcription (800-222-1231). *See also, Chapter 8, Courtroom Technology Considerations, Real-time Transcription of Evidence.*

Real-time Broadcasting of Depositions over the Internet.

A new technology breakthrough allows the sound, text and video of a deposition or other legal proceeding can now be sent over the Internet on a regular phone line to anyone in the world. This opens up immense strategic opportunities for the astute litigator. For the first time the live testimony of a witness such as an expert can be sent via the Internet over a secure and confidential connection to your staff back at your office, other co-counsel or to your own expert located in other parts of the country. Chat sessions can be opened for witnesses or other counsel to communicate with you during the live proceedings.

For the first time attorneys not present at a deposition can "sit in" though not physically present. This makes the decision easier whether to attend or not to attend a deposition since it saves travel and expense time.

It is different than videoconferencing, though that is the next step, in that the deposition is unilaterally broadcast to multiple users at remote locations. However, there is the capability to send e-mail or paging messages to the participants at the deposition to ask specific questions, etc.

You have a choice to send audio or text only or whether to send all three to whatever location you desire. For example you may want to analyze the way a particular witness responds to questions so you may decide to listen to the live audio only of a witness or the deposition is being videotaped so the video and audio can be sent over the Internet.

For cybercasting, the equipment, software and telecommunications needed to "attend" a deposition is quite simple. After logging into the Internet with your multimedia laptop you direct your browser to the LegalSpan site at www.legalspan.net. After downloading @ttend software you select the confidential deposition session you want to "attend" and enter a special password. After the deposition exhibits are downloaded – you are there seeing, hearing and reading everything that is being said. The audio is superb, the text transcription depending on the court reporter can be flawless, and the video is small and somewhat jerky. If you tune in late you can scroll back through the text if real-time transcription is being used or the audio or video can be archived for later playback over the Internet.

The equipment setup at the deposition can be an inexpensive camcorder, encoder device and a connection over the Internet by a regular telephone line.

The @ttend software is the software you use to view and receive the deposition broadcasts over DepoCast for real-time or archived deposition. It is one of a suite of broadcasts offered by LegalSpan (www.LegalSpan.net). The others include:

- inSession – broadcasts live or archived CLE sessions from anywhere in the country. This technology has many additional uses and provides the capability for a practitioner, law firm or company to broadcast with limited interaction any meeting, deposition, legal proceeding or CLE program. Corporate counsel could broadcast to several outside counsels at the same time; law firms can broadcast to branch offices; and state bar committees and sections can broadcast to remote members.
- ExpoCast – a virtual trade show where broadcasts include demonstrations and training sessions for legal products and services; and
- CourtCast – broadcasts of live legal proceedings from courtrooms.

Condensed Transcripts. Condensed or "traveling transcripts" literally reduce the pages so that 4-8 pages of transcript fit on one page. With the use of appropriate fonts, it is easily readable and obviously more convenient then the original transcript.

The smaller format can compress up to 8 standard transcript pages onto 2 sides of a single sheet for a bulk reduction of 93%. There are immediate benefits in reading transcripts on a plane or at a hotel and less weight in lugging the uncondensed transcript around. They are narrow enough to read rapidly because the eyes can take in each line without having to move. Also, there are reduced costs for photocopying and postage and to fax them is easier and cheaper.

These condensed transcripts are available from your court reporter for deposition transcripts.

Interrogatories, Pleadings, Motions and Request for Admissions

One of the persistent problems in managing discovery materials in a digital format in getting them or converting them into a digital form. The following interrogatory analysis can pertain to pleadings, request for admission, expert reports or any discovery material.

a.   Interrogatories - answers

One of the primary sources of case discovery is interrogatories. Succinct interrogatories enable one to determine the legal and factual parameters of the case. It will disclose witnesses, legal and factual theories, medical information and a variety of other critical information. Traditionally, interrogatory answers have been provided to the opposing attorney and for us in a paper format with attached exhibits. The answers can range from a few pages to hundreds of pages depending upon the case. It is not unusual for a second or third set of interrogatories or supplements to be filed with resulting answers.

The information in the answers to interrogatories is a nightmare to control. Generally, the answers are TYPED into the space on the interrogatories. Oftentimes the space is insufficient and continuance of the answer is on a separate document attached to the answers. Manually locating information in interrogatories is a time-consuming tedious process that rewards the firm that has a lot of staff.

In order to control interrogatories by a computer one needs first to ensure the questions, answers and any attached exhibits are in an electronic format and then use tools such as full text, databases or images to organize the answers. There are three possible ways in what format the information will be provided to you:

1.   A *full text copy of answers and exhibits* or a *full text copy of answers and a set of imaged exhibits*.

This obviously is the ideal way of receiving the answers since one can load these electronic responses into the computer and have instant control over the case information. Absent a court procedural rule in your jurisdiction that mandates this type of electronic exchange of data it is unlikely that the answers and exhibits will be provided to you in this format.

2.   Obtain from opposing counsel a *full text copy of answers* and a *set of paper exhibits* that are attached.

If you receive the answers in a full text format then if you image the paper exhibits and link them to the relevant answers then you will have the information in an electronic format.

One approach to obtaining a full text copy of the answers from opposing counsel is to offer to provide the questions in a word processing format if the questions and answers will be returned in a word processing format. For example, I have been successful in offering to save opposing counsel secretary's time by providing the questions in a full text format if they will provide the answers in a full text format. The secretary can take the questions and load them into a word processor and have as much space as she wants to type in the answers. This is much easier and faster for her then to use a TYPEWRITER to try to fit the answer into the space provided on the interrogatory or attach a continuance of the answer.

3.   Obtain from opposing counsel a *paper copy of answers* and a *set of paper exhibits* that are attached.

This is the least desirable and will require that the answers and exhibits either be converted to full text or imaged. To convert to full text will require that the answers be retyped or OCR be used. Some attorneys will scan the answers and exhibits in as images and at least have them available for viewing though not available for full text searching.

Calculating Damages

See the section on Spreadsheets in Chapter 6.

Conclusion

The steps to controlling the information in your case are very important. It reaps many benefits for you and enables you to feel comfortable about controlling the facts in your litigation. The final chapter will explore the use of technology in the courtroom and in alternative dispute conferences.

Chapter 8

Using Multimedia in Legal Proceedings

Introduction

The practice of law does not operate in a vacuum. We are permanently connected to people and society as we advocate our client's position whether in the courtroom or in other legal proceedings. This section will focus on the use of computers and multimedia presentation technology in and out of the courtroom to persuade others of our client's case.

Today, there are many varied forums for resolving our client's case - courtrooms, arbitration proceedings, mediations, administrative hearings, settlement conferences and others. In each it is important that your client's position is clearly stated and advocated. Technology can be a significant tool to assist you in your advocacy in all of these proceedings.

Benefits Using Multimedia Technology

From the day a client walks through the door the focus is to obtain a favorable result. As an advocate you must demonstrate to whomever is deciding your case the strength of your position and the weaknesses of your opponents case. To prove your case you need to persuade the factfinder, using witnesses and exhibits, of the merits of your case.

One of the most effective and important methods of persuading the factfinder is through the use of multimedia aids. Seeing and hearing is believing. Our society expects to be entertained and taught through multimedia. The preparation of multimedia visual presentations can be calculated to be persuasive of a particular position and to assist in convincing the trier of fact to reach a decision in favor of your client. Visual aids summarize, supplement and assist in conveying your message to the trier of fact.

Common sense and a substantial amount of research dollars demonstrates that advertisements, TV ads, and movies all stimulate and persuade us. Millions of dollars are spent on advertising campaigns to convince us to purchase services or products. The latest visual techniques - including color patterns - can be observed on TV on a daily basis. When you see commercial ads, use your imagination to see if they can be applied to a case. For example, the show "60 Minutes" uses persuasive techniques to highlight documentary evidence to influence you.

With the advances in digital information, the latest buzzword is multimedia. Multimedia is the integration of data, text, image, audio, or video in a single application. We are living through a digital revolution where information is presented to us in a multimedia context.

Society, factfinders and judges included, expect to be entertained and persuaded by the use of multimedia. Multimedia is both a technology and communications concept. As a technology concept multimedia is explained in the sense of using text, sound, graphics, video, and animations to persuade. Multimedia is taking the various forms of media - sound, text, graphics, video and animations - and presenting various combinations of the above to communicate and persuade a trier of fact as to your client's position.

As a communications concept, which is more important then multimedia as a technology concept, the digitization of information for use in multimedia provides a new and dynamic method of presenting your case to the trier of fact. It adds immediacy and realism to dry exhibits. Only in the last 10 years have we been able to digitize and present our case information in this new and persuasive way.

Digital multimedia for legal applications means being able to display your case documents as computer images, enlarge the relevant document sections, draw on the documents in various colors or put them side by side on a monitor to focus the jury's attention on the points that are important to your client. It means having a witness's deposition on CD-ROM for immediate access and stopping the video and bringing up a document pertaining to the witness alongside the video for the factfinder. It means using charting and presentation programs for bullet slides, organizational charts or a timeline of your case. See also, Chapter 6, Multimedia – Text, Graphics, Sound, Photographs and Video.

Multimedia presentations should be the norm in our cases. The rest of the world expects presentations that provide multi-sensory stimulus to learn and decide the merits of products and services, why not disputes?

There are many important benefits to using computer technology in your case during legal proceedings:

- *Increases juror understanding and the trier of fact remains focused on the case* - The trier of fact wants to learn and be involved in the presentation of the case. The trier of fact wants a visual presentation. It brings a case to life. It provides variety, keeps them interested, and increases their understanding of the factual and legal issues in a case.
- *Controlling the flow of your case* – Presenting your case digitally allows you to control the pace and flow of your case. You have the capability to rapidly present successive documents to a witness during examination and not be interrupted by paper shuffling with the witness or jury. For example, it is much easier to prepare and present a direct examination of your witnesses as they can see beforehand on computer monitor portions of documents that they will be testifying about.
- *Simplifying complex issues* - Demonstrative evidence can simplify voluminous and confusing facts for the benefit of a jury. The old adage of a picture is worth a thousand words definitely applies in all of your legal proceedings. Properly used, technology with graphics and other multimedia can simplify the issues and provide the tool for jurors to understand your case.
- *Instant Access and Control over the Law and Facts of Your Case*. Literally at your fingertips is access to the law and facts of your case. If you convert your case materials to a digital format you can instant access to interrogatory answers, deposition testimony or images of your documents. If you are surprised in trial then a quick search will produce answers or disclosure of material germane to your case.

> We are moving away from text-based collaboration, the limitation of narrow bandwidth. We now recognize that human communication is multidimensional. Accordingly, lawyers must become voice smiths and image smiths in the same way they are effective in oral advocacy.
> – Sam Guiberson,

- *Time savings* - One of the constant complaints by juries and judges is the wasted time in the courtroom as lawyers try to present their case. They are upset that exhibits are misplaced, the time it takes to publish and read documents, and any other delay that keeps them away from their family and jobs. The judge and jurors want an efficient and fair trial. One little known fact is that the use of technology in the courtroom can save a significant amount of time in trial. Many jurists estimate that 20% to 50% of the time in trial is saved by using a paperless approach to present a case to a jury.
- *Cost savings* - The monetary savings by saving time in the courtroom is immense. The costs of the attorneys, judges, clerks, etc. can easily amount to $5,000 a day. To save 1 day a week for a year would save $260,000 a year - more then enough to buy 5 courtroom presentation systems.
- *Changing demonstrative evidence* - You can change your presentation on the fly. As the facts are presented charts and other graphics can be changed in the courtroom to reflect actual testimony.

Persuasion Process

Through constant human interaction we are involved in the process of persuasion. From the glitzy ads to one-on-one communication we are constantly trying to convince someone of our point of view. The success or failure of convincing someone is dependent on our ability to persuade others as to our point of view. Multimedia aids help us persuade and studies support this conclusion. The issue is how can we best present case information to persuade the trier of fact as to our client's position.

However, a word of caution. The most important part of your presentation is you. How one looks and sounds still is the critical factor in the persuasion credibility process. A competent messenger must complement Marshall McLuhan's argument that "the medium is the message."

SEEING THE FACTS: Tapping the Power Of Seeing As Well As Hearing, ABA Journal
December, 1992, James W. McElhaney,

The actual photographs would come a little later. First was a verbal snapshot
of the crash that literally took the jury to the scene:

"Ladies and gentlemen, go back in time to the 14th of December, 1984. If you had been standing by the side of Highway 487 just at noon--about thirteen miles east of Carthage, Miss.--you would have seen Linda Jackson in her 1984 GMC Jimmy 4X4, taking Amanda--her six-week-old baby girl--to the doctor for her first checkup after she was born.

"Linda and Amanda had dropped off Mr. Jackson at work, and started to go on
to the doctor's office just before they passed where you're standing. If you look quickly, you can see Amanda in her new safety car seat--the backwards- facing kind that has been federally approved. Then right after they pass where you are--as they go around a gentle curve at about 50 to 55 miles per hour—you hear a bang--almost as if they hit another car. Only there's no other traffic, and there's nothing in the road they could hit. "So you look at the back of the car as it is going away from you and you see the left rear wheel strangely folded underneath the car, scraping the asphalt as it's being dragged along. The car starts to fishtail back and forth on its one rear wheel. Then it swerves and starts to flip over and over. One, two, three, four--five times. You see Momma--Linda--thrown from the car and land at the side of the road, crumpled in an odd, awkward angle, her left leg broken into the shape of a 'Z.'

"You run down the road to check on Amanda, to get her out of the car if you can. The GMC Jimmy 4X4 is on its back, its three remaining wheels spinning in the air. When you look inside, there is Amanda, still strapped in her seat—her head jammed between the back of her safety seat and the bottom of the dashboard. What you see dripping on her face is acid coming from the upside- down battery."

That "picture" is based on the opening statement by Tommy Rayburn from Oxford, Miss., in a products liability case against General Motors. It is one of a series of remarkably vivid verbal snapshots that were designed to show exactly what happened to Linda and Amanda Jackson.

It is important that we understand the persuasion process and incorporate multimedia solutions into our presentation. The dynamics of the persuasion process can be broken down into five parts:

1. attention;
2. comprehension;
3. agreement;
4. retention; and
5. action.

In order to persuade you have to gain the person's attention, ensure they understand the message, gain their agreement, and then lengthen their retention period for them to take action.

1. *Attention* - The use of multimedia and paperless presentation significantly supports the attention aspect of the persuasion process.

Factfinders want you to grab their attention and provide guidance on how the case should be decided. If you want the jury to think of you as the guide they should follow, and if you

> Studies have shown that in face to face communications your credibility upon the receiver of information is 7% verbal, 38% vocal and an astonishing 55% visual. The 7% verbal is the content of the information, 38% vocal refers to voice inflection and different tones, and 55% visual refers to facial and bodily movements.
>
> Decker says psychological studies show that only 7 percent of your credibility comes from your message itself; 38 percent comes from the qualities of your voice and speech; and 55 percent comes from the visual clues you give with your appearance, posture, gestures and body language as you speak. *Have to be Believed to be Heard,* Bert Decker.

---

want them to believe what your witnesses have to say, you have to keep their attention. This is done by the presentation that you and your witnesses make assisted by the use of multimedia in the legal proceeding.

Seeing, hearing and viewing visual stimuli captures the audience's attention. A child's attention span is 6 seconds while an adult's attention span is 8 seconds. It is important to lengthen the time you have their attention. Though you sometimes can bring them back quickly from their inattentive time they may have missed important points you were trying to convey.

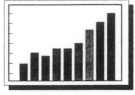

Ensure that the various trial presentation techniques you use keep the juror's attention.

2. *Comprehension* - The trier of fact must understand in a simple but effective manner the themes of your case. The impact of presentation visuals in studies showed a minimum of 10% increase in the attention, comprehension, agreement, and retention for the audience of the points that are supported with multimedia visuals. The startling statistic was that based on visuals the audiences were 43% were more inclined to take ACTION based on the visual presentation as opposed to no visual support. *Multimedia Presentations,* Robert Lindstom.

WHAT THEY BRING TO COURT: JUROR ATTITUDES IN ANTITRUST CASES, Barbara S. Swain and Dan R. Gallipeau, ABA Journal, 1994.

One of the constants of JURY RESEARCH in the antitrust area is the feeling reported by most jurors that they were overwhelmed by the economic, industrial, and policy issues presented to them. A juror who was interviewed after sitting on an antitrust case put it this way: "I felt like I just got off the plane in Tokyo. Everything looked and sounded Japanese. I was totally lost."

Jurors, like all of us, have psychological constraints on the amount of information that can be absorbed. JURY RESEARCH shows that when confronted with new, technical information that is outside of their experience and training, jurors simplify their decision-making by ignoring or distorting the importance of the information. Jurors focus on what is salient to them, not necessarily what may be legally relevant.

This often leads jurors to dismiss evidence that the trial team views as critical and to place great weight on issues that the trial team has dismissed as irrelevant. A good example is the issue of relevant market. Lawyers may spend a lot of time on defining the relevant market and proving their definition is the correct one. From the juror's perspective, the issue of relevant market remains an intangible abstraction that is ignored.

Jurors are also looking for patterns among the discrete events they hear about. They use their life experiences, attitudes, beliefs, and values to identify patterns in a complex case. They latch onto a few key ideas that are consistent with their predisposition and in turn create a psychological story based on these key ideas. In developing their psychological stories, jurors infer motivations for all parties, even if none are explicitly stated. The perceived motivations of the parties will then partially determine the information that will be salient.

In the September 28, 1992, issue of PC Week, an article entitled THE VERDICT IS IN: PC GRAPHICS WINS THE CASE, explained the success of a Houston attorney in integrating graphics in his trial to persuade the jury of his client's position. The article read as follows:

To defend a client accused of withholding critical documents from the State of Texas, a Houston attorney recently passed up the standard orations and dry paperwork in favor of PC graphics to prove his case. In 10 minutes the lawyer constructed a bar chart that compared the heights of the state capital dome, the University of Texas tower and a stack of papers representing all the documents his client had turned over to the state.

"The documents were twice as high," said William Dyer, a partner and commercial litigation lawyer for Thompson and Knight. It was simple and conveyed the message very effectively. With his success in that particular trial and in many others, Dyer has joined the emerging category of attorneys who have discovered that the easiest way to present cases is via PC software, particularly graphics programs that can crunch numbers and concepts into more effective visual aids such as bar charts and time lines.

Every picture tells a story . . . I think it's taken a lot longer to integrate computers into the [legal] field. Many lawyers thought PC's were relegated to Lexas and Nexas or case searches. For three years now, Dyer has approached the bench with . . .presentation graphics software-most recently with its windows version. "It's basically a tool to teach and simplify concepts and facts in complicated litigation, either for the judge or the jury," Dyer explained.

In another case, one of Dyer's client's had a reorganization effort under way in Chapter 11, but it was jeopardized by a $200 million back-pay claim by striking union workers. Dyer's job: to whittle the claim down to size that would permit his client to emerge from bankruptcy and not close down business.

Until minutes before the trial, the numbers were being revised by one of his witnesses - a senior partner from a Big Six accounting firm. When they were finally complete, Dyer plugged the new numbers into his laptop and popped three-dimensional charts onto a courtroom screen, while his witness took the stand to explain his conclusions.

"The real-time display at least doubled the effectiveness of the witness testimony," Dyer said." That and other charts apparently had some impact on the case: The judge eventually reduced the back-pay claim from more than $200 million to a little more than $31 million," Dyer said. Would he have won this and other trials without . . . graphics? "It's impossible to say," Dyer said. "But it is fair to say that I've been able to communicate more effectively using charts and graphs."

Dyer believes computers are an underutilized asset in today's courtrooms, a fact that is starting to change as technology begins to impact all areas of modern business life, according to industry observers.

3. *Agreement* - The trier of fact reacts to the presentation of your case in a favorable or unfavorable method. It is difficult to have a factfinder agree with your position if they are predisposed to the opposing side's position. The key is for the audience to favorably react to the presentation of your case and the themes that you present. Multimedia can support you in your quest to present your themes in an understandable, favorable manner so that the factfinder will agree with your position. As Dale Carnegie said, "The best argument is that which seems merely an explanation." Explanations can be enhanced using multimedia.

4. *Retention* -We want the trier of fact to remember the points we make for a reasonable period of time. With the myriad of witnesses, delays in the trial, days of testimony, numerous exhibits, it is imperative that the jury remember our main points to apply to their decision. The method of presentation has a significant impact as to the retention period of information.

Studies have consistently shown that people retain information longer if presented with both a visual and verbal presentation.

	Retention After 3 hours	**After 72 hours**
Telling (verbal)	70%	10%
Showing (visual)	72%	20%
Telling and Showing	85%	65%

See Presier, Demonstrative Evidence in Criminal cases, 4 Trial Dipl. J, 31(1980); Weiss-McGrath Report by McGraw-Hill, M. Dombroff, Dombroff on Demonstrative Evidence, 4, Wiley, 1983.

Seeing something also makes it more memorable. According to Kenneth L. Higbee, in "Your Memory" (2nd ed. Prentice Hall, 1988) page 38, "Picture memory exceeds word memory when measured by recall as well as by recognition. "Higbee tells of a study in which the subjects were shown 2,560 different pictures over several days. Later they were shown 280 pairs of pictures. One of each pair they had seen before, the other they had not. On the average the group correctly identified 90 percent of the pictures they had seen before.

Sarnoff A. Mednick, Howard R. Pollio and Elizabeth F. Loftus tell about it in "Learning" (2d ed. 1973) pages 140-141. "Gordon Bower told subjects to study sentences like Horse eats banana and Cow kicks ball. Some subjects were told to visualize the scene described, while others were told simply to read the sentences. The results for one experiment showed that when the subjects imagined the scene they scored 62 percent correct recall; subjects who merely read the sentences averaged 42 percent correct recall."

5. *Action* - All four of the above components must be addressed to motivate the trier of fact to take action. To take action the message must be relevant to the trier of fact. The presentation must be from a trier of fact's point of view. When an audience is actively involved and knowledgeable about the subject then a number of tools are available to the presenter. Whether it be fear, holding the trier of fact accountable, or other persuasive techniques multimedia can assist in the persuasion process.

Multimedia aids increase your ability to grab the attention of a jury, increase their comprehension, and move them toward agreement with increased retention. Finally, they are more inclined to take action in your client's favor.

Practical Considerations

The practical considerations of the impact of the technology upon the judge, lawyer and the trier of fact should not be overlooked. We have transitioned into an information technology society in a relatively short period of time compared to similar transitions to an agricultural and manufacturing economy. There has been and will continue to be change upheavals for the judge, lawyer and trier of fact. Listen and be sensitive to the practical impacts upon these parties - it may have a significant impact upon your case.

Convincing the Judge

It is imperative that you disclose to the court within a reasonable time before the proceedings of your intention to use technology in the legal proceeding. Many judges have expressed major displeasure with technology, even the addition of a single extension cord, because it changes the appearance of their courtroom. Obtaining the court's consent to use technology can be done informally or formally. Many practitioners routinely file "notices" to the court that they wish to use certain technology in the courtroom. Others raise the issue in pretrial conferences. Whether one wishes to bring a single laptop computer or a complete "paperless" presentation system one must still obtain the agreement of the court.

Many courts are adopting presentation technology in the courtroom. The driving force behind this adoption is the timesaving economics and increased juror's understanding using courtroom technology. Once court administrators and judges realize the cost savings of conducting trials in a paperless environment and the increased understanding of the jury by using technology implementation in the courtroom should accelerate. In Judge Roger Strand's federal district court in Phx, Arizona (www.uscourts.gov/phoenix/index.html) the practitioner only has to bring to court his factual and legal materials in an electronic format. This Computer

Integrated Courtroom (CIC) is completely equipped with computers, CD-ROM's and monitors. This enables the practitioner to access and use his case and legal materials and to present his case in a "paperless" format without the need to provide his own equipment.

However, since we do not all practice exclusively in Judge Strand's court, to convince the judge to use technology will partially depend upon the intended use of the technology equipment. The use of the equipment can range from having a laptop or desktop computer to a complete trial presentation system with monitors for the jury and judge and so on.

Some approaches to requesting the court to permit the technology presentation of your case are:

- Disclose early on to the court your desire to use a technology system in the courtroom. Set forth in a diagram what the requested technology is and the reasons for placement of certain equipment in the courtroom;
- Contact other judges ahead of time who are supportive of the technology to provide as references for your judge;
- Contact opposing counsel and try to convince him to share the cost and not to oppose the request to automate the litigation;
- Many judges are innovators of new ideas and techniques. Often they are called upon to speak at local or national gatherings on their experiences concerning the use of multimedia in the courtroom and "paperless trials". If you provide them a positive experience of using technology then they will become advocates of the technology; and
- Provide supportive evidence that the use of technology will save actual court time and increase the trier of fact's understanding of the issues in the case.

Focus on the Legal Proceeding

The dynamics of a trial are complex and usually very subtle. In my experience the astute trial attorney has to be aware, listen and respond to the concerns of all the participants. These include the trier of fact, judge, opposing counsel, witnesses, bailiffs, clerks, and any other person including the court reporter who may have some impact upon one's presentation in the courtroom. Their verbal and non-verbal feedback is critical to understanding their reaction to you and the presentation of your case. The extent to which the lead attorney uses technology in the courtroom depends upon his/her ability to be sensitive to the needs of the other participants. Remember that technology is only a tool and must not divert your attention from the goal of persuading and being sensitive to the trier of fact.

The question is often asked whether an attorney should take a computer into the courtroom and use it for his opening statement, direct and cross-examination of witnesses and so forth. The answer to this question depends upon a number of factors that we will explore below. Suffice it to say that there is no definitive answer to this issue.

Trial notebook integration programs have not been sufficiently developed to give you complete ease of use for locating all of your litigation material. Different programs, formats, and command structures do not inspire complete confidence in immediately locating material in a computer. Until they do I recommend a paper/paperless trial notebook. Decisions what to put into a paper vs. computer format will depend on the factual and legal issues of a case and the attorney's and court's comfort level with technology. For this reason, I generally do not suggest that lead counsel operate a computer during trial, with the exception of an easy-to-use exhibit presentation system. It is far too important to focus on the multi-faceted trial factors then to worry whether ones opening statement outline is under the OPEN.DOC or OPENCASE.DOC filename.

Remember that the computer is only a tool. It does not have a brain and think like a lawyer. It cannot prepare a clear opening statement. It cannot judge the demeanor of a witness, when to make objections, how to sell your case to a jury or the most effective way to present your evidence. It will never take the place of the attorney, but instead, it will make his or her job a lot easier.

Technology is only a tool. It should never be used as a crutch for your presentation. Your credibility and competence as an advocate are the most important ingredient in the courtroom. Use technology to enhance your presentation and to persuade.

Reaction of the Jury or Factfinder

The question is frequently posed that if you use technology in the courtroom, especially while representing a well-heeled client, will a negative reaction result from the judge or the trier of fact?

Our society, including the judges and juries, is exposed to an onslaught of technology in their lives. It is nearly impossible to go through a day without hearing or seeing information about the Internet, computers, Windows 95/98, Microsoft, or other technology. Our kids, relatives, and a variety of people we come in contact with are being challenged to utilize technology in their businesses, schools and for home use. It is estimated that in the year 1998 alone 30,000,000 computers will be sold. An amazing 1/2 of those will be purchased for home use. Judges and juries are part of this society and generally are not intimidated by the use of technology.

In fact, a positive reaction from the use of computers can result if the court and the trier of fact are shown the benefits of using technology. Many trial practitioners attest to the efficiency and time savings of using technology to provide accurate and immediate legal and case information and the capability of focusing the factfinder's attention during the proceedings. For example, if one uses the computer to present their case through the use of monitors and it saves a day of trial per week the trier of fact will react favorably toward you. This would be especially true if the opposing party is given the opportunity to use the more efficient technology for no or little cost and declines to do so. Then the trier of fact will get a negative reaction toward the party who wastes their time by continuing to use the paper presentation method. Another example is if the court needs immediate and accurate caselaw then locating legal authorities on a CD-ROM in the courtroom

> Will oral advocacy alone bore Generation X jurors? This question was raised in the ABA article Generation X Jurors a Challenge. The X generation is those people born between 1961 to 1981 and will account for 4 out of 10 Americans by the year 2000. Baby Boomers, those born between 1943 to 1960, and Generation Xer's results were similar as to those who own, use or access electronic machines such as VCR's, personal computers and so forth. However, seniors, those born before 1943, the results were significantly lower in there ownership, access or use of electronic machines. Of significance is the popularity of information sources for these three groups. The seniors were very dependent upon newspapers for their information - 79% and decreasing to 60% for Baby Boomers and down to 52% for Xers. Though not asked one can only assume that Xers are receiving almost half of there information from TV which is significant for the type of presentation one makes to this group. Is it not reasonable that they would give greater credibility to evidence that was presented using TV monitors? Generation X Jurors a Challenge, ABA Journal, October, 1995.

will assist the judge in making decisions.

The effect of the well-heeled client's use of technology in the courtroom will be the same as their high end use of some of the best attorneys, demonstrative evidence, animations and other tools in trial. If your client because of his economic status is perceived as taking advantage of a less fortunate opponent then the use of technology in the courtroom will have a negative effect upon your client.

Digital Trial Notebook

A trial notebook is a system for organizing trial materials, legal and factual, to assist you in establishing your case. Trial notebook organization and use vary as to the practitioner. What works for you in your preparation and use for trial should be retained. A digital trial notebook should merely reflect the function of your manual trial notebook. Such a format will provide immediate access to the organization of the facts and law of your case. It should literally be your command post to locate and retrieve the relevant information in your case. The following sections will explore in what form, paper vs. electronic, case information should be available to the litigator in the courtroom.

Legal Materials

In any case certain legal material needs to be accessible to the practitioner. The pertinent caselaw, statutes and rules of procedure are some of those materials. To what extent should the legal material one uses at trial be in an electronic or paper format? If the court wants the exact wording in a rule of evidence to support the admission of evidence does one locate the information on the computer or have it available in a paper format? The answer to this question will depend on a number of factors:

- *How voluminous is the paper format of the legal information?* Caselaw and statutes for all jurisdictions are available on CD-ROM. Caselaw for a particular jurisdiction is usually found in several hundred-reporter volumes. This same material can be stored on one or two CD-ROM disks for immediate access in the courtroom. One CD-ROM disk holds approximately 300,000 pages of full text data. If opposing counsel or the court raises a legal issue during the proceedings then the caselaw can be searched within minutes to locate relevant cases on the issue and can then be printed out. On the other hand the rules of evidence can be in a small paper booklet and may be more accessible and useful in a paper format.
- *How long will it take to locate the information in an electronic format as opposed to a paper format?* Again, this generally will depend upon the amount of material. In an electronic format the material can be accessed in seconds or minutes. It would be beneficial to have predefined searches for the legal issues important to your case. In a paper format the amount of material determines the time to locate the specific legal information needed.
- *Is the paper equivalent available nearby and accurate with up-to-date supplements?* Many courts have law libraries that may or may not be accessible to the practitioner. Assuming the court grants you permission to use their legal materials have they been updated with the latest supplements and advance sheets? After locating the materials do you have access to a copier to copy the materials? Other issues are the physical location of these materials in the courthouse and whether the materials are complete and up-to-date.
- *Will the court want to see an actual copy of the materials?* If the court and opposing party want to see the authorities in a paper format one needs a printer attached to your computer to print out the relevant case, statutes or other material.
- *Is one able to reasonably anticipate the court's questioning regarding particular legal issues?* If one can anticipate the legal issues to be raised in the courtroom it would be advantageous to have the legal materials and copies available beforehand in a paper format for the court and opposing parties so that time will be saved.
- *Is the legal information available on-line?* If you have a useable telephone or cellular connection in the courtroom or nearby then one could call up the on-line service for caselaw or statute access. However, will the court permit you access to their telephone system for access to a legal on-line database? How long does it take to dial up the service? What happens if I am cut off and unable to use the service?

Case Materials

Set out below is a discussion of what case materials to have available in a paper or digital format. The decision whether to have paper or electronic copies of motions, documents, and other materials will depend on:

1. Importance to Your Case. Case materials for legal proceedings generally will be important or only marginally relevant. Through discovery proceedings, pretrial statements, exhibits' lists and so forth the critical information in whatever form for both parties will generally be identified before the legal proceeding. These important documents should be available in an electronic and paper format.

2. Cost of Converting to an Electronic Format. The two primary methods of storing case data are in a full text or in an imaged format. Full text format are the words of a document in a word processing or ASCII format. In this format individual words of the document can be searched and the location in the document can be rapidly accessed. Court reporters will provide ASCII disks of depositions for approximately $25.00. To convert existing paper documents to ASCII text can be quite expensive so the decision to convert documents to this format must be judiciously made. The conversion process involves sending the paper through a scanner with Optical Character Recognition (OCR) software and then correcting the errors manually in the text.

Converting paper documents into an imaged format is generally inexpensive with a cost of approximately 15 cents per page through a service bureau. However, the individual words in an imaged document cannot be searched with a full text software program so a database type indexing system must be set up which provides sufficient information to enable one to locate the imaged document.

The following table reflects a suggested trial notebook and which case materials would be in a paper or electronic format for use in the legal proceeding. The Digital Format (Options) section provides different computer formats that the data can be in. The documents in a digital format can be used in pretrial proceedings as well as trial proceedings.

Case Materials	Paper Format	Digital Format(Options)	Source of Material
Trial Plan	YES	YES - (Word Processing)	Internal
Witness List/Trial Order of Witnesses Plaintiff's Witnesses Defendant's Witnesses	YES	Yes - (Word Processing)	Internal
Opening Statement	YES	Yes - (Word processing)	Internal
Direct/Cross Examination Outlines	YES	Yes – (Word Processing)	Internal
Exhibits List/Order of Proof, Exhibits	YES	Yes - (Database, Images)	Internal & Opposing Counsel
Complaint/Answer	YES	YES - (Full text, Images)	Internal & Opposing Counsel
Motions in Limine Trial Briefs and Memorandum	YES	YES - (Full Text, Images)	Internal & Opposing Counsel
Orders/Stipulations	YES	YES(Full Text, Images)	Internal, Opposing Counsel & Court
Interrogatories and Answers	YES	YES(Full text, Images)	Internal & Opposing Counsel
Request for Production and Actual Documents	YES, if important to case	YES - (Images)	Internal & Opposing Counsel
Requests for Admission/Responses	YES	YES - (Full Text, Images)	Internal & Opposing Counsel
Depositions	YES	YES - (Full Text, Images)	Court Reporter

Depositions Summaries	YES	YES - (Full Text)	Internal
Damages	YES	YES - (Full Text, Spreadsheets)	Internal & Opposing Counsel
Jury Profile Jury Questionnaire & responses	YES	YES - (Full text, Databases, Images)	Internal & Court
Jury Instructions	YES	YES - (Full Text, Word Processing)	Internal, Opposing Counsel & Court
Final Argument	YES	YES - (Word Processing, Databases)	Internal

Computer Equipment & Software

The intended use of courtroom technology falls into two primary areas:
- A practitioner's access to legal and factual material in his case; and
- Presenting trial exhibits, demonstrative evidence and other material to the factfinder during trial. (This will be covered in Part E of this chapter entitled *Presenting Your Multimedia Case*.)

The type and amount of technology equipment that is used in the courtroom to access ones legal and factual material will depend upon:
- court's consent to the use of the technology;
- technology equipment already available in the courtroom;
- practitioner's capability to bring in equipment and technical assistance;
- complexity of the case; and
- the comfort level of the practitioner.

If the intended use of courtroom technology is to access your legal and factual material it requires at a minimum a laptop or desktop computer (preferably with a CD-ROM reader) and a small printer. This will provide complete access to any of the legal or case information that is in a digital format. The printer provides the capability to print out hard copies of imaged exhibits, graphics, notes, jury instructions, settlement agreements, closing arguments or other material for the judge, witnesses or opposing counsel. The printer should be equipped to print either paper or transparencies. For example, if a document becomes in issue, locate it on the CD-ROM, print it out on a portable printer and attach a trial exhibit sticker to it. Transparencies of exhibits would be used with an overhead projector for witnesses, opening statements or for closing arguments. The basic system described above provides the capability to access your entire legal and factual case if it is in an electronic

> COURTABLE PORTABLES, ABA Journal, April, 1993, David P. Vandagriff
>
> Someone once said, "Computers can never replace lawyers, but lawyers with computers can replace lawyers without them." No-where is this more evident than in the courtroom.
>
> A lawyer who uses a computer effectively in court has a significant advantage over one who doesn't. A computer can provide instant access to an enormous variety of critical information, ranging from a statement made by a witness during a five-day deposition to the text of the latest Supreme Court decision.
>
> While litigators would like to anticipate every bit of information they will need, every attorney who has spent much time in court has been surprised. Being able to search for information electronically, instead of manually, is a wonderful antidote for the unforeseen.
>
> In addition to locating data, a courtroom computer can present information in a powerful visual format, making it more persuasive than oral presentation alone. Yes, lawyers have been using DEMONSTRATIVE EXHIBITS and charts for years, but today's presentation graphics programs allow anyone using a computer to construct and show detailed graphic representations quickly and easily.

format.

Tips on using computers in the courtroom:

- ❑ The computer must be unobtrusive;
- ❑ It must be small;
- ❑ Bring along extra charged batteries;
- ❑ Bring along a substitute computer with the same programs and legal and factual material on both computers;
- ❑ Have your case material backed up on tape, Zip or regular disks;
- ❑ Print a copy of your trial outline, witness notes, etc.;
- ❑ Bring extra printer toner cartridges;
- ❑ Print transparencies of documents, charts and graphs for use with an overhead   projector;
- ❑ Make sure your keyboard is quiet; and
- ❑ Turn off the sound on the computer.

Visual Digital Aids

Introduction - Multimedia

Cutting edge multimedia trials are becoming commonplace. With the overwhelming evidence establishing that people are influenced dramatically by the use of multimedia we will continue to see significant increases in its use by legal professionals in a variety of legal forums. As one attorney stated to me who participated in a paperless multimedia trial, "In my opinion it is legal malpractice not to use an in-court presentation system if the opposing side is using one!"

Sam Guiberson of Houston, Texas presents his closing arguments "on the cheap" using shareware and other low cost software. He takes the audience through the facts of a case using a variety of multimedia tools. He uses imaged documents, text, graphics, sound, and video to provide strong support for his customary eloquent verbal presentation. As Sam stated, " Look not for multimedia, but for multiple uses of media to persuade a jury".

Why did the late Honorable Carl Rubin, federal judge for the Southern District of Ohio, The Honorable Roger Strand and The Honorable Richard Bilby, federal judges for the District of Arizona, encourage the use of computers in their courtrooms? They all think that the use of computers enhances the jury's understanding of the case, results in significant timesaving and prevents the paper warehouse effect in their courtroom. What do Brian O'Neil, lead plaintiff's attorney in the Exxon Valdez case, Michael Manning, lead plaintiff's attorney in the Keating trials and Jim Wagner, lead counsel in the Washington Public Power case, all have in common? They all felt they had a definite competitive edge over their adversaries by presenting in a multimedia format their documents, video depositions and other digitized case evidence during trial.

> The infamous "Titanic" closing argument multimedia video depicts the outer edge of how multimedia is used in trial. This video was actually used in the plaintiff's closing argument in an Arizona case. The video paralleled the warnings the titanic received and ignored about the iceberg with the warnings the defendants allegedly received and ignored about the financial condition of one of their clients. The video that runs for approximately 18 minutes used all available multimedia - text, sound, graphics and video - in this persuasive presentation to the jury. It was interesting to note that the defendants were not permitted to see the video before it was presented to the jury since this was part of the plaintiff's closing argument.

Multimedia software enables one to present graphics, images, sound, video, full text and animations to a jury in a digital format. Generally each type of multimedia evidence is displayed using a specific type file format. For example, sound is usually contained in WAV files and images in a TIF format. To display digital information such as a WAV and TIFF file special display software must be used. Display software such as Microsoft's PowerPoint or inData's TrialDirector can display the different type of file formats for your multimedia factual and legal information.

Documents & Pictures

The most common case materials to present in trial are documents and photographs. In order to present these documents in a digital format to draw, enlarge, or place side by side it is necessary to convert them into a digital format. Imaging software is used to convert documents and photographs into a digital format.

Imaging software's primary function is to provide the user with the ability to scan a piece of paper, photograph or other document into a computer resulting in an image of the document. This "electronic snapshot" of the document then is available to view, enlarge, draw on and present in a legal proceeding.

Two imaging software programs are TrialDirector and Watermark. Both programs enable one to view and present documents after they have been scanned into the computer using a scanner. Software imaging features to look for are: the ability to redact parts of the image, add annotations, link to database or other programs, and the capability to enlarge. TrialDirector™ (www.indatacorp.com) and Watermark™ (www.filenet.com).

See also Chapter 6, Imaging.

AT THE CREATION, ABA Journal August 1994, Mark Curriden. *With the Generative Power of a Computer, Lawyers Can Shape an Adam or Eve to Demonstrate All Sorts of Medical Conditions. And What They See is Good.*

David Shuman knows the power of a good medical illustration. A defense lawyer in Charleston, W.Va., Shuman was defending a personal injury case in which the plaintiffs were seeking million-dollar damages. The case depended upon which medical expert jurors would believe.

Days before the scheduled trial, Shuman decided to gamble and take his demonstrative evidence-a series of professionally prepared medical illustrations-to a pre-trial conference to argue a motion. The risk paid off. The plaintiffs' lawyers marveled at the artwork and, more importantly, at the story it told. "We had talked settlement before, but the two sides were far apart," Shuman recalls. "The sight of the medical illustrations told the plaintiffs we were serious and ready to go to trial. Their demands dropped like a rock."

Charts & Graphs

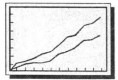

There are generally three types of software to assist you in creating charts and graphic exhibits: graphics, CAD and paint programs.

1. Graphics Software. Graphics software enables the user to create a graphic exhibit that will give a visual impression to the viewers. Bar graphs, pie charts, timelines, organization charts and a host of other graphical depictions provides the viewer with a visual impression by use of pictures and data. It can be used to represent and emphasize any kind of data or image. Charts can combine words and vivid graphic images to call attention to important detail.

2. CAD software. Another type of graphics software is a design program commonly called CAD, Computer Aided Design, that allows one to draw the interior of a home, manufacturing plans, roads, etc.

3. Paint software. Finally, there are paint programs such as Microsoft Paintbrush™ that enables you to draw freehand the picture of your choice using a mouse or other pointing device.

Presentation graphics programs like Microsoft PowerPoint™ and Harvard Graphics™ provide a number of user friendly features including tutorials, predefined graphic templates, and clip art. They offer a good basic set of drawing and annotation tools. These programs are designed for all industries and do not come with specific legal templates or examples. They provide the capability of creating bullet slides, graphs and inserting clip art to explain your client's legal position. They generally come with a "screenshow" feature that enables you to arrange the created slides and present them in whatever order you desire. These programs also allow you to create multimedia presentations by inserting graphics, sound, text, animations and even live video as an OLE object.

Special "niche" graphics software can provide valuable assistance in your cases. Two such graphics niche packages are VISIO™ and FlowCharter™. VISIO™ is a graphics program that is complementary to general presentation graphic programs such as Microsoft PowerPoint™ and enables the user to create specific relationship "type" charts. The program provides numerous stencils to assist with "relationships" that are important in your case. For example the stencils include workflow, house objects, roadway icons and host of other commonly used objects that can be used in the creation of your exhibits. Another niche program is FlowCharter™ that provides the capability to do timelines and other "flow" type representation for work or other concepts. Visio™ (www.visio.com) and FlowCharter™ (www.micrografx.com/flowcharter/).

DQ² Exhibit Bank™ is an easy to use CD-ROM library of legal graphics. These graphics are visually compelling and show how legal concepts can be presented in an easy to understand manner. Nearly 2000 professionally rendered charts present specific circumstances, conditions, or sets of data presenting visual graphic examples of how to present your legal arguments.

The CD-ROM is organized by case type: anti-trust, banking/lending liability, construction, contracts, insurance, intellectual property, labor/employment, personal injury, product liability, professional malpractice, securities and toxic tort. It also provides specific categories for damage exhibits, highly used exhibits and medical exhibits.

Once a case type is selected the graphic screen appears enabling the user to select from bar, chronology, document, flow, illustration, line, map, organizational, pie and text graphics. Once a graphic type is selected you can view many excellent completed graphics of the chart type. For example if you choose case type for personal injury and the chronology chart type you have over 20 charts to view. These include a chronology of medical injuries to a plaintiff, medical malpractice timeline, prior notice of safety problems, history of safety problems involving a product, percentage of workers injured on a particular job site and so on. You can see the colors, data configuration and viewer appeal of these professional graphs.

Each graph can be printed, customized to your case and then ordered from DecisionQuest, the maker of the DQ² Exhibit Bank™. Prices range from approximately $100 to $400 depending on the complexity of the chart. A chart can be ordered as a 3' x 4' court board, 8 ½" x 11" color print or a 8 ½ " x 11" color overhead transparency, or as a computer file.

This product is manufactured by DecisionQuest (www.decisionquest.com) (800-826-5353) and cost $99.00. Individual charts can be purchased for approximately $100 - $400. Also, consider Genigraphics (owned by inFocus) for your graphic needs. Requests made by 10 PM Central Time are shipped the next AM delivery anywhere in the US by FedEx. (www.genigraphics.com/)(800-790-4001).

Video

Video, like a video deposition, can be digitally converted onto a CD-ROM disk or laser disk. The conversion then enables the user to access any part of the video instantaneously and freeze-frame any picture. This is contrasted with the videotape method of fast forwarding to the area in the transcript using the conventional VCR method. Also, it is important to remember that this video can now be synchronized with the full text translation of the voice of the witness. This synchronization enables one to search in the full text for the particular evidence and then switch immediately to the digital video portion of the testimony at that location. For example if you are questioning a witness on the stand and you want to bring up part of the deposition involving a discussion of the word diabetes, search for the word and it will take you immediately to the video spot where the witness said this word.

Video allows a jury to listen to and read a witness. Video brings parties to life much better than written testimony. Video can be used for a variety of purposes in your case:

- Witness preparation;
- Settlement brochure;
- Day in the life documentation;
- Deposition;
- Site evaluation;
- Surveillance; and for
- Video stills.

One product that synchronizes video and text is DepositionDirector™ (www.indatacorp.com). *See also Chapter 6, Multimedia and Chapter 7, Video Depositions.*

Animations

An animation is a three-dimensional, scientifically accurate, computer-generated series of still graphic images. In motion, they provide a simulation or recreation of an event or process. Once the animation is constructed you can show it from different camera angles. Autodesk 3-D Animator™ software (www.autodesk.com) has the capability to create and then view a two-car accident from the viewpoint of the driver, overhead, behind, to the side, or any angle which will most effectively display your version of how the accident happened, as long as it is supported by evidence.

Animations can be used to reconstruct or simulate events, simplify complicated systems, and take the viewer "inside" an object. They have been used in construction, financial, medical malpractice, oil and gas, patent infringement, personal injury and toxic tort cases.

Animations can be used during different stages of litigation:

- Exhibit to summary judgment;
- Settlement tool;

> Working Model – Knowledge Revolution (www.krev.com) is a software program that will simulate automobile crashes. It will simulate gravity, air drag, acceleration and collisions on a particular object. These can be automobiles, machinery or humans. The simulations can be saved as QuickTime movies.
>
> 3D models of people, places and things can be purchased from Viewpoint (www.viewpoint.com). Examples include skeletal anatomy, internal anatomy, cars and many others including the dancing baby.

- Part of witness's testimony; and as a
- Closing statement exhibit.

Generation and Admissibility of Computer Graphics and Animations. There are several steps to qualifying computer-generated animations for use in court:

1. Pretrial Strategy - Disclose the use of animation exhibit at least 60 days before closure of discovery. This will give the judge enough time to analyze the applicable case law and how the rules of evidence will apply. Opposing counsel will have time to request the foundational basis for the animation and to retain expert assistance, if desired.
2. Qualify the Expert - The expert must possess important credentials to support the reasonableness of the data, how the data was inputted, the computer hardware and software, and the results obtained.
3. Qualify the Hardware - It is best to use commercially available hardware. It should be available for non-litigation use and accepted and used by the engineering community.
4. Qualify the Software -Commercially available software is the best to use. Emphasize this point showing its nonlitigation use by the engineering community.
5. Qualify the Data - What was the source of the data? How was the accuracy of the data checked? How was it inputted into the computer? What assumptions were made for the model? How was data input checked? Vouching for these factors that provide the basis for the animation is extremely important. If some of your data is incorrect, this can provide fruitful and deadly cross-examination. Sources of data originate from eyewitness testimony, physical measurements, design drawings, data recorders, black boxes from planes, expert witness calculations and opinions.
6. Qualify the Processing Operation of the Software - An expert can do benchmark tests, perform a smaller calculation comparing it with a calculator, or use the certifications that sometimes accompany the software.
7. Qualify the Accuracy of the Presentation Media - The media that displays the animation or other form of output must be qualified. They must demonstrate that the display is accurately depicted.

Animations can be extremely useful for certain types of cases. However, they are generally expensive.

Virtual Reality

You can fly to the moon by pointing your finger. With a flick of your wrist, see the world through the eyes of a child. Reach out and grasp furniture, windows, or walls that exist only within the silicon memory of a PC. Wave your hand to create virtual paper on an empty desktop, a simulated skid in a nonexistent car, or X-rays of the human body.

- PC Computing

VR (virtual reality), according to VR theorists William Bricken and Brenda Laurel, is, respectively, "an electronically mediated experience" and "a multisensory representation." As generally agreed, virtual reality refers to having the ability to interact with data in a way that provides the user to "enter" and navigate through a computer-generated 3-D "world" or environment and change your viewpoint and interact with objects within that environment. The user can move around the virtual reality, examine things from different perspectives and gain a greater understanding of the reality being simulated. Virtual Reality is characterized by "immersion"

> "Virtual worlds are meant to be perceived by touch, shattering the barrier between the computer screens and worlds beyond." - PC Computing

into an artificial world created through vision, sound and touch. Virtual Reality is interactive and the participant enjoys autonomy, or freedom to move around and manipulate virtual objects at will. Today, in virtual reality, you can see and hear, point and move, pick up things and throw them, and sometimes touch and feel.

The history of virtual reality is a history of computers. With computers, we moved from 1-D (inputting text one character at a time), to 2-D (Graphical User Interface), to 3-D (multimedia), to Virtual Reality. Virtual Reality is meant to emulate the life that you create.

The legal applications in the legal field are obvious and immense. Finally, we can take jurors to the "actual" scene of the accident, and they can view with through their own eyes a reconstruction of the accident. They would be able to move their hands to enter a car. The computerized reconstruction would start, and the jurors could see the accident from the driver's perspective. It could be programmed to slow down or increase the speed of the car by moving a finger on the glove. The jurors could move the location of a pedestrian by grabbing the pedestrian with their hands and moving the person to a different location.

Equipment. To experience virtual reality or a personal reality simulator, you don special headgear the size of a tissue box. Look into this headgear and you will see a stereoscopic 3-D image of the "virtual reality." Move your head to the side or up and down and the computer shifts the display to realistically match your point of view. You are in the scene, not an outside observer.

Next you have to slip a glove onto your hand. The glove is calibrated for the individual participant. The glove uses fiber optics to keep track of the basic motions of the user's right hand. On the back of both the glove and the helmet are magnetic sensors that monitor motions and send them to computers. When moving your hand and the fingers, you see a disembodied image of the glove. The display moves in the direction you do. Point the glove straight up and the room appears to fall away. With your feet still on the ground, you're flying. Point your finger toward the ground and you return. Move toward a wall and you go through it to the outside.

Dr. Michael McGreevy who guided NASA's entry into virtual reality has secured funding for a project called Visualization for Planetary Exploration that will result in virtual environments of the moon and the planets. Visual data recorded by satellites and space probes are used to create computer models of the planets.

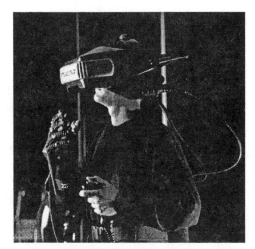

See (www.seas.gwu.edu/faculty/musgrave/sci_viz.html) and (http://olias.arc.nasa.gov/publications/McGreevy.AFO.WWW/SIGCHI.89/SIGCHI.89.html .com) It is anticipated that when it is completed, you can hold the moon or planet in your hand and point to where you want to go. The computer will place you in the surrounding area of the planet. You will feel like you were there.

Using the same virtual reality application, you could visit exotic places, resorts, ride roller coasters, or experience any "virtual" reality.

8 - 19

Presenting Your Multimedia Case

Introduction

There were some very excellent observations in one of the first paperless trials about using computers in the courtroom from the participants in the <u>Ayers. et al v. Sutliffe, et al</u>, No. C-1-90-650, Southern District of Ohio case. In FROM THE BENCH, **A Paperless Trial**, the late Carl B. Rubin, United States District Judge, Southern District of Ohio, wrote:

> I have seen the Courtroom of the Future. I have even had the good fortune to use it. When it becomes the Courtroom of the Present, everyone will benefit. It will cost the litigants less. It will permit clearer presentation of evidence, and it will be far easier for the presiding judge to administer. Such a courtroom will substitute computer monitors for the customary avalanche of paper.

J. Michael Rediker, attorney for the plaintiffs in this case stated:

> Witness examinations moved quickly, and the computers allowed the rapid questioning on numerous documents. We were also able to dispense with the expensive and time-consuming process of putting together a dozen multi-volume sets of hard copies of the trial exhibits.
>
> * * * * *
>
> Our sense was that the jurors much preferred the computers over the hard copy, a notion that was confirmed during the defense portion of the case. The defendants declined to use the computers. They insisted on the traditional method of presenting blow-ups and passing documents to the jurors. The result was vacant stares and grimaces. If the outcome of the case is any indication, the jury verdict was a strong endorsement of the computers - the jury returned a plaintiff verdict with regard to every defendant.
> * * * * * *
>
> Our experience with computers in the courtroom has several important lessons for trial lawyers. Computers can be extremely effective tools in presenting a complex case to a jury -- any jury. The jurors in our case represented a true community cross-section; only two of the nine had college degrees. Although not unusually sophisticated, they did accept -- and were not intimidated by -- the computers. The technology is accessible and is becoming more adaptable every day; concerns about operating failures should not inhibit its use. We did encounter occasional glitches, but they were addressed promptly and without any material impact on the case. Resistance to the use of computers may place trial lawyers at an extreme disadvantage if they find themselves confronted with an opponent who is computer literate.

The presentation of your digital case in court requires some forethought but will pay significant dividends. Studies have shown that the party that uses visual aids significantly influences the "60 minute" TV generation trier of fact. We have become a multimedia society and expect presentations - legal or otherwise - to include a multi-sensory approach.

Preparing Case Themes and a Visual Presentation Plan.

In all of your cases a multimedia visual plan should be developed along with your trial themes.

Considerations should be given to what type of multimedia to use to support your case strategies at the same time you are developing the theory, themes and labels for your case including your witness examinations. Your visual trial plan should include the plaintiff and defendant's main contentions and the key points you wish to make in support of your case or in opposition to the opposing party's case.

- *Organize your presentation.* It is imperative that you build your case story one step at a time. Explain to the jury each point you are making and how it fits into the overall presentation of your case. When you move from one point to the next tell the jury what you are doing. It is effective if you can have one visual for each point you are making to the jury. Then as you build your case during opening statement each point will be in front of them as you present the themes of your case. Do not make your case complex for a jury to understand.

- *Opening Statement Considerations.* Provide your main points in the opening but do not provide a laundry list of all the evidence. Instead make your main points and support them by key evidence, analogies or anything that will simplify the points and increase the juror's understanding of your case. Again, well thought out graphics for your major points will be especially useful during your opening statement. Be flexible and creative in your opening using a variety of visual exhibits to keep the jury's attention.

- *Build Your Case around Three to Five Themes.* The themes of your case should make the jury want to decide in your favor as being the only right thing to do. The themes if properly supported by visuals will always be in front of the jury. It will be the points they remember when they go back to the jury room.

- *Use simple but strong visuals.* The jury will view your visuals as important so make sure they convey in a simple way the major points of your case. List the type of demonstrative evidence and how they will be used in your case. For example determine if you will be using graphic exhibits in your opening statement. If so, then determine the conclusion you want the trier of fact to take with them after seeing the exhibit. What is the message of the exhibit and in what format —charts, graph, etc. – should the visual evidence be in. These visual exhibits can be used in pretrial with clients, expert witnesses, and members of your team and for trial itself.

Organization charts, documents blowups all lend credence to your presentation. However, a word of caution is that too many may distract from the main points of your presentation. Always maintain a link or thread throughout your exhibits so that the jury follows your argument.

Some of the ways to maintain the thread is to use consistent colors and style for all of your demonstrative evidence. For example, you may wish to provide a consistent color and only one graphic for each of the important points of your case. For example red can be used for evidence impeaching the other parties' contentions. So if you have three graphics impeaching the evidence they should have red as a common color.

You should tightly weave your opening statement with your demonstrative evidence. These exhibits should be used throughout the trial with expert witnesses, etc. The jury will then tie it together as they continually see the exhibits.

Visual Exhibit Considerations and Goals.

❑ *Clear and Understandable Message.* Ads on TV give a clear and understandable message. They are eye-catching and succinct. Your message should supply information as to the themes in your case as opposed to pure factual data. If possible, do not make the jurors draw their own conclusions from the graphic.

❑ *Gestalt Grouping Principles.* When we view a graphic display, we have a tendency to group or organize the elements on a chart. Some elements stand out and others become part of the background. It is important to ensure that the elements you want the jury to focus on and remember do not get lost in the background. If you put to much information on an exhibit then the jury will search through all the information trying to understand all the points and in effect diluting your message.

❑ *Simple and straightforward.* Do not overload the juror with too much information. Do not require them to read and select the information they will remember.

❑ *Cues.* People will immediately draw conclusions from seeing a graphic exhibit. Those conclusions and the theme should be reinforced throughout the trial with different witnesses or during different stages of the proceeding.

❑ *Free of Distracting Information.* Ensure that the exhibit does not distract or direct the jurors to points that are irrelevant. The jurors will lose the effect of your exhibit if they focus on something different.

❑ *Attention Grabbing.* Jurors will pay attention to something they are conditioned to or enjoy. Try to utilize their real life experiences to convince and persuade them. Use visually exciting graphics - bold and distinctive shapes, use of color contrast, and familiar objects.

❑ *Repetition.* During different parts of a trial, reaffirm the general themes and conclusions you want them to draw.

❑ *Color.* Plan for cohesive color and style for all demonstrative evidence. It is helpful for organizing diagrams, charts, and other visual aids. Each important subject should have its own color code to present to the jury. For example, red might be used to show damaging testimony by opposing party. Blue might be used to reflect one particular element in a case. Color can also be used to differentiate between elements in a presentation - enabling comparisons and highlighting trends. Too many colors tend to dilute value.

❑ *Support Data/Technical Data.* Be sure and have exhibit data available. The scale, who drew it, whether the measurements were received from an expert, and who generated the definitions. For example, a copy of a deposition or medical chart from which an enlargement was made.

Equipment and Multimedia Checklist

There are a wide variety of multimedia presentation technologies available to assist you in presenting your case. From the simple blackboard to a sophisticated animation all have certain advantages and disadvantages. Remember that one of the foremost goals is to maintain the attention of the jurors so a mixing of the different multimedia options will keep their attention. Mix it up and keep your presentation lively.

There are several factors in deciding which particular piece of software and hardware to use:

- Simplicity – ease of use is usually near or at the top of all lists;
- Reliability – attorneys expect the equipment to work;
- Budget Limitations – each attorney and their practice will differ as to the amounts they can afford to spend on presentation equipment;
- Flexibility – if the equipment can be used for a variety of presentation needs then it will be used more for a lower cost;
- Functionality – the equipment should not interfere with the legal proceeding, in fact it should support the court atmosphere of searching for the truth; and
- Results – are you getting a good return on your investment?

Below is a checklist of different equipment and multimedia technology.

Chalk and Blackboard or Dry Erase Board.
Pros:

- Easy to use
- Inexpensive
- Can easily annotate
- Easy to transport

Cons:

- Does not stay in front of jury throughout trial and it can be erased.
- Must be able to write legibly
- Limited use of colors and graphics

FlipBoards.
Pros:

- Stays in front of jury if writing on paper is removed and mounted on poster board.
- Inexpensive.
- Can easily annotate.
- Easy to transport

Cons:

- Must be able to write legibly
- Limited use of colors and graphics.

Digital Flipchart. Using a computer, a LCD projector and the Digital Flipchart or whiteboard a computer can be controlled at the whiteboard by the touch of your finger. It is the same as standing at a blackboard (here a whiteboard) and touching the screen to control the computer and to present and write on images, documents, etc. (www.smarttech.com).

Pros

- Can easily annotate on the whiteboard itself.
- Reflects what is on the computer screen.
- Controls computer from whiteboard
- Screen is bright so lights do not have to be dimmed.
- Can print out screens to save
- Graphics can be used

Cons:

- Need to purchase or rent LCD projector and digital flipchart
- Transportation – due to its size can be difficult.
- Cost is around $4000 for digital flipchart

Whiteboard. A whiteboard is a computerized blackboard. After writing on computer "whiteboard" with a dry eraser the writing can be automatically printed onto an 8 ½ by 11-inch piece of paper.
Pros:

- Easy to use
- Writing can be saved and given to jury for later use.
- Easy to annotate

Cons:

- Expensive – approximate cost is $5,000 to $10,000.
- Transportation – due to its size can be difficult.
- Must be able to write legibly
- Limited use of colors and graphics

Overhead projector and transparencies. (See below for further discussion)

Pros:

- Widespread use, easy to use.
- Generally easy to fix if bulb burns out.
- Can easily annotate and draw on transparencies.
- Can produce transparencies in the courtroom with laptop printer.
- Generally do not have to dim the lights.
- Color or B/W.
- Can enlarge to 8' by 10' or larger.
- Graphics can be created beforehand.
- Easy to transport

Cons:

- Projector noise can be distracting, unless you have a newer model.
- Exhibits do not stay in front of jury

Blowups - graphics & documents:

Pros:

- Stays in front of jury throughout trial and maybe in jury room.
- Can annotate if clear sheet is placed over blowup.
- Size of posterboard blowups is determined by budget
- Can be inexpensive
- Relatively easy to transport

Cons:

- Cost can be expensive depending on who prepares and the complexity of subject matter such as medical illustrations

Visual Presenter (See below for further discussion). Video camera that projects objects, photographs or paper to a monitor or to a screen using a projection device.

Pros:

- Easy to operate.
- Can project objects, paper or photographs.
- Can annotate on paper or photographs with special pens.
- Saves cost of enlarging photographs and documents.
- Objects can be enlarged.
- Many courts have visual presenter as part of courtroom equipment.
- Focuses everyone's attention on what is being shown on monitor.

Cons:

- Presentation setup cost is approximately $4,000. However leasing the equipment would be considerably cheaper.

Video Cassette Recorder (VCR)
    Pros*:*

- Widely available.
- Easy to operate
- Tape can be shown on regular TV monitor.

    Cons:

- Video production is expensive
- Have to fast forward or rewind to get to specific location. (However, if digitized, it can be played from a computer and any part can be instantly accessed).
- Difficult to edit and annotate.

Graphs, charts, bullet slides and other visual exhibits:
    Pros:

- Inexpensive to create, software packages start at $100
- Supports verbal points to jury
- Can be displayed as poster board, 35-mm slide, colored printout, transparency, slideshow presentation etc.

    Cons:

- Display method may be expensive – depends on choice.
- Complexity may increase cost

Computer presentation software (Display documents, graphics and/or video)(See below for a further explanation of presentation software).
    Pros:

- Allows for instant flexibility in the retrieval of documents or graphics.
- Allows one to quickly shift from one document or graphic to the next.
- Can draw everyone's attention simultaneously to specific parts of a document.
- Can place documents side by side and enlarge.
- Easy to annotate and save annotation
- Cost of imaging documents and photographs is small.
- Can synchronize video, audio and documents together such as the video, text and sound of a deposition.

    Cons:

- Cost of setup:
- Software cost - $100 - $1,000
- Computer equipment – can use your office equipment
- Presentation method – LCD projector; lease $125 a day; purchase $4,000 and up.

Scale Models
    Pros:

- Provides for a realistic three-dimensional view of the object, scene, etc.
- Provides for a "picture" that may be worth a thousand words.

    Cons:

- Difficult to annotate
- Expensive

Animations and Simulations
    Pros:

- Provides for a two or three-dimensional view of the object, scene, etc.
- Can view object or scene from many different viewpoints or angles.
- Provides for a "moving picture" that may be worth a thousand words.

    Cons:

- Difficult to annotate.
- Expensive
- Need to carefully lay foundation for use in the courtroom.

Overhead Projector. Transparencies are still the most widely used visual aid because of the cost and relative ease of use. All that is needed to display them is a high powered projector which many judges permit in the legal proceeding. With the introduction of low cost and quiet printers transparencies can now be printed in the courtroom as the trial is proceeding. After printing your transparencies it is suggested that one attach paper borders which can be purchased at office supply stores. Paper border transparencies are easier to handle, blocks out light and one can write on the edges. To build your presentation, place pieces of paper over the points until they are discussed.

Projecting transparencies up on a screen provides important control of the trial proceedings. Once projected, the overhead becomes the focal point of the litigants, witness and most important the jurors. The trial is a mini drama and if the overhead projector can add to the drama by projecting a "bigger then life" image of a document up for all the jurors to see then that very well may be the piece of evidence that will be remembered by the trier of fact. Also, one can draw on the transparencies to highlight important evidence. Turning down the lights for key evidence will further focus the trial with these types of multimedia aids. To get your point across quickly, cleanly and inexpensively transparencies may be the answer.

Visual Presenter. The visual or "Elmo™" presenter is a video camera attached to a metal arm pointed downward to project images onto a color monitor or a LCD projector. Anything can be placed beneath the camera for projection onto monitors in the courtroom. Actual objects, pictures, x-rays, blueprints, charts, tables, hospital records and documents can be prominently displayed with this piece of equipment. The visual presenter can be turned into a "wireless" display system by purchasing low cost transmission equipment at Radio Shack. A VCR can capture all of the proceedings and exhibits displayed on the visual presenter for later playback. Images that are displayed can also be printed whether it is a document picture or video frame.

The camera can be turned sideways to focus on models such as accident scenes, vehicles, human parts or other real evidence or people to capture them on the monitors. Very little preplanning needs to be done and the one-time price is approximately $3,000. One technique for showing deposition text is to have it printed in a mini-transcript layout. When placed under a visual presenter it enlarges it to provide a controlled and useable focus on the text of a deposition. With an overhead projector transparencies show full text better but is incapable of showing many of the things this equipment can display.

There is no need to plan which photo to enlarge since merely placing them under the cameras will show it enlarged many times over on the monitor. You can zoom in on any part of the picture and show the smallest detail and enlarge it to the size of the monitor. Elmo™ visual presenter (www.elmo.com).

Presentation Software Features

After you have created visuals for a case or imaged in documents, then presentation software is needed to display these digital exhibits to the trier of fact. The presentation software you choose should enable you to easily retrieve the digitized evidence and then use specialized tools to enhance and draw attention to specific portions of the exhibit for the legal audience's benefit. The capability to focus the trier of fact upon the specific portions of a document or other digitized evidence for everyone to view simultaneously cannot be overstated. A word of caution, whatever presentation software you use ensure that it will display the graphics or images in the file format that you captured or created the documents in.

There are some presentation software programs that were developed specifically for the needs of the legal profession and are available for purchase. For example Trial Director™ and Summation Vupoint™ both are presentation software. Trial Director™, formerly called Trial-Link™, was originally designed for the Charles Keating trials and is able to display demonstrative exhibits, animations, graphics, sound, video and any other type of information that has been digitized. It has also been used in the Exxon Valdez and O.J. Simpson trials. It enables you to retrieve the digitized evidence by bar codes or touchscreen and has many other features that are explained below. TrialDirector™ (www.indatacorp.com) and Summation Vupoint™ (www.summation.com.).

General graphics or image software packages have some limited built in presentation features that may fulfill your presentation needs. For example PowerPoint™ enables you to create a "screenshow" to show your bullet slides, charts or graphs created within the program.

There are a number of graphic, image and animation service bureaus that will prepare your images and graphics for presentation in the courtroom. Along with this service they will provide customized presentation software and equipment for the duration of the case. They are generally experts in the preparation of graphics and animations and will provide in-court assistance for the presentation of your case. Some service bureaus to consider are inData (www.indatacorp.com) and Z-axis (www.zaxis.com).

Presentation Software Features - It is important that when you present a case to a legal audience that the digitized evidence can be highlighted, annotated or displayed in a way to persuade the factfinders of your client's position. For this reason, it is important to focus upon the available features of presentation software so that your key points are emphasized for the trier of fact. Some of the most utilized features and techniques are discussed below.

<u>Retrieving graphics and images</u> - The most common method of accessing document exhibits in your case is to use bar code technology. This is the same technology that is used in grocery stores to obtain prices off the food you buy. In the courtroom you would move a pen type bar code scanner over a bar code. Once read, the document would appear on the screen. The bar codes are preconfigured to access a particular document exhibit when the bar code is read. The bar codes are easily created and can be printed on peel away stickers. Then the bar code sticker can be placed on your direct examination outline for a witness and "read' at the appropriate time or placed in any other part of your trial notebook. Using this type of program demonstrates to the trier of fact that you are in control of your case, saves time, and drives home your points.

Another retrieval method would be to go into an imaging program and locate in the computer directory the particular computer file that contains the demonstrative exhibit. This is somewhat slower and assumes that your exhibit files are properly organized to ensure they are timely located. During trial, this can be a distraction depending upon who is accessing the exhibits for presentation purposes.

Finally, one presentation system referred to as a touchscreen enables you to touch the computer screen that contains certain menuing choices to locate an exhibit. You would essentially touch the computer screen on a particular menu choice and the image would appear. This has to be preconfigured and has shown to be an effective and reliable way of accessing your exhibits.

<u>Drawing on Exhibit</u> - One of the most powerful ways of focusing a jury on the important parts of your evidence is to draw on the critical parts of the document or exhibit. This can be done by using a pen based drawing instrument such as a light pen that connects into your computer, a mouse or if you are using a touchscreen your finger. It generally permits you to draw on the exhibit in a variety of colors and block portions of the exhibit for highlighting in different colors. Also, arrows, circles and other highlighting features are available.

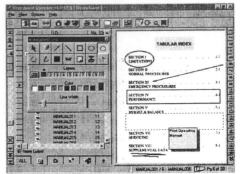

<u>Exhibit Manipulation</u> - Trial presentation systems permit you to manipulate the size of an exhibit and place two or more exhibits together on the same screen.

- <u>Enlargement</u> - Once your exhibit is on the screen you can use a mouse, pen based system or touch screen to mark off the portion that you want enlarged and do it instantly. Once enlarged you can discuss with the jury the impact of the particular document section on your case. Also, you can then draw on the enlarged portions with the tools noted above.

- <u>Side-by-Side or Top and Bottom Display</u> - One effective technique is to bring up two different exhibits side-by-side or one on the top and one on the bottom. This would be done to show the inconsistencies in the two documents or how they both are supportive of the same point. You can have up to four images on the same screen at the same time.

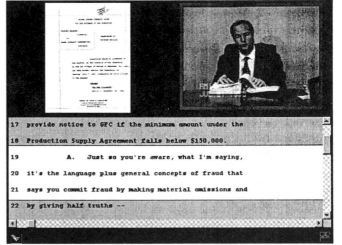

<u>Photographs</u> - Photographs can be shown electronically and enlarged and colored similar to a document exhibit.

<u>Video</u> - video depositions can be stored on CD-ROM and accessed by the trial presentation systems described above. They generally can be stopped at any point for discussion by experts or in your opening or closing statements. The advantage over using a VCR to show the video is that when it is on CD-ROM any portion of the video can be accessed in a few seconds. With a VCR you have to wait for the VCR to reel to the place where the significant video is located. This can take several minutes depending on where the video is located. Also, on CD-ROM the EXACT portion of the video can be configured to present to the jury. This is important when the court has ruled that only sentence 5 on page 34 through sentence 12 on page 36 of the video deposition can be shown.

The screens can also be split to show video, synchronized text, exhibits and sound at the same time. Annotations can be made to the video and other digitized content and then saved to a computer file.

Other Presentation Software Features – Other features include note searching, video review and editing capability, scanning capability, organization of documents by witness folders and cases, and scripting or layering capability with markup save features.

Digital Presentation Equipment

After creating your digital presentation the next step is deciding how you are going to display it to your legal audience and how should the courtroom be configured for the greatest impact upon the factfinder. The key factor in any choice one makes for presentation equipment is the QUALITY of the display to your audience. The equipment in the courtroom for a presentation will vary depending on whether it is a trial to the court or to the jury as well as what type of evidence you will be presenting.

The three primary types of digital presentation equipment are monitors, LCD panels and projectors, and CRT projectors. These display devices can generally be used with any of the computer operating programs. Ensure that the necessary connectors and input/output signals are compatible. Quality display equipment will be able to show video, graphics, images and any other form of multimedia including sound.

Monitors

Presentation monitors provide a direct view and good image quality depending on its resolution. Monitors are different then televisions in that they have higher resolution capabilities and are able to handle a variety of digital formats such as video, graphics, images, sound, etc. Resolution is the measure of the sharpness of the image it produces. The higher the resolution the sharper the image. Televisions generally have low resolution. Presentation monitors range from 640 X 480 to 1024 X 780 resolution and higher. The high resolution is required for viewing of graphics and case documents. Monitor sizes range from 10" to over 40". High resolutions are available in all sizes. The weight of the monitors increases as the size increases. It is not uncommon to need 3 people to lift and set a 37" monitor. One law firm solved this problem by placing the monitors in shipping crates that included a hydraulic lift. When the crates were taken to a courtroom the crates would be opened and the hydraulic lift would raise the monitor to the desired viewing height. A skirt could be placed around the equipment to hide the lift and wires.

The cost of a monitor depends on its size and resolution quality. The smaller Sony 10" monitors generally cost around $600. A quality stand to hold the 10" monitor can cost as much as the monitor itself but is needed to ensure that it does not get damaged. The larger 37" monitors sell for around $5,000. Prices for rental of presentation monitors vary widely in each city as well as the part of the country that you are located. One of the lowest cost larger computer monitors is sold by Gateway Computer company for approximately $1200. Visit their web site at www.gateway.com.

LCD Projectors and Panels.

Liquid Crystal Display (LCD) technology has been integrated into projectors and panels and is the most popular display technology

Using TV monitors to display digital video

One of the problems with digital video is the capability of displaying it to an audience. With regular video we display it by using a standard TV monitor in a NTSC (National Television Standards Committee) format. However, we cannot display digital video onto a standard TV monitor without converting the digital signal to an analog or NTSC format. Video scan converters are available to enable you to convert the signal to a NTSC format. The conversion can result in inferior picture quality. The most notable difference is the lack of sharpness. This technology is evolving at a rapid rate so check out the latest equipment. Prices range from $200 to several thousand dollars. One product to consider is the Pocket scan converter (www.aitech.com).

LCD projectors are being combined with visual presenters into one unit. For example Toshiba's Mediastar 311 (www.toshiba.com) has a built in document camera that captures three dimensional objects, graphs and video for multimedia presentations. It also has the traditional features of an LCD projector, plus the flip down document camera.

for computers. The latest models can handle full motion video, can display millions of color and project at a 1024 X 768 or higher resolution. LCD projection systems require a projection screen. Some systems come with "player" software that enables you to run your presentation off a floppy disk that is inserted into the LCD projector.

These systems can be used in a variety of legal settings and for in-house training. They are easy to move and setup and can be carried onto a plane. The major limitation is that the lighting conditions in the room may have to be controlled for display purposes. Some courts do not have shades or the ability to control lighting and some judges do not want a darkened courtroom during trial. However, there have been significant breakthroughs for these systems so it would be in your best interest to see an actual demonstration before deciding upon whether to use the system. If possible, insist upon previewing the system in the legal setting in which you will be using it.

LCD projection panels sit on top of overhead projectors. The overhead projector must have high lumens rating of 3,000 or more. They can fit inside of a briefcase and weigh less than 10 pounds. The portability of LCD devices has made them a popular display tool for settlement conferences and in other legal settings. Prices range from $1,000 for black and white projection to approximately $5,000 for color and full motion video features. Many audio/video service bureaus will rent LCD panels for approximately $150 per day.

LCD projectors are a display device that combines the LCD panel and overhead projector into one unit. This provides for a brighter, crisper display and lessens the need for a darkened room to display your presentation. Certain models can be carried onto a plane and weigh less than 20 pounds. Prices range from $4,000 to $8,000. They normally rent for approximately $150 to $300 per day.

> Keystoning occurs when the projected image is wider at the top than at the bottom. Keystoning happens when the light from the projector strikes the screen at an angle rather than squarely. It is a problem with most projection systems. This problem increases when the projector is close to the screen and the projection head is tilted upward. One can minimize this problem by moving the projector further from the screen or raising the projector so it is near the center of the screen. This cause new problems such as blocking the audience's view of the screen. The best solution is to tilt the screen forward until it is at a right angle to the angle of the projector head. Some screens have special brackets that extend allowing one to tilt the screen forward.

Many of these systems have remote control capability. If you don't like standing at a podium and the judge allows you to wonder – a remote control mouse may be the answer depending on the circumstances.

LCD Purchasing Considerations and Products.

One of the most used presentation devices is the LCD projection system. They are getting brighter, smaller and less expensive. They will continue to grow in popularity as we increase our use of computers in presentations. Some important buying considerations:

❑ *Demo* – always get a demonstration preferably under the conditions similar to those in which you'll use the projector. You'll need to see it operate with the kind of images and multimedia you'll typically use. Compare models side by side if you can.

❑ *Resolution* – the sharpness and clarity of projected images are determined by a projector's resolution. Resolutions available include VGA 640 X 480, SVGA 800 X 600, XGA 1024 X 768 and SXGA 1,280 X 1,024. Digital images are made up of dots or pixels that make up an image. Resolution refers to the number of dots or pixels that make up an image. The higher the resolution the sharper the image. If you are only showing slideshow and occasionally pictures you do not need the high resolution. However, showing CAD drawings or documents the high resolution is needed.

> Digital Light Processing (DLP) is a new technology breakthrough for LCD projectors. Developed by Texas Instruments, Infocus, nView, Proxima, and Davis are all using the technology in their projectors.

❑ *Computer Compatibility* – you must determine whether the

projector matches the resolution of your computer-input device. Most notebooks have SVGA screens today and some have XGA screens. If your projector only projects VGA then you have to use special technology to compress your computer SVGA or XGA into a VGA screen causing it to look less clear.

❑ *Portability and Weight* – If you travel weight is an important factor. Consider buying an under 12 lb. portable. They feature excellent resolution and image quality. However, if the machine will be fixed in one location focus on brightness, uniformity, contrast and color.

❑ *Brightness* – Most of your presentations should be delivered in rooms where people can see your face so brightness is critical. Brightness is measured in ANSI lumens. However, manufacturers enhance lumen numbers so they are unreliable. Instead, pay close attention to the brightness during the demonstration. The brightness should be uniform across the image and not just in the center.

❑ *Contrast* – contrast is the difference between the brightest and darkest areas on your image. It should be high enough for video and images.

❑ *Color* – Judge the color during a live demonstration. It is best to compare it to your computer screen. Are the pinks still pink or have they turned into yellow or oranges?

❑ *Image quality* – this refers to the overall look of the image. Are the corners of the image in focus at the same time as the screen center? Does an ugly hot spot occur somewhere? Is it crisp and clear or does the image seem to be hidden behind a dull film? Do the pixels separate at the edge? Test it with an all black screen. Is it all black? Do the same with the other primary colors. Do the colors stay intact?

❑ *Dual computer and video hookups.* How many computers and VCR's can be hooked into the projector at once? More than one will prevent having to switch cables for speakers or media.

❑ *Video format* – does it accept both NTSC and S-video?

❑ *Ceiling mounted* – Can it be mounted in a permanent location on the ceiling?

❑ *Built in computer* – does it have the capability to play back a presentation off of a floppy without the need for a computer?

❑ *Bulb replacement.* Lamp replacement cost – prices range from *$25 to $1000*. What will you do if a bulb burns out and a technician has to install a new one?

❑ *Rear projection capability.* Will you have a need to place it behind a rear projector screen?

❑ *Hand held remote* – Are the content buttons and on-line menu intuitive?

Products: inFocus (www.infocus.com) and Proxima (www.proxima.com).

CRT Projectors.

Cathode Ray Tube (CRT) projectors are generally used for large-scale presentations. These projection units can weigh as much as 150 pounds and cost upwards of $20,000 or rent for $400 to $1000 a day. They are relatively impractical for traveling purposes and require an audiovisual technician to set them up and ensure that the interfaces are proper for the computers.

Techniques and Benefits in Displaying Exhibits

After you have tried a number of cases using paper document exhibits and demonstrative exhibits you become familiar with what techniques are best in front of the trier of fact. For example, it is always suggested that an exhibit of your main points always be in front of the jury to permit them to focus on the themes of your case. But what do you do when the exhibits are "paperless"? What techniques are now available with trial presentation equipment to have the jury focus on the points you are trying to make? Do you place two of the exhibits side by side to show clear inconsistencies in the opposing sides' case? What drawing colors do you use on the exhibits to draw the jury's attention to the points you want to make? Do you let the jury play with the trial presentation system during trial? What about setting up the equipment? How should the courtroom be configured?

The proper display techniques are not always apparent from reading or discussing new technology presentation systems. In order to appreciate the power of these systems you need to observe an attorney using a system in front of a jury to see the impact upon a jury. In addition, it is important that you get as much "time" on one of these systems as possible for you to have confidence in the system as well as having confidence in your ability to use it in front of a jury. Finally, to reduce your stress level you need to understand that sometimes a technical problem could develop. Generally, such problems are short-lived and your presentation will go on. The jury is understanding of such problems and will ignore it if your preparation is apparent throughout the trial. If a problem develops be prepared to address the situation immediately by requesting a short recess or move to a different part of your case using printed material.

> **Don't forget the main visual aid is you, one should never take a backseat to your multimedia aids.**

Presentation Tips, Techniques and Benefits Checklist.
- *Advise judge.* Advise the judge and defense counsel ahead of time that you will be using monitors or a LCD projector to display exhibits. Explain that it will supplement the usual method of displaying the documents and will not replace the normal practice of authentication and admission of documents. Compare it to the overhead projector method of displaying materials.
- *Equipment storage.* Don't take for granted that the equipment can be stored in the courtroom during the trial some judges may expect you to remove it each day.
- *Electrical Power Supply.* Does the courtroom have sufficient power to run your equipment? Will the courtroom become overheated with all the electronic equipment?
- *Practice beforehand.* The jury will appreciate an efficient and effective presentation.
- *Let the jury use the equipment.* After checking with the judge and opposing counsel allow the jury to use the equipment.
- *Check Equipment Beforehand.* Set up the system in trial a few days before to check if it is operating properly and displaying the documents clearly under normal courtroom conditions.
- *Line of Sight for Trier of Fact.* Consider the location of the monitors so that the jury can see the witnesses' face when he or she sees a document and is testifying about it. Also, ensure that the jury has an unobstructed view of the document on the monitors.
- *Authenticate Documents.* Authenticate the documents and then show them the document on the screen so that the jurors can follow the witness as he or she testifies about the substance of the documents.
- *Admit documents and then Publish to the Jury.* Don't display a document to the jury before the judge has admitted it.
- *Equipment performance and controlling witnesses.* Make sure your computer and display system can bring up images rapidly so it does not hinder your fast paced cross-examination. Providing a rapid succession of documents to a witness gives the examiner the control.
- *Blackout screen.* Generally leave the document on the screen while the witness is testifying about it. When the witness moves on to another topic the old document or even a white screen may be distracting, black the screen out. Blacking out the screen will have the jury's attention redirected back to you. An exception is when a key document is on the screen you may want to change your technique as to this document.
- *Use a mix of Audiovisuals.* Use a mix of the available audiovisuals for the courtroom. Some of your most important documents should be blown up and left in the courtroom as the trial proceeds.
- *Assistance in using Equipment.* During opening and closing you may want someone else to call up the exhibits.
- *Renting instead of Buying.* Consider renting a system if the cost is too high to purchase.

- *Capture the jury's attention.* The presentation of the evidence on monitors will allow you to control the jury's attention paid to documents. Highlighting and zooming in will increase their attention.
- *Introduce and set up your visuals.* Introduce every visual – easier on listener. Tell them you are drawing attention to a particular part of your visual. Learn to talk and work with your visuals at the same time. Practice, practice and practice.
- *Choose the best presentation system.* Consider the audience, purpose, situation, environment and budget. What are the lighting conditions? Are their electrical outlets?
- *Make it interesting.* Just because TV is in the courtroom it doesn't make it interesting. The jury may tune it out just like at home.
- *Engage all learning senses.* The more senses you engage the better understanding the jury will have of the issues.
- *Efficient Presentation.* Paperless presentation saves time when a witness is testifying about several documents. It makes it an organized, clear and efficient presentation. Treat the system as an efficient way to display documents to a jury. Paper can be a distraction – finding, handing, publishing, etc. – can take several minutes.
- *Do not overuse the technology, jurors will lose their attention.*
- *Leading witnesses.* Highlighting portions of a document before questioning a witness allows you to "lead" a witness.
- *Witness video credibility.* If you want the jury to see the deponent's video face do not show the full text of the testimony at the same time - people will read the text and not look at the video.
- *Notify the jury ahead of time what you will be doing.* Tell the decision maker(s) about the equipment and that it may have glitches or that you may make a mistake but do not apologize.
- *Backup equipment.* Make sure and have backup light bulbs and know how to change or switch to the backup bulb, tape down wires, have a backup marking pen and other backup items for your visual presentation.
- *Backup presentation.* If you have problems with your presentation continue with it using paper backup. Use paper manuscript, slide handouts or handouts for yourself. Cover a different area. If you absolutely need them, recess.
- *Determine and communicate multimedia needs.* Identify your multimedia needs and communicate them clearly. Verify that your multimedia needs have been understood and implemented. Does the legal proceeding site have preset presentation rules? Arrive early to check out equipment and room. View your presentation on the actual equipment in the actual room before the presentation.
- *Keep extra digital copies of your presentation in your briefcase.* Do not leave them back at the office.
- *Visual aids are aids.* The strongest impact upon an audience is the person presenting.
- *Official looking Documents.* You may want to keep official documents with seals in their original format.
- *Check out your presentation on the computer equipment to be actually used in the proceeding.* If you design a presentation on a desktop and then use a different computer to present it may not have the same program version, fonts, etc.
- *Attention to detail is important to success.* The devil is in the details.

Some of the benefits from presenting your case digitally:

- No dead time or confusion searching through exhibit boxes.
- No dead time in lifting poster board exhibits off an unsteady easel.
- Jurors do not have vacant stares, grimaces and amusements.

❑ Jurors perceive you have better control with a visually exciting presentation.

❑ Jurors acknowledge outwardly by body language attention and mood their satisfaction or misery with the pace of the case.

❑ You never lose momentum or attention of jurors.

❑ No downtime by a witness hunting through multiple pages of an exhibit.

❑ No uneven breaks in an examination to publish a document to the jury.

❑ Enhances the visual clarity of exceptionally poor materials and writings on checks and other documents by zooming and enlarging a symbol, number, signature sentence or word.

❑ Move effortlessly from one exhibit to another in a controlled organized fashion.

❑ No walking to and from witness stand to hand deliver to him or her and then wait for a witness to read the exhibit which may be of poor quality.

Conclusion

The presentation of your digital case in court requires some forethought but will pay significant dividends. Studies have shown that the party that uses visual aids significantly influences the "60 minute" TV generation trier of fact. We have become a multimedia society and expect presentations--legal or otherwise--to include a multisensory approach.

Courtroom Technology Considerations

Computer Integrated Courtroom (CIC)

The CIC courtroom should be designed to provide "paperless" trials and insure the efficient and effective handling of evidentiary materials and testimony as well as meet judicial administrative needs. As the attached judicial function chart indicates, the computer integrated courtroom should not only make available to the judge his case notebook but also should integrate and be connected to minute entries, juror instructions, docketing, testimony of witnesses, paperless trials and so forth.

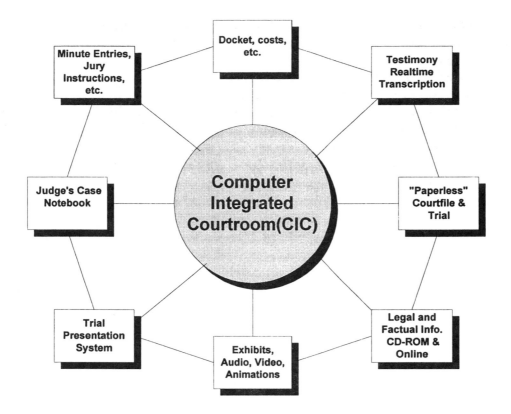

Benefits

The benefits from a CIC are:

1. **Significant reduction in the number of days in trial** - Early comments from a number of the top litigators and judges around the country indicate that the ability to try a "paperless" case provides significant cost savings. Litigators and judges estimate that 20% to 50% of trial time is saved in having the ability to view and display documents to the jury, judge, witnesses and parties through computer monitors in the courtroom. This eliminates much of the problems with trials is locating, transferring, and reading of exhibits to the interested parties in a lawsuit. With monitors strategically placed in the courtroom, this is done instantaneously and provides all interested persons the ability to view the documents immediately.
2. **Compliance with the American Disability Act Using Real-time Transcription** - Real time transcription of testimony is the ability to transcribe the witnesses' testimony instantaneously into written form for viewing on a computer monitor. Litigants or other parties having hearing problems would be able to review the testimony in "real-time" and thus comply with ADA mandates.
3. **Judicial Efficiency** – A CIC contributes to the efficient handling and organization of the case via the judge's case notebook, minute entries, docket, juror instructions, and access to judicial caseload.

4. **Connectivity** - Connectivity to outside judicial, legal and factual information sources increases the efficiency and productivity of the trials. The connectivity of the courtroom to outside law firms and other legal and factual information sources would enhance the efficiency and communication of the parties. For example, if a litigant or judge desired to research a particular point of law then they could go on-line and locate the information. In addition, since most of the information of a legal or factual nature are being reproduced on CD-ROM, the availability of CD-ROM readers in the courtroom for the litigants in the court will provide instantaneous assess to legal cases, statutes and case materials

5. **Enhance Jury Understanding** – Trial presentation systems will enhance the abilities of the litigants to present their case in an easy to understand manner for the trier of fact by displaying exhibits, video, documents and audio.

One of the critical questions as we proceed down the path automating litigation is the level of computerization in the court where you will be trying your case and the judge's support of this technology.

> Two teaching CIC facilities are the Courtroom of the Future and Courtroom 21.
>
> The "Courtroom of the Future" project located at the University of Arizona Law School is designed as a "working low cost technology courtroom". The project supports empirical studies of the use of technology upon jurors. Not only used as a teaching facility for law students the courtroom has been visited by court personnel and legal practitioners from across the country to learn how to effectively use low cost technology in courtrooms. Professor Winton Woods, head of the project, frequently consults with federal and state courts from across the country to determine the best technical layout for CIC courtrooms. (www.law.arizona.edu/courtroom.html).
>
> Courtroom 21, located in Williamsburg, Va., is the world's most technologically advanced courtroom. It was designed to demonstrate how advanced technologies could help courts. The courtroom is frequently updated with new hardware and software to determine its effectiveness in the administration of justice. (www.courtroom21.net/index.html)

Some court's like The Honorable Roger Strand's CIC in the Federal District Court of Arizona are fully automated and support "paperless" trials. Others may not be so receptive of the technology and may not want their courtroom turned into a technology courtroom.

Courtroom Technologies

Courtroom Configurations. The configuration of the display equipment in the legal proceeding is important to assuring that your digital presentation has the maximum impact upon the factfinder or audience. For example, if you place a monitor for a witness which prevents a jury from seeing his reactions when certain portions of documents are brought to his attention then the credibility of the witness is not as easy to judge. If the monitors are placed as to partially block the view of a juror then the risk is higher that the juror will not understand your legal position. If the monitor is to far away from a juror who has poor eyesight and the resolution is low then a witness may not disclose that he is unable to view the documents on the monitor. The rewards for a digital presentation are valuable but require forethought to minimize any problems.

Below are three courtroom configurations that have been used.

This configuration was used in The Federal District Court for the District of Arizona. This system fully installed with cabling is just under $27,000.

This configuration was used in a case in the Maricopa County Superior Court in Phoenix, Arizona. The parties purchased the system for under $19,000. inData Corporation in Gilbert Arizona installed the system.. (www.indatacorp.com).

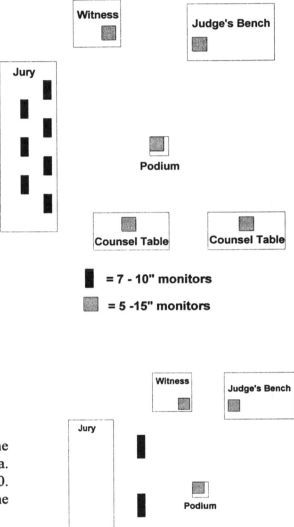

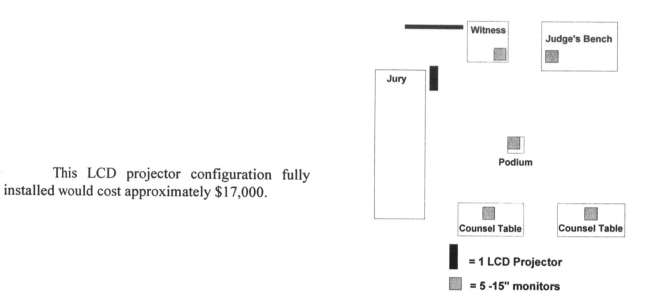

This LCD projector configuration fully installed would cost approximately $17,000.

One of the recurring questions asked is how can you afford to provide display equipment for a courtroom. Courts, state bar associations, court administrators and practitioners across the country are entering into joint funding arrangements to buy the equipment for the courtroom or the litigants will buy the equipment and donate it to the court after the case is completed. Once court administrators realize that presenting your case in an electronic format saves at a minimum 1 day of trial time per week than more systems will be installed. They will pay for themselves in a short period of time and limit the number of new courts being built.

Videoconferencing

Defense counsel: If it please the court, the defendant offers witness Edward Diamond's deposition into court. The deposition excerpts contains evidence relevant to this case.

Plaintiff's counsel: Objection, your honor, we request that the witness be present to give his testimony.

Defense counsel: Your honor, the witness is out of state and unavailable to testify here today.

Plaintiff's counsel: Your honor, the witness is available.

At the flip of a switch the witness, Edward Diamond, appears by video from out of state.

Witness
(Edward Diamond):   Good morning your honor.

Judge: Good morning, Mr. Diamond

Defense counsel: Your honor, we still object since it is necessary to have his testimony under oath and there is no one with the witness to administer the oath in person.

Plaintiff's counsel: Your honor, a court reporter is with the witness and as an officer of the court is ready and able to administer the oath. Further, the court reporter will take down the witness's testimony and transmit to our court via real-time transcription.

Judge: Everything seems proper, would the court reporter please administer the oath to the witness and let the testimony begin.

This type of "virtual" witness videoconferencing took place using Intel Video Conferencing software. The witness and court reporter were connected to the "court" using ISDN lines. ISDN lines are digitized phone lines. Normal copper phone lines are already in place throughout the United States. In order to convert the lines to ISDN lines the phone companies add some additional switching equipment and software to "digitize" the line. Where available, the cost to the consumer is approximately $150 to install and $80 a month rental, and approximately the regular cost per minute of a business call. With the cost barriers rapidly diminishing the use of video conferencing for client contact, depositions, witness testimony and many other uses will increase greatly over the next year. For further discussion on data transmission rates refer to Section 4, The Internet and Telecommunications.

Video Broadcasting or Cybercasting

A text, audio and/or video of a legal proceeding can now be broadcast over the Internet using a regular telephone line. Counsel or the court may find this strategically important for a number of reasons. Counsel may send the live court proceedings back to their office, to co-counsel, clients or their expert witnesses you are not present in the courtroom. This would obviously save immense amount of time and money to allow these parties to not have to travel to the courtroom to hear the proceedings.

The court may decide to have the trial broadcast publicly for the benefit of the community. One product that provides this technology is CourtCast™ provided by LegalSpan Corporation. (www.legalspan.net). *See also, Section 7, Real-time Broadcasting of Depositions Over the Internet.*

Real-time Transcription of Evidence

A second technology employed in courtrooms is the *real-time transmission* of the witness's testimony. The witness's testimony is transcribed into English onto the computer screen seconds after a witness testifies. This provides the court with a copy of the witness's testimony as well as being able to broadcast the testimony to counsel in the courtroom as well the capability to transmit the testimony back to their law offices for other members of the firm to review. See also, *Chapter 7, Depositions and Trial Testimony, Real-time Translation of Testimony.*

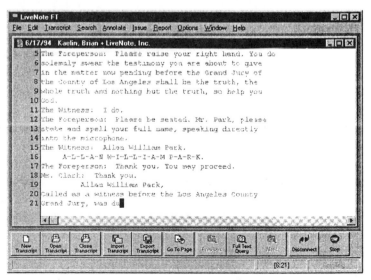

Benefits

- **Reading Back the Testimony Is Eliminated** - The court reporter does not have to read a witness's testimony back since the previous testimony can be viewed on-screen immediately.
- **Actual Testimony Can Be Viewed While Considering an Objection** - The court can now refer to the precise testimony when considering an objection.
- **Crowded Bench Conferences are Eliminated** - Clerks, associates, paralegals, and others can be "present" while viewing the discussions on-line.
- **Hearing Impaired Litigants and Jurors Can Now Participate** - Viewing the testimony and other proceedings on-screen enables hearing impaired litigants to participate in court proceedings.
- **Witness Control is Enhanced** - Testimony can be immediately searched for redirect, cross-examination, closing argument, and so on.
- **An Uncertified Copy Can Be Printed Out** - Commonly referred to as a "dirty" copy of the testimony this uncertified copy can be immediately printed out for review or discussion with one's clients.
- **Testimony can be Transmitted Worldwide** - The actual witness testimony can be distributed real-time to other law firm personnel back at the law firm or to clients and experts located anywhere in the world over the Internet using a regular phone line.
- **Examinations, Motions and Closing Arguments are Supported by Actual Witness Testimony** - Since all testimony and court rulings are available in a searchable format testimony can be reviewed for factual support for court proceedings.
- **Translation to other Languages Enhanced** - Interpreters can view the testimony on-screen and interpret for the benefit of a witness or other party.

Checklist - In-court Real-time Reporting

- **Determine if you want to use real-time reporting.**

Explore the benefits of using real-time technology. Reading back the testimony is eliminated; witness control is enhanced; actual testimony can be viewed while considering an objection; crowded bench conferences are eliminated; witness testimony can be immediately printed out; hearing impaired litigants and jurors can now participate; testimony can be transmitted worldwide; examinations, motions and closing arguments are supported by actual witness testimony; and translation to other languages is enhanced.

- **Formulate best strategy to obtain consent to use in court.**

Is opposing counsel cooperative? Should you request real-time reporting for the first time in pretrial conference without notice to the opposing counsel? Do you know the judge or clerk's attitude toward real-time reporting? Should you file a pleading outlining the technology and benefits? Should a demonstration be given to the court? Have available technical and practical benefits material for court. Do you wish transmission to a remote location such as your office, expert witnesses' office and so on? Does the court have an extra phone line(s) for your on-line connect needs? If long distance how are you going to pay for any charges?

- **Determine if court reporter can translate testimony in real-time.**

Transcription of live testimony to real-time cannot be done by all court reporters. Most court reporters do not write in real-time which result in many untranslates in the transcript that lessens the utility of the technology. It is relatively a recent technology in which most court reporters cannot write in real-time. The court reporting industry has a certifying process for certifying real-time reporters. Can the court's reporter write in real-time? Will it cause undue resentment if a real-time court reporter is requested to write the case instead of the regular court reporter? Is there an extra charge for real-time reporting? Can you download the daily-uncertified transcript for use? Will the same court reporter be doing the whole trial? Is the court reporter capable or someone else available to ensure their equipment is correctly transmitting the testimony to your computer and to fix any problems?

- **Select and purchase real-time software and train litigation team and, if needed, the court personnel.**

Select real-time software that is non-proprietary, open, easy to use and can be connected to any of the different computer aided transcript (CAT) machines that court reporters use. The real-time industry has been hampered with software from vendors that only works with certain CAT systems forcing court reporters to upgrade and purchase certain CAT systems. In the last few years new non-proprietary real-time software has become available which works with any CAT system. Provide training to your staff on the software features and the strategy for capturing and controlling witness's testimony. If possible practice under actual conditions with a connection to a court reporter's machine. Don't forget to ask the judge, clerk, law clerks and any other court personnel whether they need training or assistance in selecting appropriate software. Helping them making their jobs easier will be appreciated. Software selection criteria should include whether the notes, cross-references, searches can be saved and subsequently used in your full text program and whether the real-time annotations will be linked to the final certified transcript or whether you have to re-enter the notes.

- **Select hardware equipment needed for the courtroom.**

To view and actually control the transcripted testimony each person needs a computer, monitor and be connected to the court reporter's CAT system. Will you need to bring in a computer or does the court have them installed? Does the judge need one? Do you have a backup system? If more than one person will be using the real-time do you have the necessary equipment to split the signal or transmit it to remote locations? Can you cover the cables for safety and make them blend in with the courtroom? Will it be part of an in-court presentation system? If so, how many monitors will I need?

- **Install and test system with court reporter, judge or his computer, and other connections two weeks before trial.**

With the court's consent set a time for all the parties to test their equipment in the courtroom. Find out ahead of time the court's attitude toward having equipment in the courtroom and their preferences. The judge's bench area should be configured in a way that does not interfere with his other judicial duties nor take away from the dignity of the courtroom. If sending testimony to a remote location test the system.

Can remote users transmit messages back to you in the courtroom via the computer? Have a laptop or other computer configured and tested as a backup in case of problems.

- **Test two days before trial.**

With the court's consent set a time for all the parties, including the court reporter, to complete a final test of their equipment in the courtroom. Find out from the court who has access to the equipment and whether you can work on it at night or over the weekend if the need arises.

- **Using real-time during trial.**

Have a specific strategy as to who will be viewing real-time testimony and your legal objectives. If you are alone in the courtroom, have easy to use one keystroke commands available to mark important testimony. Don't forget to watch the non-verbal communications of the witness. Make sure witnesses excluded from the courtroom do not view the real-time testimony. Have the judge explain to jury the real-time technology and why they will or will not be using the technology. Print out important actual testimony on paper or on a transparency with a portable printer to display to the trier of fact with an overhead projector or with an in-court presentation system. Try to review the real-time testimony during breaks, while the witness is reviewing a document or any other time when your full attention is not required on the proceedings.

Conclusion

This has been the final section of an examination of an exciting time in our profession. The employment of technology in the courtroom can provide a significant advantage if properly used. However, the never-ending objective must be on convincing the trier of fact of your position. Technologies are tools in a courtroom to assist you in your case. They should never be used as a crutch. They can display legal and factual information in a fast, easily accessible form, assist in maintaining the attention of the trier of fact, and enable one to keep the factfinders's focus on the theories, elements and factual propositions of your case. The reaction of the participants to the use of technology must be monitored to ensure one is not perceived as overreaching and that the technology is not interfering with your communication with the jury.

Glossary

As you begin working with computers and software programs, you will discover that certain words are unique in the computer industry. Words such as directory, subdirectory, filename, cursor and others will begin to appear in the materials that you read. To help you in understanding these words, a list of commonly used computer terms and their definitions are contained below.

Analog – is a derivative of the word "analogous" meaning "similar to". Analog devices such as analog video and audio recording devices record real events in real time using film or audiotape. Digital translates the real event into 1's and 0's for computer use.

ANSI – stands for **American National Standards Institute**. This institute develops standards for items like computers and software that are purchased or sold by the government.

API – Application Program Interface is a term used to describe the "hooks" available to "integrate" programs with each other. Fort example API's are available for Microsoft Access to integrate or communicate with an image program.

Applications Program Software - computer programs that perform a wide range of tasks and generally designed for specific purposes. Microsoft Word and WordPerfect were designed for word processing, Summation II for database and full text document search and retrieval, Lotus 123 for spreadsheet and Watermark for graphic images. Also referred to as *application* or *program.*

Archive – archiving is the process of putting data on disks for long term storage. Backups are used to ensure data is saved in case of data loss.

Artificial Intelligence (AI) is the field of computer science in which computers are programmed to exhibit characteristics of human intelligence. It attempts to model the way humans think.
Knowledge based systems, expert systems, virtual reality are some of the components of AI.
The objective is to simulate factual patterns for consistency among decision-makers. For example, legal decisions involve a large number of factors, many with complex interactions. As a result outcomes are oftentimes inconsistent. Artificial intelligence attempts to prevent the inconsistencies by consistently noting the factors of a particular decision and leading to the same conclusion under the similar set of facts. These also are commonly referred to as "knowledge based systems" or "expert systems". They capture the expertise of decision makers , convert it to a set of rules, and apply the rules to routine decisions. JEDA - Judicial Expert Decision Aid - is an expert decision system designed for judges in black lung cases.

ASCII format - American Standard Code for Information Interchange was a code developed through the cooperation of several computer manufacturers whose objective was to develop a standard code for all computers. It facilitates the exchange of data between computer and application programs. This is the standard format for a DOS text file. Computer files in ASCII can generally be imported to most DOS based computer programs. Request a copy of a deposition from a reporter in ASCII (pronounced "as key") format unless there is a particular full text program that you will be using.

AUTOEXEC.BAT file. This is a MS-DOS file containing commands that automatically execute whenever you start the computer. For example you can put in an autoexec.bat file a command to automatically start Windows. This file is not available with the Windows 95 program.

Back up. This is a duplicate copy of your data or application program files placed in a safe and separate place in case of loss of your original data. It is important that you back up important data or program files. If the original files are damaged then one can use the backup files.

Bar Code – is a system of accessing data through a series of machine-readable lines. Bar code readers can read the bar codes and can retrieve documents for viewing or presentation in the courtroom.

Bernoulli Box – is a storage disk system that uses fluid dynamics to keep the disk floating in the air as data is accessed or written to the disk.

BIOS. Acronym for Basic Input/Output System. BIOS are instructions that tell the computer how to control the information between computers and peripherals. In some operating systems, this part of the system is customized for specific computers.

Bit. Bit is an abbreviation for **binary digit**. It is the smallest unit of measurement for a computer. A bit can be either on or off in a computer. Eight bits equal one byte or the equivalent of one character.

Bitmap – represents characters or graphics by individual pixels or dots. They are arranged in columns and rows and can be altered with paint programs. Bit map graphics, also called raster graphics, are images created with pixels.

Blowbacks – is a slang term for printing images off of a CD-ROM disk.

Boot/Reboot. This is the start up procedure for a computer. It causes the execution of start up files such an autoexec.bat file. When your computer locks up then you need to reboot the computer generally by holding down the **CTRL** and **ATL** and then pressing the **DEL** keys at the same time.

Bps. Bps stands for bits per second. It is the transmission speed between two computers.

Browser – A browser is software like Internet Explorer used to view web pages on the Internet or Intranet. It is the client software used to view sites located on servers running web server software.

Bulletin Board Service (BBS). The early forerunner to group computing systems. They permit users to exchange e-mail, retrieve files and share other computer functions between individuals who share common interests.

Byte. This is the primary unit of measurement for computer storage. It denotes the amount of space needed to store a single character of text. One byte equals 8 bits.

Boolean Search - A Boolean search uses NOT LOGIC to prevent specific words from being retrieved with a search request, such as L*<legal>, which would find all words starting with L except legal.

Cache. This is part of the memory that temporarily stores frequently used data. Information that is likely to be read or altered is stored here. Cache can significantly speed the processing of some programs.

CAD – Computer Aided Design – means having computers design products, buildings, houses, highways and so forth.

CD-ROM. Acronym for **C**ompact **D**isk **R**ead-**O**nly **M**emory. This is a type of optical disk that looks and uses the same basic technology as the popular CD audio disks. This read only technology can store 650 MB of information per disk.

CGI – Common Gateway Interface – is the standard used for connecting web pages with underlying data. A CGI script has the capability of calculating mortgages, accessing databases for reports, etc.

Character – A character is equal to a byte and is a single letter or number.

Character Recognition – or OCR is the ability of a scanner to read human readable text into ASCII text like a word processor.

Client / Servers - refers to decentralized, usually desktop computers, loosely connected to a central depository called the server. This system is contrasted with mainframes. In an Intranet or Internet system the client software is like Netscape and the server software would be Netscape Suitespot or something comparable.

Communications Program - software that controls the transfer of data from one computer to another. Programs are available to transfer data over telephone lines. Some programs permit you to operate a particular desktop computer from anywhere linked by a telephone line.

Computer File - A computer file is a collection of computer   commands and information stored in a file.

Compatibility. The capability of a piece of hardware or software to operate with another piece of software or hardware. For example word processing files from WordPerfect are not compatible with Microsoft Word word processor unless the conversion program is used first.

Communications protocol is a set of instructions, which enables two computers to talk to each other. A protocol suite is a set of instructions to handle a variety of computer tasks such as printing, file transferring and so on. TCP/IP is a protocol suite that is used on networks and on the Internet. It has become one of the key defacto standards for tying together computers. Hence, the popularity of the Internet and the communication is large part due to this protocol. It is part of the UNIX operating system. FTP is an acronym for File Transfer Protocol and is a service for transferring files.

Computer. A computer is an electronic device consisting of a central processing unit, monitor and keyboard to store, retrieve and process data.

Compression – is the ability of some software programs to shrink or compress the images and other computer files.

Config.sys file. This file automatically executes each time you boot the computer and generally configures peripheral devices attached to the computer. For example, the config file can be coded to activate a sound card when the computer is started. Windows 95 does not have this file but instead automatically configures attached hardware with a new plug and play feature which automatically recognizes attached devices.

CPU. Acronym for **C**entral **P**rocessing **U**nit. This is the main core of a computer. Oftentimes called the brain of the computer. It controls the interpretation and execution of computer instructions.

Cross-references - Cross-references are enhancements that you can imbed in full text documents. They are used to delineate words or phrases that mean the same thing.

Cursor - A cursor is the small dash on the computer screen that constantly blinks. This is the location that the next character will appear when you begin typing.

Data. Information that is processed or transmitted by a device like a computer.

Data Communications – is the transfer of data between two computer points.

Database - A database is a collection of data or information stored in computers that can be used for more than one purpose. It is data that has been organized and structured for particular purpose such as a document management system.

Database Management Systems (DBMS) - This is the task of managing data in databases and retrieving information from that database.

Data Transfer Rate (dtr). This is the rate of data transfer from one device to another. CD-ROM's can transfer information to a computer at 1000 kbps and higher. The higher the transfer the faster the access to the data.

Device driver - are drivers that control attached peripheral devices such as a mouse. Device drivers will oftentimes come with devices that are subsequently added onto computers.

Digital – is the recording of information in a binary manner. Information is recorded as 1's and 0's for use by a computer. Analog records information real time in file and tape. It does not convert the data to a new format. Text in a word processor is in a digital format, images or graphics is in a bit map or digital format and so on.

Digital Cameras – are new cameras that translate real events or pictures directly into digital data.

Digitize – is the process of converting information such as a document into binary code. Documents are converted into a digital format using a scanner. They can be in a image digital format or in ASCII text – both digital formats.

DAT – Digital AudioTape – is a technology that records digital audio onto magnetic tape.

Directory - is the location where files and subdirectories are located on the computer. The data in your computer is stored and organized using a file and directory structure. A file is a collection of information such as a word processing file or containing program executable instructions. Each file has a name associated with it. Pre Windows 95 filenames were limited to 8 characters, a period, and a 3-character extension. Windows 95 permits long file names without an extension. Files are stored in directories and directories can contain files and subdirectories. The first directory is called the root directory. A directory sequence that leads to a particular file is called a path. A typical path would be C:\document\letter1.doc for a word processing file.

Diskette - is the data storage device for your computer. Removable magnetic disks usually come in 3 1/2 or 5 1/4 size. Hard disks come in assorted sizes and are usually nonremovable. The newest disk is the optical disk that stores in essence more data on the same size disk as the magnetic disks.

Disk Drive - device that enables a computer to read and write data on a disk.

Disk File - See Computer File

Document Retrieval – The ability to locate and view a document on a computer screen.

DPI – Dots Per Inch – This is a measurement of output resolution and quality. It measures the number of dots per square inch. A 600 dpi document is much sharper than a 200 dpi document but restores more storage space.

Dot Pitch (DP). The amount of space between dots of color or pixels on a monitor is called dot pitch. The lower the dot pitch, such as .28, the clearer and crisper is the picture.

Enhancements/Annotations- Enhancements are codes that you can imbed within the text of a full text document to add in the summarization of documents and the preparation of reports. The enhancements are notes, cross-reference codes, issue codes, and markers.

Ethernet is the operating protocol for a LAN. On a LAN computers are physically connected together using Ethernet cards and software. It is relatively inexpensive and also provides the connection for Intranets to information. It has a relatively large bandwidth.

Expansion card. Expansion cards are integrated circuit cards that can be added to your computer to expand its capabilities. A network card can be added to your computer to give it the capability to connect it to a network.

Fax/Modem. This modem can send or receive faxes without printing the document first.

Fiber optic cable – is cable made from thin strands of glass through which data is transported. Excellent conduit to transfer data for medium or long distances but is more expensive than normal cable.

Field - is the location on a computer input form to collect specific data such as document number, document condition, etc.

Field Name - a labeled area on the screen input form such as DCNO (document number), DATE (document date), SUMM (summary), etc.

File. A file is a collection of information such as a word processing file or containing program executable instructions. It generally describes one document or image. Files are stored in directories and directories can contain files and subdirectories. The first directory is called the root directory. A directory sequence that leads to a particular file is called a path. A typical path would be C:\document\letter1.doc for a Microsoft Word processing file.

Filename. Each file has a name associated with it. Pre Windows 95 filenames were limited to 8 characters, a period, and a 3 character extension. Windows 95 permits long file names without an extension.

Firewall. Generally used to describe a security system for an Internet or Intranet web site. Its purpose is to preclude intruders from viewing or changing sensitive data. It will preclude access or allow it only for authorized users.

Fixed disk is another name for a hard drive.

Form - a computer input screen that contains fields where information is to be entered. After information is entered, it is called a record.

Full Duplex – is a communications protocol for describing the transmission of data simultaneously in both directions.

Full Text - This is the "full" or complete text of a document. This term usually refers to a document that has been converted for use on a computer. A "full text" document can be a deposition, memo, brief, interrogatories, rules of procedure, evidence and so forth since it is the "full text" of the document.

Full Text Search – is the capability of searching text files for words, phrases or patterns of characters. An image cannot be full text searched. It has to be retyped or OCR'ed into the computer.

GB (gigabyte) - A gigabyte is 1,073,741,824 bytes or 1024 megabytes. This unit of measurement reflects computer memory or disk storage.

Graphics – are primarily pictures and drawing either created into the computer or which are scanned and entered into a computer.

Graphical User Interface (GUI) - a computing environment that enables one to execute commands or interact with a program using graphical symbols on the screen.

Groupware – is software designed to assist groups in working together using computers. Lotus Notes is the most popular example. With the recent emergence of Intranets groupware will take on significant importance due to "open" standards, less expensive and easier to use.

Gooey – slang for GUI – which stands for Graphical User Interface.

Handwriting Recognition – is the technology that converts human handwriting into machine-readable ASCII text.

Hard Drive. A storage device generally inside the computer used to store information. You save your documents to a hard drive.

Half Duplex – is a communications protocol that allows transmission in both directions, but only in one direction at a time.

Hardware. The actual physical parts of a computer are its hardware.

HDTV – High Definition TV – is a new standard for broadcast TV. A typical TV set contains 336,000 pixels. An HTVD TV will contain over 2,000,000 pixels.

High resolution – is a description of the enhanced viewing quality of documents that have been imaged.

Home Page – This is the gateway into a web site. It usually contains the main menu that directs the visitor to other parts of the site that can include documents, graphics, newsletters, other links, etc.

HTML – Hypertext Markup Language is the language used to create hypertext, the language used to create Internet, Intranet and Extranet pages. HTML's commands direct a browser like Netscape how to display web pages. These commands pertain to graphics, text and links to other pages or web sites.

Hypertext Linking - A hypertext link is the capability to link together any two separate sources of digital information and then jump to the secondary source whenever necessary. For example, if you decide to "publish" a motion for summary judgment to your fellow attorneys then when they review it and they decide to read the case you cite in the motion they can click on the case name and it will appear for review

Hz (hertz) A unit of measures which indicates frequency in cycles per second. The higher the megahertz of a computer is the faster it will run. Hertz is a measurement of frequency that is defined as one cycle per second. A megahertz is 1,000,000 cycles per second. Microprocessors run at speeds that are measured in MHz or millions of cycles per second. The higher the MHz the faster the computer runs.

Icon – is a picture that when clicked upon will activate a program or other computer functions. This is the foundation for a GUI desktop.

Image – is an "electronic picture" of a document that is in a digital format.

Image Resolution – refers to the sharpness of an image as it is being scanned. Usually ranges from 200 to 400 dpi.

Imaging is the process of using a scanner to convert a document into a computer readable form.

Index – is generally a set of structured data information associated with documents or other information. Indexing is used to link images with the data for instant viewing. This an integral part of locating documents that have been scanned as images.

Indexing - Some full text programs create an index whenever a document is converted for use within the program. It generally will increase the speed of searches and reports.

Infrared Technology. These are invisible radiation wavelengths. This enables wireless transfer of capabilities between portables and desktop computers and also the sending of commands from a wireless keyboard or mouse to a computer.

Ink Jet Printer. A printer which sprays ink from tiny jet nozzles. It produces high quality printouts in black and white or color.

Install. Computer hardware or software is installed or set up for operation. Hardware installation is generally done by connecting hardware such as a sound card into the appropriate sockets inside or outside a computer. Software is generally installed from application programs that include their own installation programs. These installation programs are started by running a setup.exe or install.exe file that usually copies all the files and sets up graphical user icons for execution.

Interlaced Resolution. Interlaced monitors scan every other line and are not as clear and are generally less expensive then non-interlaced monitors. These monitors scan the entire screen and are considered flicker-free

Issue Code - An issue code is an enhancement code used in full text or databases to indicate a specific topic or area of interest for use within reports and searches.

Java – is a new programming language owned by Sun Microsystems that lets programmers create web add-ons or pages that can be viewed by browsers. Generally it is used in conjunction with HTML for add-on features with web pages, though it can be used alone to create web pages.

JEDDI - Electronic Filing and Judicial Document and Data Interchange

JPEG – is a standard for still image compression.

Jukebox – is a device that holds multiple optical disks that can be accessed through a computer.

KB (Kilobyte) - This unit of measurement equals 1,024 bytes. This unit of measurement denotes computer memory or disk storage.

Laser Printer. This printer uses a light beam to transfer the image to a piece of paper. It prints a whole page at a time, as opposed to one line.

Legacy Systems. Most businesses currently have present computer systems in place such as databases system, etc. These systems can be connected to Intranets or Internets and are often referred to as "legacy" systems.

Load. When a program is copied from the hard disk or diskette into RAM memory the program is *loading*. This occurs whenever you start a program. When you turn on your computer the operating system program *loads*.

Magnetic-Optic – refers to an erasable recording method. It is similar to a magnetic hard disk.

Menu - A menu in a computer program is a list of options that you choose from to do different computer functions. Summation is a "menu driven" program.

Megabyte - this unit of measurement equals 1,048,576 bytes or characters or 1,024 kilobytes. This unit of measurement reflects computer memory or disk storage.

Megahertz - see hertz

Memory - is space within the computer for storing electronic data.

Microprocessor. This is the chip inside the computer that is the center of all the activity. The chip controls all the operation s of a computer and is used to execute program commands. It is also known as a *processor*.

MIPS - Millions of Instructions Per Second – this is a measurement of computer speed.

MIS – Management Information System – is generally the department responsible for digital information systems.

Modem. This internal or external computer device connects to a telephone for the purpose of sending or receiving information from other computers.

Mouse - This is the primary pointing device for the Windows operating system. When you move the mouse over a flat surface the cursor or arrow makes a movement on the screen. It is a hand held device that allows you to control the location of the cursor with some programs and allows some commands to be executed by pushing buttons.

MS-DOS. Stands for Microsoft Disk Operating System. It is a single tasking, single user operating system. Windows 95 is a multitasking operating system.

Multitasking Operating System - This is an operating system that enables the user to perform more than one task at a time. Windows 95 and OS/2 are multitasking operating systems.

Multimedia - delivery of information in multisensory ways through the integration of previously distinct media - text, graphics, computer animation, motion video, and sound - in a single presentation under the control of the computer. Refers to using computers to create and distribute communications enhanced with voice, sound, images, video, graphics, and text. Since we are a multimedia society the multimedia approach is the powerful force of the future in how we will communicate with our clients, jurors, or the judge.

Network - A network is when two or more computers are linked together to share data, programs and hardware resources. Specialized hardware and software is required to network computers.

Non-Interlaced Resolution. These monitors scan the entire screen and are considered flicker-free. The other type, Interlaced monitors, scan every other line and are not as clear and are generally less expensive.

Notes (Annotations)- Notes are enhancements that allow you to make an extended comment anywhere in a document. Notes are very valuable as a summarization and preparation tool and will save you the time of taking handwritten notes and looking for them later.

Object Linking and Embedding (OLE). Store images as an object in a database. The object can execute code or cause another program to execute code. Objects that represent images, graphics, videos, etc. are stored in the database and when activated by clicking on the mouse can launch other applications that store the OBJECT as a computer file. This solves the problem of having to switch your present and computer files applications to new software but instead embedding these files in different software to activate when needed.

Occurrences - Occurrences are the number of times a particular search request occurs throughout a full text document

Off-line. This is when a peripheral device does not have an active communications link with the computer. For example, when a printer is off-line it is unable to communicate and thus print a document from a word processing program. Recently, a number of commercial services such as CompuServe suggest that you work off-line creating your mail before connecting to CompuServe to send it thus saving connect time charges.

On-line. Equipment, devices and other services that are in direct communication with your computer. One can be on-line with a printer or the Internet.

Operating system - is the master set of software programs that manages and controls access to the computer by other programs. It controls input and output to the mouse, keyboard, printer and all other devices connected to the computer. DOS is a operating system. Microsoft '95 is the new operating system which has combined DOS and Windows.

Optical Character Recognition -is the process of using a scanner and software of converting paper into a searchable machine readable text like a word processing document.

Optical Drives – is a storage device that is written and read by laser. There are certain types of disks such as CD-ROM which is read only, **WORM** – that can be written to once and read many times and WRRM which stands for Write Many, Read Many or is Erasable.

Operating system - controls the overall operation of the computer. The operating program directs and coordinates the commands between your computer and other hardware components such as printers, video, sound boards and so on. It also coordinates the flow of commands between application programs and the computer.

Parallel Port - A port generally located in the back of the computer which transfer data through multiple wires. Eight bits are transferred simultaneously. A printer is generally connected to a parallel port. It is usually designated with the letters LPT1.

Parallel processing - is the process that enables a computer or a large number of processors to attack a problem simultaneously. Ten computers working together to solve a problem will solve the problem faster then one computer working on the problem. The processing of data in a parallel manner will not be a problem. Operating and application software to run parallel processors will be the hurdle to overcome.

Path - This is the directory sequence the computer must search to locate a particular file or directory. See also directory and file.

Pen-based computing – is a method of entering data into a computer using an electronic stylus.

Plug and Play - The new plug and play standard in Windows 95 lets you add peripherals to your computer without worrying about jumpers, dip switches, or any other hardware adjustments. The software will search for any new hardware components on startup and then configure the appropriate drivers to play the device. Plug and play configures your PC for you

Port - This is a connector to a computer that allows data to be exchanged with other devices such as a printer, mouse, CD-ROM reader or external modem.

Processor. See Microprocessor.

Proximity Search - A proximity search is used to find words or phrases that are within a specified number of lines of another word or phrase.

Program - See Application Program.

Prompt - Usually shown as C:\ or A:\ that indicates that the computer is ready to accept input.

RAM (Random Access Memory)- is the memory available for user's programs and data when a computer is turned on. Information can be randomly accessed very quickly. RAM memory is emptied each time you turn the computer off. If you turn the computer off without saving the information in your RAM memory it will be lost. RAM is generaly measured in megabytes. For windows based programs 8 to 16 megabytes of RAM is suggested. See also ROM.

Raster Graphics – or bit map graphics are pictures defined as a set of pixels in columns or rows.

RDBMS (Relational Database Management System)

ROM_(Read Only Memory)- This computer memory stores instructions permanently. The ROM contains instructions that the computer uses to run properly. It cannot be changed and are executed each time the computer is turned on.

ROM BIOS - These are chips that contain the BIOS code and the system configuration for the computer.

Root Directory. - This is the first level directory on a computer. All other directories are subordinate to the root and are referred to as directories or subdirectories. See also directory.

Record - after information has been entered in a form and the form is saved, it is called a record.

Resolution. This reflects how sharp the images are on your computer monitor. The higher the number the sharper and clearer the image. Images are usually scanned at 200 to 400 dpi. It also refers to the output resolution on a monitor. The resolution 1024 X 768 is the number of pixels horizontally and the number of lines vertically on a computer monitor.

ROM – Read Only Memory – is usually stored in your computer. It can be accessed or read but not erased or altered.

Scan – is the process of converting a document into an image or using OCR software converting it to machine-readable text.

Scanner – is a device that converts a document or picture into an image or machine-readable text.

SCSI – "scuzzy" – Small Computer System Interface – is the standard for connecting peripherals to your hardware CPU unit.

Serial Port - This connector port on a computer sends and receives data one bit at a time. A modem, printer or mouse can be connected to your serial port. It is usually denoted as COM1. See also parallel port.

Single Tasking Operating System - An operating system that only performs one task at a time such as MS-DOS. See also multitasking and operating system. It can only be used on a single computer.

Software - is a collective term for computer programs. Programs can be application or operating system software programs. Software is a series of instructions to operate the computer and perform specialized tasks. It is generally used to refer to specific application software programs such as word processing, spreadsheets and so on.

Spreadsheet program - is a program that manipulates numbers and data in a table arranged in columns and rows. Lotus 123 and Quattro are two spreadsheet application programs.

Streaming video – allows one to see the video as it's downloading to your machine. While a bigger bandwidth is preferable all you need is a 28.800 modem and a free software plugin.

Subdirectory - A subdirectory is a computer directory within another directory.

Synonym Search - A synonym search is used to locate words or phrases that mean the same thing as other words or phrases.

Tape Backup Unit. (TBU). This device is used mainly to back up the large amounts of data on your harddrive. It is similar to an audiotape.

TCP/IP - Transmission Control Protocol / Internet Protocol is the operating protocol by which all Internet and Intranet computers communicate with each other. It is the operating language directing how the packets of information will be sent over the network wire or wireless systems.

Text Management – are the techniques for creating, storing, organizing, controlling and retrieving text files in a logical fashion.

Text search – is a technique for searching text files for occurrences of certain words or phrases.

TIFF – Tagged Image File Format – is the industry standard bit map file format for describing and storing images in a black and white format.

Unzip - refers to decompressing a file using the popular PKUNZIP software.

Vaporware – slang term referring to the announcement of software but not ready for delivery to customers.

Voice Recognition Technology - Refers to the capability of a computer to "hear" a word and convert the word automatically to usable computer text. This technological breakthrough has immense promise for automating the practice of law. We would simply command the computer to open up the word processing program, dictate a letter and print and/or fax the letter and envelope for mailing. If you have electronic mail - then just transmit it to whomever you wish. Some law firms have " voice recognition" software in place and many others are considering applications for its use.

Wildcard - The wildcard is the asterisk (*). It takes the place of any number of letters within a word. For example, *ar** could be used to represent all words that begin with the letters *ar*, regardless of their length. It also can be used any other character in a filename such as *smith*.**.

Windows – is the Microsoft operating system that features multitasking and a graphical user Interface.

Word Processing - software designed to prepare a letter, brief or other documents.

WYSIWYG – What You See Is What You Get. Refers to a word processor or graphics program that displays images on the screen exactly how they will appear on paper.

Zip – refers to compressing a file using the popular PKZIP software program.

On-line Glossaries

Internet:

http://www.webfoot.com/advice/

http://www.matisse.net/files/glossary.html

Index

A

B

C

Book Order Form

The Digital Practice of Law

A Practical Reference Applying Technology Concepts to the Practice of Law

Copies	#	Cost/Each		TOTAL
1 - 4	_____	X $49.95 =	_____	
5-10	_____	X $44.95 =	_____	
11+	_____	X $39.95 =	_____	

Tax   _____

DC Residents add 5.75%
AZ Residents add 5.75 %   _____

Shipping/Handling per Book   _____

1 - 4	_____	X $6.00 =	_____
5-10	_____	X $5.00 =	_____
11+	_____	X $4.00 =	_____

_____

TOTAL: _____

_____
Name

_____
Firm/Organization

_____
Street Address

_____
City/State/Zip:

_____
Area Code/Daytime Phone & e-mail (In case we have a question about your order)

Payment:

☐ Check Enclosed, Payable to Law Partner Publishing

☐ MasterCard ☐ Visa ☐ American Express

_____
Card Number   Expiration Date

_____
Signature Required

Mail Orders to: Law Partner Publishing, 15819 N. 5th Avenue, Phoenix, AZ 85023, PH: 602-993-1937